BRITISH INSTITUTE AT ANKARA
Monograph 31

# ANATOLIAN IRON AGES 5

Proceedings of the Fifth Anatolian Iron Ages Colloquium
held at Van, 6–10 August 2001

Edited by
A. Çilingiroğlu and G. Darbyshire

Published by
BRITISH INSTITUTE AT ANKARA
10 Carlton House Terrace, London SW1Y 5AH

© British Institute of Archaeology at Ankara 2005
ISBN 1 898249 15 6
ISSN 0969-9007

Typeset by Gina Coulthard
Printed by Stephen Austin & Sons Ltd, Hertford

*Cover illustration: Erzincan-Sırataşlar fortress (photo: Alpaslan Ceylan)*

# Acknowledgements

We were delighted to meet our colleagues who, in 2001, participated in the Fifth Anatolian Iron Ages Colloquium at Van, the Iron Age capital. It is encouraging to see that enthusiasm for the Colloquium series has not declined since the first conference held in 1984. This continued interest confirms the correctness of our decision to commence the series.

The organisation of the Fifth Anatolian Iron Ages Colloquium involved a great deal of work. The Yüzüncü Yıl University at Van kindly provided all kinds of facilities. We wish to express our deep gratitude to the University Rector, Prof. Dr Yücel Aşkın, to the Assistant Rector, Prof. Dr Zühre Şentürk and to Nuray Karayel. We are also very honoured that Prof. Dr Kemal Alemdaroğlu, Rector of Istanbul University, attended the Opening Ceremony of the Colloquium. For financial support we wish to gratefully thank Roma Istituto per gli Studi Micenei ed Egeo Anatolici and its Director, Prof. Mirjo Salvini. We are much indebted to the British Institute at Ankara for the publication of the Colloquium proceedings. We are also greatly beholden to all the people of the village of Ayanis (Ağartı) for their hospitality. For their dedicated contribution to the organisation of the conference, we wish to thank Özlem Çevik, Aylin Erdem, Fulya Dedeoğlu, Atilla Batmaz, Dilek Öztürk and all the students.

Our deepest gratitude extends to the conference participants without whom, since 1984, there could have been no Colloquium series.

*Prof. Dr Altan Çilingiroğlu*
*Colloquium Secretary*

During preparation of the conference for publication, the expertise, kind assistance and support of Gina Coulthard, Dr Jim Coulton, Dr Hugh Elton, Dr Yaprak Eran, Gülgün Girdivan, Steffi Sutherland, and an anonymous referee, have been particularly appreciated. We thank these people, deeply.

*Dr Gareth Darbyshire*
*British Institute at Ankara*

# Teşekkür

Anadolu Demir Çağları Sempozyumu'na katılan meslektaşlarımız ile 2001 yılında bir Demir Çağ başkenti olan Van'da yeniden bir araya gelmek bizi çok mutlu etti. İlk sempozyumun düzenlendiği 1984 yılından bu yana sempozyuma duyulan yakın ilginin azalmamış oluşu sevindirici idi. Bu ilginin varlığı sempozyumu düzenleme amacımızın ne kadar doğru olduğunun da ifadesi idi.

5. Anadolu Demir Çağları Sempozyumu'nun hazırlanmasında çok kişinin yoğun emeği vardır. Van Yüzüncü Yıl Üniversitesi bize her türlü olanağı sağladı. Rektör Prof. Dr Yücel Aşkın'a, Rektör Yardımcısı Prof. Dr Zühre Şentürk'e ve Nuray Karayel'e içten teşekkür ederim. İstanbul Üniversitesi rektörü Prof. Dr Kemal Alemdaroğlu'nun sempozyumun açılışına katılarak bizi onurlandırmasına minnettarız. Sempozyuma maddi destek sağlayan Roma Istituto per gli Studi Micenei ed Egeo Anatolici'ye ve bu enstitünün müdürü Prof. Mirjo Salvini'ye teşekkür ederim. Sempozyum bildirilerinin yayınlanmasını sağlayan Ankara İngiliz Arkeoloji Enstitüsü'ne teşekkür etmek bir borçtur. Misafirlerimizin Ayanis (Ağartı) Köyü'nde ağırlanmasındaki zahmetleri için tüm köy halkına şükranlarımı borçluyum. 5.Anadolu Demir Çağları Sempozyumu'nun düzenlenmesinde görev alan ve fedakarca çalışan Özlem Çevik, Aylin Erdem, Fulya Dedeoğlu, Atilla Batmaz, Dilek Öztürk ve tüm öğrencilerime teşekkür ederim.

En içten teşekkürlerimi sempozyuma katılan veya bildiri sunan meslektaşlarıma sunmak isterim. Anadolu Demir Çağları Sempozyumu'nu 1984 yılından beri kesintisiz olarak düzenleyebilmemizin en büyük destekçileri bu kişilerdir.

*Prof. Dr Altan Çilingiroğlu*
*Sempozyum Sekreteri*

Bu yayının basıma hazırlanması sırasında uzmanlıklarından, değerli yardımlarından ve desteklerinden yararlandığımız Gina Coulthard, Dr Jim Coulton, Dr Hugh Elton, Dr Yaprak Eran, Gülgün Girdivan, Steffi Sutherland ve Sayın danışmanımıza en içten teşekkürlerimizi sunarız.

*Dr Gareth Darbyshire*
*Ankara İngiliz Arkeoloji Enstitüsü*

# Contents

# Research on Early Iron Age fortresses and necropoleis in eastern Anatolia

## Oktay Belli
*Istanbul University*

### Abstract

These Early Iron Age fortresses and necropoleis were used by the Nairi and Uruatri principalities, before the Urartian kingdom was founded around the middle of the ninth century BC. The cuneiform Assyrian royal annals begin providing information about these principalities from the first quarter of the 13th century BC. For instance, the Assyrian king, Shalmaneser I (ca. 1274–1245 BC), relates that Uruatri consisted of eight kingdoms (principalities), while from Tukulti-Ninurta I (ca. 1244–1208 BC) we learn that Nairi had 60 kings (princes). Such information indicates that, from the beginning of the second half of the second millennium BC, eastern Anatolia was ruled by principalities and that there was not yet a central authority for the region.

### Özet

M.Ö. 13 yüzyılın ilk çeyreğinden beri çivi yazılı Asur kaynakları, Doğu Anadolu'da Urartu Krallığı'nın proto tarihini oluşturan Nairi ve Uruatri Beylikleri hakkında çok önemli bilgiler vermektedir. Örneğin Asur Kralı I. Salmanassar (M.Ö. 1274–1245) Uruatri'nin 8 krallıktan (beylikten) oluştuğunu, I. Tukulti-Ninurta (M.Ö. 1244–1208) ise Nairi'nin 60 kralının (beyinin) olduğunu bildirmektedir. Bu önemli bilgilerden, M.Ö. 13 yüzyılın başlarından beri Doğu Anadolu Bölgesi'nde çeşitli boy ve budunların oluşturduğu Beylikler Döneminin bulunduğunu ve merkezi bir yönetime geçilmediğini öğrenmekteyiz. Beylikler Dönemine ait herhangi bir arkeolojik kazı ve yüzey araştırmasının henüz yapılmamış olması, birçok çözümlenmemiş sorunun günümüze kadar gelmesini sağlamıştır.

The mighty Urartians, who ruled in eastern Anatolia, Transcaucasia and northwestern Iran from the ninth to the sixth centuries BC, also had a fairly developed grave-chamber architecture. Due to the low number of studies focusing on the origin and development of this grave-chamber architecture, the subject still has questions pending (Sevin 1987: 35–6). However, recent studies of second millennium BC cultures in northeast Anatolia (Belli, Bahşaliyev 2001: 25-32; Belli, Konyar 2001a; Özfirat 2001: 17) have rendered it possible for many settlements to be located, and the archaeological excavations at Ernis, Karagündüz and Yoncatepe in the Van region, and at the Hakkari Early Iron Age necropolis, have given us some idea of the origin of Urartian grave architecture. To shed more light on the subject, surveys in eastern Anatolia have been undertaken by the author from 1997 onwards, with financial support provided by the Istanbul University Research Fund (fig. 1). The aim of these surveys has been to discover similar Early Iron Age graves in the regions of Ağrı, Iğdır and Van, which are parts of the same cultural and geographic environment as Nakhichevan, where such graves are quite often encountered (Belli, Sevin 1999: 25, 35).

### Yürek fortress and tomb

Yürek fortress is situated 58km southwest of Iğdır, east of the road between Abbasgöl dam and the village of the same name. Abbasgöl canal runs northwards along the western skirts of the fortress terrace walls. 500–600m west of Yürek is Papaz fortress (Belli 1999: 275–6). The terrace walls on the western slopes of Yürek fortress have survived as two or three rows of stones. These walls have striking similarities with those of Keçikıran, an Early Iron Age fortress to the north of lake Van. Large blocks with well worked outer surfaces were procured from rich andesite beds nearby. The fortresses of Yürek and Papaz were built in the Early Iron Age; the Abbasgöl dam belongs to the seventh century BC.

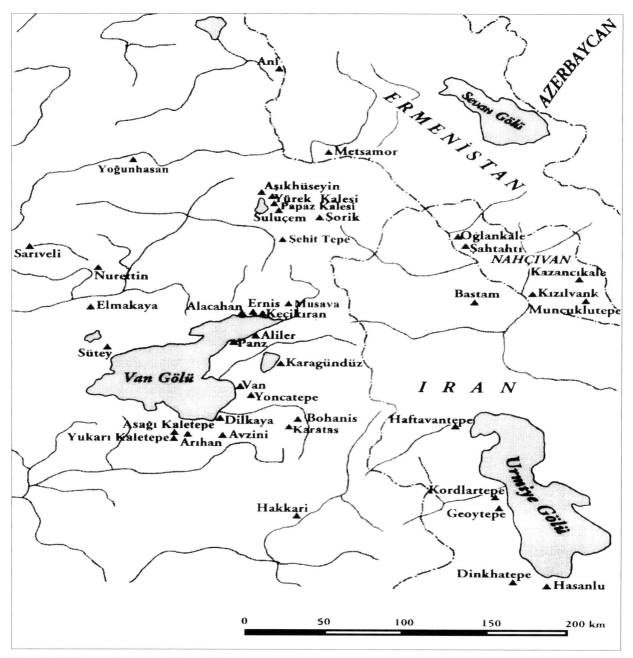

*Fig. 1. Early Iron Age necropoleis and fortresses in eastern Anatolia and neighbouring regions*

The environs of the dam constitute the most important highlands of the region, and their rich pastures and meadows have attracted nomads throughout the ages.

A large grave is situated on the flat area which lies 30–40m east of the fortress terrace walls (fig. 2). This is one of the best examples of such Early Iron Age tombs. Orientated north-south, the chamber is built of andesite blocks which have roughly worked outer surfaces, set into a pit cut into the earth, and measures 1.80m by 5.50m across; however, due to earth infill, its depth could not be calculated. There is no dromos, and its walls are built with the corbelling technique. Large, roughly-worked andesite lid-stones were laid on top of the chamber in a west-east direction, each measuring up to 1.5m by 2.5m across and weighing 1–1.5 tons (fig. 3). Smaller stones were originally placed between the larger ones but these have since fallen down into the chamber. In addition, the layer of gravel and earth covering the tomb has eroded away. Despite the lack of human remains, the size of the chamber raises the possibility that it was used for multiple burials. No similar grave has been encountered in the vicinity (Belli, Konyar 2001a: 332).

*Fig. 2. Grave at Yürek fortress*

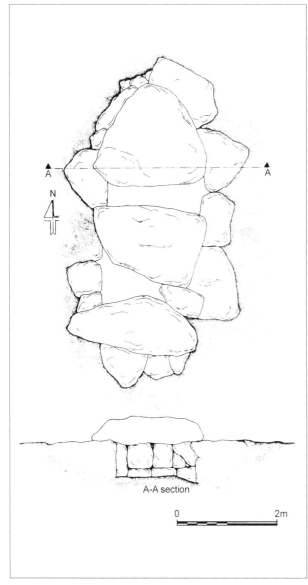

*Fig. 3. Grave at Yürek fortress: plan and section*

A-A section

0                    2m

## Aşıkhüseyin fortress and tomb

Aşıkhüseyin fortress is situated 32km south of Iğdır's Tuzluca district, atop a double-peaked hill. The upper citadel is approximately 50m north of the lower one; both are dated to the seventh century BC (Belli 1997: 178).

The tomb lies at the northeastern skirts of the fortress; unfortunately, it has been illegally excavated by villagers (fig. 4). The chamber, set into the earth, measures 2.50m by 1.75m across and has side walls of flat slabs built up in the corbelling technique; the depth could not be measured accurately due to earth infill (Belli, Konyar 2001a: 332). A single very large andesite block was used to cover the entire chamber. The grave does not have a dromos, and the chamber is entered by lifting the heavy stone lid at its north end. Potsherds, including several of metallic grey ware, and human remains, dug out of the chamber by illegal excavators, demonstrate that the grave belongs to the Early Iron Age and housed multiple burials (Belli 1997: 178, fig. 19).

*Fig. 4. Grave after an illegal excavation, Aşıkhüseyin fortress*

## Panz fortress and necropolis

Panz fortress lies 51km north of Van city, 1km east of lake Van and 1km west of the Van-Erciş highway; Çolpan village, 400m to the east, is the nearest modern settlement. The fortress is located on an approximately north-south orientated andesite hill and is surrounded by the quite fertile land which runs along the shores of lake Van. The defences follow the natural, roughly rectangular course of the hill except on the west side, facing the lake, where the presence of a steep ridge has obviated the need to build fortifications (the absence of fortifications where steep ridges occur is a customary feature of fortresses of the Late Bronze Age and, especially, the Early Iron Age in Nakhichevan and eastern Anatolia). The eastern side of the fortress is the weakest and thus strong walls were built here (fig. 5).

*Fig. 5. East wall of Panz fortress*

*Fig. 6. Acropolis of Panz fortress*

The southwestern part was also well fortified, with a 2.7–2.8m thick wall. The large, roughly worked andesite blocks used for the fortification walls, as well as the blocks used for other buildings and for the tomb, were procured from the rich andesite beds in the vicinity. The fortifications have survived as one to three rows of stones.

The fortress is highest on the northwest side towards the middle (fig. 6): this area became a hillock once the mud-brick fabric on top of the stone walls had deteriorated. The remains here are thought to be those of either an acropolis or a temple of the fortress. The northwest walls of the buildings in this area are visible; they are faced on both sides with worked stones with a core of smaller stones, and at 3.4–3.5m thick they are the thickest walls to be seen on the site. They extend to the northwest to form a terrace. Heaps of deteriorated mud-brick and small filling-stones obstruct a closer examination of the lesser structures (Belli, Konyar 2001a: 333).

The position and layout of Panz fortress are similar to those of the Avzini, Nurkök, Evditepe, Keçikıran, Şorik, Papaz, Aliler and Yoncatepe Early Iron Age citadels in the Van region. These fortresses were built on high rocky hills whilst the civil settlements and necropoleis lay on the surrounding slopes. Panz is a more expanded and developed example. It was reinforced during the Urartian kingdom period, which is the reason for the

presence of two different masonry techniques used for the walls. The characteristics of the walls of the southeastern section of the fortress clearly show that they belong to the Early Iron Age: they are built with larger and more roughly worked blocks, with huge gaps between them; furthermore there are no offsets to reinforce the walls and improve the defence. By contrast, the walls in the other parts of the fortress are more carefully built with blocks displaying higher quality craftsmanship, and these walls have offsets that strengthen them and improve their defensive value, although in this case the offsets are not placed at equal intervals. The sections with finer workmanship belong to the early period of the Urartian kingdom. There is a rock-marker 1.5m in diameter made by levelling the surface of the rock about 200–250m south of the fortress. Such circular rock-markers are to be seen near the fortresses and irrigation canals built by the Urartian king Menua (ca. 810–786 BC) (Belli 1989: 73); hence it is understood that Panz fortress was enlarged during the reign of this king, directly following the Early Iron Age. The layout of Panz most closely resembles the fortresses at Ernis-Evditepe and Aliler, which were likewise enlarged in Menua's time.

A necropolis and wall remains are found on the southeastern skirt of the fortress. However, many parts of the walls have been damaged by the construction of summerhouses, and some graves have been dug illegally. These graves are surrounded by monoliths forming elliptical or circular dolmen-like arrangements which measure 3m by 3m, 2m by 3m, or 3.75m by 2.50m across (figs 7–9). Where the monoliths are placed in an upright position, the height of some graves exceeds 1m, though the earth layer on top has eroded away. Similar graves are to be seen on high mountains south of lake Van, at Ernis-Evditepe (Belli 2001b: figs 1–3; Belli, Konyar 2003b: figs 8–11), and at Shakhtakhty in Nakhichevan (Bahşaliyev 1997: 33), and at Shiesheh in Iran (Khanzaq et al. 2001: 29, fig. 5).

*Fig. 7. Grave surrounded by monoliths*

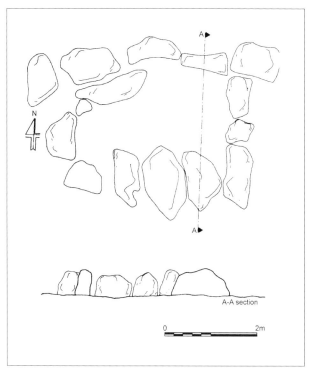

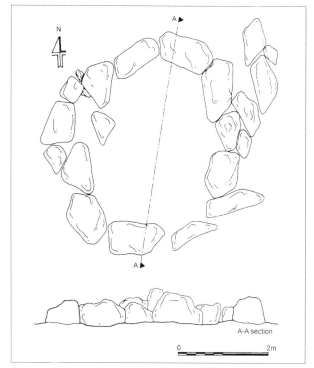

*Fig. 8. Grave at Panz fortress*

*Fig. 9. Grave at Panz fortress*

## Şorik fortress and necropolis

Şorik fortress and its necropolis are located 11km northwest of Doğubayazıt; the site is reached by turning west at a point 9km along the Doğubayazıt-Ağrı highway, passing through Sağlıksuyu (Arzep) village, and then proceeding about 400–500m west of the village. This area is called Şorik (sour) because of the high salt content in the soil.

Like other Early Iron Age sites, Şorik has a fortress surrounded by a settlement and necropolis. The fortress is located on a high andesite hill 1,790m above sea level, and its environs have very rich pastures and meadows. Now as before, stock breeding is more important than agriculture in the economic life of this area. The stones used for the walls are unworked andesite monoliths which are understood to have been gathered from creek beds. Unfortunately treasure hunters have damaged the fortifications and the buildings therein and consequently, unlike the Yoncatepe, Avzini, Nurkök, Panz, Aliler and Evditepe fortresses, the extremely denuded condition of Şorik has prevented us from retrieving even the most basic structural plan (Belli, Konyar 2001a: 334).

A settlement and necropolis are located on the northeast, north and northwest skirts of the fortress (fig. 10). The necropolis extends over a wide area as at Ernis-Evditepe (Erzen 1964: 570). Unfortunately most of the graves have been plundered by treasure hunters, who lifted the lid stones (figs 11, 12). Pottery placed as gifts, votive offerings of iron, jewellery and weapon fragments, as well as human bones, have been found scattered around the graves. The extremely corroded ironwork appears to have held little attraction for the robbers. The large number of finds and human bones suggest the graves contained multiple burials. As at Karagündüz (Sevin, Kavaklı 1996: 25) and Yoncatepe (Belli, Kavaklı 1999: 437), it is highly probable that here too vessels filled with drink and food were deposited as burial gifts.

As at other Early Iron Age necropoleis, the graves were constructed with walls built in pits dug into the earth. Heavy lid-stones were used to cover the graves (figs 13, 14). The rectangular tomb chambers measure 1.75m by 4m, 3m by 1.60m, or 2.6m by 1m, with filleted corners and sidewalls built using the corbelling technique. These tombs do not have a dromos and access into the chamber is gained by removing the lid-stone at the short side. The depths of the chambers could not be measured due to the earth infill present.

One of the plundered graves was surrounded by monoliths set in an elliptical fashion, similar to the graves on the west skirts of the Panz fortress; clearly such graves were originally covered with earth. Within the 3m wide ring of monoliths there is a chamber measuring 2.6m by 1m across (fig. 15); the outer surfaces of the andesite blocks used for the chamber walls are roughly worked. These graves are smaller than the one at Yürek.

*Fig. 10. Settlement and necropolis, Şorik*

*Fig. 11. Grave after an illegal excavation, Şorik fortress*

*Fig. 12. Grave after an illegal excavation, Şorik fortress*

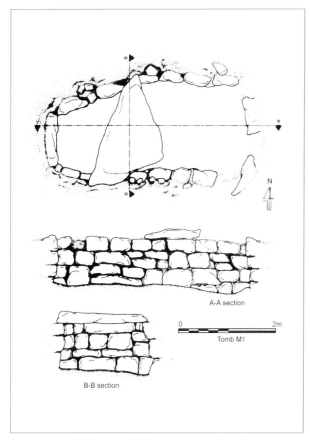

*Fig. 13. Grave at Şorik fortress: plan and section*

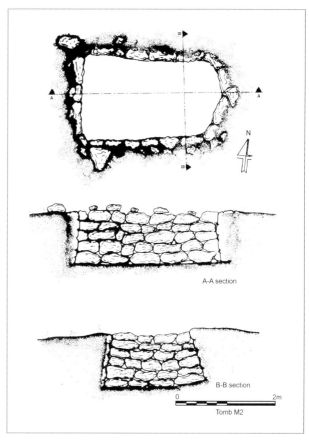

*Fig. 14. Grave at Şorik fortress: plan and section*

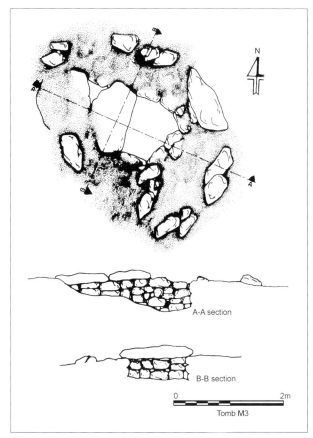

*Fig. 16. Grave after an illegal excavation, Şehit Tepe*

*Fig. 15. Grave at Şorik fortress: plan and section*

*Fig. 17. Grave after an illegal excavation, Şehit Tepe*

## Şehit Tepe necropolis

The necropolis is located at and around Şehit Tepe, 2km north of Atadam (Gredin) village in Ağrı's Diyadin district, on the northern slopes of the volcanic Tendürek mountain (2,863m above sea level). The northern section of Tendürek is not as steep as the southern and has rich water sources. The region is a typical plains settlement and is covered with pastures and mountain grass: herding still plays an important role in the economic life of the people.

Şehit Tepe lies at 2,170m above sea level. Nearly all the tombs were constructed with andesite stones, which are abundant in the vicinity and have become visible as a result of soil erosion. The largest tomb, which gives the necropolis its name, had been destroyed by the locals during illegal excavations (figs 16, 17). It lies on a rocky hill and resembles a tumulus. The cover-stones and walls of the tomb were destroyed and it is difficult to determine the plan because of the piles of stone and soil in the tomb. Nevertheless, the coursing of the stones can be clearly seen. The thousands of stones on the tomb appear to have been placed deliberately in lieu of soil (fig. 18). Externally it resembles the stone architecture characteristic of Suluçem kurgans (Özfırat 2001: 71–3, figs 28, 29).

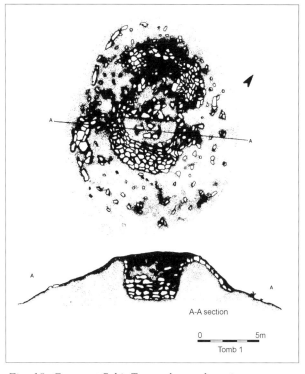

*Fig. 18. Grave at Şehit Tepe: plan and section*

There is no indication of a fortress in the vicinity but there are other tombs here that have a specific plan. For instance, there is a roughly rectangular tomb, orientated east-west and 7.5m long (fig. 19). Its western extremity has been destroyed, but fortunately the remaining stones have been left virtually undisturbed (Belli, Konyar 2003a: 103).

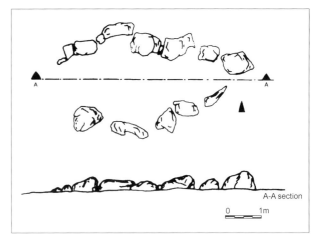

*Fig. 20. Musava tomb: plan and section*

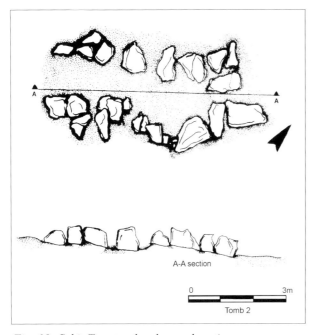

*Fig. 19. Şehit Tepe tomb: plan and section*

*Fig. 21. Grave with elliptical plan, Musava*

**Musava tomb and the Melik monumental building**

Musava tomb lies to the northeast of lake Van and 75km from Van city. Duruktaş (Isveran) village is the nearest modern settlement, 2km to the north.

This single tomb is sited on the southern slope of a rocky hill and during our survey we did not encounter any other tomb or fortress in the vicinity. It is roughly elliptical in plan, orientated east-west and 6m long by 3.5m wide (figs 20, 21). Because it was built on a slope, the soil covering the tomb has shifted to the south revealing the stone surround; the blocks were obtained from the rich andesite beds in the vicinity. This undis-turbed tomb resembles the ones in Ernis-Evditepe necropolis.

Approximately 300m east of the grave, on the southern slopes of the mountains at Melik, there is a construction, roughly square in plan with wall remains on three sides. These walls are long and regular despite the rocky and sloping terrain: the west wall is 460m long, the north 480m, and the east 453m (fig. 22). Only the southern part, looking to the Muradiye (Bargiri) plain, has no wall. Little damage has been done to the masonry by the rainwater and floods running south from the high northern hills, and only the eastern walling has

*Fig. 22. North wall of Melik*

been robbed by villagers for use in house construction. The extant remains are not very high due to collapse, the highest surviving section standing at 1m, and their original height is unknown, though they must have been higher than 2m because the fallen stones around form large piles.

No towers or projecting walls were constructed. The wall thickness is approximately 3.5m in every section (figs 23, 24). Large andesite stones, presumably obtained from the abundant andesite deposits in the vicinity, are used for both the outer faces and the inner core of the walls, and they and their joints are roughly worked (fig. 25); the spaces between the stones are filled with mud and small stones. It is thought that the walls never had a mud-brick superstructure. It is unknown whether or not wall-beds were carved in the living rock for the walls to stand on.

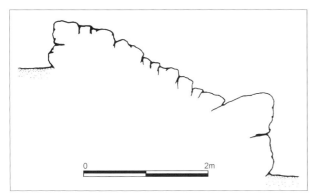

*Fig. 23. The Melik wall section*

*Fig. 24. Remains of the Melik wall from the south*

*Fig. 25. East wall of Melik*

Although the extant remains do give a reasonable idea about the original appearance of this monumental building we do not know the reasons for constructing it with such a strong wall, or its use. The hilly area to the north is still used as mountain pasture; the southern slope of the building descends gradually towards the Muradiye plain. In the Urartian period there were vineyards on these southern slopes, and the channel built by the Urartian king Menua for irrigating the Muradiye plain passes 95m to the north of the monumental structure. Today, the villagers call the empty area enclosed by the walls, which measures about 5.5 acres, 'Melik's vineyard'. No sherds or architectural remains from the locality, other than the Musava tomb, can assist in dating the monumental building. What is interesting is that we have not encountered anything similar in eastern Anatolia even though we have been surveying this region for 35 years. Long and thick walls of the same type can be observed at Çalhankale and Kazancıkale in Nakhichevan Autonomous Republic, dating to the Late Bronze and Early Iron Ages (Belli 2001a: 413–15), though unlike the Melik structure these have bastions and protruding walls to strengthen the fortifications. Since the Melik wall lacks any comparanda in the Urartian period, we believe that it was built in the Middle Bronze Age or, more likely, in the Late Bronze Age (Belli, Konyar 2003a: 104).

**Arıhan tomb**

The tomb is situated 71km southwest of Van, the nearest modern settlement being at Arıhan which lies east of Uzuntekne (Kahnımiran) village on the Pasandaşt plain (4km$^2$), one of the two important plains to the south of lake Van, the other being the Görentaş plain (6km$^2$) (Saraçoğlu 1956: 81). The Pasandaşt plain and lake Van are separated by the northeastern part of the Taurus range, which rises up like a wall between them. The plain, surrounded by high mountains and covered with rich pastures, is one of the main areas for herding in the district (Belli 2002: 240).

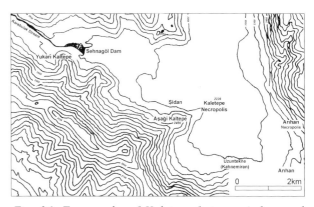

*Fig. 26. Topography of Kaletepe fortress, Arıhan and Kaletepe necropoleis*

Arıhan tomb is located 500m east of Arıhan in the vicinity of Soravan (fig. 26). Standing 2,350m above sea level, it lies on the northern slope of a rocky andesite hill. The tomb, orientated north-south, is surrounded by a single row of stones to prevent soil erosion (though this precaution proved ineffective). The thick and regular andesite cover-stones are roughly worked. Unfortunately, this monumental tomb was plundered in the Middle Ages after removal of the cover-stone at the north end (fig. 27). No harm was done to the architecture save for cross signs and Armenian names carved on the stones. The tomb, 6.30m long and 2.5m wide internally, has a height of 2m (fig. 28), although stones inside it prevented us from observing the floor. The ceiling and the walls bear soot-marks from fire. The south wall is carved out of the living rock; by contrast, the east and west walls are corbelled (Belli, Bahşaliyev 2001: figs 55, 56).

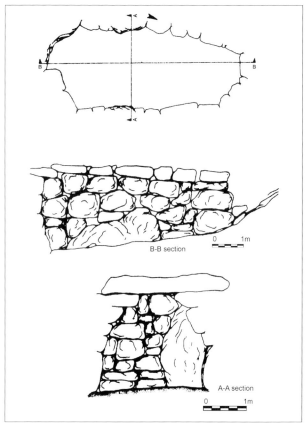

Fig. 28. Grave at Arıhan: plan and section

Fig. 27. Grave after an illegal excavation, Arıhan

## Kaletepe fortresses and necropolis

Kaletepe fortresses and necropolis are located 2.5km northwest of Arıhan and 1.0–1.5km northwest of Uzuntekne (Kahnımiran) village. The nearest modern settlement is Şidan, 1.5km northwest of Uzuntekne village.

The Kaletepe settlement was built on two separate hills, lying east/west of each other, with the highest point reached in the west. Thus we have named the eastern settlement lower Kaletepe, and the western and higher of the two as upper Kaletepe. Lower Kaletepe, at 2,456m above sea level, sits on a rocky area sloping towards the Pasandaşt plain to the northeast. It is evident that every section of this wide and calcareous hill had been settled. The walls of the houses were of roughly worked stones. However, no clear house-plans are evident because so many stones have been removed. In the easternmost area of the hill, there exists a single row of stones aligned east-west, although again part of this has been removed (fig. 29). There are no traces of a settlement in the steep calcareous area between upper and lower Kaletepe.

Fig. 29. North wall of lower Kaletepe fortress

Fig. 30. General view of upper Kaletepe fortress

The ruins of upper Kaletepe stand on an oval-shaped rocky calcareous hill, 2,550m above sea level (fig. 30). The east side of the hill opens to lower Kaletepe via another hill, rough and rocky, whilst the relatively plain eastern and northeastern parts are connected to other hills by a pass. The northern part is the steepest whilst the easiest approach is on the west and the northwest. It is thought that upper Kaletepe was intended as the last place of defence for the lower Kaletepe settlement.

The walls have fallen down on the south and southeast sides, to form heaps of stones which mostly consist of the walls' core material (fig. 31). The most important feature is that these core-stones are roughly worked rather than unworked. The walls took in the high points of exposed rock formations wherever possible. Upstanding walling is extant on the north and northeast sides, connecting with two rocks on the north. The walling would have served as a windbreak as well as a security measure. To the north of the collapsed stonework in the southwestern part of the site, there is another wall, mostly surviving as a single row of stones though occasionally as two rows. Here again the wall connects two rocky prominences. As it gradually descends towards the southeast its thickness varies between 2.60m and 2.70m. The stones of the outer face are more elaborately carved than the more roughly worked inner face. Mud was used as a binding agent between the stones. We do not know if the living rock was carved in order to level a foundation bed for the walls. The use of small stones in the wall is similar to the constructional technique found at Avzini fortress, though the latter site has a regular plan, in contrast to upper and lower Kaletepe which incorporate natural rock formations in their layout and hence exhibit an irregular arrangement. The two fortified Kaletepe settlements are the most important Early Iron Age centres in the vicinity. Built gradually over time, they hint at the dimension of perceived threats.

On the eastern slope of lower Kaletepe is the necropolis (Belli 2002: 240). The tombs were formerly obscured by a thick layer of soil washed down by rains and floods, but 19 years ago, as a result of road construction, several tombs were revealed, some of which were destroyed by the roadworks (fig. 32). The tombs are mostly orientated east-west like other tombs in the vicinity.

Fig. 32. General view of Kaletepe necropolis

Tomb I (figs 33, 34) lies at the eastern extremity of the necropolis and is 6.5m long and 2.20m wide internally. It has corbelled side walls and seven large, heavy, worked andesite cover-stones, each aligned north-south and closely resembling those at the Yürek Kalesi tomb. We entered the tomb by removing the easternmost cover-stone. Tomb II (fig. 35) lies immediately west of tomb I and has the same orientation. It is 7.20m long and 2.5m wide internally, with corbelled side walls. Its most important feature is a 50cm wide niche in the west wall (fig. 36); the only similar example known is from Karagündüz necropolis (Sevin, Kavaklı 1996: 15). It has not been robbed.

Fig. 31. Southeast wall of upper Kaletepe fortress

Fig. 33. Tomb I, after an illegal excavation, Kaletepe fortress

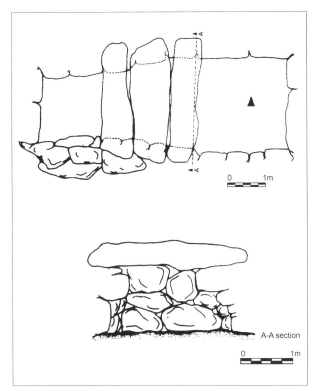

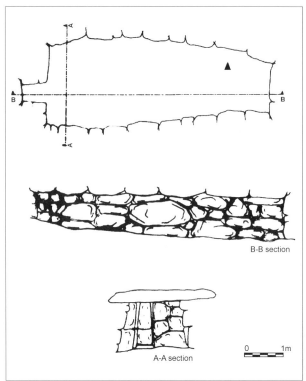

*Fig. 34. Kaletepe tomb I: plan and section*

*Fig. 36. Kaletepe tomb II: plan and section*

*Fig. 35. Tomb II, Kaletepe fortress*

*Fig. 37. Another tomb filled with soil, Kaletepe fortress*

The cover-stones of other tombs are only partially visible because the excavated soil from the road building operation was dumped over the area (fig. 37).

**Conclusion**

These Early Iron Age fortresses and necropoleis were used by the Nairi and Uruatri principalities, before the Urartian kingdom was founded around the middle of the ninth century BC. The cuneiform Assyrian royal annals begin providing information about these principalities from the first quarter of the 13th century BC. For instance, the Assyrian king Shalmaneser I (ca. 1274–1245 BC) relates that Uruatri consisted of eight kingdoms (principalities), while from Tukulti-Ninurta I (ca. 1244–1208 BC) we learn that Nairi had 60 kings (princes). Such information indicates that, from the beginning of the second half of the second millennium BC, eastern Anatolia was ruled by principalities and that there was not yet a central authority for the region.

Some scholars have suggested that the Urartian tomb chamber architecture originated in Assyria, the enemy to the south (Öğün 1978: 676). However, as the Early Iron Age graves clearly show, there are significant similarities between the graves of the principalities and the early examples of Urartian tomb chambers. Further studies will help to shed more light on this relationship.

**Acknowledgements**
This work was supported by the Research Fund of the University of Istanbul: Project Number 1411. Our survey team included Dr Alpaslan Ceylan, Dr Erkan Konyar, Gamze Yılmaz, Dr Anıl Yılmaz, Can Avcı, Gürkan Ergin, İ. Zeynep Konuralp and İsmail Ayman. Plans of the fortresses and tombs were drawn by E. Konyar, C. Avcı, A. Yılmaz and İ. Ayman. I would like to thank all my colleagues, who worked with great enthusiasm.

**Bibliography**

Bahşaliyev, V. 1997: *Nahçıvan Arkeolojisi — The Archaeology of Nakhichevan* (Arkeoloji ve Sanat Yayınları). Istanbul

Belli, O. 1989: 'Urartu kalelerindeki anıtsal kaya işaretleri — monumentale felszeichen in bereich Urartäischer festungsanlagen' *Anadolu Araştırmaları* 11: 65–122

— 1997: '1996 Yılında doğu Anadolu bölgesinde Urartu baraj ve sulama sisteminin araştırılması' *Araştırma Sonuçları Toplantısı* 15.2: 163–98

— 1999: '1997 Yılında doğu Anadolu bölgesinde Urartu baraj ve sulama sisteminin araştırılması' *Araştırma Sonuçları Toplantısı* 16.2: 267–91

— 2001a: 'Istanbul University's and Turkey's first international project in archaeology: archaeological surveys in Nakhichevan' in O. Belli (ed.), *Istanbul University's Contributions to Archaeology in Turkey (1932–2000)*. Istanbul: 411–17

— 2001b: 'An Early Iron Age cemetery in the Van region: Ernis-Evditepe' in O. Belli (ed.), *Istanbul University's Contributions to Archaeology in Turkey (1932–2000)*. Istanbul: 145–9

— 2002: '2000 Yılında doğu Anadolu bölgesinde Urartu baraj, gölet ve sulama kanallarının araştırılması' *Araştırma Sonuçları Toplantısı* 19.2: 239–56

Belli, O., Bahşaliyev, V. 2001: *Nahçıvan Bölgesinde Orta ve Son Tunç Çağı Boya Bezemeli Çanak Çömlek Kültürü — Middle and Late Bronze Age Painted Pottery Culture in the Nakhichevan Region* (Arkeoloji ve Sanat Yayınları). Istanbul

Belli, O., Kavaklı, E. 1999: '1998 Yılı Van-Yoncatepe Kalesi ve Nekropolü kazısı' *Kazı Sonuçları Toplantısı* 21.1: 435–48

Belli, O., Konyar, E. 2001a: 'Archaeological survey on Early Iron Age fortresses and necropoleis in northeast Anatolia' in O. Belli (ed.), *Istanbul University's Contributions to Archaeology in Turkey (1932–2000)*. Istanbul: 331–5

— 2001b: 'Excavations at Van-Yoncatepe fortress and necropolis' *Tel-Aviv* 28: 169–212

— 2003a: *Doğu Anadolu Bölgesinde Erken Demir Çağı Kale ve Nekropolleri — Early Iron Age Fortresses and Necropolises in Eastern Anatolia* (Arkeoloji ve Sanat Yayınları). Istanbul

— 2003b: 'The largest Early Iron Age necropolis in eastern Anatolia: Ernis-Evditepe' *Tel-Aviv* 30/2: 167–203

Belli, O., Sevin, V. 1999: *Nahcıvan'da Arkeolojik Araştırmalar 1998 — Archaeological Survey in Nakhichevan* (Arkeoloji ve Sanat Yayınları). Istanbul

Erzen, A. 1964: 'Ünseli (Ernis) Mezarlığı' *Belleten* 111: 570–2

Khanzaq, R.B., Biscione, R., Hejebri-Nobari, A.R., Salvini, M. 2001: 'Haldi's Protection. The newly found rock inscription of Argishti II in Shiesheh, near Ahar (Azerbaijan, Iran)' *Studie Micenei ed Egeo-Anatolici* 43/1: 25–37

Öğün, B. 1978: 'Die urartäischen bestattungsbräuche' in S. Şahin, E. Schwertheim, J. Wagner (eds), *Studien zur Religion und Kultur Kleinasiens für F.K. Dörner zum 65. Geburstag am 28. Februar 1976*. Leiden: 639–78

Özfırat, A. 2001: *Doğu Anadolu Yayla Kültürleri* (Arkeoloji ve Sanat Yayınları). Istanbul

Saraçoğlu, H. 1956: *Doğu Anadolu I*. Istanbul

Sevin, V. 1987: 'Urartu Oda-Mezar Mimarisi'nin Kökeni Üzerine Bazı Gözlemler' in A. Çilingiroğlu (ed.), *Anadolu Demir Çağları — Anatolian Iron Ages* I. Izmir: 35–55

Sevin, V., Kavaklı, E. 1996: *Bir Erken Demir Çağı Nekropolü Van-Karagündüz — An Early Iron Age Cemetery* (Arkeoloji ve Sanat Yayınları). Istanbul

# Urartu and the east and north

## Charles Burney
*c/o British Institute at Ankara*

## Abstract

A wide ranging essay attempts to suggest certain lines of enquiry into the background of the kingdom of Urartu, touching on chariotry, horses and horsemanship and the affinities of the Hasanlu gold bowl. On this last, an unorthodox interpretation is suggested. The influence of Assyria is seen as over-stressed. Recent fieldwork in Armenia suggests likely origins of Urartian irrigation canals and fortresses, given their relatively earlier dating than in the Van region.

## Özet

Bu çalışma Urartu Krallığı'nın geçmişine ilişkin olarak bilinen ve inanılan belli bazı kalıpları sorgulamak üzere yapılmış geniş kapsamlı deneme girişimlerinden oluşmaktadır. Savaş arabaları, atlar ve binicilik ve Hasanlu altın kasesiyle ilgili bilgiler yeniden değerlendirilmiştir. Sonuncusu ile ilgili olarak şimdiye kadar alışılmamış bir açıklama önerilmiş. Asur etkilerinin abartıldığı ortaya konmaya çalışılmıştır. Ermenistan'da yapılan yakın tarihli arazi çalışmaları Urartu sulama kanalları ve savunma duvarlarının benzerlerini ortaya çıkarmış ve bu yapılara Van Bölgesi'ndekilerden daha erken tarihler öngörülmüştür.

The abiding question mark over Urartu, how to explain its origins and peculiar characteristics, is generally known. The adoption of the cuneiform script by Sarduri I used to lead many astray into seeing Assyrian inspiration as the dominant formative factor for Urartian civilisation. One may hope that this view has had its day, but nothing has yet adequately replaced it.

Well known are the linguistic investigations into Hurro-Urartian links, with Urartian not so much a direct descendant as a cousin of Hurrian, sharing a common linguistic substratum (Diakonoff, Starostin 1986; Salvini 1978; 1992). But for the cavalier attitude of some philologists and linguists, the latter in their efforts to reconstruct prehistoric or proto-languages, we archaeologists might be inclined to pay closer attention to ideas from that quarter. For our part, we must keep our feet on the ground, notably in matters of geography and chronology, space and time. Linguistic evidence has to be employed, where relevant, for no clues can be ignored.

Archaeology can of course reveal much of the static and the permanent — settlements, fortresses, temples and even irrigation works — but is notoriously inadequate as a source for the transient and temporary, the history and movements of nomadic groups, only intermittently illuminated by written sources (Kupper 1957; Cribb 1991; Marchese 2001). Urartu is perhaps best known for its massive fortresses, familiar to all. So much has been revealed of these since my relatively amateur reconnaissances in the 1950s! (Burney 1957; Burney, Lawson 1960). Thus we may gain ever closer insights into the skills of the Urartian builders, almost certainly of native stock, and no doubt also into the wisdom of the kings and governors who were their employers or patrons. Urartian defensive planning is therefore by now quite well understood, from the siting and design of each fortress. Offensive military operations are altogether another matter, with only hints to be gained from the frustratingly laconic Urartian royal inscriptions. Sargon II's account of his famous eighth campaign excepted, there is scant evidence of Urartian deployment on the battlefield, still less of movements across country or of personnel, supply and military formations (Luckenbill 1926: paras 153–5; Smith 1994).

In one respect, however, there is considerable evidence, at least indirectly, illuminating this whole problem, in relation to horses and horsemanship. The personal skill of Menua and other kings was a point of great pride (*UKN* 110). One can look on this as an outcome of the establishment of the Urartian kingdom or alternatively as a major factor behind that development. Here a few arguments are put forward in support of the latter alternative.

There seems to be fairly general agreement that horse riding cannot have emerged from the Near East, but must have been introduced from a region or regions beyond. Before examination of the development of cavalry and indeed of chariotry, some comment is called for on the matter of the earliest domestication of the horse. A recent controversy has blown up, between advocates of an origin in the plains of south Russia and eastward through the steppes and others questioning the evidence, suggesting instead an origin in central Europe (Hänsel, Zimmer 1994; Mallory 1998). While it is true that horses were widely hunted, the weight of Russian archaeological opinion, supported by Western specialists such as David Anthony, strongly favours the more eastern origin for the domestication of the horse (Anthony 1986). Emergence of the domesticated horse as a source of meat in the fifth millennium BC along the Dnieper is agreed, while in a late fourth-millennium context at Botai, east of the Urals, 99% of no fewer than 300,000 animal bones analysed have been identified as horse. Bit wear indicates that by that period horse riding was widespread (Anthony, Brown 2000).

What then of the emergence of the horse-driven chariot? It would be mistaken to suggest that its military uses were paramount. In central Asia and Siberia there are hundreds of rock drawings depicting flimsy vehicles with two spoked wheels, at times associated with cattle (Sorokin 1990). Heavy wagons and carts, drawn by oxen rather than horses, performed the essential function of freight and personnel carriers over the wide landscapes of the steppes, moving alongside their livestock (Mallory 1989: 163; Piggott 1992: 17–36). These vehicles, with their solid wheels, were far more rudimentary in their construction than those light vehicles with two spoked wheels, the chariots of the Indo-Iranian tribes. These moved out of the region now called Kazakhstan southward into India and southwest into Iran, ultimately bringing about the introduction of the chariot far to the east of the Indo-European zone, in China (Sun Tzu; Piggott 1992: 63–8).

It is generally accepted that the Hurrians played a major role in introducing chariotry into the settled communities of the Near East (Diakonoff 1984; Moorey 1986). The role of the small, intrusive element of Indic

origin in the kingdom of Mitanni has probably been exaggerated: the population of that short-lived state was of course predominantly Hurrian. Yet they were willing to receive this alien element, whose traditions had much in common with Aryan India (Jankowska 1981; Wilhelm 1989: 17–40).

Where does all this background evidence link up with Urartu? Essential clues surely lie in the ruins of Hasanlu. I will put my head above the parapet by repeating a recently published suggestion concerning the identities of the gods depicted on the gold bowl. As the only person privileged to have drawn it in the flesh, I had long held to what amounts to the orthodox view of its context as Hurrian and more specifically Mannaean. Only lately have I proposed a radically different interpretation, identifying the leader of the three charioteers, clearly divine, no longer as Teshub, the Hurrian storm god, but as Indra, the war god of the Rig-Veda, where he is described as a bull (Frye 1962: 25; Burney 1999: 5–7).

The interpretation of the enigmatic themes of the Hasanlu gold bowl as linked with the myth of Kummarbi, and thus as essentially Hurrian, may well still be valid (Porada 1959; Winter 1989). Yet the above alternative explanation surely deserves consideration. This centres primarily on the focal subject of the whole design, the contest of the figure armed only with knuckle-dusters with the three headed monster emerging from the rock. A Vedic or Indic interpretation, with the hero as Trito ('third') is intriguing: after losing his cattle to the monster, he gains the support of the Indo-European war-god (Indra?) in defeating the creature, here depicted as a dragon rather than a serpent, and duly recovers his cattle (Mallory 1989: 137). If the leading figure in the procession of charioteers is indeed Indra, the sun god following him — one of three such gods in the Rig-Veda, described as drawn in cars by many horses — may be Suriya, sometimes said to be dependent on Indra (Bettany 1890: 182–3). In any event, on this reconstruction it would seem that a war god rather than a storm god (Teshub) led this procession on the Hasanlu bowl. It is worth reminding ourselves that in the Urartian pantheon — first recorded at Meher Kapısı, just after the initial Urartian contacts with the Urmia basin — it is a war god (Haldi) not a storm god (Tesheba) who heads the list (Salvini 1994).

Hasanlu may surely be accepted as having a significant cultural influence on Urartu in the ninth century BC, before its sack by Menua, and possibly on the immediately preceding generations. It is hard to distinguish the precise details of the chariots on the Hasanlu bowl; but they appear more closely to resemble the design favoured, for example, by the Hittites, with the axle placed centrally for weight and armament. Later

Urartian chariots often appear more similar to the type fashionable earlier in Egypt, with the axle placed well to the rear, making for greater speed and manoeuvrability but allowing less weaponry for the heat of battle (Littauer, Crouwel 1979: 101–10).

It is well known, if only from Sargon II's eighth campaign, that the Urmia region was noted for its horses, their breeding and training (Luckenbill 1926: para. 158; Zimansky 1990). Here was a vital component for any first-class army, and one developed to their best abilities by the rulers of Urartu. The above mentioned story from the Rig-Veda — originating in the second millennium BC but, like Homer, not written down for some centuries — hints at the crucial importance of livestock for the Indo-European tribes. While conditions were seemingly beginning to favour sheep over the hitherto dominant cattle, and while the acceptability of sheep as ritual offerings is demonstrated on the Hasanlu bowl, let us not overlook the economic role of wheeled vehicles, from heavy solid wheeled carts and wagons to light chariots. Military use of the chariot surely evolved out of its economic functions, not vice versa (Lincoln 1981; Mallory 1989: 117–20, 137–8; Diebold 1992).

The Near Eastern evidence, notably from Mitanni, indicates that the horsemanship of that kingdom derived from central Asia, with the well known Indo-Aryan élite, but that it was the Hurrians who did most to advance the deployment of chariotry in warfare and as an aid to occupation of new territories. This is of course not an original opinion, but it needs to be given an Urartian dimension. This growth of horsemanship and chariotry indicates a strong, if epigraphically undocumented, eastern influence on the evolving kingdom of Van. It is admittedly difficult to pinpoint other clues to possible links with central Asia. It has been suggested that representations of doorways — as with certain open-air shrines in Urartu (Tarhan, Sevin 1975) — while indeed associated with temple entrances, are a long surviving manifestation of the Proto-Indo-European concept of the patrilinear family, with the dichotomy between 'inside' and 'outside' in relation to the family dwelling (Margueron 1976; della Volpe 1990; Polomé 1992; Burney 1997: 182). Another aspect is one form of the cult of the ancestors, implied by the custom of tying rags to trees, and occurring not only in Van but as far east as Mongolia (Ujiyedin, Stuart 1997). This may well be of later derivation, and often linked with prayers for recovery from sickness, especially of a child. Yet this illustrates how customs can travel over vast distances of the continent of Asia. Over the steppes and plains mere distance has long been no barrier to contact.

More relevant may be evidence of nomadic groups not far removed from Urartian territory, though largely antedating Urartu by two centuries or more. The Meshkinshahr stelae were recorded on a survey in eastern Azerbaijan in 1978, in a region where cemeteries outnumber contemporary settlement sites of the early first millennium BC (Iron II in Iranian terms) (Ingraham, Summers 1979; Sevin 2000). Whether these stelae recorded enemy dead or local warriors is uncertain: but the dagger each wears suggests no peaceful context. It can fairly be objected that the Meshkinshahr stelae, with comparable examples from a vast zone beyond the Caucasus, cannot be seen to have influenced Urartu. The same cannot, however, be said of southern Trans-Caucasia, lying within that zone termed by the linguists East Caucasian, and seen on linguistic evidence as a focal area of Hurrian ancestry (Diakonoff, Starostin 1986). While the Syunik rock drawings and the Lchashen burials with their wagons and carts demonstrate the prevalence of wheeled vehicles in the second millennium BC, these, as already stated, were by no means all for military purposes (Burney, Lang 1971: 104–7; Piggott 1983: 66–82; Rijksmuseum 2001). But an Urartian debt to Trans-Caucasia for chariotry is less certain from the quadrigae on the bronze belt from Astkhi-Blur, owing to its late date (ninth or eighth century BC): here the chariots are involved in a stag hunt (Piggott 1983: 136).

Of far more profound significance for the whole problem of the emergence of the Urartian state is recently discussed evidence from areas including the Yerevan plain and the surrounding hills (Smith 1999). Here are numerous fortresses built on steep rocky sites at some altitude above the Yerevan plain, in some areas having associated irrigation works. Unlike the fortresses sited at the edge of the plain, and thus at lower altitudes, these appear to date to the Early Iron Age, those near the plain being of Urartian construction. Having no first-hand acquaintance with the evidence, I have to trust this dating: I have no hesitation in doing so. There follows a highly significant indicator to the inspiration behind two leading features of Urartian civilisation, namely, the fortresses with their cyclopean walls and the irrigation canals. The Urartian annals reveal that Etiu was a formidable obstacle to Urartian expansion into the Yerevan plain; and it must have enjoyed a sophisticated material culture at least by the end of the second millennium BC (*UKN* 127–31, 155A; Burney, Lang 1971: 137; Zimansky 1985: 57–8). Moreover, the cattle breeding so fundamental to the expansion of Indo-Iranian tribes across the steppes out of their homeland in the Andronovo cultural zone, modern Kazakhstan, was evidently a mainstay of the economy of the land of Aza, the Yerevan plain, not without reason the most productive territory in the whole of Urartu (*UKN* 142; Zimansky 1985: 82 [tablet no. 10 from Karmir Blur]; Kuzmina 1993). Why the Urartian kings were such enthusiastic irrigation engineers remains something of a mystery. Neither for sheep rearing nor for viticulture was irrigation required. Rich pastures would, however, have sustained more extensive herds of both cattle and horses, the latter for the army.

Few, least of all the present writer, would wish to underrate the achievements of the Urartian kings and the wealth of their major citadels in and beyond the central region around lake Van. The discoveries at Ayanis alone underline the wealth of this civilisation at its centre, in the period of reconstruction under Rusa II (Çilingiroğlu, Salvini 2001). But generations of scholars have tended to look to the south, to militaristic Assyria, as the dominant external influence on the kingdom centred on Van. Admittedly the earliest depiction of an Urartian fortress occurs on the bronze reliefs of Shalmaneser III from Balawat (King 1915); and of course the cuneiform script was imported in the reign of Sarduri I, the initial inscriptions even being written in Assyrian. It is true also that the Assyrian annals and letters reveal more than can be gleaned from the laconic Urartian inscriptions.

Nevertheless, this evidence as a whole does not amount to proof of Assyrian cultural dominance. It seems that one must look elsewhere, to east and to north, for vital formative elements in Urartian civilisation.

What about indigenous development, it may he argued? Is it not merely a matter of time before Early Iron Age sites comparable with those in southern Trans-Caucasia are discovered and recorded in eastern Anatolia? Subject always to recent, unpublished discoveries, this seems doubtful, mainly owing to the higher altitudes in eastern Anatolia. The higher terrain north of lake Van is too bleak to have supported perennial settlements of any size, nor are irrigation canals likely to be traced there, though admittedly canals with earthen banks would long since have completely vanished. The famous Shamiram-Su (Menua canal) has been restored repeatedly over the centuries. But cyclopean fortresses should be detectable. One such, albeit of rough construction, does indeed stand high in the foothills of the Süphan Dağ: this is Kefir Kale (to be distinguished from Kefkalesi), which stands two and a half hours' riding and climbing distance above Adilcevaz, with patches of snow on the site on 1 August 1956. This was, however, a mere *Fluchtburg*, a temporary refuge, not to be compared with the Early Iron Age sites above the Yerevan plain (Burney 1957: 51, pl. vi C).

In this paper a number of kites have been flown, which may well be shot down; and some of the questions may soon he answered. Yet the exercise has seemed worthwhile. It does seem as if we are slowly coming closer to an understanding of the origins of Urartu, in part deriving from indigenous developments hinted at by cemeteries in the Van region (Sevin 1999), but conceivably stimulated by the arrival of highly mobile, horse riding groups, among whose tribes an ascendancy was quite rapidly achieved. This would have made possible the achievements, military and economic, of the population of southern Trans-Caucasia and, less certainly, of the Urmia basin and beyond in northwestern Iran. The archaeological record, unfortunately, is predictably silent on such mobile intruders, in the absence of burial mounds such as those left in south Russia by the Scyths.

Urartu was in the ancient Near East but not of it, at least not till Assyrian intrusions compelled a closer, if uncomfortable, relationship with the south.

## Acknowledgements

I must end by thanking both Professor Altan Çilingiroğlu for organising such a fruitful and happy gathering in Van in August 2001 and all the participants, each one a contributor to the success of the Fifth Anatolian Iron Ages Symposium.

## Bibliography

*Abbreviation*

*UKN* = Melikišvili, G.A. 1960: *Urartskie klinoobraznye nadpisi (Le iscrizioni cuneiformi urartee)* (second edition). Moscow

Anthony, D.W. 1986: 'The "Kurgan Culture", Indo-European origins and the domestication of the horse: a reconsideration' *Current Anthropology* 27: 291–314

Anthony, D.W., Brown, D.R. 2000: 'Eneolithic horse exploitation in the Eurasian steppes — diet, ritual and riding' *Antiquity* 74: 75–86

Bettany, G.T. 1890: *Encyclopedia of World Religions*. London

Burney, C.A. 1957: 'Urartian fortresses and towns in the Van region' *Anatolian Studies* 7: 37–53

— 1997: 'Hurrians and Indo-Europeans in their historical and archaeological context' *Al-Rafidan* 18: 175–93

— 1999: 'Beyond the frontiers of empire: Iranians and their ancestors' *Iranica Antiqua* 34: 1–20

Burney, C.A., Lang, D.M. 1971: *The Peoples of the Hills*. London

Burney, C.A., Lawson, G.R. 1960: 'Measured plans of Urartian fortresses' *Anatolian Studies* 10: 177–96

Çilingiroğlu, A., Salvini, M. 2001: *Ayanis I: Ten Years' Excavations at Rusahinili Eiduru-kai 1989–1998* (CNR Istituto per gli Studi Micenei ed Egeo-Anatolici. Documents Asiana 6). Rome

Cribb, R. 1991: *Nomads in Archaeology*. Cambridge

della Volpe, A. 1990: 'From the hearth to the creation of boundaries' *Journal of Indo-European Studies* 18: 157–84

Diakokoff, I.M. 1984: *The Prehistory of the Armenian People* (revised edition). Delmer, New York

Diakonoff, I.M., Starostin, S.A. 1986: *Hurro-Urartian as an Eastern Caucasian Language* (Münchner Studien zur Sprachwisenschaft Beiheft 12 NF). Munich

Diebold, A.R. 1992: 'The traditional view of the Indo-European palaeoeconomy' in E.C. Polomé, W. Winter (eds), *Reconstructing Languages and Cultures — Trends in Linguistics* (Studies and Monographs 58). Berlin, New York: 317–67

Frye, R.N. 1962: *The Heritage of Persia*. London

Hänsel, B., Zimmer, S. (eds) 1994: *Der Indogermanen und das Pferd* (Archaeololingua Hauptreibe 4). Budapest

Ingraham, M.L., Summers, G.D. 1979: 'Stelae and settlements in the Meshkin Shahr plain, northeastern Azerbaijan, Iran' *Archaeologische Mitteilungen aus Iran* 12: 67–102

Jankowska, N.B. 1981: 'Life of the military élite in Arraphe' in M.A. Morrison, D.I. Owen (eds), *Studies on the Civilization of Nuzi and the Hurrians in Honor of Ernest Rene Lacheman*. Winona Lake: 195–200

King, L.W. 1915: *Bronze Reliefs from the Gates of Shalmaneser, King of Assyria B.C. 860–825*. London

Kupper, J.R. 1957: *Les Nomades en Mésopotamie aux Temps des Rois de Mari*. Paris

Kuzmina, E.E. 1993: 'Les steppes de l'Asie Centrale à l'époque de Bronze — la culture d'Andronovo' *Les Dossiers d'Archéologie* 185: 82–9

Lincoln, B. 1981: *Priests, Warriors and Cattle*. Los Angeles

Littauer, M.A., Crouwel, J.H. 1979: *Wheeled Vehicles and Ridden Animals in the Ancient Near East*. Leiden

Luckenbill, D.D. 1926: *Ancient Records of Assyria and Babylonia. Volumes 1 and 2*. Chicago

Mallory, J.P. 1989: *In Search of the Indo-Europeans*. London

— 1998: 'Review of Hänsel, B., Zimmer, S. (eds) 1994' *Journal of Indo-European Studies* 26: 199

Marchese, R. 2001: 'Camels and weaving: interconnective impact on nomadic material culture' *Anatolica* 27: 171–81

Margueron, J. 1976: 'Maquettes architecturales de Meskene-Emar' *Syria* 53: 193–232

Moorey, P.R.S. 1986: 'The emergence of the light, horse-drawn chariot in the Near East, c.2000–1500 BC' *World Archaeology* 18: 196–215

Piggott, S. 1983: *The Earliest Wheeled Transport — From the Atlantic Coast to the Caspian Sea*. London

— 1992: *Wagon, Chariot and Carriage — Symbol and Status in the History of Transport*. London

Polomé, E.C. 1992: 'Comparative linguistics and the reconstruction of Indo-European culture' in E.C. Polomé, W. Winter (eds), *Reconstructing Languages and Cultures — Trends in Linguistics* (Studies and Monographs 58). Berlin, New York: 369–90

Porada, E. 1959: 'The Hasanlu bowl' *Expedition* 1.3: 19–22

Rijksmuseum, Leiden: *Exhibition — centred on one of the Lchashen wagons, freshly conserved*. For four months from 2 November 2001

Salvini, M. 1978: 'Hourrite et Urartéen' *Revue Hittite et Asianique* 36: 157–72

— 1992: 'Nuovi confronti fra Hurrico e Urartaeo' *Studi Micenei ed Egeo-Anatolici* 29: 217–25

— 1994: 'The historical background of the Urartian monument of Meher Kapısı' in A. Çilingiroğlu, D.H. French (eds), *Anatolian Iron Ages 3* (British Institute of Archaeology at Ankara Monograph 16). Ankara: 205–10

Sevin, V. 1999: 'The origins of the Urartians in the light of the Van/Karagündüz excavations' in A. Çilingiroğlu, R.J. Matthews (eds), *Anatolian Iron Ages 4* (*Anatolian Studies* 49): 159–64

— 2000: 'Mystery stelae' *Archaeology* 53 (July–August): 46–51

Smith, A.T. 1999: 'The making of an Urartian landscape in southern Transcaucasia: a study of political architectonics' *American Journal of Archaeology* 103: 45–71

Smith, J.B. 1994: 'A tactical re-interpretation of the battle of Uaush: Assyria and Urartu at war 714 BC' in A. Çilingiroğlu, D.H. French (eds), *Anatolian Iron Ages 3* (British Institute of Archaeology at Ankara Monograph 16). Ankara: 229–39

Sorokin, S. 1990: 'Horse-drawn vehicles of the Eurasian forest-steppe in pre-"Centaurian" times' *Iranica Antiqua* 25: 97–147

Sun Tzu (ca. 500 BC): *The Art of War*. Translation by Y. Shibing and commentary by General T. Hanzhang. Ware

Tarhan, M.T., Sevin, V. 1975: 'The relation between Urartian temple gates and monumental rock niches' *Belleten* 39: 401–12

Ujiyedin, C., Stuart, K. 1997: 'Mongol tree worship' *Archiv Orientalni* 65: 275–91

Wilhelm, G. 1989: *The Hurrians.* Translated by J. Barnes. Warminster

Winter, I.J. 1989: 'The "Hasanlu gold bowl": thirty years later' *Expedition* 31: 87–106

Zimansky, P. 1985: *Ecology and Empire — The Structure of the Urartian State* (Studies in Ancient Oriental Civilization 41). *Chicago*

— 1990: 'Urartian geography and Sargon's eighth campaign' *Journal of Near Eastern Studies* 49: 1–21

# The Erzincan, Erzurum and Kars region in the Iron Age

## Alpaslan Ceylan
*Atatürk University, Erzurum*

### Abstract

The northeastern Anatolian provinces of Erzincan, Erzurum and Kars lie mostly in a continental climatic zone with winter extending over more than half the year. The mountain ranges, which rise to over 3,000m from plateaux at over 2,000m, are a rich source of minerals. The rivers Çoruh, Aras, Kür and Euphrates/Fırat, important water suppliers, run through this region. Remains of juniper, pine and oak trees found in archaeological excavations, especially at the settlement mounds of Karaz, Güzelova, Pulur and Sos, suggest that in former times the region was more forested and with a greater variety of trees than today. The faunal remains from these mounds show that animal husbandry was the main means of human survival for a very long period. The area is rich in minerals and there are also many obsidian beds, which provided an exchange medium for goods long before metals came into use. This quantity of minerals was one of the reasons why powerful states periodically took an interest in the area. From the research carried out in the three provinces, it appears that the area was well populated in the Iron Age. This paper provides a brief overview of the region and a catalogue of the Iron Age settlements/fortresses to be found there.

### Özet

Kuzeydoğu Anadolu Bölgesi'nde yer alan Erzincan, Erzurum ve Kars illeri çoğunlukla karasal iklim kuşağında yer aldığı için yılın yarısından çoğu kıştır. 2,000m.nin üzerinde platoların, 3,000m.nin üzerinde dağ zincirlerinin olduğu bölge maden açısından da zengindir. Anadolu'nun önemli su kaynaklarından olan Çoruh, Aras, Kür ve Fırat nehirleri bu bölgededir. Karaz, Güzelova, Pulur ve Sos Höyük'te yapılan arkeolojik kazılarda bulunan ardıç, çam ve meşe gibi ağaç türlerinin bulunması bölgenin ormanlık alanının bugünkü alanından daha geniş ve çeşit olarak da daha zengin olduğunu göstermektedir. Yine aynı yerlerden çıkan hayvan kalıntıları hayvancılığın çok uzun zamandır bu bölgenin geçim kaynağını oluşturduğunu göstermektedir. Maden açısından da bölge oldukça zengindir. Madenin kullanılmaya başlamasından çok önceleri ticarette takas aracı olarak kullanılan obsidyenin yatakları da oldukça fazladır. Madenin bolluğu dönem dönem güçlü devletlerin dikkatini buralara yönlendirmesine sebep olmuştur. Adı geçen illerde yapılan araştırmalar sonucunda buralarda oldukça yoğun Demir Çağı yerleşmeleri saptanmıştır. Araştırma bölgemizin batı bölümünü oluşturan Erzincan'da belirlenen Demir Çağı yerleşmeleri Altıntepe, Küçük Höyük, Saztepe, Çadırkaya (Pekeriç), Ozanlı Kalesi, Sırataşlar Kalesi ve Şirinlikale'dir. Araştırma bölgesinin ortasında bulunan Erzurum'daki Demir Çağı yerleşmeleri, Sos Höyük, Küçük Çağdarış, Umudum Tepe (Kalor Tepe), Tepeköy (Piralibaba) Kalesi, Uzunahmet Kalesi, Pasinler (Hasankale) Kalesi, Marifet, Sürbahan, Güzelhisar (Avnik) Kalesi, Harami Kale, Aydınsu, Hasanova, Çelikli, Sukonak, Yazılıtaş ve Delibaba'dır. Araştırma alanımızın doğu bölümünü oluşturan Kars'taki Demir Çağı yerleşmeleri ise, Kırankaya (Asboğa) Kalesi, İnkaya (Micingirt) Kalesi, Süngütaşı (Zivin) Kalesi, Köroğlu Kalesi, Toprakkale ve Yoğunhasan Kalesi'dir.

---

Our research area comprises the eastern Anatolian provinces of Erzincan, Erzurum and Kars (fig. 1). Most of this region lies in the continental climatic zone and hence more than half of the year is winter. However the lower lying regions of the Kelkit-Çoruh valley, the Erzurum plain and the Tortum-Uzundere-Oltu area have a milder climate (Erinç 1965: 5; Atalay 1983: 116). The main geological and geomorphological features of the region are: 1. mountain ranges reaching heights of over 3,000m, rising from plateaux over

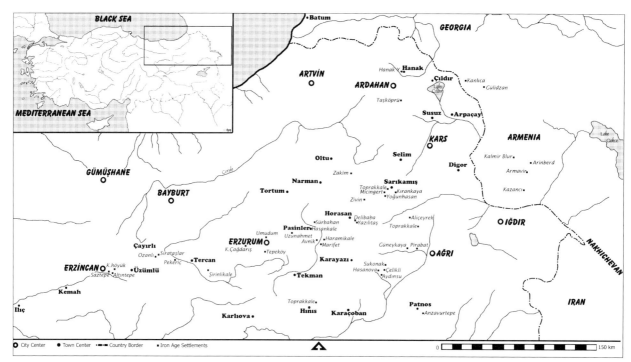

*Fig. 1. Map of the Erzincan, Erzurum and Kars region*

2,000m high; 2. mineral beds of high economic potential, conferring strategic and trade importance on the region. Various rivers rise in the region, specifically the Çoruh (the ancient Harpassos; see Xenophon, 18–19; Strabon, 15, 30), the Aras (the ancient Araxes; see Strabon, 8; Herodotus, 202; Xenophon, 25), the Kür (the ancient Kyros) and the Fırat (the Euphrates; see Herodotus, 52; Xenophon, 27–37). As today, these water sources have played an important role in human history (Erinç 1965: 43ff; Sözer 1974; Tarkan 1974: 19; Toynbee 1978: 77ff; Esin 1979: 29ff; Doğanay 1983: 210ff).

Nowadays the forested part of this region lies in the eastern Black Sea mountains and in the Sarıkamış area (İnandık 1965: 22, 41; MTA 1980). However archaeological excavations at Karaz (Koşay 1943: 165; 1984: 1ff; Burney 1958: 157; Koşay, Turfan 1959; Koşay, Vary 1964: 1ff; 1967: 1ff; Yakar 1985: 302), Pulur (Koşay, Vary 1964; Koşay 1984; Pehlivan 1984; Yakar 1985: 302; Güneri 1987), Güzelova (Koşay, Vary 1967: 1ff; Yakar 1985: 302) and Sos (Sagona et al. 1997; Sagona 2000) show that there used to be a wider area under forest, and with a greater variety of tree types such as pine, juniper and oak, than at present. Grain found at these excavations also demonstrates that agriculture was carried out in the past.

The main source of income for the region today is animal husbandry. The wide, fertile plain of the Erzurum and Kars plateau, in particular, stays green for most of the year and the area is a centre for cattle rearing. Historical and archaeological sources demonstrate that animal husbandry has been practised here for many millennia, with a variety of domesticated animals (Tarkan 1974: 18; Doğanay 1983: 388ff). Evidence comes from the excavations at Karaz, Pulur, Güzelova and Sos and from the records of the campaign of the Hittite king Murshili II (1344–1306 BC) (for Murshili II's campaigns of the seventh year of his reign see Goetze 1967: 97ff), and the taxes claimed by Argishti I of Urartu (786–766 BC) from the land of Diauehi (König 1955–1957: 81; Melikišvili 1960: 128; Payne 1995: 75–6, 80).

The other particular feature of this region is its mineral beds. Even before metals were utilised by man, the obsidian of the region was used for exchange. When metal came to be used, these mineral veins began to be worked (Ryan 1960: 22; MTA 1977; 1980; Slattery 1987). The value of these minerals in the Iron Age can be understood from Urartian inscriptions referring to this area. For example, the inscriptions of Argishti I refer to an annual tax of 20.5kg of gold, 18.5kg of silver and 5 tons of copper. Evidence from Altıntepe also indicates that the area was rich in minerals (Luckenbill 1926–1927: 499; Ryan 1960: 17ff; Esin 1969: 107; Sevin 1979: 105, n. 112; Slattery 1987: 3ff; Belli 1986; 1991; Merhav 1991; Çilingiroglu 1994: 67, n. 160).

We have studied the area since 1998 in order to define all the extant Iron Age settlements (Ceylan 2000a; 2000b; 2001a: 37ff.; 2001b; 2002; 2003).

## Iron Age settlements in Erzincan province

This province forms the western part of our study area. Iron Age settlements include the following sites.

### Altıntepe

Altıntepe is located 20km east of Erzincan on the north side of the main Erzurum-Erzincan road. It is known that it was built by the Urartian king Rusa II (685–645 BC). The first finds derived from railway construction in 1935. Excavations were begun in 1959 by T. Özgüç. The fortress is an important source of information about Urartu (Steinherr 1958; Özgüç 1961; 1963; 1966; 1969; Azarpay 1968: 43, 46, 69; Emre 1969; Piotrovskii 1969: 24, 32, 37, 127–8; Özgüç 1974; Merhav 1991; Ceylan 2000a) (fig. 2).

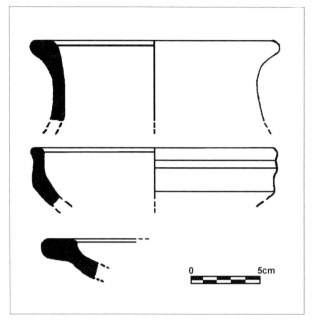

Fig. 3. *Pottery from Erzincan–Çadırkaya*

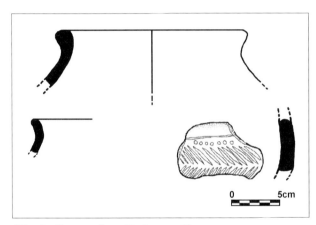

Fig. 2. *Pottery from Erzincan–Altıntepe*

### Küçük Höyük

Küçük Höyük lies 2km to the north of Altıntepe, between there and the town of Üzümlü. Our survey found large quantities of Iron Age pottery sherds (Özgüç 1961: 257; Emre 1969: 281; Ceylan 2000a: 183).

### Saztepe

Saztepe is 2km to the west of Altıntepe on the way to Erzincan. Its modern name derives from the reed (saz) beds in the area. Large quantites of Iron Age material have been found here but unfortunately the fortress is too badly damaged to ascertain its plan (Ceylan 2003: 313)

### Çadırkaya (Pekeriç) fortress

Çadırkaya lies about 104km east-northeast of Erzincan, in the district of Tercan. This Iron Age fortified settlement has Urartian rock-cut tombs, rock-cut symbols and a rock-cut stepped water tunnel (von Gall 1967: 504ff; Işık 1987; Belli 1989: 65ff; Ceylan 2000a: 185) (fig. 3).

### Ozanlı fortress

This fortress is situated 4km southwest of Ozanlı village in the district of Çayırlı, 117km northeast of Erzincan. There are wall foundations carved from the living rock, a rock-cut stepped water tunnel and rock-cut rooms (Ceylan 2000a: 185) (fig. 4).

Fig. 4. *Erzincan–Ozanlı fortress*

### Sırataşlar fortress

The fortress lies 8km northeast of the town of Çayırlı. The masonry work carried out on the living rock is noteworthy, including a 'blind window'. There are also cyclopean citadel walls, a water canal and a water tunnel (Ceylan 2002: 166) (figs 5, 6).

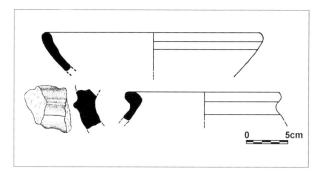

Fig. 5. *Pottery from Erzincan–Sırataşlar*

Fig. 6. *Erzincan–Sırataşlar fortress*

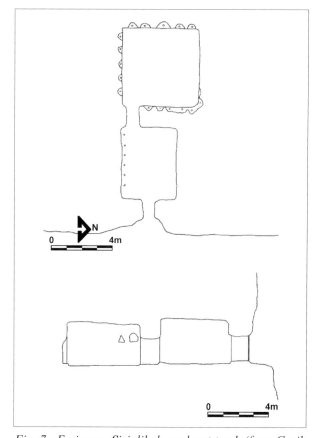

Fig. 7. *Erzincan–Şirinlikale rock-cut tomb (from Çevik 2000)*

## Şirinlikale

The fortress of Şirinlikale is built on a high rocky outcrop at the entrance to a valley 50km southeast of Tercan. Together with vast quantities of Iron Age pottery, there is a rock-cut stepped water tunnel and two rock-cut tombs (Işık 1987; Çevik 2000: 120ff) (fig. 7).

## Iron Age settlements in Erzurum province

This province is in the centre of our study area. Iron Age settlements include the following sites.

### Küçük Çağdarış fortress

The fortress lies in the district of Aşkale on the main Erzurum-Erzincan road, approximately 45km west of Erzurum. There are wall foundations carved into the living rock, an open-air cultic site and a rock-cut stepped water tunnel (Işık 1987; 1995: 14; Ceylan 2003: 315) (fig. 8).

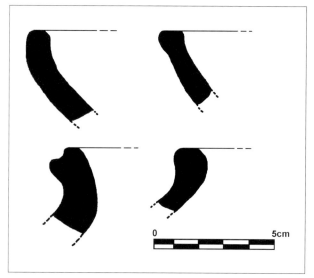

Fig. 8. *Pottery from Erzurum–Küçük Çağdarış*

### Umudum Tepe (Kalortepe)

2km west of Umudum village and 18km north of Erzurum, the fortress stands on a rocky outcrop overlooking the Erzurum plain. Citadel walls and rock-cut tombs can be seen there. The graves appear to be from two different periods (Çilingiroğlu 1980; Işık 1995: 10, 29; Çevik 2000: 121ff).

### Tepeköy (Pir Ali Baba) fortress

Lying 2km southeast of the village of Tepeköy (which is 12km south of Erzurum), on mount Eyerli, the fortress occupies two hills: an upper and a lower one. Citadel walls, other architectural remains and Iron Age pottery have been found (Başaran, Sevin 1976–1977; an article on this fortress is currently in press).

*Uzunahmet fortress*

The fortress stands on a hill 18km east of Erzurum. There are large quantities of Iron Age pottery sherds and remains of a citadel wall (Güneri 1987: 45ff; Ceylan 2003, 315, fig. 5) (fig. 9).

*Sos Höyük*

This mound lies 18km east of Erzurum on the Erzurum-Pasinler main road. Excavations revealed that one level (Sos II) of the mound belongs to the Iron Age (Sagona et al. 1997; Sagona et al. 1998; Sagona 1999; 2000).

*Fig. 9. Erzurum–Uzunahmet fortress*

*Pasinler fortress*

The fortress, 40km to the east of Erzurum in the Pasinler district, is built on a steep rocky outcrop and has an inscription of the Urartian king Minua (810–786 BC), remains of Iron Age citadel walls, rock-cut tombs and a water tunnel (König 1955–1957: no. 44; Melikišvili 1960: 69; Payne 1995: no. 5.3.3; Çevik 2000: 124; Erkmen, Ceylan 2003; Ceylan 2003: 315) (fig. 10).

*Marifet rock-cut tomb*

An Iron Age settlement and rock-cut tombs lie on a rocky hill west of Marifet village which is 44km south of the town of Pasinler (Başgelen 1985; Çevik 2000: 123; Ceylan 2003: 315).

*Demirdöven rock-cut tomb*

This tomb came to light during the construction of a reservoir. It lies on the top of Hasandede mountain, 10km north of the town of Pasinler (Çevik 2000: 123; Ceylan 2003: 314).

*Güzelhisar (Avnik)*

This fortress lies on a rock outcrop by Güzelhisar village, 38km south of Pasinler. An inscription of the Urartian king Sarduri II (764–734 BC) was found here (Orthmann 1968–1969; Aydın 1991; Ceylan 2003: 315).

*Harami fortress*

Harami fortress is sited on a steep rocky hill 3km east of the Güzelhisar fortress. It has Iron Age characteristics including a rock-cut stepped water tunnel (Başgelen 1985: 17; Ceylan 2003: 315).

*Toprakkale*

This fortress lies to the south of the village of the same name, northeast of the town of Hınıs. Iron Age pottery has been found along with ceramics from various periods (Başgelen, Özfırat 1996).

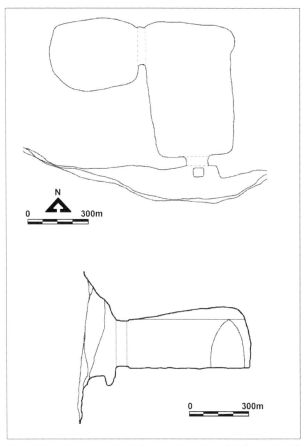

*Fig. 10. Erzurum Pasinler rock-cut tomb (from Çevik 2000)*

*Aydınsu rock-cut tomb*

The tomb is to be found 5km south of the village of Aydinsu which lies 30km southeast of the town of Karayazi. It is known to be of Iron Age date (Çevik 2000: 128).

*Hasanova rock-cut tombs*

Three Iron Age rock-cut tombs have been found in Hasanova, 22km southeast of the town of Karayazı. Two of the tombs lie in the village, the third is about 5km to the west (Başgelen 1985; Çevik 2000: 123).

*Yazılıtaş*

A Urartian inscription of king Minua is carved into the steep rock face at the village of Yazılıtaş, 18km southeast of Horasan (König 1955–1957: no. 23; Melikišvili 1960: no. 36; Sevin 1979: 103ff; Belli 1982: 156; Pehlivan 1984: 86ff; 1991: 34ff; Payne 1995: no. 5.1.7, 39ff; Ceylan 2001b).

*Delibaba (Dellal) fortress*

This settlement lies to the east of the Dellal pass, 17km southeast of Horasan. There is a rock-cut stepped water tunnel. An inscription of the Urartian king Minua was found here but is now lost (König 1955–1957: no. 43; Melikišvili 1960: no. 68; Payne 1995: no.5.3.2, 48ff) (fig. 11).

*Fig. 11. Erzurum–Delibaba (Dellal) fortress*

**Iron Age settlements in Kars province**

This region constitutes the eastern part of our study area. Iron Age settlements include the following sites (see Kökten 1971–1972).

*Kırankaya (Asboğa) fortress*

The fortress sits on a rocky outcrop 18km southeast of the town of Sarıkamış on the main Erzurum-Kars road. Citadel walls and Iron Age pottery have been found (Kırzıoğlu 1958: 52; Ceylan 2001a: 60; 2003: 316).

*İnkaya (Micingirt) fortress*

Twenty two kilometres southwest of Sarıkamış, İnkaya resembles other fortresses of the region with a water cistern and citadel walls (Ceylan 2001a: 60; 2003: 316).

*Süngütaşı (Zivin) fortress*

The fortress lies on a 40m high rocky outcrop, 35km southwest of Sarıkamış. Two water cisterns, a rock-cut stepped water tunnel and an inscription of the Urartian king Minua (810–786 BC), which provides details of his campaign in the north, have been found. This is one of the most important fortresses of the region (König 1955–1957: no. 24; Melikišvili 1950: 27ff; 1960: no. 37; Kleiss, Hauptmann 1976: 15; Tarhan 1980: 101; Diakonoff, Kashkai 1981: 165ff; Pehlivan 1991: 34ff; Çilingiroğlu 1994: 7ff; Payne 1995: no. 5.1.8.40; Salvini 1995: 5ff; Ceylan 2001a: 62ff, figs 19, 20; 2003: 317).

*Toprakkale*

The site lies to the east of the main Erzurum-Kars road, 8km southwest of Sarıkamış. The wall construction technique and the pottery indicate that the fortress was used in the Iron Age (Ceylan 2001a: 53, figs 7, 8; 2003: 316, fig. 7) (figs 12, 13).

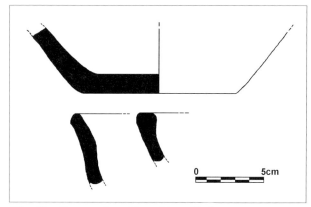

*Fig. 12. Pottery from Kars–Toprakkale*

*Fig. 13. Kars–Toprakkale fortress*

*Yoğunhasan fortress*
This fortress lies 5km west of the village of Kars and 40km southwest of Sarıkamış. Remains of the citadel wall and rock-cut tombs can be seen. A small Urartian reservoir has also been identified about 500m south of the fortress (Ceylan 2001a: 55–9; 2003: 316, figs 6, 7) (figs 14, 15, 16).

Our work in the area has shown that it was intensively settled in the Iron Age, and we hope to increase our knowledge of this period in the region by further surveys in the forthcoming years.

**Acknowledgements**
I would like to thank those team members who have taken part in the surveys made from 1998 onwards.

**Bibliography**
Atalay, İ. 1983: *Türkiye Vejetasyon Coğrafyasına Giriş.* Izmir

Aydın, N. 1991: 'Güzelhisar Urartu kitabesi' *Belleten* 213: 323–9

Azarpay, G. 1968: *Urartian Art and Artifacts.* Los Angeles

Başaran, S., Sevin, V. 1976–1977: 'Bibliyografya' *Anadolu Araştırmaları* 4–5: 500

Başgelen, N. 1985: 'Doğu Anadolu'da Demir Çağına ait bazı yeni bulgular I' *Arkeoloji ve Sanat* 28–31: 15–18

Başgelen, N., Özfırat, A. 1996: 'Erzurum'da bir Demir Çağı merkezi: Toprakkale' *Anadolu Araştırmaları* 14: 143–59

Belli, O. 1982: 'Urartular' *Anadolu Uygarlıkları, Görsel Anadolu Tarihi Ansiklopedisi* I: 139–208

— 1986: 'Doğu Anadolu Bölgesinde antik demir metalürjisinin araştırılması' *Araştırma Sonuçları Toplantısı* 3: 365–78

— 1989: 'Urartu kalelerindeki anıtsal kaya işaretleri' *Anadolu Araştırmaları* 11: 65–88

— 1991: 'Ore deposits and mining in eastern Anatolia in the Urartian period: silver, copper and iron' in R. Merhav (ed.), *Urartu: A Metalworking Center in the First Millennium B.C.E.* Jerusalem: 16–41

Burney, C. 1958: 'Eastern Anatolia in the Chalcolithic and Early Bronze Age' *Anatolian Studies* 8: 157–209

Ceylan, A. 2000a: '1998 Erzincan yüzey araştırması' *Araştırma Sonuçları Toplantısı* 17.2: 181–92

— 2000b: 'Çayırlı'da tarihi ve arkeolojik araştırmalar' *Atatürk Üniversitesi Türkiyat Araştırmaları Enstitüsü Dergisi* 15: 277–91

— 2001a: *Sarıkamış-Tarihi ve Arkeolojik Araştırmalar.* Erzurum

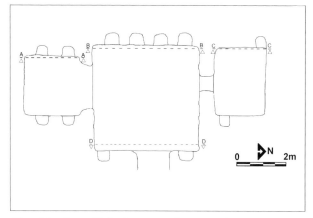
Fig. 14. *Kars–Yoğunhasan rock-cut tomb*

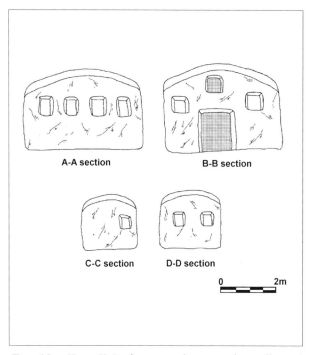
Fig. 15. *Kars–Yoğunhasan rock-cut tomb: walls and niches*

Fig. 16. *Kars–Yoğunhasan fortress*

— 2001b: '1999 Yılı Erzincan ve Erzurum yüzey araştırmaları' *Araştırma Sonuçları Toplantısı* 18.2: 71–82

— 2002: '2000 Yılı Erzincan ve Erzurum yüzey illeri araştırmaları' *Araştırma Sonuçları Toplantısı* 19.2: 165–78

— 2003: '2001 Yılı Erzincan, Erzurum ve Kars illeri yüzey araştırmaları' *Araştırma Sonuçları Toplantısı* 20.2: 311–24

Çevik, N. 2000: *Urartu Kaya Mezarları ve Ölü Gömme Gelenekleri*. Ankara

Çilingiroğlu, A. 1980: 'Umudum Tepe (Kalortepe)' *Anadolu Araştırmaları* 8: 191–203

— 1994: *Urartu Tarihi*. Izmir

Diakonoff, M., Kashkai, S.M. 1981: *Geographical Names According to Urartian Texts*. Wiesbaden

Doğanay, H. 1983: *Erzurum'un Şehirsel Fonksiyonları ve Başlıca Plânlama Sorunları*. Unpublished Associate Professorship thesis. Erzurum University

Emre, K. 1969: 'Altıntepe'de Urartu seramiği' *Belleten* 33: 279–89

Erinç, S. 1965: *Doğu Anadolu Coğrafyası*. Istanbul

Erkmen, M., Ceylan, A. 2003: '2001 yılı Pasinler Kalesi kazısı' in T.C. Kültür Bakanlığı, Anıtlar ve Müzeler Genel Müdürlüğü, *Müze Çalışmaları ve Kurtarma Kazıları Sempozyumu* 13: 17–28

Esin, U. 1969: *Kuantitatif Spektral Analiz Yardımıyla Anadolu'da Başlangıcından Asur Kolonileri Çağına Kadar Bakır ve Tunç Madenciliği*. Istanbul

— 1979: *İlk Üretimciliğe Geçiş Evresinde Anadolu ve Güneydoğu Avrupa I: Doğal Çevre Sorunu*. Istanbul

Goetze, A. 1967: *Die Annalen des Mursilis* (Mitteilungen der Deutschen Orient-Gessellschaft). Berlin

Güneri, S. 1987: 'Erzurum çevresindeki höyüklerin yüzey araştırması' *Araştırma Sonuçları Toplantısı* 5.2: 45–75

Herodotus: *Heredot Tarihi 1*. Translated by M. Ökmen. Istanbul 1983

İnandık, H. 1965: *Türkiye Bitki Coğrafyasına Giriş*. Istanbul

Işık, F. 1987: 'Şirinlikale. Eine unbekannte urartäische Burg und Beobachtungen zu den Feldenkmälern eines Schöpferischen Bergvolks Ostanatoliens' *Belleten* 200: 497–533

— 1995: *Die Offenen Felsheiligtümer Urartus*. Rome

Kırzıoğlu, F. 1958: *Kars Tarihi*. Istanbul

Kleiss, W., Hauptmann, H. 1976: *Topographische Karte von Urartu*. Berlin

Koşay, H.Z. 1943: 'Karaz sondajı' *Türk Tarih Kongresi* 3: 165–9

— 1984: *Erzurum ve Çevresinin Dip Tarihi*. Ankara

Koşay, H.Z., Turfan, K. 1959: 'Erzurum Karaz kazısı raporu' *Belleten* 91: 349–413

Koşay, H.Z., Vary, H. 1964: *Pulur Kazısı*. Ankara

— 1967: *Güzelova (Tufanç) Erzurum Kazısı 1961*. Ankara

Kökten, I.K. 1971–1972: 'Kars çevresinde dip tarih araştırmaları ve yazılıkaya resimleri' *Atatürk Konferansları* 5: 95–104

König, F.W. 1955–1957: *Handbuch der chaldischen Inschriften* (Archiv für Orient Forschung, Beiheft 8). Graz

Luckenbill, D.D. 1926–1927: *Ancient Records of Assyria and Babylonia 1–2*. Chicago

Melikišvili, G.A. 1950: 'Diauehi' *Vestnik Drenaj İstorii* 34.4: 26–42

— 1960: *Urartkie Klinoobraznye Nadpisi*. Moscow

Merhav, R. 1991: 'Everyday and ceremonial utensils' in R. Merhav (ed.), *Urartu: A Metalworking Center in the First Millenium B.C.E.* New York: 200–43

M.T.A. 1977: *Maden Tetkik Araştırma*. Ankara

— 1980: *Türkiye Orman Envanterleri*. Ankara

Orthmann, W. 1968–1969: 'Eine Urartäischer Inschrift in Avnik' *Archiv für Orientforschung* 22: 77–8

Özgüç, N. 1974: 'The decorated bronze strip and plaques from Altıntepe' in E. Akurgal, U.B. Alkım (eds), *Mansel'e Armağan — Mélanges Mansel 2*: 847–60

Özgüç, T. 1961: 'Altıntepe kazıları' *Belleten* 25: 253–90

— 1963: 'Altıntepe Urartu mimarlık eserleri' *Anatolia* 7: 43–57

— 1966: *Altıntepe 1*. Ankara

— 1969: *Altıntepe 2*. Ankara

Payne, M. 1995: *Urartu Yazılı Belgeler Kataloğu*. Unpublished Masters thesis. Istanbul University

Pehlivan, M. 1984: *En Eski Çağlardan Urartu'nun Yılışına kadar Erzurum ve Çevresi*. Unpublished PhD thesis. Erzurum University

— 1991: *Daya(e)ni-Diau(e)hi*. Erzurum

Piotrovskii, B.B. 1969: *Urartu*. Geneva

Ryan, C.W. 1960: *A Guide to the Known Minerals of Turkey*. Ankara

Sagona, A. 1999: 'The Bronze Age – Iron Age transition in northeast Anatolia: a view from Sos Höyük' *Anatolian Studies* 49: 153–9

— 2000: 'Sos Höyük and the Erzurum region in late prehistory: a provisional chronology for northeast Anatolia' in C. Marro, H. Hauptmann (eds), *Chronologies des Pays du Caucase et de l'Euphrate aux IVe–IIIe Millenaires: Actes du Colloque d'Istanbul, 16–19 December 1998* (Varia Anatolica 11). Paris: 329–73

Sagona, A., Erkmen, M., Sagona, C., Howels, S., McNiven, I. 1998: 'Excavations at Sos Höyük 1997: fourth preliminary report' *Anatolica* 24: 31–64

Sagona, C., Erkmen, M., Howels, S. 1997: 'Excavations at Sos Höyük 1996: third preliminary report' *Anatolica* 23: 181–226

Salvini, M. 1995: *Geschichte und Kultur der Urartäer.* Darmstadt

Sevin, V. 1979: *Urartu Krallığının Tarihsel ve Kültürel Gelişimi.* Istanbul

Slattery, D.J.G. 1987: 'Urartu and the Black Sea colonies: an economic perspective' *Al Rafidan* 8: 1–30

Sözer, N. 1974: 'Erzurum coğrafyası: tabii ve beşeri özellikler' in Z. Başar et al. (eds), *50. Yıl Armağanı Erzurum ve Çevresi.* Erzurum: 27–38

Steinherr, F. 1958: 'Die Urartäischen Bronzen von Altıntepe' *Anatolia* 3: 97–102

Strabon: *Geographica.* Translated by A. Pekman. Istanbul 1993

Tarhan, M.T. 1980: 'Urartu devletinin kuruluş evresi ve kurucu krallardan "Lutupri=Lapturi" hakkındaki yeni görüşler' *Anadolu Araştırmaları* 8: 69–114

Tarkan, T. 1974: 'Ana çizgileriyle Doğu Anadolu Bölgesi' in Z. Başar et al. (eds), *50. Yıl Armağanı Erzurum ve Çevresi.* Erzurum: 7–23

Toynbee, A. 1978: *Tarih Bilinci 1.* Istanbul

von Gall, H. 1967: 'Zu den Kleinasiatischen-Treppentunneln' *Archaeologischer Anzeiger* 504–27

Yakar, J. 1985: *The Later Prehistory of Anatolia: The Late Chalcolithic and Early Bronze Age. Part ii* (British Archaeological Reports International Series 268). Oxford

Xenophon: *Anabasis.* Translated by H. Örs. Istanbul 1984

# Ritual ceremonies in the temple area of Ayanis

## Altan Çilingiroğlu
### *Ege University, Izmir*

### Abstract

The various ritual ceremonies that must have taken place within the temple area of Ayanis fortress are considered, utilising the evidence of the small finds recovered from the temple area excavations and epigraphic sources.

### Özet

Bu çalışmada, tapınak alanı kazılarında bulunan küçük buluntulara ve epigrafik kaynaklara dayanılarak, Ayanis Kalesi tapınak alanında gerçekleşmiş olması gereken çeşitli dini merasimler incelenmektedir.

The *susi* temple that was dedicated to the god Haldi occupies a 30m² area, situated on the highest point of Ayanis fortress (1,861m above sea level) (fig. 1). The temple area consists of a square core-temple (12.45m by 13m across, the cella measuring 4.58m by 4.62m), and a portico with ten pillars parallel to its south, north and west walls, with a circular structure in the middle of the courtyard. The entrance to the temple area is by a gate on the east side. Another gate on the north side connects the temple area to adjacent structures. The arrangement whereby two pillars project from the south and north walls of the core-temple is so far attested only here at Ayanis, likewise the existence of two hearths uncovered adjacent to these walls. A wooden portico evidently surrounded the courtyard area in front of the core-temple, except on the east side (fig. 2) (for details of the temple see Çilingiroğlu 2001a).

Two alabaster bases, both with a hole in the middle, were unearthed on the flanks of the temple area's east gate. It is likely that these bases held painted wooden sacred trees. Similar bases with such trees are known from the stone relief from Adilcevaz Kef Kalesi (for a recent drawing of this relief see Çilingiroğlu 1997: fig. 32). Two bronze foundation discs (Sağlamtimur et al. 2001: 244, pl. III:49, 50), measuring 7.1cm in diameter and 3.7cm high, were recovered from directly beneath the floor surface at a point 0.8m from the bases and 0.7m from the east wall. The inscriptions on these discs testify that the temple complex was erected for the god Haldi.

To Haldi, his lord, Rusa, the son of Argishti, dedicated (Salvini 2001a: 275).[1]

The inscription (Salvini 2001b: 253–70) carved on the façade of the core-temple, occupying eight basalt blocks, likewise mentions that the temple was built for Haldi.

*Fig. 1. The fortress of Ayanis on the eastern shore of lake Van*

---

[1] According to Salvini (2001b: 260), *susi* and the Gate of Haldi refer to the same building, namely the tower-temple of Ayanis. I believe that the *susi* and the Gate of Haldi should refer to different parts of the temple: *susi* may be the temple itself and the Gate of Haldi only the recessed doorway of the temple.

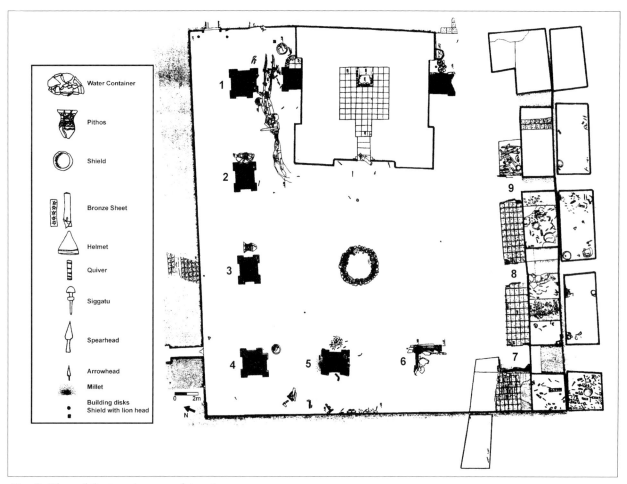

*Fig. 2. Plan of the temple area of Ayanis*

To Haldi, his lord, Rusa, the son of Argishti, has built this *susi*, also a Gate of Haldi to perfection in Rusahinili Eidurukai has erected and constructed to Haldi… (Salvini 2001b: 259).

The temple inscription and other inscribed objects suggest that there must have been one or more types of ceremony held in the temple area. Various golden rosettes, decorative objects and miniature stone vessels that were found on the floor had fallen down from a second storey (Çilingiroğlu 1994; Sağlamtimur et al. 2001: 222, 225, figs 7–10, 12–15); however, we are uncertain whether or not these artefacts were used in the ceremonies.

It would be useful to consider the character and locations of the small finds in the temple area, since these might provide clues regarding the possible ceremonial use of the objects (fig. 2). On the east side of pillar 1, two swords and a fragmentary shield were found and another complete shield was unearthed on the southwest side; it is certain that these shields were originally hung from the pillar. Another important group of small finds comes from the northeast area of

the core-temple's wall, where a lion-headed shield, a quiver and a bone object filled with millet were found. It is highly likely that these objects were associated with the hearth next to the projecting pillar on the north wall of the core-temple, an interpretation supported by the inscription on the shield. Another hearth was situated adjacent to the pillar on the south wall of the core-temple.

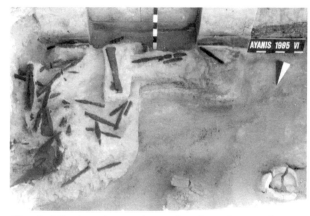

*Fig. 3. Libation altar and spearheads in the temple area*

Between pillar 1 and the north pillar of the core-temple, hundreds of iron spearheads were found; the existence of such a cluster should have a meaning. A limestone libation altar lies close to the southwest corner of pillar 1, associated with a channel that runs parallel to the north wall of the core-temple; the altar would have sat on the wooden beams that originally covered the channel (fig. 3).

On the east side of pillar 2, a broken terracotta basin was found, measuring 1.2m by 0.8m by 0.6m. On the east side of pillar 3, a pithos was uncovered bearing a hieroglyphic inscription; similar pithoi with the same decoration are depicted on Urartian belts (Merhav 1991: 227, figs 6.2, 6.3). Near to the door that leads to the rooms on the north side of the temple area were found three bronze helmets, one inside the other and bearing dedicatory inscriptions. Near pillar 4 there was a shield which must originally have been hung from the pillar. Standing parallel to the west wall of the temple area is pillar 5, around which was a large number of quivers. Significantly, none of the other pillars were associated with quivers. In the same area there were many spearheads and arrowheads and, in addition to the metalwork, millet seeds were scattered all around the pillar and filled the quivers.

The courtyard of the temple is damaged on the south side. The storage structures that were built below the temple area here are entirely exposed (figs 4, 5; see also Çilingiroğlu 2001a: fig. 26). A large quantity of weapons and armour was found in the various parts of the storerooms: shields, helmets, quivers, arrowheads, spearheads and decorated bronze plates. It is obvious that a number of shields were originally hung from the south wall of the temple area, and some of them were crushed after they had fallen down from the wall. However, the shields and weapons lying *in situ* on the storeroom floors had been stored in the rooms; some of the shields were found stacked one against the other, leaning against one of the walls (fig. 6).

In front of the core-temple's west façade and near its recessed entrance there was a number of artefacts, including four inscribed *sikkatu* that were probably once situated on the temple wall (Sağlamtimur et al. 2001: 243, pl. II:18), a bronze plate decorated with rosettes (Sağlamtimur et al. 2001: 232, fig. 3), mushroom-headed bronze nails and decorative mosaics. No weapon was found inside the cella, which contained alabaster ornaments, intaglio decoration on the walls, stone mosaics and numerous bronze nails. However, excavation revealed a large quantity of animal bones in this room at a depth of 3.12m. Unfortunately, the significance of these animal remains is uncertain because of the plundering of the cella which accompanied and followed its destruction. The interpretation which we suggest is that body parts of sacrificed animals were brought into the room.

*Fig. 4. Storeroom in the temple area*

*Fig. 5. Bronze shield in a storeroom of the temple area*

*Fig. 6. Bronze shield leaning against a wall in a storeroom*

Between the western pillars and the core-temple façade there is a circular structure, probably the one called 'sirhanini' in the Ayanis temple inscription (Salvini 2001a: 260), with important evidence of painted frescoes. We assume that this building was used by the priests during ceremonies. In the courtyard, between the circular structure and the temple, and connected to a channel running underneath the floor, there was a hole which contained pieces of an andesite altar. Other fragments of this altar were found in the storerooms to the west of the temple complex; these had probably been moved for re-use by medieval settlers.

We can classify the objects that were found in the temple area into four groups.

1. Libation items and solid offerings
2. Dedicatory weapons and armour
3. Fire cult items
4. Sacrificial altars

The cultic ceremonies which took place within the temple area (fig. 7) most probably included the offering of libations (water or wine) and solids (e.g. millet). The libation pithos which was found near pillar 3 could have contained wine or water; in this connection we may note the two wine filled cauldrons which stood before the Temple of Musasir,

*Fig. 7. Temple area and core-temple of Ayanis*

. . . belonging to the kings of Urartu, [used] for offering sacrifices before Haldi, [and] which were full of sacrificial wine . . . [and] . . . three large basins of bronze which held inside them 50 measures of water... (Luckenbill 1927: 173).

The altar on top of the channel mentioned above would presumably also have been used for libations during ceremonies. The millet found around pillar 5 and the north wall of the core-temple, in some of the quivers and in an animal bone, indicates that this material too was considered sacred and was used as an offering. It is uncertain whether or not the terracotta basin on the east side of pillar 2 was used for libations. In our opinion, this vessel probably held water which was used for ritual cleansing by those about to participate in ceremonies; it seems likely that the king, prince, administrators or priests would have purified themselves in this way as soon as they entered the temple area and that the ceremonies would have commenced following this act.

Some of the best archaeological evidence regarding libation ceremonies comes from the site of Altıntepe (Özgüç 1969: pls xxvi, xxvii, 1–4) where four stelae were found standing on a stone platform, with a stone libation altar in front of them.[2] Other important evidence derives from the seal impressions from Toprakkale, which depict a person standing just in front of a platform with three stelae on it; and on one of the sealings the one handled libation container is visible (Lehmann-Haupt 1907: fig. 54; Işık 1986: fig. 2a). It is unknown whether the libation constituted only part of a ceremony or was a complete ceremony in itself. We prefer to think that it was almost certainly a part of the ceremony which took place following the cleansing ritual mentioned above.

Since 1989 a number of different types of metal arms, armour and other equipment have come to light in the Ayanis excavations: 14 shields, 34 quivers, ten helmets, four *sikkatu*, 108 spearheads, 399 arrowheads, two swords, one sword sheath and two bronze discs. Almost all of these are from the temple area: 13 shields, 33 quivers, nine helmets, all four *sikkatu*, 84 spearheads (81 in iron and three in bronze), 145 iron arrowheads, 160 bronze arrowheads, the two swords, the sword sheath and the two bronze discs; the shield found at the Monumental Gate was presumably taken from the temple area too. Most of these artefacts bear inscriptions which tell us that they were dedicated to the god Haldi. The following translations are representative examples (Salvini 2001a: 272–6; Çilingiroğlu, Salvini 1999).

To Haldi, [his] lord, Rusa, the son of Arghisti, made and dedicated this shield for his life. He put it in Rusahinili Eidurukai . . . (on a shield)

To Haldi, [his] lord, Rusa, the son of Arghisti, dedicated . . . (on a helmet)

To Haldi, [his] lord, Rusa, the son of Arghisti, made and dedicated this lance [sword] for his life (on a sword)

To Haldi, [his] lord, Rusa, the son of Arghisti, dedicated (on a bronze spearhead)

To Haldi, [his] lord, Rusa, the son of Arghisti, dedicated (on two bronze discs)

To Haldi, [his] lord, Rusa, the son of Arghisti, dedicated (on four bronze *sikkatu*)

There are three incribed quivers which, although much damaged, plausibly bear similar wording.

---

[2] It is possible that stelae were introduced to Urartian art from Hasanlu following the capture of that site by Menua.

As can be comprehended from the contents of these inscriptions, all of this equipment had been dedicated to the god Haldi. Were these dedicatory offerings made after the libation ceremony had taken place; and did both these ceremonies in fact represent parts of just one ceremony? The answers to these questions remain uncertain.

Most of the weapons and armour which were dedicated to Haldi were unearthed in the courtyard of the temple (figs 3, 8) or in the storerooms beneath the southern part of the courtyard (Çilingiroğlu 2001b: figs 1, 2). The majority were hung either on the temple walls, on other walls or on the pillars within the temple area. No weapons or armour were found inside the cella, though it is possible that they had been there originally but were later plundered by thieves. It is probable that the weapons and armour dedicated to Haldi would first have been placed on the cella podium (fig. 9) and then later taken back to their places on the walls of the temple area. Arms and armour used for years in such ceremonies could be retired to the storerooms. New weapons and armour were produced for new ceremonies. It is interesting to note that only the king is attested as making these dedications, not other élites, not even other members of the royal family. However, not all of the inscriptions state that the dedication was made by the king himself.

*Fig. 8. Bronze shields on the floor of the temple area*

*Fig. 9. Cella and podium of the temple*

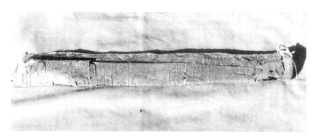

*Fig. 10. Bronze quiver filled with millet*

We lack information regarding when, in which month of the year and on what occasions, these dedication ceremonies took place. It can be proposed that they were part of ceremonies held before or after military campaigns, a suggestion supported by the fact that Haldi was the main war god and leader of the army.

In addition, the deliberate placement of millet in some of the military artefacts suggests a relationship between fertility and military equipment (fig. 10). From their own written sources we know that the Urartians celebrated and made sacrifices during the cultivation of new vineyards and for the harvest season (*UKN* 65). We surmise that such ceremonies took place in the temple area of Ayanis fortress. Millet, a symbol of fertility, is assumed to be one of the most common cereals in the Urartian kingdom, and indeed in some of the mountain villages around Van today it is used to make bread. Other archaeological evidence related to dedicatory military equipment and fertility is found with the two hearths adjacent to the northern and southern walls of the core-temple (fig. 2). The northern hearth has an outer surface of mud-bricks and the traces of its fire are still visible on the temple wall and the adjacent pillar. Directly beside it was found a lion-headed shield, together with a quiver and a bone object both filled with millet, all of which we assume were hung on the temple wall. The shield bears an inscription familiar from the other inscribed objects, but with one ununsual expression which deserves mention here.

> To Haldi, [his] lord, Rusa, son of Argishti, made and dedicated this shield for his life . . . Rusa says: he who takes this shield, he who throws it, he who . . . water, he who . . . he who th[rows] earth on fires and [or: of the] earths, he who effaces my name and puts his name, may God Haldi destroy him . . . (Salvini 2001b: 272).

The inscription mentions a fire which under any circumstances must not be extinguished. This unusual reference, together with the close physical association of the hearth and the inscribed shield, suggests that the concepts of fire, fertility and military equipment were brought together in the same context, in other words in the same ceremony. It is not possible to trace back the origins of such a ceremony, since Ayanis is the only site with a temple providing clues about a fire cult. Furthermore, not a single Urartian inscription mentions a fire cult or sacred hearths.

In western Iran the plans of the Achaemenid fire-temples are strikingly similar to those of Urartian temples. Most probably the temple plans of Zendan-i Suleyman in Pasargadae, and Ka'bah-i Zardusht in Nagah-i Rustem, were derived from the Urartian examples. Although it would be premature to suggest a direct correlation between the use of fire at the Ayanis temple and the fire cult ceremonies of Iran, it is highly likely that there were other cultural interactions between eastern Anatolia and Iran in addition to the architectural influences which are apparent. Iranian interaction with, and influence on, Urartu could have occurred when the Zoroastrian religion appeared in Iran in the seventh century BC. It is also striking that the representations of the god Haldi with winged sun disc (Merhav 1991: 96, 98, 109, figs 62, 63, 13.2–4, 73; Çilingiroğlu 1997: 118, fig. 68) and of Ahuramazda are very similar. This issue should be re-examined in the future, in light of the new data from the Ayanis excavations.

As noted above, a hole in front of the Ayanis core-temple was connected to a channel beneath, which runs alongside the core-temple wall towards the southern part of the temple area, and fragments of an andesite altar were found in the hole as well as in the storerooms in the western quarter of the fortress. When these fragments were brought together, the diameter of the altar measured 0.8m with a hole in the middle to let the blood flow. A similar altar was found at the north side of the İrmuşini temple courtyard at Çavuştepe (Erzen 1978: 11), and this too was connected to a channel running towards the exterior of the temple courtyard.

Many Urartian inscriptions, including the temple inscription from Ayanis, contain orders regarding ceremonial sacrifices (Salvini 2001b: 259). The gods which required such sacrifices included Haldi, Teisheba, Arubani, Hutuni, the Moon God and the Sun God. The gods specified on the Ayanis inscription are Eiduru (=Mount Süphan), Baba, Adia, Sarki and Inuani; the inscription also indicates that Haldi's weapons and Gate were to be offered sacrifices too. Deities aside, the Ayanis inscription also mentions that 'a young kid' should be sacrificed for new buildings erected.[3] As the

*Fig. 11. Lion head from a bronze shield*

inscription makes clear, the sacrifices had to be performed in front of the temple (Salvini 2001b: 259–60). In order to obey the inscription's orders an altar was needed: it is possible that the andesite fragments that were found just across from the core-temple entrance belonged to that very altar.

The Ayanis inscription indicates that a part of the sacrificed animal was given to king Rusa.

> . . . he who sacrifices in front of the Gate of Haldi . . . has to give a heart to Rusa . . . (Salvini 2001b: 260).

Other inscriptions likewise mention that some parts of the sacrificed animals were to be given to the kings visiting fortresses; for example:

> What goes for an offering of all [that is] in the Haldian Gates, the liver and the heart let one give to Rusa . . . When the king should be in Teisheba's city, from the sacrificial meat, from the carcass the liver let one give to the king . . . (Diakonoff 1991: 15, 16).

Butchered pieces of sacrificed animals might have been placed in the Ayanis cella, more specifically, on the podium within the cella; and one can find expressions in Urartian inscriptions to support this idea, for example, ' . . . the liver let one give to the king . . .' (Diakonoff 1991: 16). Despite the large number of animal bones found in the Ayanis temple cella, it is uncertain whether or not these are the remains of butchered sacrificial animals, though we suggest that they are, as noted earlier.

---

[3] It is not clear from the wording whether these new buildings lay within the fortress or in the outer town. However, the Ayanis gate inscription has a blank space one and a half lines long which we think was reserved for the addition of the name of a new building to be erected within the fortress; see Çilingiroğlu, Salvini 1995: 118–19.

To conclude, various ceremonies must have taken place in the temple area of Ayanis, including libations, fire rituals, offerings of military equipment, animal sacrifices and fertility ceremonies, with their varied concepts and procedures. As revealed by the inscriptions, the offering of military equipment was performed for the god Haldi alone. Other deities received animal sacrifices. Erecting a new building at the fortress also required ceremonies and sacrifices. Animal sacrifices were to be made to the mountain god Eiduru, whose first attestation is in the Ayanis inscription. Sacrifices were also needed for the weapons and Gate of Haldi. Another sacrificial occasion was when the king visited the fortress.

It is most likely that these various ceremonies for different gods and occasions took place at different times of the year, and we are inclined to believe that ceremonies in the temple area were frequent, although how frequently the same kinds of ceremonies were repeated is unknown. The Ayanis inscription informs us that at least 30 animals were sacrificed at the site, not including the sacrifice orders on the Meher Kapı inscription. We have no direct evidence as to how the animal meat was used after the sacrifice but from an economic viewpoint it must have been fully consumed (compare Diakonoff 1991: 17).

## Bibliography
*Abbreviation*
UKN = Melikišvili, G.A. 1960: *Urartskie klinoobraznye nadpisi (Le iscrizioni cuneiformi urartee)* (second edition). Moscow

Çilingiroğlu, A. 1994: 'Decorated stone vessels from the Urartian fortress of Ayanis' *Tel Aviv* 21: 68–76
— 1997: *Urartu Krallığı: Tarihi ve Kültürü*. Izmir
— 2001a: 'Temple area' in A. Çilingiroğlu, M. Salvini (eds), *Ayanis I. Ten Years' Excavations at Rusahinili Eiduru-kai 1989–1998*. Rome: 37–65
— 2001b: 'The excavation of Ayanis fortress in 2001 season' *Studi Micenei ed Egeo-Anatolici* 43.2: 275–9
Çilingiroğlu, A., Salvini, M. 1995: 'Rusahinili in front of mount Eiduru: the Urartian fortress of Ayanis (seventh century BC)' *Studi Micenei ed Egeo-Anatolici* 35: 111–24
— 1999: 'When was the castle of Ayanis built and what is the meaning of the word "suri"?' in A. Çilingiroğlu, R.J. Matthews (eds), *Anatolian Iron Ages 4* (*Anatolian Studies* 49): 55–60
Diakonoff, I.M. 1991: 'Sacrifices in the city of Teiseba (*UKN* 448) — lights on the social history of Urartu' *Archäeologische Mitteilungen aus Iran* 24: 13–21
Erzen, A. 1978: *Çavuştepe I*. Ankara
Işık, C. 1986: 'Neue Beobachtungen zur Darstellung von Kultszenen auf urartäischen Rollstempelsiegeln' *Jahrbuch des Deutschen Archaologischen Instituts* 101: 1–22
Lehmann-Haupt, C.F. 1907: *Materialien zur alteren Geschichte Armeniens und Mesopotmiens*. Berlin
Luckenbill, D.D. 1927: *Ancient Records of Assyria and Babylonia II*. Chicago
Merhav, R. (ed.) 1991: *Urartu: A Metalworking Center in the First Millennium BCE*. Jerusalem
Özgüç, T. 1969: *Altıntepe II*. Ankara
Sağlamtimur, H., Kozbe, G., Çevik, Ö. 2001: 'Small finds' in A. Çilingiroğlu, M. Salvini (eds), *Ayanis I. Ten Years' Excavations at Rusahinili Eiduru-kai 1989–1998*. Rome: 219–50
Salvini, M. 2001a: 'Royal inscriptions on bronze artifacts' in A. Çilingiroğlu, M. Salvini (eds), *Ayanis I. Ten Years' Excavations at Rusahinili Eiduru-kai 1989–1998*. Rome: 271–8
— 2001b: 'The inscriptions of Ayanis (Rusahinili Eiduru-kai): cuneiform and hieroglyphic' in A. Çilingiroğlu, M. Salvini (eds), *Ayanis I. Ten Years' Excavations at Rusahinili Eiduru-kai 1989–1998*. Rome: 251–70
Zimansky, P. 1979: 'Bones and bullae: an enigma from Bastam, Iran' *Archaeology* 32.6: 53–5

# Water supply for cities in the late eighth and seventh centuries BC: Assyria and Urartu

## Stephanie Dalley

*Oriental Institute, Oxford University*

## Abstract

Some scholars have claimed influence emanating from Urartu to Assyria for innovations in water supply, and others have claimed the reverse. Since evidence from Assyria is much more abundant than that from Urartu or Iran, no fair judgement is yet possible. Evidence from Assyrian inscriptions and archaeological remains is collected to show the kinds of installations that might be expected on Urartian sites. In particular, qanat-like tunnels with vertical shafts, huge underground drains in cities, terracotta piping in palaces and probably aqueducts are described together with the vocabulary for them, and their context as a display of royal control.

## Özet

Bazı araştırmacılar su sağlama sistemlerinde yapılan yeniliklerde Asurluların Urartulardan etkilendiğini, bazıları ise bunun tam tersini savunmaktadır. Ancak Asurlularla ilgili bilgilerin, Urartular ve İran'la ilgili bilgilere kıyasla daha çok olması nedeniyle, henüz kesin bir karara varmak olası değildir. Asur yazıtlarından elde edilen kanıtlar ve toplanan arkeolojik buluntularla Urartu yerleşimlerinde karşılaşılabilecek olası donanım ve düzenekler ortaya konmaya çalışılmıştır. Özellikle dikey kuyulu 'qanat' benzeri tüneller, yerleşimlerdeki çok büyük yeraltı pis su kanalları, saraylardaki pişmiş toprak borular ve olası su kanalları, bunlar için oluşturulmuş terminoloji ve bunlar üzerindeki krallık kontrolü anlatılmaya çalışılmıştır.

---

Archaeologists and historians of the ancient Near East sometimes claim priority or originality for their own field of investigation — the 'first' irrigation of fields, the 'origins' of monotheism, the 'earliest' discovery of alloying — putting their own work, or the history of their own country, at the starting point of global development. Moortgat seems to have been the first to claim that Urartian waterworks were a source of inspiration to the kings of Assyria in the eighth to seventh centuries, and he was followed by Laessøe, Seidl and Boehmer among others (Boehmer 1997). Whether or not they were right can only be evaluated if we can produce from both sides data of similar quality and secure interpretation of the evidence. It is clear to me that we cannot yet do so. Moreover, Assyria and Urartu are not the only players on the field: western Iran and the achievements of the Elamites should also be taken into account, but this is impossible because much of the basic work has not yet been done. Neither Urartian nor Elamite inscriptions can match those of Assyria for detailed information, nor are sculptured landscape scenes available from Urartu or Elam as they are from Nimrud, Khorsabad and Nineveh. In addition, despite the splendid work done recently on Urartian dams and canals (Belli 1995), there is much that cannot be closely dated to give the precision of sequence that we have from Assyria. As Zimansky (1985: 67) has pointed out, there are enormous difficulties in identifying and dating canals which are often obscured by erosion, by being buried in deposition, and by the consequences of earthquakes.

Recently the huge book *Assyrische Wasserbauten* by Ariel Bagg (2000) claimed to show the superiority of Assyrian water technology, but it could not present in an even-handed manner the evidence from Urartu because the evidence available is weighted heavily in favour of Assyria. Moreover, Bagg ignores the Iranian contribution by not mentioning the 50km canal which supplied a finely constructed reservoir, built by the Elamite king Untaš-Napiriša at Choga Zambil in western Iran (Ghirshman 1968: 96–100). The latter dates from the 14th century, and so is much older than the great 'Semiramis' canal works of Menua in the ninth century (Salvini 1992) or of Sennacherib in the seventh (Jacobsen, Lloyd 1935). The fact that the 14th century Elamite canal is now popularly attributed to Darius reminds us that we have very little evidence for pre-Achaemenid waterworks in western Iran — but they certainly existed, and may have influenced developments in Urartu.

My aim here is to present some further information with a view to showing the level of expertise reached under the neo-Assyrian kings. This is particularly crucial for the late eighth to early seventh centuries because at that time city sizes seem to have increased (Stronach 1994), implying perhaps new solutions to water supplies, and it is also a period for which there is good evidence for public and royal recognition of engineering. We shall particularly look at possibilities that flowing water, whether underground through tunnels or overground by aqueducts, reached the heights of citadels. This would mean that the great cities were not simply dependent on wells and cisterns for their water, and would not have to leave the protection of city walls to fetch water from rivers.

First, the qanat system. Most scholars are now agreed that certain lines of text in Sargon's eighth campaign, described in the famous letter to the gods, cannot be understood to describe an Urartian qanat. The old interpretation, proposed by Laessøe half a century ago with the work of Lehmann-Haupt in mind, has yielded to a better understanding of technical vocabulary, and should definitely be abandoned (Dalley 2002b). Salvini has shown that Lehmann-Haupt was mistaken in attributing qanats in the region of Van to Urartians, and that traceable qanats in the region are not linked to Tušpa or Toprakkale; nor is an appropriate word found in Urartian inscriptions, in which water projects are often described (Salvini 2001: 143–4). But we may still keep an open mind for other sites, particularly lower towns and field systems, because some old and some newly found evidence indicates that qanat-type constructions were known in seventh century Assyria.

The Negoub tunnel scheme which brought water from the upper Zab to Nimrud, initiated in the ninth century by Assurnasirpal II and finalised in the seventh by Esarhaddon, has all the characteristics of the qanat except that it channels river water rather than collecting underground water, and is larger in scale than more recent, traditional qanats (Davey 1985). The same may be true of Sennacherib's qanat-like tunnel at Arbela, a city which lies in an area later riddled with qanats. Both these schemes are dated by inscriptions found *in situ*. The Assyrians would not necessarily have made the modern distinction between a tunnel with shafts collecting ground water and a tunnel with shafts collecting river or canal water.

Together with these innovative works we may mention an intriguing profession which appears for the first time in neo-Assyrian texts: LŰ *ša* UGU *qanâte*, 'the man in charge of *qanâte*', whatever *qanâte* might mean. The profession is attested for the first time in 700 BC (*ADD* 112:9 = Kwasman 1988: no. 356) for a man with the Assyrian or Babylonian name Nabu-kašir, and later, in 657 BC (*ADD* 618.r.9 = Kwasman 1988: no. 334) for a man with the Assyrian or Babylonian name Nusku-ahu-iddin. The term is also found in the Assyrian version of the lexical list of professions (Landsberger et al. 1969: 240, line 18), but not in earlier professions lists, of which many versions are extant. We cannot be sure what the profession means; but Goblot (1979: 19) in his wide-ranging book on the qanat has pointed out that the word seems to be Akkadian in origin; and the Syrian Arabic word for a qanat engineer is *qanawāti*. In Akkadian the word *qanû*, plural *qanâte*, like many technical words concerning water, has a wide semantic range, and can also mean pipes of any kind as well as reeds and a linear measure. It is possible, but unprovable, that the material remains at Negoub and Arbela correspond with the Assyrian profession.

Quite likely dated to the same period around the seventh century is a row of vertical shafts beautifully lined in pink granite at Babylon, all connected by an underground channel that brought river or canal water from northeast of the city — recorded by Rassam (1897: 352–4). Any one of the following kings may have installed this system: Sargon II, Esarhaddon, Assurbanipal, Nabopolassar or Nebuchadnezzar II, with dates 709–562 BC.

Taken as a whole, this is a useful group of evidence gathered from Assyrian cities, texts and from Babylon, which shows that the Assyrians had either adopted or invented qanat-type tunnels by 700 BC, and probably had a new, specialist profession to promote them. The profession is held by men with Akkadian names, in contrast to horse experts who were definitely Urartians at that time (Dalley 1985).

Normally Assyrian royal inscriptions do not mention engineers or the details of technical work. The king is represented as sole instigator and completer of great building works. Exceptional in this respect are Sargon II, Sennacherib and Esarhaddon. Sargon attributed the inspiration for his new city at Khorsabad to the little-known god Mušda written <sup>d</sup>ŠITIM, patron of engineers, the *šitimgallu* or 'great ŠITIM engineer' of Enlil. Mušda is a god known from texts of the late third millennium BC, but not thereafter until he was found recently by collation of a text of Sargon II (Fuchs 1994: 41, line 60). Sometimes the Sumerian logogram ŠITIM is translated as 'builder, mason'; but the Akkadian word for a canal engineer *sēkiru* is sometimes represented by the logogram ŠITIM followed by a qualifying word. Sennacherib spoke, surprisingly, of the work of the human *šitimgallu* in his building work for Nineveh, and so did Esarhaddon for Babylon. This small cluster of information suggests that particular importance was accorded to the work of the *šitimgallu* in the late eighth and early seventh centuries, just at a time when innovations in canal and tunnel works can be identified.

Sargon's water supply works outside Khorsabad are described in his royal inscriptions, but some remarkable construction work inside the city, on the citadel, admirably recorded by Victor Place (1867: 275–9, pls 38, 39), is omitted from all accounts of Mesopotamian waterworks that I have read. A system of baked brick and bitumen underground channels, still in perfect condition when excavated, is still hard to understand; Place admitted that he could not understand it, and I have not had any better success despite asking colleagues who have greater expertise than I do. The channels were big enough for two men inside to pass each other. The construction has a right angle bend in it, and lay below the paving of a terrace between the ziggurrat and the palace; but it was not there simply to collect and drain away water from rain falling on the ziggurrat and the terrace. The size is so great that the channels were presumably cleared by flowing water; buckets filled from shadufs or with pulleys would have been inadequate. Does this imply that the canal, which Sargon built to bring water from the springs in the nearby mountain, would have brought flowing water into the citadel at the required height? Or is there another way of interpreting the evidence, connected with ritual and ceremonial processions on the ziggurrat terrace?

Terracotta pipes for conducting fresh water in the Assyrian palace at Samal have been compared by Belli with terracotta pipes to bring water from the Aygir lake in Urartu to irrigate fields, definitely part of a gravity-flow system in both places, but for their different purposes. Fine water supply or drainage systems have been found in many Assyrian palaces, and belong to a much older tradition that goes back into the Early Dynastic period in Mesopotamia, but they have not been studied systematically. The men who planned them are unlikely to be the LÚ *ša* UGU *qanâte*, because this profession is not found in the standard professions list, but occurs first in an Assyrian version of the list, apparently as a new or Assyrian profession.

Turning now to Nineveh and the question of water supply to the citadel of Kuyunjik: as David Stronach pointed out in a recent discussion, the citadel is very high above the level of the plain, yet most interpretations of the garden scene on a relief sculpture of Assurbanipal agree that water flows into the garden beside the Southwest

Palace along an aqueduct. One might suggest that the aqueduct is the one at Jerwan, greatly telescoped for artistic purposes; but as Bagg (2000: 156, but compare 199) has pointed out, inscriptions of Sennacherib seem to mean that the garden was on the citadel and that water from the Khosr was brought artificially 'into the middle of the city, above and below', over a bridge or aqueduct (the word *titurru* can have either meaning) of baked brick. This appears to Bagg so implausible that he suggested the garden on the Nineveh sculpture is at Arbela, although he agreed with the general consensus that the adjacent palace is at Nineveh. A collage of scenes from different places on a single sculptured composition is not, however, attested in Assyrian tradition. The plain interpretation of the text and the sculpture is that Sennacherib managed to bring flowing water on to the citadel with aqueducts. The text says,

> *aššu mušê íd Husur qereb āli mālak mê eliš u šapliš ina agurri kīri maši titurri abtani šapalšu ina mehret abulli qabal āli ina agurri pīli peṣê ana mētiq narkabti bēlūtiya ušēpiš titurru*
> In order [to bring] the outflow of the river Khosr within the city [and] a course of water above and below, I built twin(?) aqueducts with kiln-baked bricks. Below it facing a city gate in the middle of the city I had a bridge made of baked brick [and] white limestone for my royal chariot to pass along (Frahm 1997: 66–89).

Is there any possible interpretation of this, other than to deduce that water from the mountains was very carefully given a gradient that would allow it to enter the citadel of Kuyunjik at just the right height? Bagg usefully notes that the outer wall to the east of Nineveh is not debris from digging a ditch, since it consists of hard conglomerate rock, so it may be a natural formation which was incorporated into the design for the city's defences; it was as high above ground level as the citadel of Kuyunjik (Bagg 2000: 191–2) and so perhaps may be considered in connection with supplying water from the east and northeast of the city. This would mean the water crossed the moat outside the east wall of Nineveh, and then crossed through the main wall of the city, a possible location for the crossing being at the Shibaniba gate where Steel and MacGinnis (1990) found stones from a likely bridge or aqueduct. Sennacherib's inscription seems to say that he made a second bridge near to it but lower, made of baked brick and stone, for his royal chariot to drive along. This text shows that we need not interpret the aqueduct on the garden relief as being the one at Jerwan, since the citadel of Nineveh was, in some way, supplied with water directly from an aqueduct of similar construction except in baked brick rather than stone.

The way in which a bridge for passengers could be constructed as a draw-bridge so as not to weaken the city's defences is described by Herodotus for Babylon (*Histories* 1.185–6).

> She [Nitocris] built a bridge over the river with blocks of stone . . . using iron and lead to bind the blocks together. Between the piers of the bridge she had squared baulks of timber laid down for the inhabitants to cross by, but only during daylight, for every night the timber was removed to prevent people from going over in the dark   . . .

A different construction would have to be devised to bring aqueduct water through the city walls, and we may resist the temptation to speculate. Strabo (*Geography* XVI.1.2), in connection with the works of Semiramis, wrote of 'the construction of fortifications with aqueducts therein, and of reservoirs for drinking water   . . . and bridges'. The picture that emerges from these pieces of evidence is one of a great city supplied with running water brought in on a long destroyed aqueduct of great length, built of baked brick and bitumen, probably on the north side of the river Khosr, which bridged the moat, perhaps with a pair of bridges at different levels, and came through the city wall to bring water to the Southwest Palace and its gardens.

In connection with an Elamite contribution, already mentioned is the great 14th century canal of Untaš-Napiriša, the Elamite king, at Choga Zambil. I would like also to mention an Elamite achievement in bronze casting which has implications for my own research into the problem of the Hanging Gardens and its water supply. I summarize that research by stating that the origin of the legend seems to lie in Sennacherib's palace garden at Nineveh, and that a technical passage in his inscription seems to show that he brought continuous water to the upper levels of the gardens by casting in bronze one or more water raising screws of a kind later attributed to the genius of the Greek inventor Archimedes, who lived 400 years later (Dalley 1994; Dalley, Oleson 2003). This interpretation would match Strabo's account (*Geography* XVI.3) of the Hanging Gardens, which he said were watered with a screw. Several scholars have denied that Assyria could have made such a bronze screw at that time. But in a programme of experimental archaeology with the BBC we managed to cast a small screw in very primitive conditions. Our bronze caster Andrew Lacey, with whom I discussed the inscription and the technical difficulties, showed that the cylinder and its internal screw would surely have been cast together — it was the moulds which were two separate items, not the castings. This eliminated one of the main difficulties in my initial attempt at interpretation (Dalley 2002a: 71–2).

The Elamite evidence which shows that large scale castings of this kind were feasible is the pair of bronze barriers, inscribed by Šilhak-Inšušinak in the 12th century BC, which consist of hollow cylinders in bronze, single castings more than 4m in length, with square terminals added as separate castings welded on to the ends of the cylinder (Harper 1992: 134). One of them is on display in the Louvre.

It is self-evident that nobody would cast a machine such as a large water raising screw in bronze unless it already existed and worked in a less expensive medium, in this case presumably timber. Urartians were expert both in bronze casting and in carpentry, so it is worth keeping a look-out on Urartian sites for installations connected with raising water by means of screws, whether wooden or bronze, in the seventh century if not earlier. Such an installation within a citadel or a lower town would consist of two tanks, lying one above the other, offset on terraces, so that a screw would lie between them at an angle of about 35 degrees. A shaped bedding for the screw might be found at the bottom. One could not hope to recover evidence on the bank of a canal where the screw would rest on the bank and raise water into a channel on the other side of the bank, so the main chance of finding evidence is limited to urban sites.

In this case when we look for evidence of influence, we certainly cannot find proof from data that are so one-sided and biased against Urartu and Elam. And we can emphasise that Sennacherib almost certainly did not invent the water raising screw at the same time as he cast one in bronze, having invented a new method for making the casting rather than inventing the mechanism itself.

Relevant to this period is the tunnel of Hezekiah in Jerusalem. Bagg has suggested Palestine as a source of inspiration for Assyrian developments in water supply. The suggestion seems inherently unlikely, because the terrain of Palestine, and the traditions of water supply for cities since the Early Bronze Age, are utterly different from those of both northern and southern Mesopotamia; and Palestine has no tunnels of this date built with a row of vertical shafts.

Although in modern times scholars have either suggested, or declared as fact, that Hezekiah built his tunnel in Jerusalem as a defensive measure against an impending siege by the Assyrian army, neither the *Old Testament* nor the tunnel inscription suggest such a connection. Ussishkin (1995: 302–3) has recently suggested that it was made as a peacetime achievement in emulation of Sennacherib's work at Nineveh. The *Bible* mentions it long after the account of Sennacherib's invasion, as if it belonged to the deeds of Hezekiah's latter years (2 *Kings* 20:20; 2 *Chron.* 32:30; *Ecclesiasticus* 48:17). Hezekiah's act of defiance in preparation for the Assyrian attack was to block spring water so that it would not be available to the Assyrians outside the wall. Two further arguments support Ussishkin's suggestion. The inscription, which speaks of the workmen and their triumph in making the two ends meet, is unusual in describing labour from the labourers' point of view, much as Sennacherib does in his account of waterworks and bronze castings for Nineveh. This interpretation would put Hezekiah's tunnel into the same category as some Assyrian and Urartian waterworks — prestige engineering which enhanced the peace time reputation of the king as a pioneer in water schemes and fitted the fashion of the period with an inscription that described in detail how the workmen achieved their goal.

This paper has given evidence for several ways in which kings in the late eighth and seventh centuries BC made a conspicuous display of power through the management of water, and has proposed extending our understanding with new possibilities at a time when cities became much larger. Their achievements were highly visible both on citadels and in the surrounding countryside, and they honoured publicly their designers and engineers, taking a royal interest also in the tribulations of their workforce. The relationship between Urartian and Assyrian technology remains to be clarified, but seems to belong within a much older and more extensive tradition.

## Bibliography

*Abbreviation*

ADD = Johns, C.H.W. 1898: *Assyrian Deeds and Documents*. Cambridge

Bagg, A.M. 2000: *Assyrische Wasserbauten* (Baghdader Forschungen 24). Mainz

Belli, O. 1995: 'Neue Funde urartäischer Bewässerungsanlagen in Ostanatolien' in U. Finkbeiner et al. (eds), *Beiträge zur Kulturgeschichte Vorderasiens, Festschrift für Rainer Michael Boehmer*. Mainz: 19–48

Boehmer, R. 1997: 'Bemerkungen bzw. Ergänzungen zu Gerwan, Khinis und Fahdi' *Baghdader Mitteilungen* 28: 225–49

Dalley, S. 1985: 'Foreign chariotry and cavalry in the armies of Tiglath-pileser III and Sargon II' *Iraq* 47: 31–48

— 1994: 'Nineveh, Babylon and the Hanging Gardens' *Iraq* 56: 45–58

—2002a: 'More about the Hanging Gardens' in L.A.-G. Werr et al. (eds), *Of Pots and Plans: Papers on the Archaeology and History of Mesopotamia and Syria Presented to David Oates in Honour of his 75th Birthday*. London: 67–73

— 2002b: 'Water management in Assyria from the ninth to the seventh centuries BC' *ARAM* 14: 443–60

Dalley, S., Oleson, J.P. 2003: 'Sennacherib, Archimedes and the water-screw. The context of invention in the ancient world' *Technology and Culture* 44: 1–26

Davey, C.J. 1985: 'The Negub Tunnel' *Iraq* 47: 49–55

Frahm, E. 1997: *Einleitung in die Sanherib-Inschriften* (Archive für Orientforschung Beiheft 26). Vienna

Fuchs, A. 1994: *Inschriften Sargons aus Khorsabad*. Göttingen

Ghirshman, R. 1968: *Tchoga Zanbil, Mémoires de la Délégation Archaéologique en Iran, XL volume II*. Paris

Goblot, H. 1979: *Les qanats. Une technique d'acquisition de l'eau*. Paris

Harper, P.O. et al. 1992: *The Royal City of Susa*. New York

Herodotus: *The Histories*. English translation by A. de Sélincourt (revised edition). Harmondsworth 1972

Jacobsen, T., Lloyd, S. 1935: *Sennacherib's Aqueduct at Jerwan* (Oriental Institute Publications 24). Chicago

Kwasman, T. 1988: *Neo-Assyrian Legal Documents in the Kouyunjik Collection of the British Museum*. Rome

Landsberger, B., Reiner, E., Civil, M. 1969: *Materials for the Sumerian Lexicon XII*. Rome

Place, V. 1867: *Ninive et l'Assyrie. Volume 2*. Paris

Rassam, H. 1897: *Asshur and the Land of Nimrod*. Cincinnati

Salvini, M. 1992: 'Il canale di Semiramide' *Geographia Antiqua* 1: 67–80

— 2001: 'Pas de qanats en Urartu!' in P. Briant, (ed.), *Irrigation et drainage dans l'Antiquité, qanats et canalisations souterraines en Iran, en Egypte et en Grèce*. Paris: 143–55

Steel, L., MacGinnis, J. 1990: 'Notes on Nineveh' *Iraq* 52: 63–74

Strabo: *Geography*. English translation by H.L. Jones (Loeb Classical Library 8 Volumes). London, New York 1917–1932

Stronach, D. 1994: 'Village to metropolis: Nineveh and the beginnings of urbanism in northern Mesopotamia' in S. Mazzoni (ed.), *Nuove Fondazione nel Vicino Oriente Antico*. Pisa: 85–114

Ussishkin, D. 1995: 'The water systems of Jerusalem during Hezekiah's reign' in M. Görg (ed.), *Meilenstein, Festgabe für Herbert Donner = Aegypten und Altes Testament* Band 30. Wiesbaden: 289–307

Zimansky, P. 1985: *Ecology and Empire: the Structure of the Urartian State*. Chicago

# Gordion re-dating

## Keith DeVries[1], G. Kenneth Sams[2] and Mary M. Voigt[3]

[1]University of Pennsylvania Museum, Philadelphia, [2]University of North Carolina, Chapel Hill,
[3]College of William and Mary, Williamsburg, Virginia

## Abstract

This paper presents a summary of the recent revision of the chronology of the Early and Middle Phrygian periods at Gordion.

## Özet

Bu çalışmayla, Gordion'daki Erken ve Orta Frig dönemleri kronolojisi ile ilgili olarak yapılmış yeniden gözden geçirme çalışmaları özetlenmektedir.

In January 2001, Bernd Kromer of the Heidelberg Akademie der Wissenschaften reported a series of radiocarbon determinations for samples taken from the Yassıhöyük stratigraphic sounding excavated in 1988–1989. These were submitted by Peter Kuniholm on behalf of Mary Voigt. Included were five samples of seeds, each sample taken from a different pot recovered from the floor of a destruction level building (TB2A). Three different plant series were represented. The seed samples produced a calibrated range extending from 835 to 800 BC at the 1 sigma level, with a slightly larger but compatible range at the 2 sigma or 95% level of confidence. Thus these short-lived samples consistently indicated a date for the great fire at Gordion that is a century or more earlier than the commonly accepted date of ca. 700 BC. The 700 BC date stemmed from an assumption that Gordion was destroyed during a Kimmerian incursion. Evidence for the incursion and its timing was obtained by combining the late antique chronographer Eusebios' placement of the death of Midas in 696 BC with the report by the Augustan writer Strabo that Midas died at the time of a Kimmerian invasion of Phrygia.

We had submitted the radiocarbon samples because a discussion by DeVries, Sams and Voigt in January of 1999 had led to a rejection of the 700 date based on recent stratigraphic analysis as well as a re-study of finds and publications from the Rodney S. Young excavations. We agreed that the Early Phrygian destruction level had to be significantly earlier than 700 BC, and we thought that the carefully selected carbon samples would give us guidance. With the new dates in hand we have begun a thorough re-checking of artefacts from the destruction level (phase 6A in the Yassıhöyük stratigraphic sequence), the Middle Phrygian Period (YHSS 5) and the tumulus burials. We have found nothing to contradict the new radiocarbon dates and much to support them. For example, we had been aware of a discrepancy between the artefacts deposited in tumulus MM, often considered to be the tomb of Midas, and those of the destruction level, with destruction level finds being typologically earlier. A close scrutiny demonstrates that the pottery and bronzes of the destruction level find their best correspondences well back in the sequence of Gordion tumuli, after the earliest excavated tumulus, W.

A few artefacts from the destruction level independently indicate a late ninth century date. For example, a set of north Syrian ivory horse trappings from one of the terrace buildings resembles recently published horse trappings bearing inscriptions of Hazael of Damascus, who reigned from 842 to ca. 805 BC. A bronze griffin handle attachment from the richly furnished megaron 3 has a parallel in a bird attachment from the burned level of Hasanlu period IVD, itself dated ca. 800 BC by shortlived radiocarbon samples. Dates for the Middle Phrygian rebuilding at Gordion again support our re-dating. Pottery imported from Greece recovered from two distinct Middle Phrygian contexts dates to the late eighth and early seventh centuries as previously reported by DeVries.

As the archaeological evidence casting doubt on the conventional Gordion chronology began to accumulate, we went back to the historical sources which had played a pivotal role in constructing the old sequence. We found that the literary evidence that had been thought to bear upon the destruction and its date is very weak. The entry of 696 for the death of Midas in Eusebios is compromised by a questionable correlation with the reign of Gyges of Lydia (dated by Assyrian records to the 660s BC) and by demonstrably wrong correlations with regnal years of an Egyptian pharoah and a Judean king. A passage in Strabo which links Midas' suicide to a Kimmerian invasion is an isolated account and much less telling than usually supposed.

Strabo tells us that Midas died as a result of drinking bull's blood, as do several other sources, none earlier than the Roman period. But none of the sources except Strabo cites the Kimmerians as the cause of Midas' suicide, and Strabo himself says nothing about a destruction of Gordion or even a ruination of the Phrygian state. Clearly there was in antiquity no firm historical tradition associating Midas and his death with the Kimmerians.

The radiocarbon and dendrochronological evidence provides a firm and consistent absolute chronology for ninth and eighth century Gordion. Thus far, the relative chronology obtained from a study of artefacts from the Gordion sequence as well as more distant independently dated sites is consistent with these absolute dates. We look forward to discussion of the Gordion results with scholars working at Early Iron Age sites across Anatolia.

**Acknowledgements**
We would like to thank Lynn Roller for reading out our statement at the conference, and Altan bey for allowing us to share with our colleagues new evidence for the chronology of the Early and Middle Phrygian periods at Gordion, in advance of a formal and more detailed publication of the data.

# Legitimacy, identity and history in Iron Age Gurgum*

**Lynn Swartz Dodd**

*University of Southern California and University of California, Los Angeles*

## Abstract

The Iron Age kingdom of Gurgum included the Kahramanmaraş valley in southern Turkey, the target of a survey directed by Elizabeth Carter of the University of California, Los Angeles, during the 1990s. The survey results for the Early and Middle Iron Age are summarised here. These data show that the kings of Gurgum faced a radically changed landscape in and around their territory during the ninth century BC. The appearance in this kingdom of a new text type, the extended kinglist, and a system of decorum in display monuments, are seen as interrelated elements in a strategy of legitimation. Faced with a bleak future that included competition from Aramaean kingdoms and impending conquest by the Assyrians, the kings of Gurgum began to reach into the past to buttress their position in the present.

## Özet

Bir Demir Çağ Krallığı olan Gurgum Türkiye'nin güneyinde yer alan Kahramanmaraş vadisini de sınırları içine almaktadır. 1990'lı yıllar boyunca Los Angeles/Kaliforniya Üniversitesi mensuplarından Elizabeth Carter burada yüzey araştırmaları gerçekleştirmiştir. Burada, bu araştırmaların Erken ve Orta Demir Çağ dönemlerine ait sonuçları özetlenmektedir. Araştırmanın sonuçları M.Ö. 9. yüzyılda Gurgum krallarının krallık sınırları içinde ve dışında belirgin farklara sahip bir siyasi coğrafya ile karşı karşıya olduklarını ortaya koymaktadır. Krallık içinde yeni bir döküman tipi ortaya çıkmıştır. Kral adlarından oluşan geçmişe dönük uzun bir liste ile teşhirdeki anıtlarla ilgili olarak oluşturulan yeni bir muaşeret adabı sisteminin birbirleriyle ilişkili olduğu düşünülmüş ve bunlar oluşturulmaya çalışılan yasallaşma stratejileri içinde yerlerini almışlardır. Böylece Arami Krallıkları ile rekabet etmek ve Asurluların yaklaşan fetihleri gibi unsurları da içeren ümitsiz bir gelecekle karşı karşıya kalan Gurgum kralları mevcut durumlarını destekleyebilmek amacıyla geçmişlerinden güç almaya çalışmışlardır.

---

Kahramanmaraş (fig. 1) is located northeast of Cilicia, between central Anatolia and Syria, in a valley bordered by the Anti-Taurus mountains (Ahır Dağı) to the north, by the Amanus mountains (Nur Dağları) to the west and by lower hills to the south and east. The Aksu and Erkenez Su rivers flow through the valley, and the Gavur Gölü is situated at its southwestern edge. In the southeastern portion of the valley, numerous springs flow from the hills and base of the northern Arapdere Dağ. Here the natural drainage is sometimes insufficient and marshy areas existed in the past. The valley contains a high percentage of arable land, alternating with rocky outcrops that serve as barriers to travel across the valley floor. These outcrops also provide stone and other resources and are used for sheep/goat herding.

The Kahramanmaraş valley was subject to the cultural and political influence of the Hittites during the Late Bronze Age. Subsequently, during the Early Iron Age, it became part of an independent political entity, a kingdom named Gurgum. In the Middle Iron Age the valley again came under the cultural and administrative influence of an external power, Assyria.

* This article is a revision of the paper presented at the Symposium. The author has been engaged in a detailed study of the Late Bronze Age and Iron Age pottery for her PhD dissertation (Dodd 2002) under the direction of Elizabeth Carter (UCLA), with whom the author is preparing the final report on the Kahramanmaraş survey for publication.

*Fig. 1. Map of region*

The Kahramanmaraş Valley Survey, directed by Elizabeth Carter of UCLA, provides the most intensive, systematic archaeological view of an area otherwise known largely from Luwian (Hawkins 2000), Phoenician and Neo-Assyrian display inscriptions and texts.[1] However, whilst the inscriptions are a precious source of detail, the archaeological data extend into temporal and social domains that the inscriptions do not. In particular, no textual data from the kingdom of Gurgum bridges the Late Bronze Age to Early Iron Age period. Also, the survey data provide a view of the settlement pattern outside the main city, Kahramanmaraş, where the major centre for the valley is presumed to have been located. The survey identified settlements of all sizes and their location across the landscape, and thereby allows the relationship between the settlements of the Late Bronze Age and those of the Iron Age to be specified. The data from the survey are used here, in conjunction with textual material, to explore elements of continuity and innovation in the Early Iron Age kingdoms of north Syria. Of particular

interest here are the ways in which élite and corporate identities were constructed and buttressed within Gurgum, whose literate members used Luwian in their display inscriptions.

By the late tenth century BC, the Luwian kingdoms (that is, those polities in which the predominant language for monumental texts was Luwian, in contrast to those kingdoms in which Aramaean or Phoenician dominated the inscriptions) had defined themselves in a configuration that would endure until they were absorbed into the Assyrian empire between the ninth and seventh centuries BC. By the Middle Iron Age, nearly a dozen Luwian and Aramaean polities were paying explicit homage to the symbolic systems and structures of the defunct Hittite empire — even though some of them had never even been part of that original tradition. The Hittite past was deliberately invoked in order to maintain the unequal power relations of the preceding period, but on a significantly localised scale. The period between the Late Bronze Age and the Early Iron Age is one of ferment and reconstruction, which includes the reassertion of local traditions that had been suppressed under Hittite rule during the second half of the Late Bronze Age.

**Survey**

The overwhelming majority of the UCLA survey activities were concentrated on the valley floor and in certain of the rocky outcrops within the valley (Carter 1995; 1996; Carter et al. 1999). Based on the survey data, the following chronological scheme has been adopted.

| Period | Time Span |
|---|---|
| Terminal Late Bronze Age | end of the LBA to the 12th and early 11th centuries BC |
| Early Iron Age | early 11th to late tenth century and perhaps earliest ninth century BC |
| Middle Iron Age | ninth to seventh centuries BC |
| Late Iron Age | sixth century BC onward until the Hellenistic period |

These chronological divisions are based on an interpretation of the ceramic traditions in Kahramanmaraş, and reflect an understanding of continuity and change at the turn of the second to first millennium BC, from the Late Bronze Age to the Iron Age. The chronology adopted here is similar to that suggested by Müller (1999) for Lidar Höyük, but it is not intended to suggest uniformity of cultural or ceramic traditions between the two areas, although there are some similarities. In summary, this chronology reflects the persistence of a

---

[1] The Incirli inscription (Carter 1996; Kaufman, Zuckerman in preparation) contains Phoenician, Neo-Assyrian, Greek (a palimpsest) and possibly a small eroded Luwian text.

version of the Late Bronze Age ceramic traditions into the early 11th century BC, when the sparsely attested Early Iron Age wares finally appear. In contrast to the few Early Iron Age ceramic types, numerous examples of Middle Iron Age material were found during the Kahramanmaraş survey.

## Summary of Early Iron Age pottery and settlement pattern

Early Iron Age pottery was located at only seven sites in the Kahramanmaraş valley (fig. 2), all of which lie on, or to the south of, the Aksu river's mid-valley bend. This is a notable distribution, especially in comparison with the dispersed settlement pattern that characterises all other periods. The imbalance in the site locations and in their quantity leads me to suspect that there is an as yet undefined local Early Iron Age ceramic assemblage within our survey collections. Unfortunately, the lack of single period sites for the late second millennium/early first millennium BC makes identification of these local wares problematic at present. The situation may be clarified once controlled excavation is undertaken in the valley.

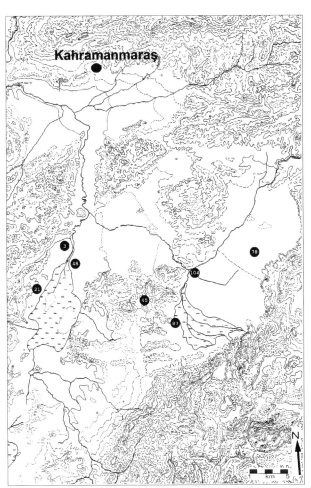

*Fig. 2. Map showing Early Iron Age sites*

The Early Iron Age sites were identified by a restricted number of exemplars. Overall, the following may be said of the Kahramanmaraş Early Iron Age ceramic assemblage. Pottery is rarely painted; the notable exception is a vessel with a sloppily painted surface treatment (fig. 4C), which is known as 'random line designs' at Tille Höyük (Blaylock 1999) and as 'Kindergarten ware' at Kilise Tepe, and which may also be similar to examples found at Lidar (Müller 1996: Taf. 130) and possibly at Hama (Riis 1990: 147, 437). As a corpus, Early Iron Age vessels are often tempered with a combination of chaff and calcareous grit, or chaff and sand. Early Iron Age wares with coarse chaff alone are not common in Kahramanmaraş. Those shapes and wares that might be viewed as developments from the Late Bronze Age drab ware tradition frequently lack chaff tempering, or have only fine chaff tempering alongside grit or sand. Surface treatments include slips, either a sometimes thick, light coloured slip (fig. 3B), or a reddish slip that ranges from light to dark (fig. 3A, C, D). Attested forms include cooking pots (fig. 4A), jars (fig. 4B), and cups and open bowl or plate forms (fig. 3A–C). Kahramanmaraş's plain wares share characteristics with assemblages known from a fairly extensive array of sites, ranging from the dam areas on the Tigris and Euphrates, to Cilicia, the Göksu (Brown 1967) and northern Syria.

The identification of Early Iron Age wares in the Kahramanmaraş valley is possibly complicated by continuity between Late Bronze Age and Early Iron Age types and forms. Though the Early Iron Age corpus is limited, the ceramic repertoire has some affinity with Late Bronze Age traditions, suggesting a local evolution of vessel shapes and wares. For example, several Kahramanmaraş bowls and pots are similar to examples known from Late Bronze Age Tarsus (Korbel 1987: Taf. 33:243, 29, 28:343, 17:110). Despite any socio-political upheaval during the transition, a certain continuity of Late Bronze Age forms and wares, especially of the so-called drab wares, may have persisted for a limited time at sites such as Tille, Tell Afis, Boğazköy, Kuşaklı, Karahöyük/Elbistan and Kilise Tepe (see Genz, this volume, for further discussion). A similar continuity has also been noted at Lidar, where new features were introduced to an otherwise locally evolving potting tradition that had developed out of Late Bronze Age practices (Blaylock 1999: 265; Müller 1999).

A characteristic shape for the first Early Iron Age ware, which is similar to Cilician buff ware, is a bowl or deep platter with a slightly thickened flat rim (fig. 3B). The paste is light brown with a grey core, and is tempered with chaff and grit with some mica. Its surface has a low burnish.

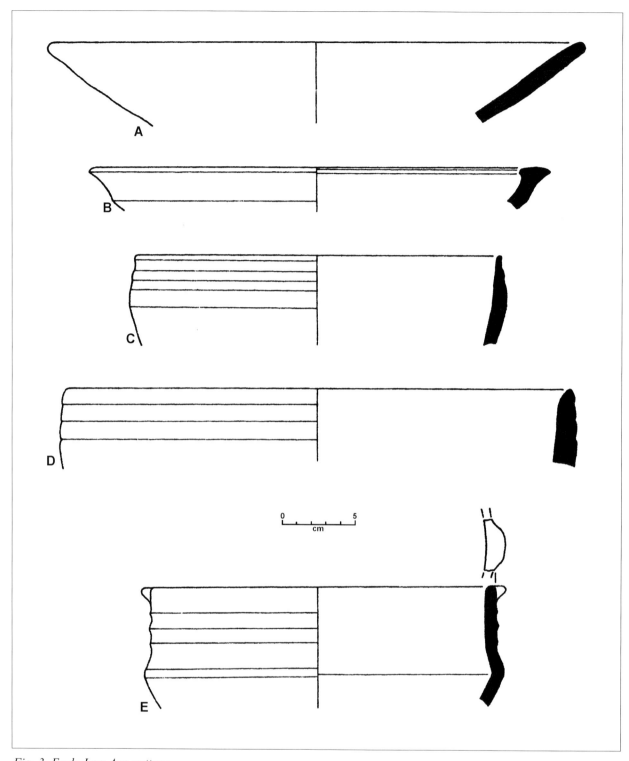

*Fig. 3. Early Iron Age pottery*

*(A) Deep platter. Wheelmade. Hard fine fabric. Reddish yellow (5 YR7/6) slip or self-slip on reddish brown (5 YR5/4) paste with medium grey core. Light interior burnish. Fine calcareous grit and fine chaff. KM 80 (149)*

*(B) Bowl. Light brown (7.5 YR6/4) slip on dark greyish brown (10 YR4/2) paste with dark grey core. Burnished. Fine sand and chaff temper. KM 45 (137)*

*(C) Bowl or pot. Reddish brown (2.5 YR5/4) slip on yellowish red (5 YR4.5/6) paste. Interior closely burnished. Calcareous grit tempered. KM 78 (192)*

*(D) Bowl or pot. Light red brown exterior slip, dark red interior slipped. Much quartzy calcareous grit, fine chaff temper. KM 78 (216)*

*(E) Lugged pot. Pink paste (7.5 YR8/4). Burnished. Fine and coarse calcareous grit temper. KM 104 (005)*

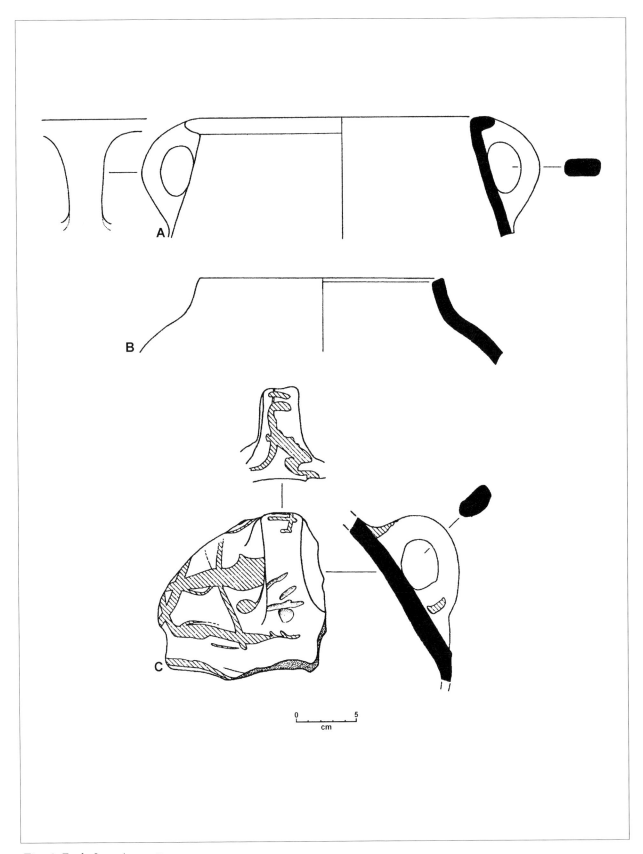

*Fig. 4. Early Iron Age pottery*
*(A) Pot. Light reddish yellow paste. Calcareous grit and chaff tempered. Light brown core. Burnished (649)*
*(B) Jar. Very pale brown (10 YR7/4) slip on dark grey (10 YR4/1) paste. Burnished. Possibly handmade. Sand and little fine chaff temper. KM 63 (091)*
*(C) Jar. Yellow-brown paste. Heavy chaff, some grit tempered. Red paint. KM 87 (195)*

This vessel shape is known from sites both east and west of Kahramanmaraş. It occurs at Early Iron Age Tarsus as Cilician buff ware 'standard bowls' (Hanfmann 1963: cat. no. 70, pl. 116), and at Lidar in the earliest Iron Age levels (Müller 1999: Abb. 5:4). Another open form, a sand and chaff tempered, partially burnished, grey cored cooking pot (fig. 4B), is a shape known from sites in the Euphrates dam areas, and at Lidar (Müller 1996: Taf. 55:10) and Korucutepe (Winn 1980: pl. 54:8). Another closed vessel form is an everted rim jar or pot with handle. Its fabric is chaff and micaceous grit tempered, and the surface is either self-slipped or smoothed. This last example has parallels to vessels found at Lidar Höyük (Müller 1999: Abb 5:7).

Corrugated ware, *Rillenkeramik*, ribbed ware or, according to a recent suggestion, groovy pottery (see Roaf, Schachner, this volume), is found in Kahramanmaraş (fig. 3C–E). The corrugated pots and bowls are generally handmade, and are tempered with chaff and either calcareous grit or quartz grit. The surface may be slipped in a reddish tone. Surfaces are generally smoothed or burnished. Colours can be mottled, and a reddish brown is most common. Colour variation between interior and exterior is sometimes notable, and usually it is the exterior that is darker, perhaps due to smoke darkening. The Kahramanmaraş examples of corrugated ware occur in a restricted range of colours, predominantly reddish browns, but also 7.5 YR8/4 (pink) (a corrugated lugged pot). Parallels for the open forms found in Kahramanmaraş are similar to shapes from the earliest Iron Age levels at Lidar Höyük (Müller 1996: Taf. 60:3, 7, 15; 1999: Taf. 48:8). Similar material has also been attested in surveys[2] and on excavations[3] at sites such as Tille Höyük (Blaylock 1999: fig 3:7), Korucutepe (Winn 1980: pls 52:5, 53:11, 58:21), Imıkuşağı (Sevin 1995: res. 13, 15; 1983: 399, Abb. 7), Norşuntepe (Bartl 1994: Abb. 6:2), Değirmentepe (Duru 1979), Köskerbaba Höyük (Bilgi 1991: fig. 02.8; 1987), Tepecik, Oylum Höyük (Özgen et al. 1997: Abb 19:4), Sakçegözü (Taylor et al. 1950: 114, fig. 25:9), Tarsus (Hanfmann 1963), Tell

Halaf (Bartl 1995: 208, 212) and Kenan Tepe (Parker et al. 2002). For a discussion of the chronological range of corrugated ware, and problems concerning its dating, see especially Bartl 1994; 2001; Roaf, Schachner this volume (and literature cited therein).

## The Middle Iron Age pottery

A substantial change occurs in both the quantity and the character of pottery in the Middle Iron Age ceramic assemblage of Kahramanmaraş. There is an increase in sites, from seven in the Early Iron Age to 48 in the Middle Iron Age (fig. 6). The Middle Iron Age pottery in Kahramanmaraş includes shapes and ware types that proliferate from Cilicia eastward to Iraq and southeastern Turkey, and southward into the Levant, thus outlining a region on which the Assyrians had a definite impact.

In the Kahramanmaraş survey, the Middle Iron Age pastes are found to be more compact than in the preceding centuries. Slips occur on a fairly wide variety of forms, in a range of colours that includes cream, very pale brown, light orange and pink, light red, dark red, reddish brown, and brown (fig. 5A, C, D, F). The tempering regimes also change during the Middle Iron Age. In Kahramanmaraş, chaff still appears in combination with other tempers, especially in the larger vessels and open forms (fig. 5F), but overall there is a bias towards calcareous grit temper in particular, or sand temper (fig. 5A–C, G, J–L). Coarser calcareous grits now appear less often in Kahramanmaraş, which constitutes a shift away from the Late Bronze Age pottery tradition known as drab ware. Fine and medium calcareous grits and fine chaff occur, and another frequent pairing is fine calcareous grit and mica. A change in tempering is also attested to the north and south of Kahramanmaraş at this time.[4]

The types of surface treatments seen in the Middle Iron Age in Kahramanmaraş include fairly simple painted decorative schemes, in black-on-buff, dark- or black-on-white, red and black bichrome, and red-on-black wares (fig. 5L). Other black-on-red decorative treatments also occur: the first has opaque black paint on a dark orange ground; the second has a finer paste in a light orange colour, and carries dark concentric circles or targets as decoration; the third type has a deep red slip (instead of a red paste) decorated with dark grey paint; examples corre-

---

[2] Surveys include: the Keban/Altınova (Winn 1980) and Ataturk and Karakaya dam areas (Özdoğan 1977: ware 4); the Sakçegözü plain (Garrard et al. 1996); Adıyaman (Blaylock et al. 1990); and the Birecik and Karkamiš dam areas (Algaze et al. 1994: 18, fig. 29-0)

[3] The Tille Höyük corrugated ware occurs in levels IV and V, which form the core of Neo-Hittite occupation during the tenth century and into the ninth (Blaylock 1999: 267; Summers 1993). In excavations such as Norşuntepe, Tepecik, Korucutepe and Değirmentepe, this corrugated ware, or *Rillenkeramik*, occurs stratigraphically between the mid-twelfth century and the end of the eleventh, or possibly to the middle of the tenth (Bartl 1994: 502).

[4] See Swift 1958: 125; Müller 1996: 285. Amuq Phase O wares are characterised by red slipped burnished ware with part mineral, part organic tempers. To the north, in the later Iron Age levels at Lidar Höyük, there is a tendency towards fewer chaff tempered wares. At Lidar, 60% of the wares found are sand tempered (with or without grit, and with or without calcareous grit). Only 25% are chaff and sand tempered (with or without calcareous grit).

spond roughly to varieties of black-on-red described long ago by Mellaart (1955: 119). In Kahramanmaraş, black and red bichrome painted pottery was found at three sites: KM 21 Sivrimine Tepe; KM 28 Orta Höyük Çakallı Hasanağa, and possibly KM 10 Özbek Karahasan. All examples are from closed vessels, such as pitchers or flasks; similar examples can be found at 'Ain Dara (Stone, Zimansky 1999: 27, 70), Kilise Tepe (Hansen, Postgate 1999) and in the Amanus at Domuztepe in its eighth or ninth century levels (Alkım 1952).

Despite the variety of painted wares just listed, the number of examples found in the UCLA Kahramanmaraş survey was extremely low for all types. In most cases there are no more than a couple of examples of each kind. Plain, unpainted pottery is by far the most common component of the entire ceramic assemblage. A small proportion of the Middle Iron Age pottery has untreated surfaces, but generally the ware of this period has a slip, or self-slip, or some burnish.

The Middle Iron Age slips range in colour and quality, although this variation can be summarised in two main categories: cream slip on buff ware; and red slipped wares. Examples of the first group include a splayed rim bowl of a type known from both Tille (Blaylock 1999) and Lidar (Müller 1999: Abb. 7:2). The illustrated example (fig. 5A) has a fine sand tempered fabric and a smoothed opaque cream slip on a buff-pink paste. Other examples of light coloured slips on buff ware include: Assyrian period ridged rim bowls, with parallels at Kinet Höyük (from the Assyrian levels; M.-H. Gates, personal communication, September 1998) and elsewhere (Seton-Williams 1961: pl. xxxviii:21; Lebeau 1983: 263, type CT16); and ring collar jars with a light brown slip on buff or brown paste (Lloyd, Gökçe 1953: 46; Ball, Tucker et al. 1989: 63). Light coloured slips also appear on orange pastes (fig. 5F). Slips in a range of reddish tones occur frequently within the Middle Iron Age assemblage at Kahramanmaraş. These red slips are often fugitive or eroded, sometimes burnished, and occur in a range of colours from pink (fig. 5D) to light red (fig. 5G) and reddish brown to dark red (fig. 5C). The regional range of red slips also varies considerably (Swift 1958: 125; Hanfmann 1963: pl. 122:419, 420; Lebeau 1983: 251: form BL16, 252: form BL24; Ökse 1988: nos 49, 60; Müller 1996: 285; Stone, Zimansky 1999: pl. ix:27).

Certain simple, open, deep plates may represent a development from the standard open bowl/plate form known since at least the Late Bronze Age (as, for example, at Tarsus). These wide platter bowls are a well attested shape at most Iron Age sites across a fairly wide area to the south, east and west of Kahramanmaraş (Ökse 1988: nos 965–9); they occur in a range of colours, from reddish yellow to pink and very pale brown, and they are often smoothed or slightly burnished on the exterior. One example found in the Kahramanmaraş survey (Dodd 2002: fig. 4.7A) is incised with a rectilinear design or possibly a potter's mark, as is seen occasionally on similar plates and other vessels from sites such as Tarsus (where these incised line designs occur both in the Iron Age and in earlier periods: Goldman 1956; Hanfmann 1963), Kinet Höyük (Gates 2001) and 'Ain Dara (Stone, Zimansky 1999).

Assyrian palace ware was not located at any of the surveyed sites. However, a Neo-Assyrian glazed vessel recovered from Hopaz (KM 178), a site now drowned in a lake, is on display in Kahramanmaraş Museum. Classic Middle Iron Age forms — such as the indented rim bowl (fig. 5C) and ledge rim bowls (fig. 5B, H) — have strong parallels across a wide geographical area that includes Lidar (Müller 1996), Tell Abou Danné (Lebeau 1983), Hama (Riis 1990), Tarsus (Hanfmann 1963) and Sultantepe (Lloyd, Gökçe 1953: figs 6, 7). A common factor affecting all these sites is contact and interaction with the Assyrians during the Middle Iron Age.

During the Middle Iron Age the ceramic assemblage of Kahramanmaraş is transformed. During the Early Iron Age, the assemblage had relatively few identifiable types, and probably also a significant local tradition existed that has yet to be clearly recognised. The Early Iron Age settlement pattern is idiosyncratic. By contrast, during the Middle Iron Age, the settlements are broadly dispersed throughout the valley, and a larger number of identifiable vessel shapes, surface treatments and wares are found. The Middle Iron Age assemblage includes forms that appear across Syro-Anatolia, north Mesopotamia and the Levant, consistent with an assumption that residents of the valley were now more integrated into, or more aware of, material cultural practices characteristic of a wider region. The composition of the Middle Iron Age ceramic assemblage reflects the intensity and orientation of this regional interaction, which is also attested in the monuments and texts of both the local rulers and the Assyrians. Significantly, the northerly orientation of the Early Iron Age ceramic assemblage becomes less prominent during the Middle Iron Age, when southern and eastern parallels are more apparent. This integration, at least to the extent that it is reflected in the ceramic assemblage, accelerates during the ninth and into the eighth centuries BC. The changes in the ceramic assemblage and the settlement pattern show the ninth century to have been a period of considerable transformation. This is in part related to an ability to recognise pottery forms in the Middle Iron Age, and while a real transformation of the ceramic assemblage is apparent, this change does not mean that the settlement pattern itself is a new creation without precedent in the past settlement traditions in the valley.

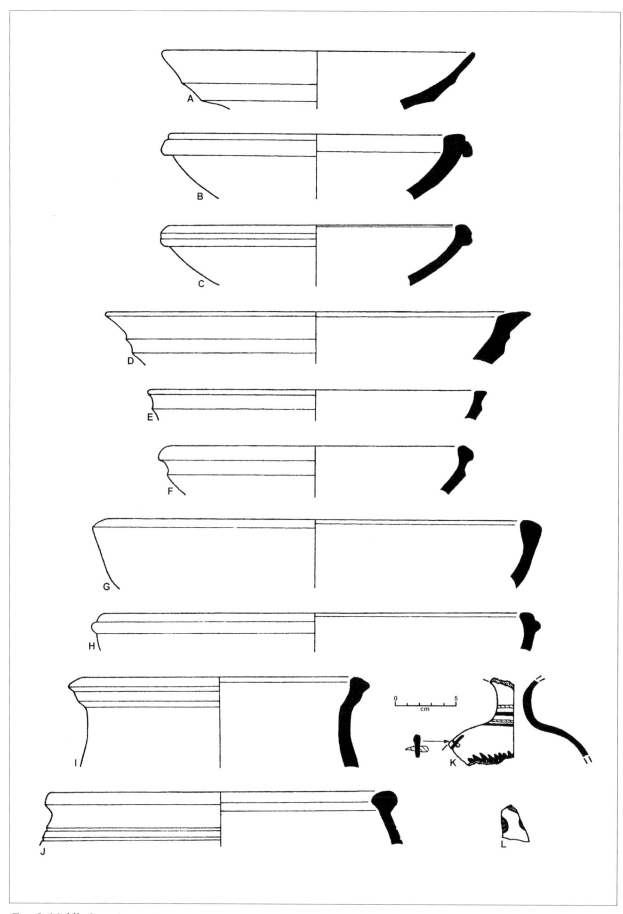

*Fig. 5. Middle Iron Age pottery*

*Fig. 5. Middle Iron Age pottery*

*(A) Bowl. Pale yellow (2.5 Y8/2) slip on very pale brown (10YR7/3) paste. Exterior lightly burnished. Fine micaceous sand tempered. KM 80 (159)*

*(B) Bowl. Dark grey (2.5 Y4/1) paste. Exterior burnished. Fine to coarse calcareous sand temper. KM 17 (640)*

*(C) Bowl. Red (2.5 YR5/6) slip on yellowish brown (10 YR5/4) paste. Grit visible on surface. Calcareous grit temper. Burnished exterior. KM 120 (659)*

*(D) Bowl. Light brown (7.5 YR6/4) paste. Grey (7.5 YR5.5/1) core. Calcareous grit and chaff tempered. Pink (7.5 YR7/4) slip or self-slip. KM 80 (148)*

*(E) Bowl. Grey (5 Y5/1) paste. Reddish brown (5 YR6/3) exterior and very pale brown (10 YR7/3) interior self-slip. Horizontally burnished. Chaff and grit tempered. KM 61 (160)*

*(F) Bowl. Pink slip (7.5 YR7/4) on orange brown (7.5 YR6/5) paste. Calcareous grit and possibly fine chaff tempered. KM 88 (182)*

*(G) Bowl. Light red (2.5 YR7/6) slip or self-slip on reddish yellow (5 YR6/6) paste. Interior burnished. Fine calcareous grit or sand temper. KM 57 (104)*

*(H) Bowl. Light brown (7.5 YR6/4) self-slipped paste with dark grey brown (10 YR4/2) core. Rim and interior burnished. Calcareous grit and possibly fine chaff tempered. KM 61 (158)*

*(I) Jar. Light brown (7.5 YR6/4) slip or self-slip on light yellowish brown (10 YR6/4) paste with dark grey (10 YR4/1) core. Grit and chaff temper. KM 91 (241)*

*(J) Jar. Dark greyish brown (10 YR4/2) self-slipped paste with thick dark grey core. Some burnishing. Calcareous grit tempered. KM 104 (189)*

*(K) Jug or pitcher, bichrome painted. Light reddish brown (5 YR6/4) paste with reddish grey (5 YR5/2) core. Painted light reddish brown (2.5 YR6/3) and weak red (10 R4/3). KM 21 (X287)*

*(L) Black-on-red sherd. Black paint on light orange paste. Very fine calcareous temper. KM 121(597)*

The degree of Late Bronze to Early Iron Age continuity in the Kahramanmaraş survey has been argued in detail elsewhere (Dodd 2002). In brief, because of the low number of sites identified for the Early Iron Age (seven sites), the impression is that there was a collapse of the settlement system at the end of the Late Bronze Age. However, these data should be compared to the Middle Iron Age, when 48 settlements existed. Among these 48 sites, 31 of them were previously occupied during the Late Bronze Age. Thus, if the longer view is taken, there is considerable continuity between the Late Bronze Age and the Middle Iron Age, and the possibility must be admitted that additional Early Iron Age sites may be identified once the local Early Iron Age assemblage is more clearly identified in future.

The historical narrative supplied by the Neo-Hittite élites of the Iron Age kingdoms, who defined themselves through a connection to Hittite predecessors, features continuity between the Late Bronze Age and Early Iron Age as its central theme. Thus, while the ceramic evidence from the Early Iron Age is scant and thus ambiguous, the settlement pattern data offer a clearer view of population continuity in the landscape over an extended time.

## Material reflections of cultural identity

Following the demise of the Hittite empire, its unitary southern territory had fractured into a number of locally ruled principalities with firmly established élites (see MARAŞ 1).[5] Thus, by the ninth century BC, the Syro-Anatolian region was transformed into a collection of competing polities, independently ruled until their incorporation into the Assyrian empire's provincial system, through which they became the northwestern frontier of that empire. Kingdoms similar to Gurgum, but attested earlier, were centered on Malatya, Lidar and Karkamiš, and were ruled by men with Luwian names and Luwian inscriptions ( Jasink 1995; Bonatz 2000; Hawkins 2000). Their claims to legitimacy were founded in part on their connection to, and creative appropriation of, the Hittite past. Previously marginal rulers were transformed into claimants of the imperial legacy. Furthermore, rulers with Aramaean names and Semitic language inscriptions had consolidated their control over neighbouring areas, including Bit-Adini, Patina and Sam'al amongst others (Sader 1987; Mazzoni 1992; Dion 1997). These élites asserted their claims of control and power in a manner similar to the Luwian or Late Hittite princes.

---

[5] All inscriptions referred to in capital letters are illustrated, transcribed and translated in Hawkins 2000. Most of the inscriptions and all the Luwian translations referenced in this paper can be found in the same work.

Throughout the tenth century, inter-group interaction had become more fully situated at the new royal cities, nodes of the territories whose boundaries the sedentary élites were motivated to defend and define.[6] In this Syro-Anatolian region a complex mixture of cultural and linguistic groups traded and competed hotly for resources and prestige.

The ninth century was the beginning of the end for the independent polities of northern Syria. Aššurnasirpal I, Shalmaneser III and finally Adad-Nirari V, made forays into Syro-Anatolia, and into the kingdom of Gurgum itself. The Banquet Stele of Aššurnasirpal is emblematic of the peer-polity competition that characterised this period, and which rapidly shifted in favour of a particular competitor, Assyria.

Assyrian expansion and aggression — territorial, administrative, diplomatic and military — pressed the frontier of their imperial influence westwards towards Gurgum (Parpola 1987: 257:12, 124:24, r.18, r.2, 253:6; Tadmor 1994: Ann. 13*:12, Ann. 27:5, St. I B:25', 38', Summ. 7:r.8, Ann. 3:5, St. IIIA:18, Ann. 17:4', Ann. 21:9', Summ. 7:45, St. I B:42', St. II B:14', T. I B:41'). Thus, during the ninth century BC and onwards, the élite of Gurgum attempted to retain power in the face of multiple assaults on its legitimacy and viability, both by adjacent Aramaean kingdoms and by the Assyrians. The Gurgumeans became increasingly mobilised in defence not only of the realm, but also of the élite establishment, and of a conceptual group identity and social space that had been created to exclude, as external alterities, the Assyrians and the Aramaeans. One means of defining who the 'we' are in Gurgum is the creative use of a past in the service of history writing — the use of the past in the present (Asad 1993; Trouillot 1995).

Formerly the borders of Gurgum had merely abutted adjacent like-sized kingdoms; now they became a frontier facing a territory controlled by a bellicose and distant Assyrian imperial centre. This transformation was perceived by the Gurgumeans as pernicious and it had significant negative consequences. This reaction is particularly visible in the élite realms, and in part it is situated in the domain of heightened use of the past to buttress the legitimacy of the rulers. Narrative creates a link by providing a story of common experiences, history and memories, allowing people in a defined space to make sense of the social world and identities (Somers, Gibson 1994; Paasi 1998). Based on the assumption that social changes are reflected in archaeological remains, identity creation should be marked by a change in material patterning within the social space under study.[7]

The challenge, to a researcher interested in the mechanisms used to define a social space and group identity, is the identification of a semiotic system that its users, the members of a group, would recognise. In the case of Gurgum, a strategy is reflected in monumental display sculpture, funerary inscriptions and sealings. Along with Gurgum's settlement pattern and ceramic corpus, these provide evidence of the recycling and localisation of legitimation strategies known from the Hittite empire, but not imported wholesale from there.[8] Royal monuments contrast noticeably with presentations on non-royal monuments. This offers an opportunity to describe a representational canon within the past — a reflection of the need to deploy images and concepts in new ways to perpetuate specific aspects of cultural identity for defined goals. No longer was wealth, military support and agricultural produce co-opted for the *god-king* in a distant imperial capital. Instead, wealth supported local élites engaged in competitive interactions with adjacent kingdoms. These new kingdoms restructured economic, political and social relationships during this period and, along with this, adopted an explanatory framework designed to support their place within it.

When authority intersects with representation, a system of *allowable* images is created, or more specifically, a system of decorum is established (Baines 1990; Marcus 1995; Yoffee 1998). This system reflects varying levels of access to ideologically powerful symbols in a society, and is mirrored by differential access to economically valuable resources.[9] This system of decorum —

---

[6] Such a case is clearly outlined in the Kilamuwa inscription (KAI no. 24).

[7] Curet 1996; Ando 2000. Karjalainen (1986) defines places as lived locations that acquire meaning through the experience of them. For Tuan (1975: 152), places are experienced along a continuum that is anchored at one end by abstract locations in space devoid of association, and at the other by nodes of extreme emotional or symbolic importance. See also Gottmann 1973; 1982; Lipsanen 2001.

[8] This study is confined to the survey results of Gurgum and the Kahramanmaraş valley, although reference is made to sealings and two royal sculptures found elsewhere.

[9] Underlying this assertion is an assumption that members of a social group build roughly similar understandings — of such domains as kinship relations, interpretation of people's behaviours, religious agencies, moral imperatives or political structure — on the basis of fragmentary cues (Boyer 1998). Thus, when ideas are taught and shared from member to member within a cultural group, they become mentally embedded and embodied and can eventually be reliably recalled when referenced. When culturally situated images appropriately refer to shared underlying concepts and narratives — such as when they are employed in display inscriptions and when these are erected publicly or when they are used in restricted or élite contexts (such as a palace or temple) — then such images become ideologically charged, culturally significant and have an understood role as authority.

articulated, visible, shared ideological assumptions and constraints on the use of symbolically important representations — linked a new corporate identity to the rationale by which wealth was symbolically, and possibly also actually, distributed.

Once identified, a system of decorum becomes a probative tool, because the deployment of cultural commodities is *not* an innocent process. Consciously or not, this process reflects a differential distribution of political and social power as people make their own history (Asad 1993; Trouillot 1995). Ideologically charged images and symbols are being used to create a coherent cultural or corporate identity. This is a culturally significant event that reflects the politics of power: an attempt by a group to mobilise resources in defined ways for its own benefit. It is communicative action (Habermas 2001).

One purpose of communicative action is to entrench and perpetuate specific components of an ideology — or an ideological system of knowledge that legitimates the social order — by building up schemes about the nature of the world that place authority at the source of all good things (Bloch 1985: 33; Marcus 1995). Rituals and display events that carry symbolism designed to support the king's authority, specifically those that emphasise the sanctity of the king and his position as intermediary between the supernatural and natural worlds, are the ones emphasised and sanctioned (Friedman, Rowlands 1977; Helms 1988; 1992; 1993). Being invoked in stone prompts actualisation or reification within the mind of the viewer through the act of looking, reinforcing in the mind of the viewer cultural conceptions about differential access to the divine (Cohen 1979; Helms 1979; 1987; Curet 1996: 123; Sturken, Cartwright 2001). How the viewers situate themselves in relation to the depicted entities, how they are perceived, is related to their adoption of a subject position, an identity.

In Gurgum, the system becomes visible when private and royal monuments are compared. Private monuments from Kahramanmaraş and nearby depict a *restricted* set of events, textually and/or figurally. A named person may be represented in a banquet scene — probably a ritual meal. As in MARAŞ 2, the deceased and sometimes a second person sit at either side of a table laden with food. Where preserved, texts on private funerary monuments generally read: 'This is...' or 'I am...[name]' followed by a biographical note. The focus is on the deceased, and the only representations are of human beings or abstractions,[10] no gods.

---

[10] An architectural motif, or abstract design, is used on the TILVESET inscription.

In private *non-funerary* inscriptions, gods can be portrayed by private authors in declarations of an *offering* to a god. In KÜRTÜL, the statue was erected to the storm god (Tarhunzas) and promises an offering of 80 measures of barley. On MARAŞ 3, the author says 'Tarhunzas heard me' and then details the offerings pledged in thanksgiving for the storm god's hearing of a prayer by this supplicant. In private inscriptions, it is permissible for gods to be represented for the purpose of identifying the focus of offerings being declared. However, divine beings do not appear in *narrative interaction* with humans in any private monuments. The clear contrast between private display inscriptions and royal monuments is visible in ISPEKÇUR, a royal monument containing a god-human juxtaposition. The apparent restriction of such images to royal authors localises the divine-human interaction specifically through the instrument of the ruling dynasty, through the person, actions and agency of the reigning king. In DARENDE we find that a king is maintained in power so that the sacral places for god-human interaction on this earth can be created and maintained. Therefore royal rule is supported by *divine order and access*, as represented in a figural narrative. The permanence of the inscribed stone material and the privileged position of these inscriptions — erected publicly or in prestige-laden contexts — situates them within a specific cultural frame of royal ideology.

Keeping this royal ideology in mind, we turn finally to display inscriptions, by non-royal people, that refer to royalty — such as the inscription of a high official, a eunuch, on MARAŞ 14. This stela describes the official's connection to the king. It is an associative act in response to the affective power of the dynasty — an acknowledgment of the king's ability to create a desirable sacral and societal order. The king maintains the landscape free from emptiness that could be filled by undesirable elements, and he improves the settlements by adding granaries, vineyards and by rebuilding. Such tropes are expressed repeatedly by Neo-Hittite rulers — as in MARAŞ 1, which dates to the end of the ninth century BC: 'I settled the devastated places and I benefited the settlements by Tarhunza's and Ea's authority' (Hawkins 2000).

Inscriptions of non-royal authors, such as the eunuch's mentioned above, thereby annex their author to the authentic source of power within this specific cultural frame — *to the king* through whom the divine order flows. This sacral access 'trickles down' then to the official ranks through the ruling dynasty. Thus, in this system of decorum, we see a major source of legitimacy for the king, one common to many ancient systems: restricted and special access to the divine and to the beneficial aspects which flow concurrently with such an ideology of restricted access.

A second source of legitimacy, invoked by Iron Age rulers, is constituted through claims of dynastic affiliation to Hittite predecessors. Connection to a former centre of sacral and political power was only useful if the audience continued to subscribe to a tangible, historically situated meaning of the importance and benefits of a particular model of kingship. The referential power was rooted in a social context where the 'signified' remained vibrantly available in the cultural and ideological vocabulary. For this Early Iron Age audience, the traditional expectation of social and political world order was framed by a model of power emanating from a palatial or imperial centre that controlled and managed interaction with subject territories.[11] Therefore, when non-royal inscriptions assert the private author's connection to the king, and thereby to the ideology of a kingship predicated on claims of dynastic affiliation to the Hittite imperial system, they show this model to have been still valid, vibrant and operative.

The ability of the Iron Age rulers to create prestige events locally, just as the Hittite overlords had done from a distance, is clearly delineated in the system of decorum described above. Claims of dynastic affiliation are another prestige commodity. However, as part of the élite's personal narrative of legitimisation, claims of dynastic affiliation are elements situated in the narrative foreground. They support the *agenda* of the narrative — in this case legitimisation — and they allow the text to fulfill its missions and to be intelligibly and appropriately received (Winter 1995: 255; Loprieno 1998). Foregrounded elements in a narrative thus reflect the overt goals of the text's producers. To put the claims from this text in context, we can begin with the seal found at Lidar Höyük, on which the ruler's dynastic affiliation is specified: 'Kuzi-Tešub, king of the land of Karkamiš, son of Talmi-Tešub, king of the land of Karkamiš, recognised by the gods'. This seal links the grandfather of a Neo-Hittite ruler to Karkamiš (a vice-regent seat held by members of the royal Hittite line), and so connects the Late Bronze Age imperial Hittite period with the Iron Age Neo-Hittite, via a specific family affiliation (Hawkins 1985).

At this point I would like to clarify that I am not about to argue for a direct translation of, or transparency between, the 'world' and the 'word', i.e. for the truth value of such dynastic affiliations. Rather, dynastic claims on seals and sculpture are statements of self-presentation, and as such they point to the choices made by Early Iron Age élites, who were selecting from, and amongst, a variety of possible affiliations in order to construct the most powerful and persuasive identity available to them given their particular audiences (Winter 1995). These choices are themselves the instructive elements, quite aside from the possible authenticity of the actual claims made. The details of the claimed affiliations offer a critique on their utility before a specific audience, and they reveal the Neo-Hittite perception of peripheral power-centres as legitimate dynastic conduits through which ruling power and élite prestige might extend from the end of the Hittite empire period onward into the Early Iron Age.

The Early Iron Age rulers chose to follow a naming convention established centuries before, one that had been used during the Hittite Imperial period according to a well established formula: name the living king and his father and occasionally also his grandfather. Although such naming conventions include claims of legitimacy (relationship to a former king as well as acknowledgment by the gods), the formulation used on the Lidar bullae is what might be termed 'narrative neutral' or 'unmarked' (in contrast to 'marked', foreground elements). The text on the Lidar bullae represents the standard late New Kingdom (i.e. later Late Bronze Age) Hittite practice, as well as standard Early Iron Age Luwian practice.[12]

In the Early Iron Age, anything other than a two-generation dynastic list can be viewed as a text that departs from a normal genealogical presentation in a specific way, in response to something outside the norm. Therefore, when (after a couple of centuries of using this two-generation system) we see a change in this practice of claiming dynastic affiliation by these Iron Age rulers, a closer inspection is warranted. Before proceeding further we should note that, in general, two types of 'historical' inscriptions were normally employed by both Imperial Hittite and post-Imperial Luwian rulers: narrative texts (myths and statements about events and personages — mostly kings); and chronicle-type texts. Chronicles — in the case of the Hittites — generally only mean annalistic texts, because king-lists were not a canonical text genre during the Imperial period (Bryce 1998: 409).[13] Narrative texts present information to answer the specific question: what is the ruler doing, or what has he recently done, for the domain he rules, for his constituencies — human and divine? *Why* does he merit kingship?

---

[11] This is an ideal construction certainly, but it does not cede ground even when confronted with the reality of rebellious regions that might require military intervention, or when faced with the documented alternative wherein the centre made concessions to win or maintain the loyalty of subject territories.

[12] It is not, however, the standard Aramaean practice; there, eponymous ancestors were identified (see, for example, Dion 1997; Sader 1987).

[13] Modern scholars have drawn up king-lists on the basis of references in annals and other types of texts, not on the basis of actual Hittite king-lists.

Narratives are a type of text that we see in Early Iron Age Gurgum from the end of the 11th to the early tenth centuries BC — the period preceding Assyrian interference. For example, on MARAŞ 8:

> I am Laramas, Astuwaramanzas's grandson, Muwatalis's son. When from my river land the houses...[text break]...burned down, I found Gurgum the river land waste...[break]... For the city I planted out vineyards, I filled granary on granary... I called forth the gods to the river (Hawkins 2000: 253).

Later, in the ninth century, ever longer dynastic affiliations begin to appear in Gurgum and these sculptures, such as MARAŞ 4 and MARAŞ 1, roughly coincide with the interference by Assyrian kings such as Aššurnasirpal II (ca. 870 BC) and Shalmaneser III (ca. 858 BC). First a hybrid appears in MARAŞ 4. This sculpture is inscribed with the standard connected narrative text with the addition of an expanded dynastic list. On this monument, Halparuntiyas II describes his valiant capture of the city of Iluwasi, and tells how he cut off the feet of the men and made the sons eunuchs, and thereby exalted himself. But in the same inscription he also invokes the memory of *four* generations of his family, instead of naming only his father and (optionally) his grandfather. There seems to be a nascent urge here to stress the depth of his familial connection. Subsequently, later in the ninth century, the transformation is complete: on MARAŞ 1 Halparuntiyas III, the grandson of the author of the last text, creates a nearly complete list of his forefathers; it includes eight generations.

Within the span of the ninth century, a new text type — the king-list — is created and utilised in Gurgum by the royal scribes. The transition moves from the 'unmarked' naming of the father (part and parcel of normal personal identification as seen on the Lidar bullae), to an invocation of four generations in the mid-ninth century and finally, at the end of the ninth century, to a detailed exposition of the whole remembered dynastic line. A dynastic list emphasises the current ruler's connection to a worthwhile, venerable past. The assertion implied is that the present king deserves support, regardless of his beneficial actions on behalf of his kingdom, simply on the merits of his dynastic affiliation to a revered past, as a line of continuity to a golden age (Loprieno 1998).

Such careful enumeration of the dynastic past evinces an attempt to mobilise a new source of political power and prestige, signalling that something new is afoot. As an innovative text type in Gurgum, these assertions of dynastic affiliation serve to promote royal display focusing not on the present, but on support for the present from the past. Thus, the shift from narrative toward chronicle in Gurgum points to the ruler's need to address new tensions. For the traditional power base, the legitimisation and maintenance strategies had been well established, requiring no adjustment for a couple of hundred years. But in the context of new, more fluid sources of social power, and in response to assaults on political prestige in the ninth century from Assyrians and Aramaeans alike, the rulers were beginning to renegotiate their public identity and presentation.

Gurgum was among those delivering quantities of tribute to the imperial Assyrian centre. Such a reorientation of productive output could certainly impact upon local sources of revenue and the independent ability of the local élite to create prestige events. During the ninth century, in the face of what might have seemed a looming crisis, with the Assyrians already invading the area and raising the possibility of an insecure territorial future for Gurgum,[14] the chosen strategy of these Luwian rulers was to assert their connection to the original source of dynastic legitimacy. This change contrasts with a multi-century long tradition, and reflects fluidity in a discourse about the use of the past, prompted by assaults on territorial integrity in the present.

This change also coincides with Assyrian activity in north Syria, and appears at a time when, across that region, new details and modes of representation filter into royal presentations, Luwian and Aramaean alike. This includes a shift toward Assyrian-style dress and postures, a phenomenon seen on both MARAŞ 1 and the slightly later Incirli inscription found in the Kahramanmaraş valley.[15] It would be extremely easy to refer to the Assyrians and their westward expansionist drive as the major reasons why rulers in Gurgum felt compelled to assert ever longer dynastic pedigrees. Similarly, it would be possible to see the impetus for these changes, and for the use of the text type, in Kahramanmaraş, as a result of simple contact with other groups that had a longer lived tradition of enumerating their ancestors; thereby attributing the changes merely to emulation. Such an interpretation ignores the active attempts of the Gurgumean rulers to redefine avenues of prestige that would support their cultural identity. It also fails to account for the multiple and fluid sources of pressure on these polities in the Middle Iron Age.

---

[14] Compare Weippert 1992. Also, the inscription of Kilamuwa (ca. 830 BC; *KAI* no. 24) describes the collusion of local élites with Assyrians.

[15] The Incirli inscription is on display in the Gaziantep Museum. This monument apparently dates to the reign of Tiglath Pileser III (Zuckerman, Kaufman in preparation; see also note 1 above).

The Kahramanmaraş survey shows that there was considerable stability and continuity in site location and quantity from the Late Bronze Age into the Iron Age. However, from the Early Iron Age to the Middle Iron Age the number of sites increases (figs 2, 6), and there is a significant addition of many new ceramic types to what is argued to have been a slowly evolving Late Bronze Age ceramic tradition augmented by the corrugated ware tradition of the Early Iron Age. Perhaps the most noteworthy feature of the Late Bronze Age to Early Iron Age transition in Kahramanmaraş is that so few identifiable Early Iron Age types (figs 3, 4) characterise the ceramic assemblage. In contrast, at the end of the ninth century and into the eighth, the Kahramanmaraş survey displays burgeoning ceramic variability, when the number of Middle Iron Age sites rises to 48, an increase of 19% from the Late Bronze Age. In terms of hectares occupied, this represents an increase of 26% from the preceding period. The variability could therefore be a reflection of a substantial augmentation of the population, if site size and population density are considered to be directly related.

These increases coincide with the increasing influence of Assyria in the region, and with an intensification of contact between the Aramaeans, Assyrians, Luwians and perhaps others; and with references to

*Fig. 6. Map showing Middle Iron Age sites*

deportations into Gurgum by the Assyrians. The result was a complex, intensely competitive market for the specialities and bulk commodities on which the Gurgumean élites depended for trade, income and prestige exchange.

Such was the situation of the Gurgumeans, and which the Assyrians confronted when they became increasingly active and bellicose in the region. Aramaean polities had been established in the interstices of the Luwian polities, and on their southern and eastern borders, creating a dynamic and shifting socio-political landscape in Iron Age north Syria. This last situation underscores the mobility of segments of the population during the Late Bronze Age to Iron Age transition. Initially, the Assyrians harnessed the inter-polity competition amongst the north Syrian kingdoms, well documented by Kilamuwa's claim to have more or less hired the Assyrians as mercenaries, in order to combat his Cilician neighbour's aggression (Fales 1979; Swiggers 1983; Çambel et al. 1998). This claim by Kilamuwa indicates that local borders were becoming increasingly mobile and contested, and that neighbouring polities were seeking any advantage they could gain for purposes of both defence and expansion, including recourse to Assyrian manpower.

Once the Assyrians had established a foothold in the north Syria region, they were able to assert an aggressive hegemonic agenda, and eventually annex kingdoms as vassal states. Rapidly during the ninth century BC, we find the local kings putting their family trees in order, and adopting Assyrianised modes of dress and presentation in their royal display monuments. Soon, the production of Luwian display inscriptions and royal seals ceases, and monuments in other languages begin to appear in Gurgum's territory. At this point, the external assault on the political legitimacy of the Luwian rulers of Kahramanmaraş is complete, and assertions of dynastic longevity tied to the Hittite past disappear, along with the use of Luwian for royal glyptic and display sculpture.

Luwian as a language continued in use in the *non-royal* realm into the eighth century BC, and even beyond. Of all the known Luwian seals, fully one-third have non-royal Luwian names on them (Hawkins 2000: pls 328–33). In stark contrast to the non-royal monumental inscriptions, none of these seals contains a title tying the owner to the royal sphere or to a palatial economy, or making any assertions of relationship to the king. The same is true in the few remaining lead letters (see Hawkins 2000: pls 306–13). Outside the context of the funerary and supernatural realms, users of the Luwian language show considerable autonomy, perhaps pointing to an increasing independence, to privatisation of trade and exchange, and to the continued demotion of the importance of the regional palatial centres, which had been loci of political and real economic power when the Hittite kings ruled. The Hittite system, although it failed, had provided a participatory and mutual relationship of obligation and client-state patronage, through which commodities moved and interstate trade was facilitated when state intervention was necessary.

In this context, the choice of dynastic affiliation is directly relevant to the maintenance of political and economic power within the independent kingdom of Gurgum. Iron Age dynasts employed legitimation strategies that were ultimately linked to an imperial past, to an empire's centralised system that had provided benefits to administrators in positions similar to those in which the Iron Age élites were situated. Nonetheless, the actions and choices of these Luwian élites actually critiqued the very system they were invoking. These rulers show a preference for decentralised, competing centres of power in the political landscape of north Syria, and in the choice of origins for political legitimacy — tied to peripheral centres, not the capital. As north Syria was increasingly infiltrated by new groups, who did not subscribe to a cultural model wherein Luwian kings or their royal pretensions meant much at all, the kings of Gurgum intensified their legitimation efforts. No longer able to project power effectively across a kingdom whose borders now lay on an imperial frontier, they projected it deeper into the past, back to a time before the Aramaeans spilled into the land, before the ninth century when the Assyrians created havoc, before the assault on the political, cultural and economic landscape of the small, decentralised Iron Age kingdoms. The mobilisation of a new cultural commodity — reverence for the depth of the dynastic link — is a response signalling that a shift in the distribution of power had already occurred. In Gurgum, the very fabric of kingship itself was so seriously devalued that it would eventually come under attack from within. For the Gurgumean king, the end was near (Hawkins 1985).[16]

## Acknowledgements

I wish to thank Elizabeth Carter for her guidance. I also gratefully acknowledge the work of Patrick Finnerty on the maps and pottery illustrations. I also wish to thank Geoffrey Summers for facilitating access to the material collected by Brown and held in the British Institute at Ankara (see Brown 1967).

---

[16] The penultimate king of the Gurgumean dynasty may have been assassinated by his son.

## Bibliography

*Abbreviation*

*KAI* = Donner, H., Röllig, W. 1973: *Kanaanäische und aramäische Inschriften.* Wiesbaden

Algaze, G., Breuninger, R., Knudstad, J. 1994: 'The Tigris-Euphrates Archaeological Reconnaissance Project: final report of the Birecik and Carchemish Dam survey areas' *Anatolica* 20: 1–96

Alkım, U.B. 1952: 'The results of recent excavations at Domuztepe' *Belleten* 16: 238–50

Ando, C. 2000: *Imperial Ideology and Provincial Loyalty in the Roman Empire.* Los Angeles

Asad, T. 1993: *Genealogies of Religion.* Baltimore

Baines, J. 1990: 'Restricted knowledge, hierarchy, and decorum: modern perceptions and ancient institutions' *Journal of the American Research Center in Egypt* 27: 1–23

Ball, W., Tucker, D., Wilkinson, T. 1989: 'The Tell Al-Hawa Project. Archaeological investigations in the North Jazira 1986–1987' *Iraq* 51: 1–66

Bartl, K. 1994: 'Die Frühe Eisenzeit in Ostanatolien und Ihre Verbindungen zu den Benachbarten Regionen' *Baghdader Mitteilungen* 25: 473–518

— 1995: 'Some remarks on the Early Iron Age in eastern Anatolia' *Anatolica* 21: 205–12

— 2001: 'Eastern Anatolia in the Early Iron Age' in R. Eichmann, H. Parzinger (eds), *Migration und Kulturtransfer, Der Wandel vorder- und zentralasiatischer Kulturen im Umbruch vom 2. zum 1. vorchristlichen Jahrtausend.* Bonn: 383–410

Bilgi, Ö. 1987: *Köskerbaba Höyük Kazısı (Lower Euphrates Project 1978–1979 Activities).* Ankara

— 1991: 'Iron Age pottery from Köskerbaba Höyük' in A. Çilingiroglu, D.H. French, (eds), *Anatolian Iron Ages. The Proceedings of the Second Anatolian Iron Ages Colloquium held at Izmir, 4–8 May 1987* (British Institute of Archaeology at Ankara Monograph 13). Oxford: 11–28

Blaylock, S.R. 1999: 'Iron Age pottery from Tille Höyük, southeastern Turkey' in A. Hausleiter, A. Reiche (eds), *Iron Age Pottery in Northern Mesopotamia, Northern Syria and Southeastern Anatolia. Papers Presented at the Meetings of the International Table Ronde at Heidelberg (1995) and Nieborów (1997) and other Contributions.* Münster: 263–86

Blaylock, S.R., French, D.H., Summers, G.D. 1990: 'The Adıyaman Survey: an interim report' *Anatolian Studies* 40: 81–135

Bloch, M. 1985: 'From cognition to ideology' in R. Fardon (ed.), *Power and Knowledge: Anthropological and Sociological Approaches.* Edinburgh: 21–48

Bonatz, D. 2000: *Das syro-hethitische Grabdenkmal: Untersuchungen zur Entstehung einer neuen Bildgattung in der Eisenzeit im nordsyrisch-südostanatolischen Raum*. Mainz

Boyer, P. 1998: 'Cognitive tracks of cultural inheritance: how evolved intuitive ontology governs cultural transmission' *American Anthropologist* 100: 876–89

Brown, G.H. 1967: 'Prehistoric pottery in the Antitaurus' *Anatolian Studies* 17: 123–64

Bryce, T. 1998: *The Kingdom of the Hittites*. Oxford

Çambel, H., Röllig, W., Hawkins, J.D. 1998: *Corpus of Hieroglyphic Luwian Inscriptions. Volume 2: Karatepe-Aslantaş. The Inscriptions* (Untersuchungen zur indogermanischen Sprach- und Kulturwissenschaft — Studies in Indo-European Language and Culture). Berlin

Carter, E.C. 1995: 'Report on the Kahramanmaraş Archaeological Survey Project from 24/9/93 to 11/11/93' *Araştırma Sonuçları Toplantısı* 12: 331–41

— 1996: 'The Kahramanmaraş Archaeological Survey Project: a preliminary report on the 1994 season' *Araştırma Sonuçları Toplantısı* 13.1: 289–306

Carter, E.C. Eissenstat, Hill, C., Dodd, L.S. 1999: 'The Kahramanmaraş Archaeological Project survey 1997' *Araştırma Sonuçları Toplantısı* 16.2: 569–76

Ciafardoni, P. 1992: 'Insedimenti aramaici e pre-aramaici nella regione del Idlib' in S. Mazzioni (ed.), *Tell Afis e l'età del ferro*. Pisa: 37–72

Cohen, A. 1979: 'Political symbolism' *Annual Review of Anthropology* 8: 87–113

Crespin, A.-S. 1999: 'Between Phrygia and Cilicia: the Porsuk area at the beginning of the Iron Age' *Anatolian Studies* 49: 61–72

Curet, L.A. 1996: 'Ideology, chiefly power and material culture: an example from the Greater Antille' *Latin American Antiquity* 7(2): 114–31

Dion, P.-E. 1997: *Les Araméens à l'âge du fer: Histoire politique et structures sociales* (Études bibliques, nouvelle série). Paris

Dodd, L.S. 2002: *Cultural Identity and the Recreation of Statehood during the Early Iron Age-Late Bronze Age Transition in North Syria*. Unpublished PhD thesis. University of California, Los Angeles

Donner, H., Röllig, W. 1973: *Kanaanäische und aramäische Inschriften*. Wiesbaden

Duru, R. 1979: *Keban Project Değirmentepe Excavations 1973*. Ankara

Eidem, J., Ackermann, R. 1999: 'The Iron Age ceramics from Tell Jurn Kabir' in A. Hausleiter, A. Reiche (eds), *Iron Age Pottery in Northern Mesopotamia,*

*Northern Syria and Southeastern Anatolia. Papers Presented at the Meetings of the International Table Ronde at Heidelberg (1995) and Nieborów (1997) and other Contributions*. Münster: 309–24

Eidem, J., Pütt, K. 1999: 'Tell Jurn Kabir and Tell Qadahiye. Danish excavations in the Tishrin Dam Area' in G. del Olmo Lete, J.-L. Montero Fenollós (eds), *Archaeology of the Upper Syrian Euphrates: The Tishrin Dam Area: Proceedings of the International Symposium Held at Barcelona, January 20–28th 1998*. Barcelona: 193–204

Fales, F.M. 1979: 'Kilamuwa and the foreign kings: propaganda vs power' *Die Welt des Orients* 10: 6–22

Friedman, J., Rowlands, M. J. 1977: 'Notes towards an epigenetic model of the evolution of civilization' in J. Friedman, M.J. Rowlands (eds), *The Evolution of Social Systems*. London: 201–76

Garrard, A., Conolly, J., Moloney, N., Wright, K. 1996: 'The early prehistory of the Sakçagözü region, North Levantine Rift Valley: report on the 1995 survey season' *Anatolian Studies* 46: 53–82

Garstang, J. 1937: 'Third report on the excavations at Sakçe Guezi 1908–1911' *Liverpool Annals of Archaeology and Anthropology* 24: 119–40

Gates, M.-H. 2001: 'Potmarks at Kinet Höyük and the Hittite ceramic Industry' in E. Jean, A.M. Dinçol, S. Durugönül (eds), *La Cilicie: espaces et pouvoirs locaux (2e millénaire avant J-C. – 4e siècle ap. J-C). Actes de la Table ronde internationale d'Istanbul, 2–5 novembre 1999. Institut Français d'Études Anatoliennes Georges Dumézil, Istanbul.* Paris: 137–57

Goldman, H. 1956: *Excavations at Gözlü Kule, Tarsus, II: From the Neolithic through the Bronze Age*. Princeton

Gottmann, J. 1973: *The Significance of Territory*. Charlottesville

— 1982: 'The basic problem of political geography: the organization of space and the search for stability' *Tijdschrift voor Economische en Sociale Geografie* 73(6): 340–9

Habermas, J. 2001: *Vorstudien und Ergänzungen zur Theorie des kommunikativen Handelns* [*On the Pragmatics of Social Interaction: Preliminary Studies in the Theory of Communicative Action*] (Studies in contemporary German social thought). Cambridge

Hanfmann, G.M.A. 1963: *Excavations at Gözlü Kule, Tarsus, III: The Iron Age*. Princeton

Hansen, C.K., Postgate, J.N. 1999: 'The Bronze Age to Iron Age transition at Kilise Tepe' *Anatolian Studies* 49: 111–22

Hawkins, J.D. 1985: 'Neo Hittite states in Syria and Anatolia' in J. Boardman, I.E.S Edwards, N.G.L. Hammond, E. Sollberger (eds), *The Cambridge Ancient History III.1* (second edition). Cambridge: 372–441

— 2000: *Corpus of Hieroglyphic Luwian Inscriptions* (Untersuchungen zur indogermanischen Sprach– und Kulturwissenschaft – Studies in Indo-European Language and Culture). Berlin

Helms, M.W. 1979: *Ancient Panama: Chiefs in Search of Power.* Austin

—1988: *Ulysses' Sail: An Ethnographic Odyssey of Power, Knowledge and Geographical Distance.* Princeton

— 1992: 'Thoughts on public symbols and distant domains relevant to the chiefdoms of Lower Central America' in F.W. Lange (ed.), *Wealth and Hierarchy in the Intermediate Area: A Symposium at Dumbarton Oaks, 10th and 11th October 1987.* Washington, DC: 317–29

— 1993: *Craft and the Kingly Ideal: Art, Trade and Power.* Austin

Henrickson, R.C. 1993: 'Politics, economics and ceramic continuity at Gordion in the late second and first millennia BC' in W.D. Kingery (ed.), *The Social and Cultural Contexts of New Ceramic Technologies* (Ceramics and Civilization 6). Westerville: 88–176

Henrickson, R.C., Voigt, M.M. 1998: 'The Early Iron Age at Gordion: the evidence from the Yassıhöyük Stratigraphic Sequence' in N. Tuna, Z. Aktüre, M. Lynch (eds), *Thracians and Phrygians: Problems of Parallelism.* Ankara: 79–106

Jamieson, A. 1999: 'Neo-Assyrian pottery from Tell Ahmar' in A. Hausleiter, A. Reiche (eds), *Iron Age Pottery in Northern Mesopotamia, Northern Syria and Southeastern Anatolia. Papers Presented at the Meetings of the International Table Ronde at Heidelberg (1995) and Nieborów (1997) and other Contributions.* Münster: 287–308

Jasink, A.M. 1995: *Gli Stati Neo-Ittiti. Analisi delle Fonti Scritte e Sintesi Storica* (Studia Mediterranea). Pavia

Karjalainen, P.T. 1986: *Geodiversity as a Lived World. On the Geography of Existence* (University of Joensuu Publications in Social Sciences). Joensuu

Kaufman, S., Zuckerman, B. (in preparation): *The Incirli Stela*

Korbel, G. 1985: *Die Spätbronzezeitliche Keramik von Norşuntepe* (Institut für Bauen und Planen in Entwicklungsländern, Mitteilungen 14). Hanover

— 1987: *Materialheft spätbronzezeitliche Keramik Tarsus (Grabung Hetty Goldman)* (Institut für Bauen und Planen in Entwicklungsländern, Mitteilungen 5). Hanover

Lebeau, M. 1983: *La Céramique de l'Age du Fer II–III á Tell Abou Danné.* Paris

Lipsanen, N. 2001: *Naturalistic and Existential Realms of Place in Roseau, Dominica* (Department of Geography, Faculty of Science, University of Helsinki). Helsinki

Lloyd, S., Gökçe, N. 1953: 'Sultan Tepe, Anglo-Turkish joint excavations, 1952' *Anatolian Studies* 3: 27–47

Loprieno, A. 1998: 'Le Pharaon reconstruit. La figure du roi dans la littérature égyptienne au 1er millénaire avant J.C.' *Bulletin de la Société Française d'Égyptologie* 142: 4–24

Marcus, M. 1995: 'Art and ideology in ancient western Asia' in J.M. Sasson (ed.), *Civilizations of the Ancient Near East.* New York: 2,487–505

Mazzoni, S. 1992: *Tell Afis e l'età del Ferro.* Pisa

Mellaart, J. 1955: 'Iron Age pottery from southern Anatolia' *Belleten* 19: 115–36

Müller, U. 1996: *Die Eisenzeitliche Keramik von Lidar Höyük* (Fakultät für Orientalistik und Altertumswissenschaften). Heidelberg

— 1999a: 'Die eisenzeitliche Stratigraphie von Lidar Höyük' *Anatolian Studies* 49: 123–32

— 1999b: 'Die eisenzeitliche Keramik des Lidar Höyük' in A. Hausleiter, A. Reiche (eds), *Iron Age Pottery in Northern Mesopotamia, Northern Syria and Southeastern Anatolia. Papers Presented at the Meetings of the International Table Ronde at Heidelberg (1995) and Nieborów (1997) and other Contributions.* Münster: 403–34

Ökse, T. 1988: *Mitteleisenzeitliche Keramik Zentral-Ostanatoliens.* Berlin

Özdoğan, M. 1977: *Lower Euphrates Basin 1977 Survey.* Istanbul

Özgen, E., Helwing, B., Tekin, H. 1997: 'Vorläufiger Bericht über die Ausgrabungen auf dem Oylum Höyük' *Istanbuler Mitteilungen* 47: 39–90

Paasi, A. 1998: *The Role of Identities and Boundaries in the Contemporary World. Fifth Nordic-Baltic Conference in Regional Science 'Global-Local Interplay in the Baltic Sea Region' 1–4th October, 1998.* Pärnu

Parker, B.J., Creekmore, A., Swartz Dodd, L., Moseman, E., Abraham, M., Schnereger, J. 2002: 'The Upper Tigris Archaeological Research Project (UTARP): year 2000 excavations at Kenan Tepe' *Kazı Sonuçları Toplantısı* 23.2: 435–44

Parpola, S. 1987: *The Correspondence of Sargon II, Part I: Letters from Assyria and the West* (State Archives of Assyria). Helsinki

Riis, P. J. 1990: *Hama 2.2: Les objets de la période dite syro-hittite (Âge du Fer).* Copenhagen

Sader, H. 1987: *Les états araméens de Syria depuis leur fondation en provinces assyriennes.* Beirut

Seton-Williams, M.V. 1961: 'Preliminary report on the excavations at Tel Rifa'at' *Iraq* 23: 68–86

Sevin, V. 1983: 'İmikuşağı kazıları 1982' *Kazı Sonuçları Toplantısı* 5: 137–42

— 1995: *İmikuşağı I.* Ankara

Somers, M.R., Gibson, G.D. 1994: 'Narrative and the social constitution of identity' in C. Calhouhn (ed.), *Social Theory and the Politics of Identity.* Oxford: 37–99

Stone, E., Zimansky, P. 1999: *The Iron Age Settlement at 'Ain Dara Syria. Surveys and Soundings* (British Archaeological Reports International Series 786). Oxford

Sturken, M., Cartwright, L. 2001: *Practices of Looking: An Introduction to Visual Culture.* Oxford

Summers, G.D. 1993: *Tille Höyük 4: The Late Bronze Age and the Iron Age Transition.* Ankara

Swift, G.F. 1958: *The Pottery of the 'Amuq Phases K to O, and Its Historical Relations.* Unpublished PhD thesis. University of Chicago

Swiggers, P. 1983: 'Commentaire philologique sur l'inscription phénicienne du roi Kilamuwa' *Rivista di studi fenici* 11: 133–47

Tadmor, H. 1994: *The Inscriptions of Tiglath-Pileser III King of Assyria.* Jerusalem

Taylor, J. du P., Seton-Williams, M.V., Waechter, J. 1950: 'Excavations at Sakçe Gözü' *Iraq* 12: 53–138

Trouillot, M.-R. 1995: *Silencing the Past: Power and the Production of History.* Boston

Tuan, Y.-F. 1975: 'Place: an experiential perspective' *The Geographical Review*: 151–65

Voigt, M.M., Henrickson, R.C. 2000: 'The Early Iron Age at Gordion: the evidence from the Yassıhöyük Stratigraphic Sequence' in E. Oren (ed.), *The Sea Peoples and Their World: A Reassessment.* Philadelphia: 327–60

Weippert, M.H.E. 1992: 'Die Feldzüge Adadnararis III. nach Syrien: Voraussetzungen, Verlauf, Folgen' *Zeitschrift des Deutschen Morgenländischen Gesellschaft* 108: 42–67

Winn, M.M. 1980: 'Phase K. The Early Iron Age' in M. van Loon (ed.), *Korucutepe 3. Final Report on the Excavations of the University of Chicago, California (Los Angeles) and Amsterdam in the Keban Dam Reservoir, Eastern Anatolia 1968–1970.* New York: 155–76

Winter, I. 1995: 'Homer's Phoenicians: history, ethnography, or literary trope [a perspective on early Orientalism]' in J. Carter, S. Morris (eds), *The Age of Homer.* Austin: 247–71

Yoffee, N. (with Baines, J.) 1998: 'Order, legitimacy, and wealth in ancient Egypt and Mesopotamia' in G. Feinman, J. Marcus (eds), *Archaic States.* Santa Fe: 199–260

# Amasya province in the Iron Age

**Şevket Dönmez**
*Istanbul University*

## Abstract

The Iron Age settlements and their ceramics recorded in the 1997–1999 seasons of surveys in Amasya province (central Black Sea region) are introduced and evaluated. Unfortunately no settlement dated to the Iron Age has yet been excavated in this area. All the pottery recovered by our surveys exhibits strong similarities to material from Samsun and Tokat provinces (central Black Sea region), and to Middle and Late Iron Age material from the provinces of Ankara, Kırşehir, Çorum, Yozgat and Kayseri (central Anatolian region). However none of the Amasya region pottery is related to ceramics from Gordion/Yassıhöyük, Boğazköy-Büyükkaya and Kaman-Kalehöyük. For the Middle and Late Iron Age we have found so-called Alişar IV ware (originating in the area of the Kızılırmak bend) and ceramics of the central Anatolian painted pottery tradition, as well as large quantities of central Anatolian plain pottery types, especially brown and grey wares. In the late phase of the Late Iron Age and in the Hellenistic period the Amasya region had close relations with central Anatolia, as indicated by the evidence of bowls bearing painted parallel band decoration and ivy leaves.

## Özet

Bu bildiride Orta Karadeniz Bölgesi'nde yer alan Amasya ili sınırları içinde 1997–1999 yılları arasında gerçekleştirilen yüzey araştırmaları sırasında saptanan Demir Çağı yerleşmeleri ile bu yerleşmelerin çanak-çömlekleri tanıtılmış ve değerlendirilmiştir. Amasya ili sınırları içinde arkeolojik kazı yapılmış herhangi bir Demir Çağı yerleşmesi olmaması nedeniyle değerlendirmeler, ne yazık ki yalnızca yüzey araştırmalarına dayanmaktadır. Yüzey araştırmaları sırasında ele geçirilen çanak-çömleklerin, Orta Karadeniz Bölgesi'nin diğer illeri olan Samsun ve Tokat illerinin yanı sıra, Ankara, Kırşehir, Çorum, Yozgat ve Kayseri illerinin Orta ve Geç Demir Çağı örnekleri ile yakın benzerlikler gösterdiği saptanmıştır. Ayrıca, Amasya ili Demir Çağı yerleşmelerinde saptanan bazı çanak-çömlek parçalarının Gordion/Yassıhöyük, Boğazköy-Büyükkaya ve Kaman-Kalehöyük örnekleri ile güçlü benzerlikleri olduğu ortaya çıkmıştır. Orta ve Geç Demir Çağı'nda Alişar IV olarak adlandırılan ve Kızılırmak kavsi içinden kaynaklandığı bilinen Orta Anadolu Bölgesi boya bezekli çanak-çömlek geleneği ile yine aynı bölgede görülen çanak-çömlekler içinde özellikle kahverengi ve gri renklilerin benzerleri Amasya ili sınırları içindeki Demir Çağı yerleşmelerinde de ele geçmiştir. Geç Demir Çağı'nın geç evresi ile Helenistik Çağ'da Amasya ili ile Orta Anadolu Bölgesi'nin ortak kültür ögelerine sahip olduğu görülmektedir. Buna en çarpıcı örnekler olarak koşut bantlar ve sarmaşık yaprakları ile bezenmiş çanaklar gösterilebilir.

---

This paper outlines the evidence for Iron Age settlements and ceramics recorded in our three seasons of survey (1997–1999) in the following districts of Amasya province (in the central Black Sea region of Turkey): Gümüşhacıköy, Merzifon, Suluova, Göynücek and the central Amasya district (fig. 1). Details of the Iron Age ceramics and their parallels are provided in the catalogue appended to the end of this paper.

## Gümüşhacıköy district
### Niyazbaba Tepesi
Located 20km northwest of Gümüş town, between the villages of Büyük Alan and Sallar, the site lies approximately 100m west of Niyazbaba turbeh after which it is named (fig. 1: site no. 1). Approximately 4–5m high and 80m by 40m across, it was previously recorded in Özsait's survey (Özsait 1990: 369).

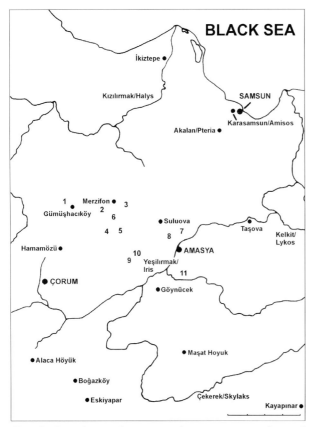

*Fig. 1. Iron Age settlements in Amasya province located during 1997–1999 surveys: (1) Niyazbaba Tepesi; (2) Alıcık Höyük; (3) Onhoroz Tepe; (4) Alacapınar Tepe (Hayrettin I); (5) Delicik Tepe (Hayrettin II); (6) Samadolu Höyüğü; (7) Yoğurtçubaba Tepesi; (8) Dereağıl Tepesi; (9) Oluz Höyük; (10) Doğantepe; (11) Gediksaray Höyüğü*

Evidence for Late Iron Age settlement includes a jug sherd decorated with painted parallel bands and festoons (fig. 2.1) (compare: Maşat Höyük level II; Kaman-Kalehöyük level IIa1; Kültepe late level). There is also evidence for Late Chalcolithic/Early Bronze Age I–II activity (Dönmez 1999: 522; 2001a: 303).

**Merzifon district**

*Alıcık Höyük*

The site lies 8km along and 3km south of the Gümüşhacıköy-Merzifon road, approximately 500m southeast of Alıcık village (fig.1: site no. 2), and is located on a natural hill. It measures approximately 25m high and 150m by 120m across (Dönmez 2000: 235; 2001a: 303). Evidence for the late phase of the Late Iron Age comprises a bowl sherd with inverted rim and a sharp carinated body (fig. 2.4) (compare: Kaman-Kalehöyük level IIa1). Late Iron Age painted pottery includes a bowl and a jug. The bowl sherd has a slightly inverted rim and a rounded circular body, decorated on

the inside with a horizontal band (fig. 2.3) (compare: Boğazköy-Büyükkale level I). The jug survives as a body sherd decorated on the exterior with triangles with central dots (fig. 2.2) (compare: Alaca Höyük). Other painted sherds indicate activity dating to Early Bronze Age II–III, the Middle and Late Bronze Ages, and the Hellenistic and Roman periods.

*Onhoroz Tepe*

Located 1.5km northeast of Yolüstü village (fig. 1: site no. 3), the site is approximately 20m high and 120m by 80m across, and was previously recorded in Özsait's survey (Özsait 1998: 149; Özsait, Özsait 1998: 460–1). Middle and Late Iron Age activity is attested (Dönmez 1999: 521–2; 2001a: 303, fig. 5). All but one of the Iron Age sherds recovered in our survey are undecorated, and include bowls, jugs and kraters. The Middle Iron Age evidence comprises: a bowl sherd with protruding lip and a shallow circular body (fig. 2.5) (compare: Boğazköy-Büyükkaya); three jug sherds, the first one having thick lips protruding both inside and outside, and an inverted body (fig. 2.6) (compare: Maşat Höyük early phase of level III; Boğazköy-Büyükkale), the second jug having a protruding lip with a projecting part at the top and a circular body (fig. 2.7) (compare: Masat Höyük: early phase of level III), and the third specimen with a protruding lip and circular body (fig. 2.8) (compare: Boğazköy-lower town); and a krater sherd (fig. 2.10) (compare: Boğazköy-Büyükkaya; Alişar Höyük). Late Iron Age ceramics are represented by a krater sherd with externally thickened lip (fig. 2.9) (compare: Boğazköy-Büyükkaya), and the body sherd of a jug decorated with a painted ladder motive (fig. 2.11) (compare: İkiztepe Mound III) — the only example of painted Iron Age pottery we have found at the site. In addition to the Iron Age material there is evidence for Early Bronze Age I–III, Middle Bronze Age, Late Bronze Age and Hellenistic period settlement.

*Alacapınar Tepe (Hayrettin I)*

Alacapınar Tepe, 2km northeast of the village of Hayrettin which lies 7km south of Merzifon (fig. 1: site no. 4), is approximately 15m high and 150m by 100m across (Dönmez 2000: 235; 2001a: 303). Late Iron Age ceramics were found including: a bowl sherd with externally thickened lip, inverted rim and a carinated body (fig. 2.13) (compare: Boğazköy-Büyükkaya level Ia); and a decorated jug sherd with everted rim and narrow neck, its entire surface decorated with thick bands of paint (fig. 2.12) (compare: Alişar Höyük) — this sherd dates to the late phase of the Late Iron Age. There is also evidence for Early Bronze Age II–III, Middle Bronze Age, Late Bronze Age and Hellenistic period settlement.

*Delicik Tepe (Hayrettin II)*

Delicik Tepe, 100m east of Alacapınar Tepe and approximately 2km northeast of Hayrettin village (fig. 1: site no. 5), is approximately 150m by 120m across and 15m high (Dönmez 2000: 235; 2001a: 303). Late Iron Age sherds were found here, all of them bearing painted decoration. Two belong to pitchers decorated with parallel bands (fig. 2.14–15), one of them (fig. 2.14) with a frame design filled with horizontal bands (compare: Akalan; Maşat Höyük level II; Eskiyapar; Kerkenes Dağ; Alişar Höyük; Kültepe), the other (fig. 2.15) decorated at the point where the handle joins the rim (compare: Hacıbektaş Höyük/Suluca Karahöyük; Alişar Höyük; Eğriköy). The body sherds of what were possibly jugs (fig. 2.16–17) (compare: Alişar Höyük; Yalıncak) have similar decoration to the pitchers, one of them (fig. 2.16) dateable to the late phase of the Late Iron Age. Middle Bronze Age, Late Bronze Age and Hellenistic period settlement is also attested.

*Samadolu Höyüğü*

The höyük is located 3km along and 1.5km south of the road from Gümüşhacıköy in the village of Samadolu (fig. 1: site no. 6). The site is approximately 15m high and 100m by 70m across (Dönmez 2000: 235; 2001a: 303). Middle Iron Age finds included an undecorated jug sherd with an externally thickened and rounded lip and a circular body (fig. 3.1) (compare: Alişar Höyük). Other surface sherds belong to Early Bronze Age I–III, Middle Bronze Age, Late Bronze Age, Hellenistic and Roman settlements.

**Suluova district**

*Yoğurtçubaba Tepesi*

The site is located 2km from Kulu village (fig. 1: site no. 7) and is approximately 20–25m high and 150m by 100m across (Dönmez 1999: 521, res. 23, 24; 2001a: 303). It has previously been recorded in Özsait's survey (Özsait 1989: 289). An undecorated Middle Iron Age jug sherd was found, with an externally rounded lip and a circular body (fig. 3.2) (compare: Maşat Höyük early phase of level III). Late Chalcolithic, Early Bronze Age I–III, Middle Bronze Age and Late Bronze Age material was also evident.

*Dereağıl Tepesi*

The site lies in the Dereağıl neighbourhood of Yüzbeyli village south of Suluova (fig. 1: site no. 8), and is approximately 15–20m high and 150m by 100m across (Dönmez 1999: 521, res. 21, 22; 2001a: 303). It was previously recorded in Özsait's survey (Özsait 1989: 289–90). Middle Iron Age evidence includes an undecorated bowl sherd with inverted rim and a shallow, circular body (fig. 3.3) (compare: Boğazköy-Kuzeybatı Yamacı). Late Chalcolithic, Early Bronze Age II–III and Late Bronze Age settlement is also attested.

**Central Amasya district**

*Oluz Höyük*

The höyük is situated 1.5km west of Oluz village which lies 3km south of the Amasya-Çorum road (fig. 1: site no. 9), and is one of the largest mounds of the central Black Sea region, being approximately 15m high and 300m by 250m across (Dönmez 2000: 234; 2001a: 303, fig. 4). Middle Iron Age and Late Iron Age settlement is evident, including two undecorated jug sherds. One of these sherds is dated to the Middle Iron Age and has an everted rim, a clearly defined neck and a globular body (fig. 3.5) (compare: Boğazköy-Büyükkaya level IIa). The other belongs to the Late Iron Age and has an externally thickened rounded rim, a short and narrow neck and a globular body (fig. 3.4) (compare: Kululu). There is also evidence for Early Bronze Age II–III, Middle Bronze Age, Late Bronze Age and Hellenistic period settlement.

*Doğantepe*

Located in the town of Doğantepe, 7km north of the Amasya-Çorum road and 25km southwest of Amasya (fig. 1: site no. 10), the site displays the remains of a large settlement, surviving approximately 40m high and 300m by 200m across. More important in antiquity than today, and characterised by a huge rock mass, the site was introduced to the archaeological world by the chance discovery of the famous Amasya-Doğantepe figurine and the well known bronze stamp seal (Alp 1963). Our project focused on the collection of surface sherds from the largely destroyed sections of the northern part of the site (Dönmez 1999: 520, res. 19, 20; 2001a: 303). Middle and Late Iron Age settlement is represented. The Middle Iron Age evidence includes an undecorated bowl with a thickened internal lip, an everted rim and a shallow, circular body (fig. 3.7) (compare: Boğazköy-Kuzeybatı Yamacı). From the Late Iron Age there is a decorated bowl, again with an internally thickened lip, an everted rim, and a shallow, circular body, the decoration comprising parallel lines on the lip (fig. 3.6) (again compare: Boğazköy-Kuzeybatı Yamacı). Other sherds belonged to Early Bronze Age II–III, the Middle Bronze Age and the Hellenistic period.

**Göynücek district**

*Gediksaray Höyüğü*

The höyük, 1km north of Gediksaray town (fig. 1: site no. 11), is another of the largest mounds in the central Black Sea region, being approximately 15m high and 350m by 150m across (Dönmez 2000: 234; 2001a: 303, fig. 6). The mound is cut in two by the modern road to Gediksaray. Middle and Late Iron Age activity is attested. The Middle Iron Age evidence includes two pot sherds: an undecorated jug with an internally and externally thickened rounded lip and an everted rim (fig. 3.8). (compare: Alişar Höyük); and an undecorated krater sherd with a substantial internally and externally thickened lip and a circular body (fig. 3.10) (compare: Boğazköy-Büyükkale). Four sherds are dated to the Late Iron Age: an undecorated jug with drawn-out rim (fig. 3.9) (compare: Boğazköy-Büyükkale level I); a krater, apparently with a drawn-out lip and a wide neck, and with the body decorated with an angular design in brown paint (fig. 3.11) (compare: Boğazköy-Büyükkale); and two jug body sherds decorated with parallel lines in dark brown paint (figs 3.12–13) (for parallels to the decoration, compare: Akalan; Alaca Höyük; Kerkenes Dağ; Çadır Höyük). Settlement dating to Early Bronze Age II–III, the Late Bronze Age and the Hellenistic and Roman periods is also attested.

## Conclusion

Excavations in recent years at sites such as Yassıhöyük/Gordion (Sams 1994: figs 1–5), Boğazköy-Büyükkaya (Genz 2000: Abb. 3–5) and Kaman-Kalehöyük (Omura 1992b: 323, res. 8/1) have begun to reveal the true character of the so-called 'Dark Age' which was formerly believed to have followed the end of the Hittite empire and the Late Bronze Age, now clearly indicating that it is in fact the early stages of the Iron Age (Early Iron Age: ca. 1190–850 BC). However the Amasya province surveys conducted both by myself and previously by others have so far found no Early Iron Age ceramics that match examples from Yassıhöyük/Gordion, Boğazköy-Büyükkaya and Kaman-Kalehöyük. In spite of this, Özsait and Özsait, conducting surveys since 1986 in the central Black Sea Region, suggest that some pot sherds found at some sites in Samsun and Amasya provinces must be dated to the Early Iron Age (Özsait, Özsait 2002a; 2002b; 2002c). These settlements are as follows. In Amasya province: Örenler in the central Amasya district; Ayvalıpınar I, Ayvalıpınar II in Göynücek district; Oymaağaç-Kalebaşı, Karatepe, Büyük Küllük Tepe, Küçük Küllük Tepe, Akkaya, Elma Tepesi, Körceviz, Kızkayası, Alacapınar Tepe, Dericik I, Civektepe, Onhoroz Tepe, Aliağa Pınarı in Merzifon district; Karacaören I, Kaleciktepe and Çaltepe in Gümüşhacıköy district; Karataş and Yeniköy in Hamamözü district; Yoğurtçubaba Tepesi in Suluova district. In Samsun province: Sarıgazel, Salur-Yüktepe in Ladik district; and finally Sivri Tepe in Havza district.

Özsait and Özsait date some of the pot sherds found at these settlements to the Early Iron Age because they have red painted decoration and a faceted appearance; and they claim that because these pot sherds look like the Early Iron Age examples from Boğazköy-Büyükkaya, they must have been made by a culture in close relations

with the Hittite cultural zone, possibly the Ghaska people (Özsait, Özsait 2002c: 536). However, when these sherds are considered from the standpoint of technical structure, shape and decoration, one cannot discern a difference between central Black Sea and central Anatolian Middle and Late Iron Age examples.

In the Middle Iron Age (ca. 850–650 BC) there were important settlements within the bend of the Kızılırmak river, including Boğazköy, Alaca Höyük, Hacıbektaş Höyük (Suluca Karahöyük), Kaman-Kalehöyük, Maşat Höyük, Kayapınar, Eskiyapar, Alişar Höyük and Çadır Höyük and, to the south of the river bend, sites such as Kültepe, Sultanhanı, Yassıdağ, Topaklı and Porsuk. This region's painted pottery group — bearing stylised deer representations in silhouette technique with concentric motifs, or sometimes with the use of geometric motifs alone — found in the main settlements and known as Alişar IV ware, is considered to be the main characteristic of the Kızılırmak bend in the Middle Iron Age. However the Amasya surveys have failed to find any pot sherds belonging to that group. Nevertheless, examples of the undecorated pottery tradition of the same period in the Kızılırmak bend region — grey ware (figs 2.10, 3.5) and brown ware (figs 2.6–7, 3.2) — have been found at the Amasya province Iron Age settlements.

During the Late Iron Age the decorative techniques used by workshops within the Kızılırmak bend and to the south of it changed considerably. The stylised deer figures began to be produced with new linear and negative painting techniques and hence assume a more natural appearance. Furthermore, the number and variety of bird representations increased and these began to be used as the main elements in compositions which included also representations of bulls, horses, donkeys, wild goat, roe deer, lions, dogs and fish. Representations of hybrid creatures such as winged bulls and sphinxes, and unidentifiable strange creatures, also appeared at this time. Human figures too, very few in number and extremely stylised in the Middle Iron Age, became important in the Late Iron Age; and Kybele, the mother goddess of the Phrygians (who was in fact worshipped in Anatolia from Neolithic times) is portrayed on the pottery of this period. It is thought that these changes in the character of products from within and beyond the Kızılırmak bend are a result of and reflect political changes in the Late Iron Age. For example, the sudden appearance of horses and horsemen figures may show the influence of Eurasian horse riding nomads at that time; double-handled undecorated pottery, and painted representations of crowned and bearded figures on other ceramics, clearly reveal Iranian — i.e. Median-Achaemenid — influence. Apart from figures and motifs, there are some other changes in decorative techniques in the Late Iron Age. Even though traditional colours such as dark red and shades of brown and black continued to be used, new styles were introduced. Frames with a white or beige background, and compositions within them, began to appear, and after some time the frame technique continued to be used without a lighter coloured background.

Of the Late Iron Age painted pot sherds recovered by our Amasya surveys, those with geometric decoration deserve special attention. This decoration appears on bowls (figs 2.3, 3.6), jugs (figs 2.11, 2.17, 3.12, 3.13), pitchers (figs 2.1, 2.2, 2.14, 2.15) and a krater (fig. 3.11).

Between the beginning of the fifth century BC and the middle of the fourth, i.e. the late phase of the Late Iron Age, some of the workshops in the Kızılırmak bend, whilst continuing to produce pottery according to traditional schemes, also acquired new methods and came under new influences, as shown clearly by those decorated ceramics with lighter coloured backgrounds, from such sites as Kara Samsun/Amisos, Maşat Höyük, Boğazköy, Alaca Höyük, Eskiyapar, Hacıbektaş Höyük, Kaman-Kalehöyük, Kırşehir Höyük, Alişar Höyük and Büyüknesfesköy/Tavium.

Three sherds dating to this late phase of the Late Iron Age have been found in our survey work (figs 2.4, 2.12, 2.16) (Dönmez 2001b: 94). In addition there is a bowl sherd in Amasya Museum, found near Gümüşhacıköy, which has ivy leaf decoration apparently from a motif resembling a tree with branches ending in small balls (Dönmez 2001b: fig. 1), one of the most beautiful examples of vegetal decoration from the Amasya region.

In Hellenistic times Amasya province had a local pottery tradition that shows strong links with the preceding Iron Age ones, demonstrated for example by an almost intact bowl with ivy leaf decoration found in Harmancık village in Göynücek (Dönmez 2001b: figs 2, 3). Clearly there was no significant cultural gap between the Late Iron Age and the Hellenistic period. Rather, a cultural continuity in pottery development can be traced and the pottery workshops, in existence since the Middle Iron Age, continued without interruption into Hellenistic times. Viewed in this light, the chronological boundary of the Late Iron Age within the Kızılırmak bend can be said to extend down to the middle of the fourth century BC.

In conclusion, pottery from the Amasya province Iron Age settlements appears to have strong links with material from Akalan and İkiztepe in Samsun province, and Maşat Höyük in Tokat province. On the other hand, it also has some similarities with the important Iron Age settlements in the Kızılırmak bend such as Kaman-

Kalehöyük and Hacıbektaş Höyük (Suluca Karahöyük) in Kırşehir province, Alaca Höyük and Boğazköy in Çorum province, and Kerkenes Dağ, Çadır Höyük and Alişar Höyük in Yozgat province. In addition, the Amasya region Iron Age pottery has some similarities with that from the settlements south of the Kızılırmak, namely Kültepe, Kululu and Eğriköy in Kayseri province and, to the west, Yalıncak in Ankara district. Furthermore, recent surveys conducted in Kastamonu, Sivas and Ordu provinces show that the local Iron Age pottery traditions there have strong resemblances to that of the Amasya region.

## Catalogue

Abbreviations used in the catalogue:
Di. = diameter
H. = height
W. = width
Th. = thickness

*Niyazbaba Tepesi*
Fig. 2.1. Jug body sherd. H. 4.1cm, W. 3.8cm, Th. 0.8cm. Light brick-red paste. Fine vegetal and fine mineral tempered. Slipped in same colour as paste. Hard fired. Slightly burnished. Decorated on the outside with very dark brown paint in parallel bands and festoons. Wheel made. Late Iron Age. Close parallels: Maşat Höyük level II (Özgüç 1982: fig. H.11); Kaman-Kalehöyük level IIa1 (Omura 1992a: lev. vi.6, res. iii.7); Kültepe late level (Özgüç 1971: res. 82).

*Alıcık Höyük*
Fig. 2.2. Jug body sherd. H. 3.6cm, W. 5.1cm, Th. 0.8cm. Red-brick paste. Fine vegetal and fine mineral tempered. Slipped in same colour as paste. Hard fired. Slightly burnished. Decorated on outside in reddish brown paint. Wheel made. Late Iron Age. Close parallels: Alaca Höyük (Koşay 1938: lev. vi.9; Koşay, Akok 1973: lev. xciv, bottom right).

Fig. 2.3. Bowl rim sherd. Di. 16.2cm, H. 4.5cm, Th. 0.7cm. Pinkish beige paste. Fine vegetal and fine mineral tempered. Slipped in same colour as paste. Hard fired. Moderately burnished. Decoration on the inside in dark red. Wheel made. Late Iron Age. Close parallels: Boğazköy-Büyükkale level I (Bossert 2000: Taf. 65.701, 704).

Fig. 2.4. Bowl rim sherd. Di. 19.1cm, H. 4.2cm, Th. 0.7cm. Light orange paste. Fine vegetal and fine mineral tempered. Slipped in brick-red. Hard fired. Slightly burnished. Decoration on the outside in dark brown and light beige. Wheel made. Late phase of Late Iron Age. Close parallels: Kaman-Kalehöyük level IIa1 (Omura 1992a: lev. vi.3).

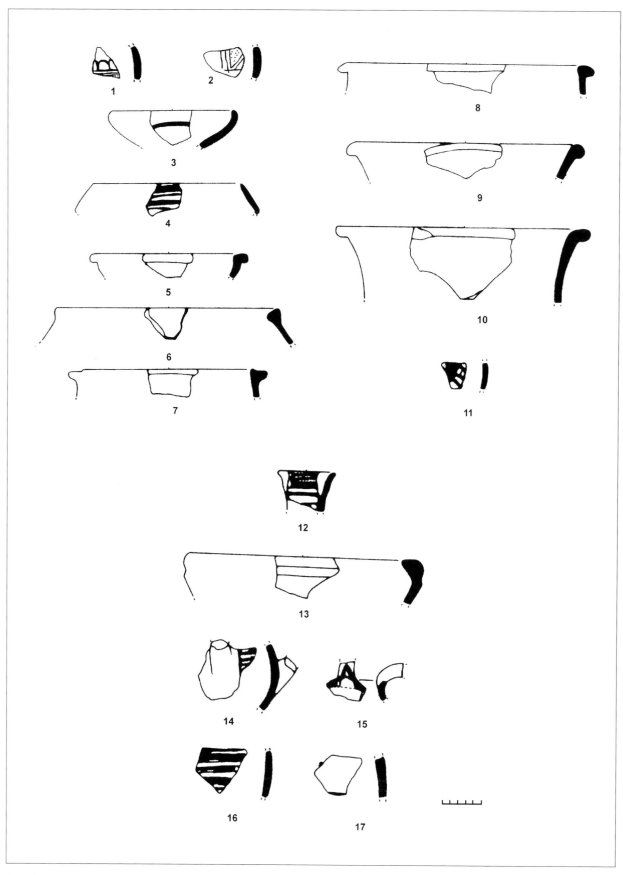

*Fig. 2. Iron Age pottery: (1) Niyazbaba Tepesi; (2–4) Alıcık Höyük; (5–11) Onhoroz Tepe; (12, 13) Alacapınar Tepe (Hayrettin I); (14–17) Delicik Tepe (Hayrettin II)*

*Onhoroz Tepe*

Fig. 2.5. Bowl rim sherd. Di. 18.2cm, H. 3.3cm, Th. 0.9cm. Brown paste. Fine and medium vegetal and medium mineral tempered. Slipped in same colour as paste. Moderately fired. No burnish. Wheel made. Middle Iron Age. Close parallels: Boğazköy-Büyükkaya (Bossert 2000: Taf. 76.892); Boğazköy-Büyükkale (Bossert 2000: Taf. 83.995).

Fig. 2.6. Jug rim sherd. Di. 27.5cm, H. 4.2cm, Th. 0.8cm. Light brown paste. Medium vegetal and medium mineral tempered. Slipped in same colour as paste. Moderately fired. No burnish. Wheel made. Middle Iron Age. Close parallels: Maşat Höyük early phase of level III (Özgüç 1982: fig. L.18); Boğazköy-Büyükkale (Bossert 2000: Taf. 29.263).

Fig. 2.7. Jug rim sherd. Di. 22.8cm, H. 3.5cm, Th. 0.9cm. Light brown paste. Fine and medium vegetal and medium mineral tempered. Slipped in same colour as paste. Moderately fired. No burnish. Wheel made. Middle Iron Age. Close parallels: Maşat Höyük early phase of level III (Özgüç 1982: fig. M.17)

Fig. 2.8. Jug rim sherd. Di. 29.2cm, H. 3.7cm, Th. 0.8cm. Pinkish beige paste. Medium vegetal and medium mineral tempered. Slipped in same colour as paste. Moderately fired. No burnish. Wheel made. Middle Iron Age. Close parallels: Boğazköy-lower town (Bossert 2000: Taf. 54.566).

Fig. 2.9. Krater rim sherd. Di. 28.8cm, H. 4.7cm, Th. 1cm. Buff paste. Fine vegetal and medium mineral tempered. Slipped in same colour as paste. Moderately fired. No burnish. Wheel made. Late Iron Age. Close parallels: Boğazköy-Büyükkale (Bossert 2000: Taf. 5.38, 24.221).

Fig. 2.10. Krater rim sherd. Di 30.4cm, H. 9.1cm, Th. 1.1cm. Greyish brown paste. Medium and coarse vegetal, and medium and coarse mineral tempered. Slipped in same colour as paste. Moderately fired. No burnish. Wheel made. Middle Iron Age. Close parallels: Boğazköy-Büyükkaya (Bossert 2000: Taf. 1.36); Alişar Höyük (von der Osten 1937a: fig. 451.1).

Fig. 2.11. Jug body sherd. H. 3.5cm, W. 3.2cm, Th. 0.7cm. Pinkish beige paste. Fine vegetal and fine mineral tempered. Slipped in same colour as paste. Hard fired. Slightly burnished. Decoration on the outside in dark red. Wheel made. Late Iron Age. Close parallels: İkiztepe mound III (Bilgi 1999: fig. 13.6–9).

*Alacapınar Tepe (Hayrettin I)*

Fig. 2.12. Jug rim sherd. Di. 7.2cm, H. 5.1cm, Th. 0.7cm. Pinkish beige paste. Fine vegetal and fine mineral tempered. Slipped in same colour as paste. Hard fired. Slightly burnished. Decoration on the outside in light brown, brick-red and light beige. Wheel made. Late phase of Late Iron Age. Close parallels: Alişar Höyük (von der Osten 1937b: pl. v.5).

Fig. 2.13. Bowl rim sherd. Di. 28.9cm, H. 5.5cm, Th. 1.1cm. Light brown paste. Medium vegetal and medium mineral tempered. Slipped in same colour as paste. Hard fired. No burnish. Wheel made. Late Iron Age. Close parallels: Boğazköy-Büyükkale level Ia (Bossert 2000: Taf. 34.315).

*Delicik Tepe (Hayrettin II)*

Fig. 2.14. Pitcher body sherd. H. 8.5cm, W. 8.1cm, Th. 0.8cm. Light brick red paste. Fine and medium vegetal and fine and medium mineral tempered. Slipped in same colour as paste. Moderately fired. Moderately burnished. Decoration on the outside in black. Wheel made. Late Iron Age. Close parallels: Akalan (Cummer 1976: fig. 2.18); Maşat Höyük level II (Özgüç 1982: fig. K.11, lev. 65.5); Eskiyapar (Bayburtluoğlu 1979: lev. 182.35); Kerkenes Dağ (Schmidt 1929: fig. 54); Alişar Höyük (von der Osten 1937b: fig. 36d.744); Kültepe (Özgüç 1971: lev. xix.2).

Fig. 2.15. Pitcher rim sherd. H. 5.2cm, W. 5.5cm, Th. 0.8cm. Yellowish buff paste. Fine vegetal and fine and medium mineral tempered. Slipped in same colour as paste. Hard fired. Slightly burnished. Decoration on the rim and handle in black. Wheel made. Late Iron Age. Close parallels: Hacıbektaş Höyük/Suluca Karahöyük (Balkan, Sümer 1968: res. 28); Alişar Höyük (von der Osten 1937a: fig. 441.4–6); Eğriköy (Darga 1959: pl. xxxi.1-1a).

Fig. 2.16. Jug body sherd. H. 6cm, W. 6.6cm, Th. 0.8cm. Light buff paste. Fine vegetal and fine mineral tempered. Slipped in same colour as paste. Hard fired. Slightly burnished. Decoration on the outside in black, dark brown and beige. Wheel made. Late phase of Late Iron Age. Close parallels: Alişar Höyük (von der Osten 1937b: fig. 38c.53).

Fig. 2.17. Jug body sherd. H. 5.5cm, W. 6.2cm, Th. 0.9cm. Dark brick-red paste. Medium vegetal and fine and medium mineral tempered. Slipped in same colour as paste. Hard fired. Slightly burnished. Decoration on the outside in dark brown. Wheel made. Late Iron Age. Close parallels: Yalıncak (Tezcan 1966: lev. xxi, bottom right).

*Samadolu Höyüğü*

Fig. 3.1. Jug rim sherd. Di. 12.3cm, H. 4.3cm, Th. 0.7cm. Pinkish beige paste. Medium vegetal and medium mineral tempered. Slipped in same colour as paste. Moderate fired. No burnish. Wheel made. Middle Iron Age. Close parallels: Alişar Höyük (Schmidt 1933: pl. vb, 1880:68; von der Osten 1937b: fig. 67.3; Akurgal 1955: Taf. 31b, top).

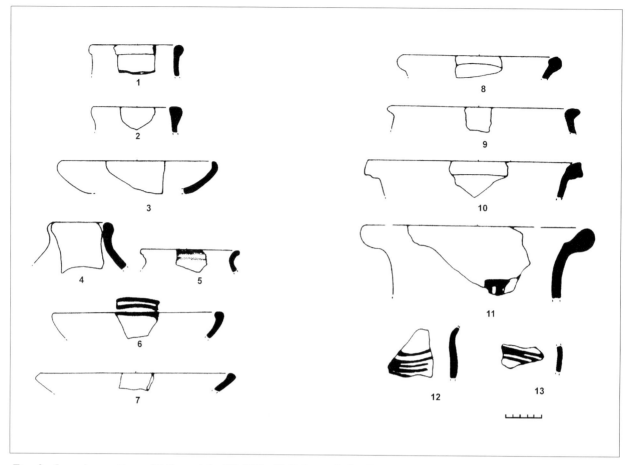

*Fig. 3. Iron Age pottery: (1) Samadolu Höyüğü; (2) Yoğurtçubaba Tepesi; (3) Dereağıl Tepesi; (4, 5); Oluz Höyük; (6, 7) Doğantepe; (8–13) Gediksaray Höyüğü*

*Yoğurtçubaba Tepesi*

Fig. 3.2. Jug rim sherd. Di. 12.1cm, H. 3.2cm, Th. 0.9cm. Light brown paste. Medium and coarse vegetal and medium and coarse mineral tempered. No slip. Badly fired. No burnish. Wheel made. Middle Iron Age. Close parallels: Maşat Höyük early phase of level III (Özgüç 1982: fig. M.8).

*Dereağıl Tepesi*

Fig. 3.3. Bowl rim sherd. Di. 22.6cm, H. 4.5cm, Th. 0.8cm. Light grey paste. Fine vegetal and fine mineral tempered. Slipped in same colour as paste. Hard fired. Slightly burnished. Wheel made. Middle Iron Age. Close parallels: Boğazköy-Kuzeybatı Yamacı (Bossert 2000: Taf. 71.808).

*Oluz Höyük*

Fig. 3.4. Jug rim sherd. Di. 8.1cm, H. 6.9cm, Th. 1.1cm. Grey paste. Medium vegetal and medium mineral tempered. Slipped in same colour as paste. Moderately fired. No burnish. Wheel made. Late Iron Age. Close parallels: Kululu (Özgüç 1975: sek. 11).

Fig. 3.5. Jug rim sherd. Di. 14.1cm, H. 3.1cm, Th. 0.7cm. Grey paste. Medium vegetal and medium mineral tempered. Slipped in same colour as paste. Moderate fired. No burnish. Wheel made. Middle Iron Age. Close parallels: Boğazköy-Büyükkale level IIa (Bossert 2000: Taf. 2.14).

*Doğantepe*

Fig. 3.6. Bowl rim sherd. Di. 24.1cm, H. 3.5cm, Th. 0.8cm. Pinkish beige paste. Fine and medium vegetal and medium mineral tempered. Slipped in same colour as paste. Hard fired. Slightly burnished. Decoration on the outside in very dark brown. Wheel made. Late Iron Age. Close parallels: Boğazköy-Kuzeybatı Yamacı (Bossert 2000: Taf. 64.692); Kululu late phase (Özgüç 1971: res. 109)

Fig. 3.7. Bowl rim sherd. Di. 27.8cm, H. 2.5cm, Th. 0.8cm. Pinkish beige paste. Fine and medium vegetal and medium mineral tempered. Slipped in same colour as paste. Hard fired. Slightly burnished. Wheel made. Middle Iron Age. Close parallels: Boğazköy-Kuzeybatı Yamacı (Bossert 2000: Taf. 64.697).

*Gediksaray Höyüğü*

Fig. 3.8. Jug rim sherd. Di. 21.8cm, H.3.1cm, Th. 0.9cm. Dark buff paste. Medium vegetal and fine and medium mineral tempered. Slipped in same colour as paste. Hard fired. Slightly burnished. Wheel made. Middle Iron Age. Close parallels: Alişar Höyük (von der Osten 1937a: figs 446.31, 447.19).

Fig. 3.9. Jug rim sherd. Di. 25.9cm, H. 3.6cm, Th. 0.9cm. Light brown paste. Medium vegetal and medium mineral tempered. Slipped in same colour as paste. Moderately fired. No burnish. Wheel made. Late Iron Age. Close parallels: Boğazköy-Büyükkale level I (Bossert 2000: Taf. 4.23).

Fig. 3.10. Krater rim sherd. Di. 30.9cm, H. 5.1cm, Th. 0.9cm. Dark brown paste. Medium vegetal and medium mineral tempered. Slipped in same colour as paste. Hard fired. Moderately burnished. Wheel made. Middle Iron Age. Close parallels: Boğazköy-Büyükkale (Bossert 2000: Taf. 5.41).

Fig. 3.11. Krater rim sherd. Di. 48.4cm, H. 10.4cm, Th. 1.4cm. Light brick-red paste. Medium and coarse vegetal and fine and medium mineral tempered. Slipped in same colour as paste. Hard fired. Moderately burnished. Decoration on the outside in very dark brown. Wheel made. Late Iron Age. Close parallels: Boğazköy-Büyükkale (Bossert 2000: Taf. 17.163).

Fig. 3.12. Jug body sherd. H. 6.9cm, W. 6.5cm, Th. 0.9cm. Brick-red paste. Fine and medium vegetal and fine mineral tempered. Slipped in same colour as paste. Hard fired. Moderately burnished. Decoration on the outside in dark brown. Wheel made. Late Iron Age. Close parallels: Akalan (Cummer 1976: fig. 1.5); Kerkenes Dağ (Schmidt 1929: figs 61, 62); Çadır Höyük (Genz 2001: fig. 4.5); Alaca Höyük (Koşay 1938: lev. vi.13); Yalıncak (Tezcan 1966: lev. xiv bottom, xxii middle).

Fig. 3.13. Jug body sherd. H. 3.4cm, W. 6cm, Th. 0.7cm. Light brown paste. Fine vegetal and fine and medium mineral tempered. Slipped in same colour as paste. Hard fired. Moderately burnished. Decoration on the outside in dark brown. Wheel made. Late Iron Age. Close parallels: Akalan (Cummer 1976: fig. 1.5); Kerkenes Dağ (Schmidt 1929: figs 61, 62); Çadır Höyük (Genz 2001: fig. 4.5); Alaca Höyük (Koşay 1938: lev. vi.13); Yalıncak (Tezcan 1966: lev. xiv bottom, xxii middle).

## Bibliography

Akurgal, E. 1955: *Phrygische Kunst*. Ankara

Alp, S. 1963: 'Amasya civarında Zara Bucağında bulunan Hitit heykeli ile diğer Hitit eserleri' *Anatolia (Anadolu)* 6: 191–216

Balkan, K., Sümer, O. 1968: '1967 yılı Hacı Bektaş (Suluca Karahöyük) kazısı önraporu' *Türk Arkeoloji Dergisi* 16.2: 15–19

Bayburtluoğlu, I. 1979: 'Eskiyapar Phryg Çağı' *Türk Tarih Kongresi* 8.1: 293–303

Bilgi, Ö. 1999: 'İkiztepe in the Late Iron Age' *Anatolian Studies* 49: 27–54

Bossert, E.M. 2000: *Die Keramik Phrygischer Zeit von Boğazköy* (Boğazköy-Hattusa Ergebnisse der Ausgrabungen XVIII). Mainz am Rhein

Cummer, W.W. 1976: 'Iron Age pottery from Akalan' *Istanbuler Mitteilungen* 26: 31–6

Darga, M.S. 1959: 'An sujet des céramiques découvertes au Höyük d'Eğriköy' *Anadolu Araştırmaları* I.2 / *Jahrbuch für Kleinasiatische Forschung* 3.2: 195–201

Dönmez, S. 1999: 'Sinop-Samsun-Amasya İlleri yüzey araştırması, 1997' *Araştırma Sonuçları Toplantısı* 16.2: 513–36

— 2000: 'Sinop-Samsun-Amasya İlleri yüzey araştırması, 1998' *Araştırma Sonuçları Toplantısı* 17.2: 229–44

— 2001a: 'The central Black Sea region survey' in O. Belli (ed.), *Istanbul University's Contributions to Archaeology in Turkey (1932–2000)*. Istanbul: 302–6

— 2001b: 'Amasya Müzesi'nden boya bezekli iki çanak ışığında Kızılırmak kavsi Geç Demir ve Helenistik Çağları çanak-çömleğine yeni bir bakış' *TÜBA-AR* 4: 89–99

Genz, H. 2000: 'Die Eisenzeit in Zentralanatolien im Lichte der keramischen Funde vom Büyükkaya in Boğazköy/Hattusa' *TÜBA-AR* 3: 35–54

— 2001: 'Iron Age pottery from Çadır Höyük' *Anatolica* 27: 159–70

Koşay, H.Z. 1938: *Alaca Höyük. 1936'daki Çalışmalara ve Keşiflere Ait İlk Rapor*. Ankara

Koşay, H.Z., Akok, M. 1973: *Alacahöyük Kazısı 1963–1967 Çalışmalara ve Keşiflere Ait İlk Rapor*. Ankara

Omura, S. 1992a: *Kaman-Kalehöyük I*. Tokyo

— 1992b: '1990 yılı Kaman-Kalehöyük kazıları' *Kazı Sonuçları Toplantısı* 13.1: 319–36

Özgüç, T. 1971: *Demir Devrinde Kültepe ve Civarı / Kültepe and its Vicinity in the Iron Age*. Ankara

— 1975: 'Kululu hakkında yeni gözlemler' *Anadolu (Anatolia)* 17: 1–18

— 1982: *Maşat Höyük. II: Boğazköy'ün Kuzeydoğusunda Bir Hitit Merkezi / A Hittite Center Northeast of Boğazköy*. Ankara

Özsait, M. 1989: '1987 yılı Amasya-Suluova tarihöncesi Araştırmaları' *Araştırma Sonuçları Toplantısı* 6: 287–300

— 1990: '1988 yılı Gümüşhacıköy çevresi tarihöncesi Araştırmaları' *Araştırma Sonuçları Toplantısı* 7: 367–80

— 1998: '1995 ve 1996 yıllarında Amasya Merzifon ve Gümüşhacıköy yüzey Araştırmaları' *Araştırma Sonuçları Toplantısı* 15.2: 143–62

Özsait, M., Özsait, N. 1998: 'Amasya'da M.Ö. II. bin yılı yerleşmeleri' *Uluslararası Hititoloji Kongresi* 3: 457–68

— 2002a: 'Les céramiques du Fer Ancien ('L'Age Obscur') dans la Region Amasya-Merzifon' *Anatolia Antiqua* 10: 79–95

— 2002b: 'Amasya'da Erken Demir Çağ keramikleri' *Arkeoloji ve Sanat* 107: 17–24

— 2002c: 'Amasya-Merzifon araştırmaları' *Anadolu Araştırmaları* 16: 527–52

Sams, G.K. 1994: *The Early Phrygian Pottery. The Gordion Excavations 1950–1973: Final Reports Volume 4* (University Museum of Pennsylvania Monograph 79). Pennsylvania

Schmidt, E.F. 1929: 'Test excavations in the city on Kerkenes Dagh' *The American Journal of Semitic Languages and Literatures* 45.4: 211–74

— 1933: *The Alishar Hüyük Seasons of 1928 and 1929, Part II* (University of Chicago Oriental Institute Publications 20). Chicago

Tezcan, B. 1966: 1964 *Yalıncak Köyü Çalışmaları.* Ankara

von der Osten, H.H. 1937a: *The Alishar Hüyük Seasons of 1930–1932, Part II* (University of Chicago Oriental Institute Publications 29). Chicago

— 1937b: *The Alishar Hüyük Seasons of 1930–1932, Part III* (University of Chicago Oriental Institute Publications 30). Chicago

# Thoughts on the origin of the Iron Age pottery traditions in central Anatolia

**Hermann Genz**
*American University of Beirut*

## Abstract

Iron Age pottery traditions in central Anatolia certainly cannot be traced back to the preceding Hittite ceramic tradition. Furthermore, their much quoted resemblance to the Balkan material is in fact quite superficial. Instead, many types and decorative elements find good parallels in the central Anatolian Early and Middle Bronze Ages. This paper examines these typological similarities and tries to explain how the earlier pottery traditions may have survived into the Iron Age.

## Özet

Orta Anadolu Demir Çağ çanak çömleğinde gözlenen özelliklerin izine, öncesindeki gelenek olan Hitit keramiklerinde kesinlikle rastlanmaz. Ayrıca bunların Balkan malzemesi ile belirgin olduğu düşünülen benzerlikleri de aslında oldukça yüzeyseldir. Halbuki bu çanak çömleğin birçok tipinin ve bezeme öğelerinin yakın benzerlerine Orta Anadolu'da Erken ve Orta Bronz Çağ dönemlerinde rastlanılır. Bu çalışma ile bu tipolojik benzerlikler incelenmiş ve erken dönemlerde gözlenen çanak çömlek geleneklerinin Demir Çağa nasıl ulaşmış olabileceği hususları aydınlatılmaya çalışılmıştır.

The paucity of archaeological data for the period directly post-dating the fall of the Hittite empire (shortly after 1200 BC) has greatly hampered our understanding of the formation processes for the Early Iron Age cultures of central Anatolia. This situation has changed considerably during the last decade, with Early Iron Age levels having been uncovered at Boğazköy (Seeher 1997; 1998; Genz 2000), Gordion (Henrickson 1993; 1994; Voigt 1994) and a number of other sites (Genz no date). In this paper, the evidence from the Early Iron Age settlement on Büyükkaya at Boğazköy/Hattuša will be presented, and the ceramic material will be used to formulate an hypothesis concerning the possible origins of the Iron Age pottery traditions in central Anatolia.

## The Early Iron Age at Boğazköy

At Boğazköy, excavations on the hill of Büyükkaya produced remains of a small Early Iron Age village (Seeher 1997; 1998; Genz 2000). The building remains uncovered are restricted to post-holes, pits and the foundation walls of small rectangular houses built of undressed stones. A stratified sequence suggests a tripartite division of the Early Iron Age into an early, a middle, and a late phase.

The pottery from the early phase is restricted to simple utilitarian forms such as bowls, hole mouth cooking pots, jugs and jars. Two basic wares can be distinguished: a finer buff ware and a coarse ware ranging in colour from brown to black. Although the majority of the pottery is handmade, still about a third is wheel made. Most noteworthy is a clear Hittite tradition, attested not only in the continued use of the potter's wheel, but also in the shapes of several vessels. The vessels exhibiting these Hittite features cannot be simply residual from the Hittite levels below, since the Early Iron Age pottery is generally defined by a better surface treatment, such as burnishing, which is very rare on Hittite pottery from the Late Empire period.

Generally, the pottery from the middle and late phases shows strong continuity from the early phase material. However, there are also several outstanding differences. The Hittite traditions disappear, and the production of wheel made pottery ceases almost completely. At the same time, new shapes and decorations appear. Typical of these are facetted rims on bowls, hole mouth pots, pots with a flaring rim and jugs. Red painted decoration, restricted to the finer buff ware, is one of the hallmarks of the middle and late phases of the Early Iron Age, though only less than 5% of the assemblage is painted. The repertoire of the painted motifs is strictly geometric, most typical being dot filled triangles. Incised decoration, although present, is remarkably rare on Büyükkaya. Other typical features of middle and late phase pottery are a variety of knobs and horseshoe shaped handles on coarse ware pots. A series of radiocarbon dates generally places the Early Iron Age levels from Büyükkaya between the beginning of the 12th and the tenth centuries BC (Seeher 2000a: 373).

## The origin of the Iron Age ceramic traditions in central Anatolia

The end of the Hittite empire, shortly after 1200 BC, was accompanied by a marked break in the ceramic traditions in central Anatolia.

The pottery of the Hittite empire is very homogenous throughout a vast region, which extends from Gordion in the west to beyond the Euphrates in the east, and encompassing Cilicia (Gunter 1991: 105; Henrickson 1995: 82; Gates 2001: 141). This pottery is the product of a highly specialised ceramic industry employing full-time craft specialists. It is entirely wheel made and well fired. Labour intensive surface treatments such as burnishing are only rarely found, and few pieces bear a red or white slip (Parzinger, Sanz 1992: 42–8). Decorative features such as painting or incisions are entirely absent. The pottery types attested in the Late Hittite empire are highly standardised.

So far, only at a few sites, notably Boğazköy, Karahöyük/Elbistan and Kilise Tepe, is there a noticeable transition between Late Bronze Age and Iron Age pottery traditions, with Late Bronze Age shapes and techniques continuing for a short period alongside the new Iron Age traditions (Genz no date). However, these Late Bronze Age traditions probably lasted for only one or two generations, and they faded away without leaving recognisable traces in the Iron Age pottery repertoire. In this respect, the statements of Bittel (Bittel, Güterbock 1935: 56) and Akurgal (1955: 25–6), to the effect that the Iron Age pottery of central Anatolia cannot be traced back to the preceding Hittite pottery, remain entirely valid today.

The Iron Age pottery differs in a number of aspects from the Hittite material. First of all, in contrast to the entirely wheel made pottery of the Late Bronze Age, most of the Early and Middle Iron Age material is handmade. Only from the later ninth century onwards, at Gordion (phase YHSS 6 [for the revised Gordion chronology, see DeVries et al. this volume]) and

Boğazköy (Büyükkale period IIb) is the use of the potter's wheel attested again (Henrickson 1994: 111; Genz 2000: 37). Through painting and polishing or burnishing, labour intensive surface finishing techniques are widely attested in the central Anatolian Iron Age. Most importantly, the geographically widespread uniformity of pottery in the Late Bronze Age gives way to marked regionalism in the Early Iron Age ceramic traditions. Despite our admittedly scanty knowledge of the central Anatolian Early Iron Age, several markedly different ceramic zones can already be distinguished (Genz 2004: 26–8) and, without doubt, ongoing research will lead to a better definition of these ceramic zones in the future.

The marked changes visible in ceramic production following the end of the Late Bronze Age are often explained as revealing new Balkan immigrants, with reference to Herodotus (VII.73) and Strabo (XIV.5.29) who mention that the Phrygians came from the Balkans to Anatolia around the time of the Trojan War. The Early Iron Age pottery from Gordion in particular has often been traced back to Balkan origins (Sams 1994: 20; Voigt 1994: 277; Muscarella 1995: 94), but Henrickson rejected the parallels as being too general in nature (Henrickson 1993: 117).

As yet, evidence of direct Balkan influence is restricted to the knobbed ware of Troy VIIB2 (Blegen et al. 1958; Bloedow 1985; Koppenhöfer 1997), but this certainly did not reach the Anatolian plateau.

If the Iron Age pottery traditions in central Anatolia cannot be connected to the preceding Hittite culture, nor to Balkanic immigrants, then where do they come from?

Already in 1935, Bittel had noticed a surprising similarity between the Early Bronze Age Alişar III pottery and the Iron Age Alişar IV pottery (Bittel, Güterbock 1935: 56). This observation is clearly illustrated by the fact that many early researchers had great difficulty in distinguishing between painted Early Bronze Age and Iron Age pottery (von der Osten, Schmidt 1930: 243; Schmidt 1932: 25–6; von der Osten 1937: 463).

Only recently has more attention been paid to these similarities (Özkaya 1995: 137). In particular, it is the discovery of Early Iron Age levels on Büyükkaya at Boğazköy which has shed new light on the connections of Early and Middle Bronze Age pottery with the Iron Age ceramic traditions (Seeher 1998: 236–9; 1999: 331). For a surprisingly large number of Early and Middle Iron Age ceramics, very close parallels can be found in the Anatolian Early and Middle Bronze Ages, not only in shapes and decorative features, but also in such details as handles and spouts.

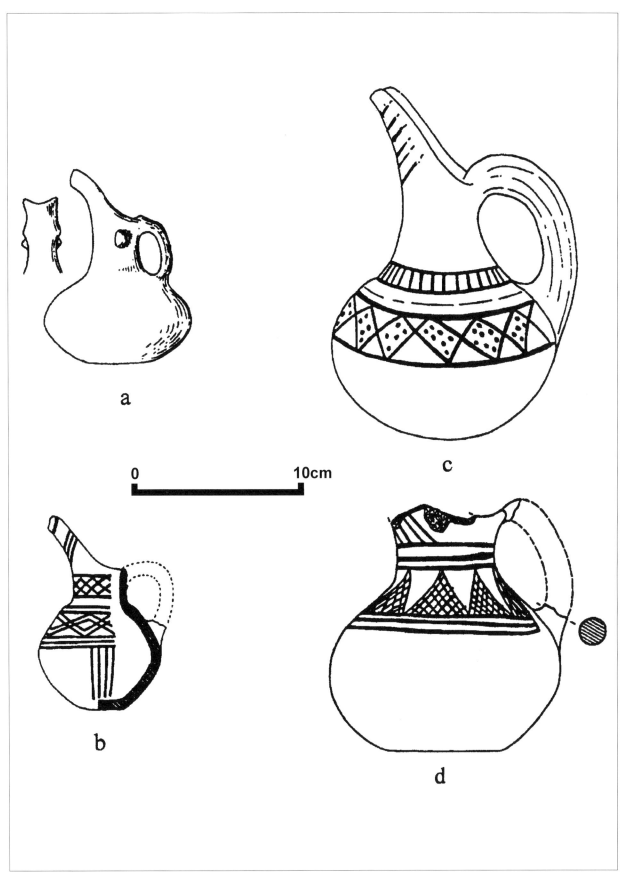

*Fig. 1. (a) Nallıhan, Early Bronze Age (Tezcan 1956: res. 1); (b) Alaca Höyük, Early Bronze Age (Orthmann 1963a: Taf. 49:11/101); (c) Eskiyapar, Early Iron Age (after Bayburtluoğlu 1979: res. 1a); (d) Boğazköy, Middle Iron Age (Genz 2004: Taf. 61:6)*

Beak spouted jugs are a common form in the Iron Age (Akurgal 1955: 11–13; Sams 1994: 64–5; Bossert 2000: 76–7; Genz 2004: 24), as well as in the Early and Middle Bronze Ages (Orthmann 1963a: 98–9; 1963b: 19–20, 26–7, 35, 42, 45; Öktü 1973: 86; Seeher 1987: 126–33; 2000b: 37–46; Efe 1988: 55–8; Kull 1988: 146–8). The proportions of the vessels, as well as the position of the painted decoration, are quite similar in both periods (fig. 1).

Iron Age trefoil mouthed jugs have good parallels in earlier periods. An example from the Early Iron Age levels on Büyükkaya, with its handle attached at a 90° angle to the spout (fig. 2b) (Genz 2000: Abb. 5:1), has almost exact counterparts from Middle Bronze Age graves at Demircihöyük-Sarıket (fig. 2a) (Seeher 2000b: Taf. 67, 68). The ordinary trefoil mouthed jugs, with the handle opposite the spout, are also quite alike in both the Iron Age (fig. 2d) (Genz 2000: Abb. 8:3) and the Middle Bronze Age (fig. 2c) (Orthmann 1963b: Taf. 34:354; Kull 1988: Taf. 23:5). A side spouted jug from the Early Iron Age levels at Büyükkaya (fig. 3b) (Genz in press: Taf. 26:6) resembles one from the Karum period at Kültepe, not only in its general shape but even in details of the painted decoration (fig. 3a) (Anatolian Civilisations 1983: 191:A500).

Several fragmentary side spouts from the Early Iron Age levels on Büyükkaya have a connection between the end of the spout and the opening of the vessel (fig. 4b–c) (Genz 2004: 24). The most convincing parallels for these spouts are found in the Early Bronze Age of southwestern Anatolia, for example at Beycesultan (fig. 4a) (Lloyd, Mellaart 1962: figs P.25:20, P32:5) and at Kuruçay (Duru 1996: lev. 122:2, 4).

Even in minor details, resemblances between Early Bronze Age and Iron Age jugs are noticeable. In both periods, beak spouted jugs sometimes show knob like protrusions on the sides of the neck, as well as a swelling at the neck; examples from the Early Bronze Age include Nallıhan (Tezcan 1956: res. 1) and Demircihöyük-Sarıket (Seeher 2000b: Abb. 22, 26, 29) and, from the Iron Age, Büyükkaya (fig. 3c–g) (Genz 2004: Taf. 36:3).

A basket handled vessel from Early Iron Age levels at Büyükkaya (fig. 4e) (Genz 2004: Taf. 19:10) has good parallels from the Early Bronze Age levels at Demircihöyük (fig. 4d) (Efe 1988: Taf. 58:1), from Early to Middle Bronze Age levels at Aphrodisias (Joukowsky 1986: fig. 444:27), from Middle Bronze Age contexts at Boğazköy (Orthmann 1963b: Taf. 32:303–5) and Kültepe (Özgüç 1959: fig. 56, lev. xxxii:2), and from Late Bronze Age levels at Beycesultan (Mellaart, Murray 1995: figs P8, P41:7, 10).

Comparisons for the horseshoe shaped handles, which are characteristic of the Early Iron Age levels on Büyükkaya (fig. 4g) (Genz 2000; 2004: 24), already appear in the Early Bronze Age at Demircihöyük (fig. 4f) (Efe 1988: Taf. 27:3, 58:5, 59:13), Kusura (Lamb 1937: pl. 83:4), and in the Middle Bronze Age at Demircihöyük (Kull 1988: Taf. 2:5, 6, 11) and Aphrodisias (Joukowsky 1986: figs 447:1, 477:14).

The small funnel shaped vessels with perforated walls from the Early Iron Age levels at Büyükkaya (Genz 2000: Abb. 5:2–3) have earlier parallels, ranging in date from the Early Bronze Age to the beginning of the Late Bronze Age. However, they are not as yet attested for the Hittite Imperial period. The comparanda include finds from the Early Bronze Age levels at Demircihöyük (Seeher 1987: Taf. 43:21, 49:19, 57:12, 13; Efe 1988: Taf. 17:8) and Aphrodisias (Joukowsky 1986: fig. 439:33), as well as examples from the earlier part of the Late Bronze Age at Alaca Höyük (Koşay, Akok 1973: pl. 30) and Tarsus (Goldman 1956: pl. 308:1057).

Even the dark burnished surfaces and the frequent occurrence of knobs and degenerated ledge handles on Early Iron Age coarse wares (Henrickson 1993; 1994; Genz 2000: 36; 2004: 42) resemble Early Bronze Age pottery traditions (Orthmann 1963a: 74–5; Efe 1988: 7–8).

The general similarity between the Early Bronze Age Alişar III pottery (Öktü 1973) and the Middle Iron Age Alişar IV pottery (Bossert 2000; Genz 2000: 37–8; 2004: 42) has already been mentioned above. This similarity, however, refers rather to the painting techniques with dark matt paint than to the actual motifs. More convincing parallels for the Early Iron Age painting traditions are to be found in the Middle Bronze Age, especially at Tarsus and Kültepe. Dot filled triangles and groups of lines on the rims of vessels, typical of the Early Iron Age red painted pottery in the central area of the Kızılırmak bend (Genz 2000: 39; 2004: 42), are common motifs on Middle Bronze pottery from Tarsus (Goldman 1956: pls 287:781, 796, 291:910, 295: 859), and the groups of lines on vessel rims are also found on Middle Bronze Age pottery from Kültepe (Özgüç, Özgüç 1953: lev. L:459–461) and Lidar Höyük (Kaschau 1999: Taf. 134:3, 162:7, 193: ). For Kilise Tepe, Symington (2001: 171) likewise notes that the red painted pottery from Early Iron Age Levels IIa and b goes back to Middle Bronze Age traditions.

It must be stressed that all the above mentioned forms, features and decorations are not, or are hardly, attested in the pottery of the Hittite Imperial period.

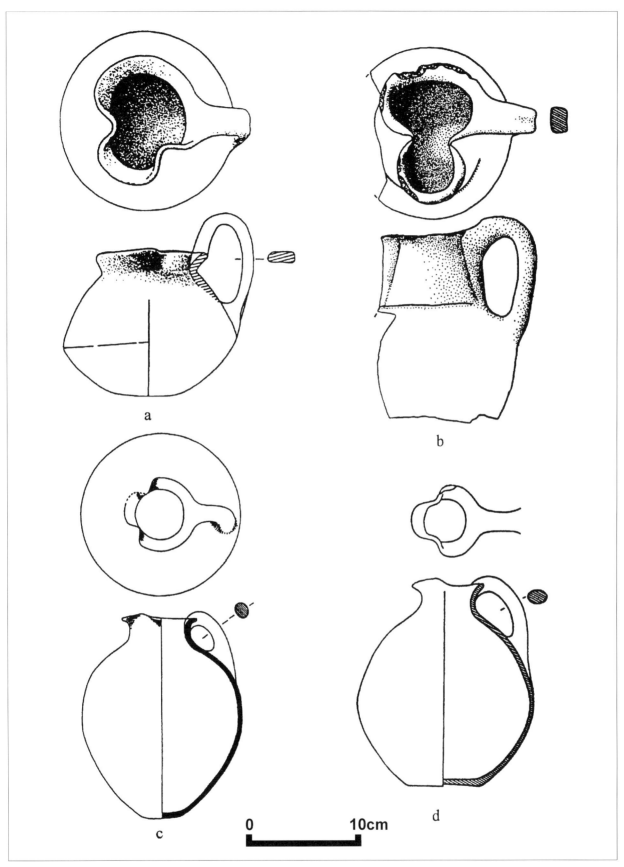

Fig. 2. (a) Demircihöyük-Sarıket, Middle Bronze Age (Seeher 2000b: Abb. 67); (b) Boğazköy, Early Iron Age (Genz 2004: Taf. 15:5); (c) Boğazköy, Middle Bronze Age (Orthmann 1963b: Taf. 34:354); (d) Boğazköy, Middle Iron Age (Genz 2004: Taf. 60:7)

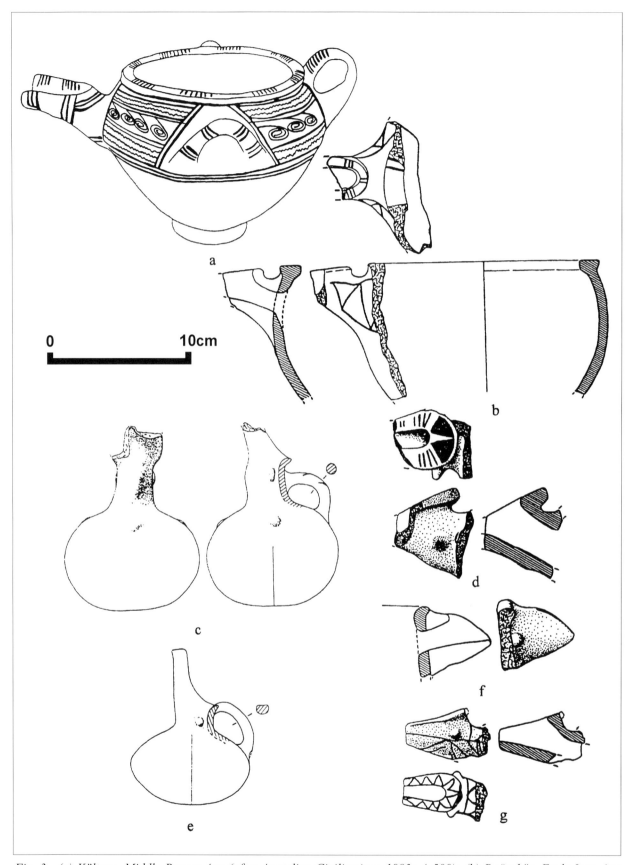

*Fig. 3. (a) Kültepe, Middle Bronze Age (after Anatolian Civilisations 1983: A 500); (b) Boğazköy, Early Iron Age (Genz 2004: Taf. 26:6); (c) Demircihöyük-Sarıket, Early Bronze Age (Seeher 2000b: Abb. 26); (d) Boğazköy, Early Iron Age (Genz 2004: Taf. 36:3); (e) Demircihöyük-Sarıket, Early Bronze Age (Seeher 2000b: Abb. 18); (f)–(g) Boğazköy, Early Iron Age (Genz 2004: Taf. 24:14, 19:8)*

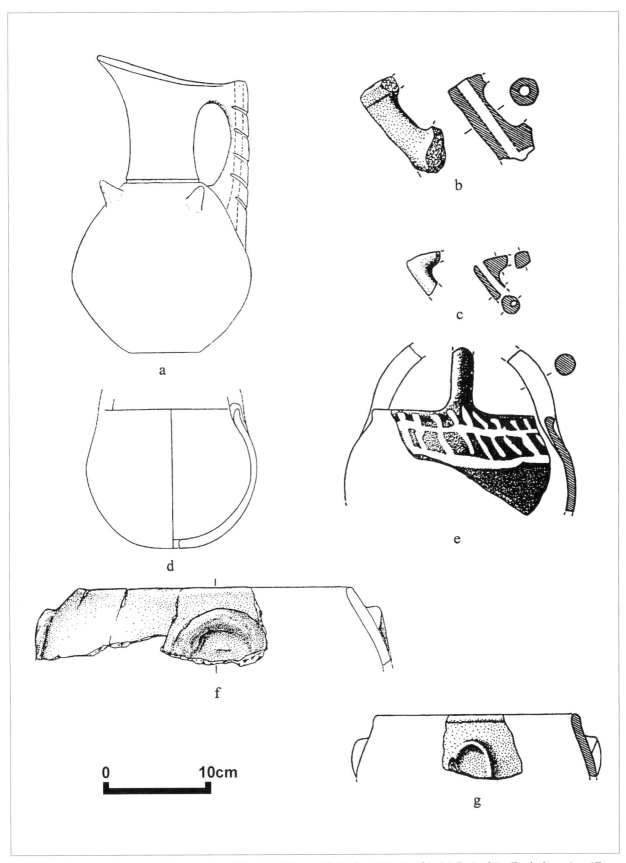

*Fig. 4. (a) Beycesultan, Early Bronze Age (Lloyd, Mellaart 1962: fig. P32, 5); (b)–(c) Boğazköy, Early Iron Age (Genz 2004: Taf. 24:13, 15:8); (d) Demircihöyük, Early Bronze Age (Efe 1988: Taf. 58:1); (e) Boğazköy, Early Iron Age (Genz 2004: Taf. 19:10); (f) Demircihöyük, Early Bronze Age (Efe 1988: Taf. 27, 3); (g) Boğazköy, Early Iron Age (Genz 2004: Taf. 22:13)*

## Interpretation

The parallels between Early and Middle Bronze Age pottery on the one hand and Iron Age pottery on the other are reasonably convincing, and the large number of comparisons precludes any attempt to explain these parallels as fortuitous. Nevertheless, the interpretation of these observations poses a number of problems.

First of all, how did the earlier pottery traditions survive into the Iron Age, with the pottery of the Hittite Imperial period clearly marking a break in an otherwise continuous development?

Two different explanations can be suggested. The older ceramic traditions may have survived in areas that remained outside Hittite control, for example in parts of western Anatolia or to the north in the area of the Pontic mountains. Another possibility is that the earlier pottery traditions may have survived within the Hittite empire, in the more remote rural areas. At present, Hittite Imperial period pottery is known mainly from the large urban centres and their immediate environs, so we can only make guesses as to what the pottery in the empire's rural areas looked like. Nevertheless, it is entirely possible that older ceramic traditions, going back to the Early or Middle Bronze Ages, continued to be manufactured in those rural areas.

The earlier parallels for the Boğazköy Iron Age pottery present a second problem: hardly any of these come from the site of Boğazköy itself, or from the area within the Kızılırmak bend. Rather, two different areas of origin can be recognised. One of these is Early to Late Bronze Age western central Anatolia, encompassing the regions from Eskişehir in the north to the lake district in the south. From this area the tradition of unpainted ceramics seems to have derived, comprising hole mouth jars with horseshoe shaped handles, different types of spouted jugs and funnel shaped vessels with perforated walls. The other region is Middle Bronze Age Cilicia and the area south of the Kızılırmak, and it is to here that the painted traditions can be traced.

It is impossible as yet to judge at what time these earlier western and southern pottery traditions arrived in the area of the Kızılırmak bend. The appearance of these new ceramic traditions may reflect population movements beginning with the end of the Hittite empire; but equally it is possible that population groups were moved around within the Hittite Imperial period, either as prisoners of war being resettled in new areas, or as corvée labourers. The ambitious building programmes carried out at Hattuša in the time of the Hittite empire surely created the need for a large work force that would certainly have exceeded the capacity of Hattuša's immediate surroundings. Textual evidence suggests the possibility that workers from other parts of the Hittite empire were sent temporarily or even permanently to the capital (Klinger 1992: 195–7). A similar explanation has been put forward for the occurrence of the handmade burnished ware in Late Helladic IIIC Greece (Bankoff et al. 1996), though that proposal is not without its problems (Genz 1997).

It is very tempting to connect the new cultural elements appearing in Early Iron Age Boğazköy with the long time enemies of the Hittites, the Kaška of the Pontic region (Seeher 1998: 239; 1999: 331). However, hardly any connections in the material culture yet known from Early Iron Age Boğazköy point towards the north. It has to be admitted, though, that the Bronze and Iron Age material culture of the Pontic region, with the exception of that from İkiztepe (Alkım et al. 1988), remains largely unknown (Orthmann 1963a: 74).

The thoughts developed in this paper certainly raise more questions than they answer, but it is hoped that they will contribute to a better understanding of the formation of the Iron Age cultures of central Anatolia.

## Acknowledgements

I would like to thank Dr J. Seeher for having entrusted me with the publication of the Iron Age pottery from Büyükkaya at Boğazköy, as well as for providing comments on an earlier version of this paper.

## Bibliography

Akurgal, E. 1955: *Phrygische Kunst*. Ankara

Alkım, U.B., Alkım H., Bilgi, Ö. 1988: *İkiztepe I*. Ankara

Anatolian Civilisations 1983: *The Anatolian Civilisations*. Istanbul

Bankoff, A.H., Meyer, N., Stefanovich, M. 1996: 'Handmade burnished ware and the Late Bronze Age of the Balkans' *Journal of Mediterranean Archaeology* 9: 193–209

Bayburtluoğlu, I. 1979: 'Eskiyapar "Phryg Çagi"' in E. Akurgal et al. (eds) *VIII. Türk Tarih Kongresi*. Ankara: 293–303

Bittel, K., Güterbock, H.-G. 1935: *Boğazköy. Neue Untersuchungen in der hethitischen Hauptstadt* (Abhandlungen der Preussischen Akademie der Wissenschaften Jahrgang 1935, Phil.–Hist. Klasse Nr. 1). Berlin

Blegen, C.W., Boulter, C.G., Caskey, J.L., Rawson, M. 1958: *Troy IV: Settlements VIIa, VIIb and VIII*. Princeton

Bloedow, E.F. 1985: 'Handmade burnished ware or "barbarian" pottery and Troy VIIB' *La Parola del Passato* 40: 161–99

Bossert, E.-M. 2000: *Die Keramik phrygischer Zeit von Boğazköy* (Boğazköy-Hattuša 18). Mainz am Rhein

Dupré, S. 1983: *Porsuk I. La céramique de l'age du Bronze et de l'age du Fer.* Paris

Duru, R. 1996: *Kuruçay Höyük II.* Ankara

Efe, T. 1988: *Demircihüyük III.II: Die Keramik II.* Mainz am Rhein

Gates, M.-H. 2001: 'Potmarks at Kinet Höyük and the Hittite ceramic industry' in É. Jean, A.M. Dinçol, S. Durugönül (eds), *La Cilicie: Espaces et Pouvoirs Locaux (2e millénaire av. J.-C. – 4e siècle ap. J.-C.) / Kilikia: Mekânlar ve yerel güçler (M.Ö. 2. binyıl – M.S. 4. yüzyıl).* Paris: 137–57

Genz, H. 1997: 'Northern slaves and the origin of handmade burnished ware: a comment on Bankoff et al. (*JMA* 9 [1996] 193–209)' *Journal of Mediterranean Archaeology* 10: 109–11

— 2000: 'Die Eisenzeit in Zentralanatolien im Lichte der keramischen Funde vom Büyükkaya in Boğazköy/Hattuša' *Türkiye Bilimler Akademisi Arkeoloji Dergisi / Turkish Academy of Sciences Journal of Archaeology (TÜBA-AR)* 3: 35–54

— 2004: *Büyükkaya I: Die Keramik der Eisenzeit* (Boğazköy–Hattuša 21). Mainz am Rhein

— no date: 'No land could stand before their arms, from Hatti .... on ...? New light on the end of the Hittite empire and the Early Iron Age in central Anatolia' paper presented at the workshop: *Philistine and other 'Sea Peoples': Aegean-style Material Culture in the Eastern Mediterranean during the 12th Century BCE.* Haifa/Beersheva. May 2001

Goldman, H. 1956: *Excavations at Gözlü Kule, Tarsus II. From the Neolithic through the Bronze Age.* Princeton

Gunter, A. C. 1991: *Gordion Excavation Final Reports III: The Bronze Age* (University Museum Monograph 71). Philadelphia

Henrickson, R.C. 1993: 'Politics, economics and ceramic continuity at Gordion in the late second and first millennia BC' in W.D. Kingery (ed.), *The Social and Cultural Contexts of New Ceramic Technologies* (Ceramics and Civilization Volume 6). Westerville, Ohio: 88–176

— 1994: 'Continuity and discontinuity in the ceramic tradition of Gordion during the Iron Age' in A. Çilingiroğlu, D.H. French (eds), *Anatolian Iron Ages III.* Ankara: 95–129

— 1995: 'Hittite pottery and potters: a view from Late Bronze Age Gordion' *Biblical Archaeologist* 58: 82–90

Joukowsky, M.S. 1986: *Prehistoric Aphrodisias: An Account of the Excavation and Artifact Studies, Volumes I–II* (Archaeologia Transatlantica 3). Court-St. Étienne

Kaschau, G. 1999: *Lidar Höyük. Die Keramik der Mittleren Bronzezeit* (Archaeologica Euphratica 3). Mainz am Rhein

Klinger, J. 1992: 'Fremde und Außenseiter in Hatti' in V. Haas (ed.), *Außenseiter und Randgruppen* (Xenia. Konstanzer althistorische Vorträge und Forschungen 32). Konstanz: 187–212

Koppenhöfer, D. 1997: 'Troia VII — Versuch einer Zusammenschau einschließlich der Ergebnisse des Jahres 1995' *Studia Troica* 7: 295–353

Koşay, H.Z., Akok, M. 1966: *Alaca Höyük Kazısı.* Ankara

— 1973: *Alaca Höyük Kazısı.* Ankara

Kull, B. 1988: *Demircihüyük V: Die mittelbronzezeitliche Siedlung.* Mainz am Rhein

Lamb, W. 1937: 'Excavations at Kusura near Afyon Karahisar' *Archaeologia* 87: 217–73

Lloyd, S., Mellaart, J. 1962: *Beycesultan I. The Chalcolithic and Early Bronze Age Levels.* London

Mellaart, J., Murray, A. 1995: *Beycesultan III.II. Late Bronze Age and Phrygian Pottery and Middle and Late Bronze Age Small Objects.* London

Muscarella, O.W. 1995: 'The Iron Age background to the formation of the Phrygian state' *Bulletin of the American Schools of Oriental Research* 299/300: 91–101

Öktü, A. 1973: *Die Intermediate-Keramik in Kleinasien.* München

Özgüç, T. 1959: *Kültepe-Kaniš.* Ankara

Özgüç, T., Özgüç, N. 1953: *Kültepe Kazısı Raporu 1949.* Ankara

Özkaya, V. 1995: *IÖ. Erken Birinci Binde Frig Boyalı Seramiği.* Erzurum

Orthmann, W. 1963a: *Die Keramik der Frühen Bronzezeit aus Inneranatolien* (Istanbuler Forschungen 24). Berlin

— 1963b: *Frühe Keramik von Boğazköy* (Boğazköy-Hattuša 3). Berlin

Parzinger, H., Sanz, R. 1992: *Die Oberstadt von Hattuša. Hethitische Keramik aus dem Zentralen Tempelviertel* (Boğazköy-Hattuša 15). Berlin

Sams, G.K. 1994: *The Early Phrygian Pottery. The Gordion Excavations, 1950–1973: Final Reports, IV* (University Museum Monograph 79). Philadelphia

Schmidt, E.F. 1932: *The Alishar Hüyük. Seasons of 1928 and 1929. Volume I* (Oriental Institute Publications 19). Chicago

Seeher, J. 1987: *Demircihüyük III.I: Die Keramik I.* Mainz am Rhein.

— 1997: 'Die Ausgrabungen in Boğazköy-Hattuša 1996' *Archäologischer Anzeiger* 1997: 317–41

— 1998: 'Die Ausgrabungen in Boğazköy-Hattuša 1997' *Archäologischer Anzeiger* 1998: 215–41

— 1999: 'Die Ausgrabungen in Boğazköy-Hattuša 1998 und ein neuer topographischer Plan des Stadtgeländes' *Archäologischer Anzeiger* 1999: 317–44

— 2000a: 'Die Ausgrabungen in Boğazköy-Hattuša 1999' *Archäologischer Anzeiger* 2000: 355–76

— 2000b: *Die bronzezeitliche Nekropole von Demircihöyük-Sarıket* (Istanbuler Forschungen 44). Tübingen

Symington, D. 2001: 'Hittites at Kilise Tepe' in É. Jean, A.M. Dinçol, S. Durugönül (eds), *La Cilicie: Espaces et Pouvoirs Locaux (2e millénaire av. J.-C. – 4e siècle ap. J.-C.) / Kilikia: Mekânlar ve yerel güçler (M.Ö. 2. binyıl – M. S. 4. yüzyıl)*. Paris: 167–84

Tezcan, B. 1956: 'Nallıhan-Beypazarı Çevresinden Getirilen Kaplar Hakkında' *Belleten* 20: 343–7

Voigt, M.M. 1994: 'Excavations at Gordion 1988–1989: the Yassıhöyük Stratigraphic Sequence' in A. Çilingiroğlu, D.H. French (eds), *Anatolian Iron Ages III*. Ankara: 265–93

von der Osten, H.H: 1937: *The Alishar Hüyük. Seasons of 1930–1932. Volume III* (Oriental Institute Publications 30). Chicago

von der Osten, H.H., Schmidt, E.F. 1930: *The Alishar Hüyük. Season of 1927. Volume I* (Oriental Institute Publications 6). Chicago

# Tavium in the first millennium BC: first survey results

## Christoph Gerber
*Heidelberg University*

## Abstract

Tavium is the easternmost of the three Galatian centres and one of the most important cities in Roman central Anatolia. The pre-Roman history of the city still remains to be elucidated. The probable identification with Tabnia and Tawiniyya in the second millennium BC, and also prehistoric surface finds, indicate that this site was a central place from earliest times. From this the importance of the city in the Iron Age can be inferred. But so far we can rely only on pottery discovered by field survey to evaluate the point. The site — although not yet excavated — was surely one of the main Iron Age settlements in central Anatolia.

## Özet

Tavium Roma Döneminde Orta Anadolu'nun en önemli şehirlerinden biri olup, üç Galatya yerleşiminin de en doğuda yer alanıdır. Şehrin Roma Dönemi öncesi tarihi halen tamamiyle açıklığa kavuşturulamamıştır. M.Ö. 2 binyılda Tabnia ve Tawiniyya ile olan olası özdeşleşmesi ve yüzeydeki prehistorik buluntular, bu yerleşimin erken dönemlerden beri merkezi bir konumda olduğunu ortaya koymuştur. Bu noktadan yola çıkarak yerleşimin Demir Çağında da önemli bir yerleşim olduğu sonucuna varabiliriz. Ancak bu durumu savunabilmek için şu anda elimizde olan tek bulgu yüzey araştırmaları sonucu bulunmuş olan çanak çömlektir. Yerleşim — henüz kazılmamış da olsa — hiç şüphesiz Orta Anadaolu'daki en önemli Demir Çağ yerleşimlerinden biriydi.

---

Tavium is located in eastern central Anatolia, near the middle of the Halys bend. It belongs to the village of Büyüknefes in the province of Yozgat and lies approximately 20km south of the Hittite capital Hattuša (fig. 1) (for detailed preliminary reports, see Strobel, Gerber 2003). The ancient city lies in hilly terrain which slopes gently down from the Zincirli Dağ in the north to the Delice Irmak in the south (fig. 2). Geologically it is a very recent formation (Strobel, Gerber 2000: 225). The basin of Musabeyli (which may also be called the Tavium basin) is situated just west of the Yozgat mountains (with heights of up to about 1,500m above sea level) and it is crossed by several valleys which run almost north–south and converge north of Yerköy near the village of Gümüşören. From historical records we know of forests surrounding the city of Tavium.

Tavium itself lies on the gently sloping southern side of a plateau, with a panoramic view deep into Cappadocia to the south and southeast. Approached from the south the city is apparent from afar, but from the north and west it is only visible from the edge of the high plain. The basis for the existence of the settlement is its richness in water. Several springs break through the slope at Tavium, giving it a greenness unique in the region today (see again fig. 2); the water is used for irrigating the vineyards and fields. The second very favourable condition for the location of the settlement is the presence of rocky outcrops south of the slope. A ridge, which emerges from the high plateau, slopes down towards the southwest, eventually disappearing in the valley. The two westernmost outcrops of this ridge provide the natural setting for the two settlement mounds called Büyükkale and Küçükkale (fig. 3). These rock outcrops not only provided natural defences for the settlements on top of them, but also formed a barrier protecting the slope and springs behind them. Thus the location of Tavium is marked by two favourable natural conditions: richness in water and a protected situation on and behind the rocky outcrops.

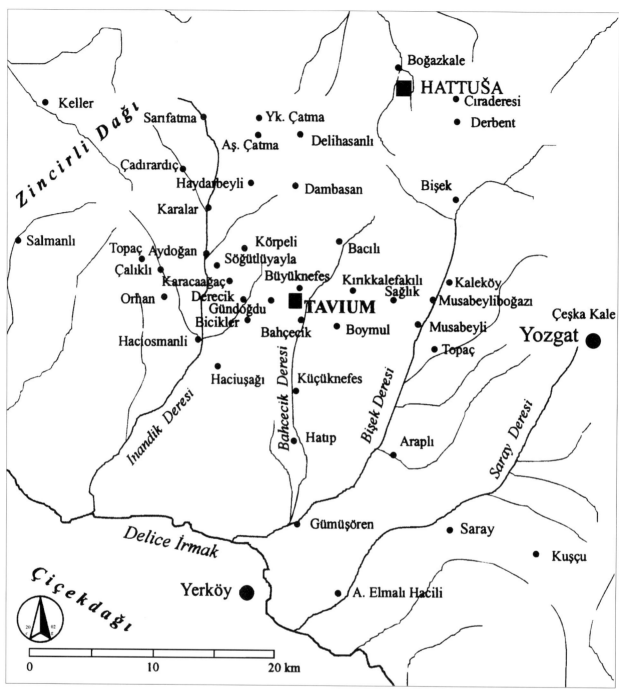

*Fig. 1. Map of the region of Tavium*

For a long time, only Büyükkale and Küçükkale and the areas immediately adjacent to them (fig. 4) were known as Tavium (Belke, Restle 1984: 229ff). The true extent of the ancient city remained unknown until our research began in 1997. Admittedly, Friedrich Cornelius had previously identified the city wall in the so-called *Hangstadt*, but his description (Cornelius 1973: 82ff) was not cited in the literature dealing with Tavium and the wall was rediscovered by us during our first campaign. The city, in fact, extends over the whole area between the streams of Kaleözü in the west and the Nefesçay in the east, and from the rim of the high plateau in the north to the region south of the two settlement mounds. The distance in both directions is around 1,500m, so the area of the settlement at its greatest extent may have covered nearly 1.5 km² (Strobel, Gerber 2000: 237ff). The city is surrounded by several necropoleis and at least nine tumuli (Strobel, Gerber 2000: 249ff).

Kurt Bittel visited the site (i.e. Büyükkale) in the 1930s and was able to identify continuous settlement since Early Bronze Age times (Bittel 1942: 29ff). Our discoveries not only confirm his results but also demonstrate that the beginning of the settlement reaches back into the Chalcolithic period. The earliest finds on Küçükkale are also from the Early Bronze Age (Strobel, Gerber 2000: 253).

The city reached its maximum extent in late Roman/early Byzantine times. Thereafter, the settled area diminished until Byzantine control over central Anatolia vanished. During our first campaign, the director of the Yozgat Museum, Musa Özcan, carried out a rescue excavation in the eastern part of the city after a grave had been robbed. This trench reached late Roman levels at a depth of 3–4m, indicating the existence of deep layers of the Byzantine period. The entire city terrace has a depth of many metres, which covered the earlier levels.

The meaning of the word 'Tavium' is unknown but it may be derived from a root *TAW–. Its origin is also unknown but already by the beginning of the second millennium BC (Assyrian Colony period) the settlement was known as 'Tawnia/Tamnia' (Balkan 1955: 73–5; Garelli 1963: 333–7; Orlin 1970: 118–23). The Hittite name was 'Tawinijja', the Hellenistic-Roman, 'Taouion/Tavium' and the Byzantine, 'Tauia/Tabia' (Strobel, Gerber 2000: 217, n. 9).

The natural conditions of Tavium favoured an important settlement at the site since earliest times. The extent of the Chalcolithic settlement remains unknown because, as yet, sherds of this period have been found only on the western slope of Büyükkale (Strobel, Gerber 2000: 254; 2003). But already in the Early Bronze Age there was a large settlement on the site. The very impressive Early Bronze Age layers at Büyükkale contain very large walls, which may have belonged to a fortress. Küçükkale was also settled, as well as the area between the two mounds. In our 2001 campaign we found, for the first time, Early Bronze Age sherds in the city terrace of the *Weststadt*. This suggests that there may have been a large settlement north of Büyükkale and Küçükkale. If this is correct, the site may have been a city as early as the third millennium BC.

In the Middle Bronze Age, Tavium may have been the 'Karum Tawnia' which is known from a Kültepe letter (Kt f/k 183 from level Ib; Balkan 1955: 73–5). This was the residence of an apparently powerful lord or king. In Hittite times the site may be identified with the important cultic centre of Tawinijja (for which see Haas 1994: 729ff). The site's natural conditions, its short distance to the capital, Hattuša, and the road between these two places (the route was later followed by the

Fig. 2. Tavium from the east, against the high plateau

Fig. 3. Büyükkale and Küçükkale from the south

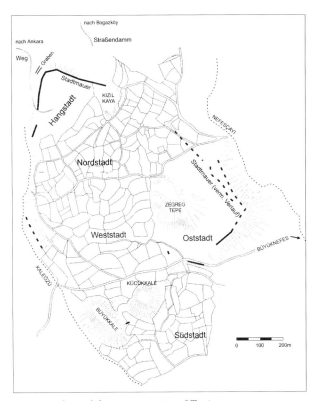

Fig. 4. Plan of the ancient city of Tavium

Roman road), support such an identification, although from Tavium itself very few finds of the Hittite period are known. The importance of the city in post-Hittite times is responsible for the depth to which the second millennium BC remains are buried. None of the other very important Hittite centres achieved an importance as great as Tavium in later times.

The rivalry between Tavium and Hattuša should be stressed here. The parallels between the two cities are remarkable: Tavium lies on a south facing slope opening far to the south, whilst Hattuša lies on a north facing slope opening far to the north. Both cities extend up the slope as far as the high plain and both are surrounded by a trapezoidal plan city wall on the slope. Of course, the city wall which can be seen today at Tavium is of late Roman date, but the parallels should not be overlooked. The discovery of some Hittite sherds in the *Hangstadt* may give a hint as to the extent of the Hittite city. Hattuša/Boğazkale seems to have been more important than Tavium only in Hittite times. After the collapse of the Hittite empire, Tavium regained its former importance as the regional centre. In the Iron Age at Boğazkale there was a settlement with a large fortress, but thereafter only in Hellenistic times (the Galatian settlement), and in the middle Byzantine period did small settlements exist (Seeher 1999: 168–74). The loss of Tavium's political primacy in Hittite times may have been compensated by the high cultic importance of Tavium/Tawinijja in the imperial Hittite religion.

For Iron Age Tavium we have to rely on survey finds, as well as on the historical importance of the site in former and subsequent times. I will return to the Iron Age later in this discussion. The history of Tavium is far better known in the period following the settlement of the Celts, also known as Galatians, in central Anatolia (Strobel 1996; 1998). The Galatian tribe of the Trocmii selected Tavium as their main centre: it was a very important cultic focus, for the worship of Zeus Tavianos. The initial results of our survey in the city area of Tavium indicate that the *Hangstadt* was settled in the late Hellenistic period. At this time Tavium was already an urban centre. This is important because the process of urbanisation in central Anatolia in the Hellenistic period is almost unknown. The theatre may also go back to Hellenistic times, although its visible remains (only the cavea at the southern slope of Zeğreg Tepe is extant) may date to the early Roman period (Strobel, Gerber 2000: 245). The emperor Augustus gave Tavium city status when central Anatolia was integrated into the Roman empire as the province of Galatia. With the introduction of Christianity the city became an episcopal see and was of great importance throughout the Byzantine period. I will not go into details of the history of the city in these later times but, before returning to the Iron Age, let me first provide a short overview of the settlement of Büyükkale and Küçükkale.

Büyükkale rests on a rocky outcrop (fig. 5). While in the south the rock stands out, in the northern part it is covered by nearly 25m of cultural deposits. The west slope was very informative for our survey. It is very steep and therefore has little vegetation. The rains have washed large amounts of pottery out of the slope and have also revealed very large walls. The richness of the ceramic material from this slope provides a rough 'stratigraphy' of the mound — a rather unusual result for a survey. Since we appreciated the presence of this opportunity at the beginning of our survey, we divided the slope into strips, each nearly 3m high, and collected the sherds accordingly. In the uppermost strip, Roman and perhaps later pottery predominated. The following two strips yielded Iron Age pottery and some Hittite sherds. In the four strips below, Early Bronze Age pottery predominated. In the two lowermost strips, the surface material consisted of sherds that had been washed down the slope, and sherds of all periods were well represented (Strobel, Gerber 2000: 252ff). The evidence indicates that the Early Bronze Age settlements of Büyükkale may have had a total depth of about 10m. The latest Early Bronze Age settlement was surrounded by a large wall, visible in the middle part of the west slope (fig. 6). Up to this level, Early Bronze Age pottery is present in large amounts, whilst above the wall very little material was found and most of this could be dated to later than the Early Bronze Age. The absence of large amounts of second millennium BC pottery may be explained by a situation like that at Alişar, where the foundations of the late Early Bronze Age walls were in use until the first millennium BC, thus preventing the erosion of the second millennium BC levels (von der Osten 1937: 287).

*Fig. 5. Büyükkale from the west*

*Fig. 6. Large wall on the west slope of Büyükkale*

On Küçükkale the cultural layers were eroded, and pottery is found in large amounts at the foot of the mound. The many fragments of marble may indicate the presence of a public building, perhaps a temple, in Roman times, and it is possible that most of the earlier cultural layers were removed during the construction of this building. Iron Age pottery is concentrated on the eastern slope, whilst late Hellenistic so-called 'Galatian ware' predominates on the western slope (Strobel, Gerber 2000: 253).

Zeğreg Tepe has provided only very few identifiable pre-Hellenistic sherds.

I shall now return to the discussion of the Iron Age. As yet, the finds are concentrated on Büyükkale and Küçükkale, indicating Iron Age occupation of at least these two mounds. However, as with Early Bronze Age sherds, it may only be a question of time before the first Iron Age sherds are found in the city terrace. Considering the importance of the site in the Early Bronze Age (pottery evidence, fortification walls at Büyükkale), in the second millennium BC (historical evidence emerging from the identification of Tavium with Tabnia and Tawinijja), in Hellenistic times (pottery evidence, extension of the city to the *Hangstadt* and the theatre) and then in the Roman and Byzantine periods (historical evidence), it should be clear that in the Iron Age too, this site was one of the most important settlements in central Anatolia. A more developed understanding of this importance can only be achieved by future excavation. Until then we have to rely on the pottery evidence from survey work.

To conclude, I will discuss some examples of the Iron Age pottery found in our survey. For the chronological subdivision I rely on the results from Boğazkale elaborated by Herrman Genz (Genz 2000; 2001).

The evidence for the Early Iron Age is very scanty. A very small number of sherds with red paint, from the lower part of the west slope at Büyükkale, may belong to this period. Pottery from the Middle Iron Age is well represented. We have many examples of matt dark brown monochrome painting with garlands, well known from Büyükkaya at Boğazkale (figs 7, 8). In the later part of the Middle Iron Age, polychrome painting begins together with painting on white slip (fig. 9) and the first examples of grey ware, known from the Büyükkaya 2 period at Boğazkale. The characteristic ware of the Late Iron Age is polished grey ware, of which we have many examples (fig. 10). Sherds with lustrous paint on a white slip that covers only part of the vessel are rare, and the polychrome painting characteristic of this late phase has not yet been identified in the Tavium survey. A major problem with the Late Iron Age pottery is the revival of Middle Bronze Age forms and wares, including the red polished wares typical of the earlier part of the second millennium BC. Thus, it is impossible (at present) to date securely such pieces to either the early Middle Bronze Age or the Late Iron Age (Hermann Genz, personal communication; Genz this volume). Such difficulties in dating surface finds of pottery can only be resolved by future excavations, at Tavium or elsewhere.

*Fig. 7. Iron Age pottery: dark brown monochrome painting*

Fig. 8. Iron Age pottery: dark brown monochrome painting

Fig. 10. Iron Age pottery: polished grey ware

Fig. 9. Iron Age pottery: polychrome painting

**Acknowledgements**

I thank Michael Roaf (München) for revising the English text. I thank Hermann Genz for the information he shared with me, both in Boğazkale and in Büyüknefes.

**Bibliography**

Balkan, K. 1955: *Observations on the Chronological Problems of the Karum Kaniš*. Ankara

Belke, K., Restle, M. 1984: *Galatien und Lykaonien* (Tabula Imperii Byzantini IV). Vienna

Bittel, K. 1942: *Kleinasiatische Studien* (Istanbuler Mitteilungen 5). Istanbul

Cornelius, F. 1973: *Geschichte der Hethiter*. Darmstadt

Garelli, P. 1963: *Les Assyriens en Cappadoce*. Paris

Genz, H. 2000: 'Die Eisenzeit in Zentralanatolien im Lichte der keramischen Funde vom Büyükkaya in Boğazköy/Hattuša' *TÜBA-AR* 3: 35–54

—2001: 'Iron Age pottery from Çadır Höyük' *Anatolica* 27: 159–70

Haas, V. 1994: *Geschichte der hethitischen Religion*. Leiden

Orlin, L. 1970: *Assyrian Colonies in Cappadocia*. Paris

Seeher, J. 1999: *Hattusha Guide. A Day in the Hittite Capital*. Istanbul

Strobel, K. 1996: *Die Galater I*. Berlin

— 1998: 'Galatia' in H. Causik, H. Schneider (eds), *Neuer Pauly IV*. Stuttgart-Weimar: 742–5

Strobel, K., Gerber, C. 2000: 'Tavium (Büyüknefes, Provinz Yozgat) — Ein regionales Zentrum Anatoliens. Bericht über den Stand der Forschungen nach den ersten drei Kampagnen (1997–1999)' *Istanbuler Mitteilungen* 50: 215–65

— 2003: 'Tavium (Büyüknefes, Provinz Yozgat) — Bericht über die Kampagnen 2000–2002' *Istanbuler Mitteilungen* 53: 131–95

von der Osten, H.H. 1937: *The Alişar Höyük. Seasons of 1930–1932. Volume II*. Chicago

# <sup>LÚ</sup>A.ZUM-*li* versus <sup>LÚ</sup>A.NIN-*li*: some thoughts on the owner of the so-called *Prinzensiegel* at Rusa II's court

## Ursula Hellwag

*Institut für Vorderasiatische Archäologie, München*

### Abstract

Well preserved cylinder seal impressions found at Ayanis show that the seal inscriptions found at other Urartian sites and previously read <sup>LÚ</sup>A.NIN-*li* are to be read either ideographically as <sup>LÚ</sup>A.ZUM-*li* or phonetically as <sup>LÚ</sup>*a·șu-li* and that they are to be interpreted not as 'prince', but as the title of a government official. These seals, therefore, cannot be used as evidence for the existence of additional Urartian kings (the fathers of the <sup>LÚ</sup>A.ZUM-*li*) who were successors of Rusa II. Most probably the <sup>LÚ</sup>A.ZUM-*li* were contemporary with Rusa and cast no light either on possible successors to Rusa or on the events that led to the fall of Urartu.

### Özet

Ayanis'te iyi korunmuş olan silindir mühür baskı yazıtları göstermektedir ki, diğer Urartu yerleşim merkezlerinde daha önce bulunmuş ve <sup>LÚ</sup>A.NIN-*li* olarak okunan mühür yazıtların, ya ideogram olarak <sup>LÚ</sup>A.ZUM-*li* şeklinde, ya da fonetik olarak <sup>LÚ</sup>*a·șu-li* olarak okunmalı ve 'prens' olarak değil, bir resmi görevlisinin ünvanı olarak tanımlanması gerektiğini ortaya koymaktadır. Bu nedenle bu mühür baskıları bilinenlere ilave edilen ve II. Rusa'nın varisleri olarak kabul edilen Urartu Krallarının (<sup>LÚ</sup>A.ZUM-*li* nin babaları) varlıklarını ispat için kullanılmamalıdır. Büyük olasılıkla '<sup>LÚ</sup>A.ZUM-*li*'ler Rusa ile aynı dönemde yaşamışlardı ve ne Rusa'nın olası varisleriydiler, ne de Urartu Krallığının çöküşüne neden olan olaylar üzerinde etkileri vardı.

---

The end of the kingdom of Urartu, and in particular the date of this, must be reconsidered in the light of the results of the current excavations at Ayanis which speak for a terminal date early in the second half of the seventh century BC (Çilingiroğlu, Salvini 2001).

Among the finds from Ayanis are four sealings, bearing cylinder seal impressions with the well known 'sacred' or 'stylised' tree motif (Salvini 2001: 316–18, figs 8b–e; Abay 2001: 323–4), whose owner was the man identified as the <sup>LÚ</sup>A.NIN-*li* from impressions found at Karmir-Blur, Bastam and Toprakkale. The sign previously read as NIN is, on the seal impression from Ayanis, for the first time clearly recognisable as the sign ZUM (fig. 1) (previously suggested in Hellwag 2000 which includes details of previous interpretations). In the Urartian cuneiform script this sign differs from the sign NIN only in three short, rather than long, horizontal wedges before the last vertical wedge, and in three additional ones after it (fig. 2). No-one had paid attention to the fact that the horizontal wedges before the vertical one were rather short, and that those after the

*Fig. 1. Seal impression from Ayanis (Salvini 2001: 316, seal Ay-3)*

*Fig. 2. (a) sign:* NIN *(UKN: 37); (b) sign:* ZUM/șu *(UKN: 37)*

wedge were destroyed or damaged on the previously known impressions, and so the sign had been wrongly read as NIN (on the photograph in Wartke (1993: 68) the sign as ZUM is recognisable).

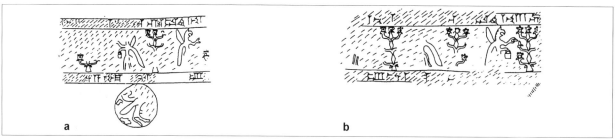

Fig. 3. (a) A1 text 1, Bastam (Salvini 1979: 119; Seidl 1979: 137); (b) A1 text 2, Bastam (Salvini 1979: 124; Seidl 1979: 137)

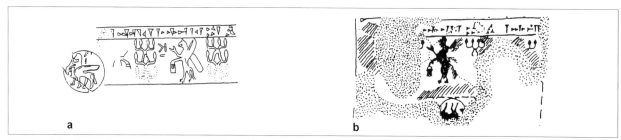

Fig. 4. (a) A2 text 3, Bastam (Salvini 1979: 127; Seidl 1979: 138); (b) A2 UPD 5, Karmir-Blur (UPD: V 1)

Fig. 5. (a) A3 seal impression, Bastam (Seidl 1988: 145); (b) A3? seal impression, Toprakkale (VA 4311, drawing by Hellwag, the original with the kind permission of R.-B. Wartke)

Fig. 6. (a) A4 seal impression, Bastam (Seidl 1988: 145); (b) A4? seal impression, Toprakkale (VA 4297, drawing by Hellwag, the original with the kind permission of R.-B. Wartke)

Fig. 7. (a) A5 seal impression, Bastam (Seidl 1988: 145); (b) A5 UPD 7, Karmir-Blur (UPD: 140)

Fig. 8. (a) A6 seal impression, Bastam (Seidl 1988: 146); (b) A6? UPD 1, Karmir-Blur (UPD: 135)

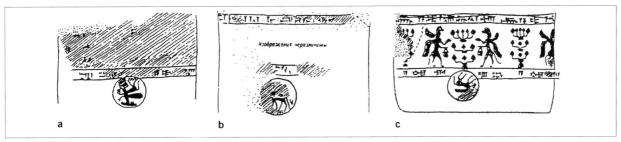

*Fig. 9. (a)* UPD *2, Karmir-Blur (*UPD*: 136); (b)* UPD *3, Karmir-Blur (*UPD*: 137); (c)* UPD *4, Karmir-Blur (*UPD*: 138)*

## Problems with the previous reading

The interpretation of this title LÚA.NIN-*li* as 'prince' was due to Igor M. Diakonoff (1963 = *UPD*: 62). He read the respective cuneiform signs in the seal legends on two clay tablets from Karmir-Blur as LÚA.NIN-*li* = Son of the Queen (*UPD*: 4 [see fig. 9c] and *UPD*: 7 [see fig. 7b]). The *Prinzensiegel* with this title were impressed on a number of official letters found in Karmir-Blur (*UPD*), on clay tablets and numerous bullae from Bastam (Salvini 1979: 123; 1988: 126–7; Seidl 1979: 137–8, 140–2; 1988: 145–6, 149, 151), and on a limited number of bullae from Toprakkale (figs 3–9) (Lehmann-Haupt 1910; 1926; Seidl 2001: 453, fig. 4). In the seal legends the names of the *Prinzen* and of their fathers are given (see table 1, nos 1–4). Were these persons merely male members of the royal family at Rusa II's court? Or were they crown-princes and their fathers reigning sover-

eigns? In this case the fathers must have been successors of Rusa II — thus extending the list of Urartian kings considerably (Arutjunjan 1974: 427–8; Salvini 1995: 115, tab. 116).

Since the scene of the stylised tree is repeated in an almost identical manner on seal cylinders it is reasonable to assume that the other cylinder seal impressions with the same motif belonged to individuals with the same title. This allows us to add another two individuals who we can suppose bore the title (table 1, nos 3, 4). Although the scene on the impression *UPD* 3 (fig. 9b) is not legible, the impression of the stamped end of the seal shows the same four legged winged horse as on the inscribed seals, and so it is probable that it too belonged to this group. If so, we can add Erimena (table 1, no. 5) to the list of *Prinzen* or their fathers.[1]

| | Seal owner | Transcription | lúA.ZUM-*li* inscribed | Findspot | Reference | Figure |
|---|---|---|---|---|---|---|
| **1** | Rusa, son of Rusa | $^mRu$-$sa$-$a$-$i$ $^mRu$-$sa$-$he$ | yes | Karmir-Blur | *UPD*: 4 | fig. 9c |
| **2** | Rusa, son of Sardu(ri) | $^mRu$-$sa$-[$a$-$i$ $^m$]$^dSar_5$-$du$-$hi$ | yes | Bastam | Bastam 1 = A1 | fig. 3a |
| | | | yes | Bastam | Bastam 2 = A1 | fig. 3b |
| **3** | Sar(duri), son of Sardu(ri)[2] | $^{m.d}Sar_5$[-$^?$] $^dSar_5$-$du$[-$ri$]-hi | no | Bastam | Bastam 3 = A2 | fig. 4a |
| | | | no | Karmir-Blur | *UPD*: 5 | fig. 4b |
| **4** | Sarduri, son of Rusa[3] | $^{m.d}Sar_5$-$du$-$ri$ $^{[m]}Ru$-$sa$ | no | Bastam | Bastam sealings = A6[4] | fig. 8a |
| | | | no | Karmir-Blur | *UPD*: 1 | fig. 8b |
| **5** | Erimena | $^m$]$E$-[$r$]$i$-$me$-$n$[$a$-$n$]$é$ ? | no | Karmir-Blur | *UPD*: 3 | fig. 9b |

*Table 1. The names of the owners and their fathers on the* Prinzensiegel

[1] See Movsisyan 2000: 133–9, who read the name as Rusa, son of Erimena, as Zimansky (1985: 80, 3) proposed. If this is correct, and my examination of the tablet confirms this reading, it would be additional evidence for Rusa (III) and for his having spent some time in Karmir-Blur as LÚA.ZUM-*li*. The stone inscriptions from Erebuni/Arin-Berd and Argištiḫinili/Armavir record the activities of a Rusa son of Erimena without any title (*HchI*: 132; *UKN*: 288; *UKN*: II 458).

[2] There is sufficient space for these signs to have been inscribed on the seal as Seidl has shown (1979: 137–8). Abbreviated writings are used in Urartian texts (although they are not

common). See Melikišvili 1971: 20; Salvini 1988: 140; 1995: 115; Seidl 1998: 509, Anm. 3 $^mAn$-$ri$ $^mAn$-$ri$-$du$-$i$.

[3] This individual is to be identified with $^{m.d}Sar_5$-$du$-$ri$-$še$ $^mRu$-$sa$-$a$-[$hi$]-$n$[$i$-$še$] mentioned in the text of the letter.

[4] See the comments of Seidl: 'Möglicherweise stammt A6 von dem Siegel der Abrollung auf *UPD* 1: Mischwesen des Stempels nach links, baumähnlich gegliedert; doch sind alle Abrollungen zu schlecht, um etwas Sicheres sagen zu können' (Seidl 1988: 149, fig. 8) and 'bei B.B. Piotrovskij, Urartu [Geneva 1969] Abb. 37 ist auch der Stempelabdruck auf der unteren Kante zu erkennen' (Seidl 1979: 141); see also Piotrovskij (1980: 27, Abb. 10).

| King | Transcription | Translation | Reference |
|------|--------------|-------------|-----------|
| Menua | *i²]-na-a-ni-e* <sup>lü</sup>*e-re-li* | 'this² king' | *HchI*: 19a; *UKN*: 32; *KUKN*: 49₄ |
| | *a-i-še-e-i* <sup>lü</sup>e-[*ri-li-e-še* ? | 'sometimes/ever the king' | *HchI*: 20; *UKN*: 38; *KUKN*: 55₅; Dinçol 1976 |
| | LUGAL *e-ri-la-a-ú-e* | 'king of kings' | *HchI*: 47; *UKN*: 72; *KUKN*: 90₆ |
| | // LUGAL LUGAL-*li-li* | 'king of kings' | *HchI*: 23; *UKN*: 36; *KUKN*: 53₂₄ |
| Sarduri II | LUGAL *e-ri-la-ú-e* | 'king of kings' | *UKN*: 168; *HchI*: 109; *KUKN*: 274₁₀ |
| Rusa II's time | *'a-al-du* LUGAL-*li* | 'protected² (be/is) the king' | Salvini 1979: 118, 123 |

*Table 2. Writings for 'king' =* e-ri/e-li *in Urartian inscriptions*

In the Ayanis report, Salvini also discussed the problem of attributing these seals to princes and its consequences for dating the end of the Urartian kingdom, and he proposes that they were used by unknown officials who were members of the king's immediate circle. Although 'Son of the Queen' together with its historical implications must now be removed, it is clear that the <sup>LÜ</sup>A.ZUM-*li* had a high position at court, since as Salvini (2001: 23–4) observed 'the persons that bear this title (<sup>LÜ</sup>*a-ṣu-li*) have dynastic names and patronyms — different from all the other officials that appear in the tablets and bullae and must therefore be considered members of the royal family'.

**A phonetic reading of** <sup>LÜ</sup>*a-ṣu-li*

K. Radner (Hellwag 2000: 27, n. 39) and Salvini (2001: 23) have both suggested a phonetic reading of the title as *a-ṣu-li*. If they are correct, the <sup>LÜ</sup>*a-ṣu-li* might be derived from an Urartian stem *a-ṣu-še* as a type of sacrifice, according to König (*HchI*: 175), or a celebration, according to Melikišvili (*UKN*: 390) and Arutjunjan (2001: 436–7), while according to Salvini the meaning is uncertain (Salvini 2001: 23, n. 67). The final -*li* might be interpreted as a Hurrian suffix denoting an office holder or profession, as pointed out by Wilhelm (1992: 244) (as far as I know, no expert in the Urartian language has discussed Wilhelm's suggestion). Diakonoff wrote (1970: 70) that he knew of no Urartian attestations for this kind of Hurrian suffix, but this could be evidence for the use of such.

This reading may be compared with the Urartian word *e-ri/e-li* 'king', normally written with the sign LUGAL or MAN, which is one of the few singular nouns ending in -*li*. In line 24 of the inscription of Menua from Yazılıtaş (*KUKN*: 53₂₄) and in line 5 from Bastam no. 1 the word for king was written LUGAL-*li* with the phonetic complement indicating the reading *ereli* (see table 2, second column, lines 3, 5). The phonetic writing of *e-ri/e-li* is attested in the eighth century inscriptions of Menua (here also as <sup>LÜ</sup>*e-ri/e-li*) and Sarduri II (table 2).

Another one of Rusa I from Topzawa (line 11), (mentioned in *UKN*: 264; *HchI*: 122 and *KUKN*: 387) is without any evidence in this case because of missing signs, according to Salvini 1984.

In a similar way <sup>LÜ</sup>*aṣuli* could represent an important member of the king's court in Ayanis, Bastam, Karmir-Blur and Toprakkale. It is possible to construct a family tree (fig. 10; see also Kroll 1984: 161, 165) for the latest Urartian kings including all the names of *Prinzensiegel*, assuming that Erimena was the son or even a brother of Rusa II. In this case they would indeed have been princes, and *aṣuli* might be the Urartian word for prince.

Titles, however, were normally written logographically and not phonetically in Urartian official inscriptions (see for example Zimansky 1985: 84; see also the so called 'king seals' of Rusa II, Seidl 1988: 146–7) and a logographic interpretation is in my opinion more likely.

**A logographic reading of** <sup>LÜ</sup>A.ZUM-*li*

If one takes the different parts of the title separately it is possible to suggest an etymology and also a possible interpretation of the duties associated with the title.

*The sign A*

In Urartian the logogram A(MEŠ) is generally (by Menua, Rusa I, Argišti II, Rusa II) equated with Akkadian *mû* (I): 'water, liquid' (*AHw*: 664; Borger 1986: no. 579; *UKN*: 38).

*The sign ZUM*

Diakonoff (*UPD*: 119, no. 231) and also König (*HchI* 1957: Taf. 103) mention the sign ZUM (= SAL/(or MUNUS) + ÁŠ) as being common in Urartian. According to the *Akkadisches Handwörterbuch* (*AHw*: 342 II b) and the *Chicago Assyrian Dictionary* (Oppenheimer 1956: 54–5 ḫalu A) this sign can be read in Akkadian as ḫialum, ḫâlu meaning 'exude', also used in Neo-Assyrian times literally and metaphorically in the context of 'giving birth/to be delivered' and according to Borger (1986: no. 555) ZUM = ḫâlu: 'to let (a liquid)

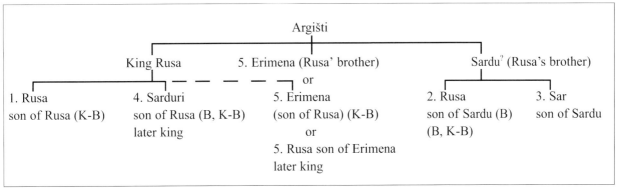

*Fig. 10. Family tree for the latest Urartian kings.  B = Bastam; K-B = Kamir Blur (see table 1)*

emerge/to let flow out'.  So, the reading ᴸᵁ̇A.ZUM-*li* could mean 'he, who lets the water flow out' — the term for an office that describes the task of the office holder.

I would like to put the 'one who lets the water flow out' in the context of the opening of the canal sluices, one of the most important tasks in an economy like that of Urartu which relied on carefully managed water supplies and irrigation.  For this there are plenty of archaeological and philological examples (Belli 1997; Zimansky 1998: 81–4; Bagg 2000: 132–5, 140, n. 154).  Bagg described in detail Urartian techniques for water management, including sluices on reservoirs, drainage pipes and canals, and expressed his admiration for their achievements.  Only the right amount of water brings optimum results and therewith economic prosperity for the people living in the areas concerned; the opening of the sluices would therefore have been an appropriate task.  The ᴸᵁ̇A.ZUM-*lis* could have been responsible for such an almost priest-like, ritual office in Urartu, conducting the sluice opening ceremony in the name of Haldi, Teišeba (the weather god) and Šivini (the sun god), the three highest deities in the Urartian pantheon.  According to König this ceremony was described on Rusa II's stele from Zwartnoths and on a stele fragment of Argišti II (*HchI*: 126).[5]

Since the same seal was used in different centres, e.g. at Bastam and Karmir-Blur and perhaps also at Toprakkale (figs 4–8), the owner must have either travelled there or the bulla/letter must have been sent from one place to the other.  If the former, then the ᴸᵁ̇A.ZUM-*li* could well have travelled with the king and

there need not have been more than one ᴸᵁ̇A.ZUM-*li* at any particular time.  If the latter, one can imagine that there were a number of experts, one at each Urartian fortress, at the same time.  They could have used either a personal seal with their name and their father's name, or an office seal for orders and letters or to document deliveries of goods and other tasks (Zimansky 1985: 81–3; Salvini 2001: 316–18, figs 8b, c, d, e; Abay 2001: 323–4).

Maybe there was a rotation system so that the office holders changed during the reign of Rusa II.  Or new appointments would have been made when previous office holders died.  This would explain the seal variations and the different occupants of the post at the time of Rusa II.

The office holder ᴸᵁ̇A.ZUM-*li* would have been — in today's terms — a 'minister for water' at the Urartian royal court.  Naturally, this explanation of the sign ZUM is speculative and can be questioned — and other explanations are possible.  Most recently Seidl (2001) closely examined the Toprakkale sealings in the Vorderasiatisches Museum in Berlin, with regard to their function.  These sealings, as well as the numerous clay bullae in Bastam, the small number from Ayanis and also the texts on the sealed tablets from there and Karmir-Blur (Zimansky 1985: 81–3) seem to have formed part of the court administrative procedures.  S. Dalley and M. Roaf have both in personal communications suggested that the title ᴸᵁ̇A.ṢU-*li* might be connected with the Akkadian ⁽ˡᵘ⁾A.ZU (ZU can be read *ṣu* or *sú*) which can be read either as *asû* 'doctor', or *barû* 'divination priest'.  Hence -*li* could be a phonetic complement for the Urartian word for doctor or divination priest.  The title ˡᵘA.ZU is also attested for a divination priest in Hurrian texts (Salvini, Wegner 1980; Haas 1984).

## Iconography

To conclude, I will investigate the iconography of the seals — the design on the cylinder and on the stamp of the seals — and show how this supports my interpretation of the role of the ᴸᵁ̇A.ZUM-*li*.

[5] Melikišvili (*UKN*: 281: [*a-še* Aᴹᴱˢ *e-ši-a ṣi-ú-l*[*i*] . . . ) and Arutjunjan (*KUKN*: 421₂₂, n. 13: [*a-še* Aᴹᴱˢ *e-ši-a-ṣi-ú-l*[*i*] ...) do not translate the verb in this passage but see a connection with the Hurrian word *eši/e* 'heaven'.  One might compare the passage in Sargon's eighth campaign which was translated by Bagg (2000: 128) '. . . Obstbäume und Weinstöcke ließ er (Ursā [=Rusa]) wie mit Regen beregnen'.

The seals used by the $^{LÚ}$A.ZUM-*li* are the typical Urartian cylinder stamp seals and all bear very similar images (figs 1, 3–9): on the cylinder surface there is a repetitive picture with almost the same iconography in all cases: a 'stylised' or 'sacred' tree (sometimes called the 'tree of life') with supernatural genies arranged antithetically on both sides, sometimes with various hieroglyphs in the field. Seidl (1988: 145–6, 151) in her Bastam catalogue distinguished six variants, A1 to A6, on altogether ten to 13 specimens. The end of the cylinder seal was engraved with the design of a winged horse carrying a small bucket, and with similar hieroglyphs to those on the cylindrical surface.

The small bucket seems to me to be one of the most important details of all the $^{LÚ}$A.ZUM-*li* seal depictions. We find it on cylinders and stamps, and even those depictions which differ in other details always show it. There are small silver and bronze buckets among the metal finds from early Urartian times (ninth and first half of the eighth centuries). Sometimes an inscription certifies that these vessels belonged to members of the royal family. Two carry the name of Išpuini, one of which was given by this king to his grandson Inušpa (Salvini 1978: 171–4; Merhav 1991: 214–19; Wartke 1993: Taf. 79); the other bucket is of the same date (late ninth century) and is decorated with a repetitive frieze which shows the typical ceremony at the 'sacred tree' (Merhav 1991: 216).

The motif of the 'sacred tree' has a long tradition in the Near East, going back hundreds of years before Urartian times (Keel, Uehliger 1992: 32). Flanked by animals and hybrid beings, it is a favourite motif on cylinder seals, especially on those of the Mittani period (and maybe the Urartian representations allude to Hurrian tradition). In Neo-Assyrian palaces, wall reliefs show the tree with human or eagle headed genies (e.g. in the northwest palace of Ashurnasirpal; see also Hrouda 1964) who hold buckets in their left hands. The interpretations of the motif vary from a fertilisation scene to one of consecration and cleansing ritual, with defence and protection (symbolised by the apotropaic genies) against the powers that threaten the royal prosperity playing an important role.

Dalley in a personal communication has mentioned that griffin and winged figures are associated with the magico-medical practices of doctors and that a bucket of the above mentioned shape is also illustrated as being used by a doctor and/or incantation priest in Egypt. The winged figures are normally identified as *apkallu* (*ūmu-*, bird- and fish-*apkallu*) or sages, with an apotropaic function involved in magico-medical practices too (see especially Wiggermann 1992: 73–8). These divine beings are also closely associated with the human sages

(experts or scholars) at the court who included in their number scribes, diviners, astrologers, etc. Wiggermann suggests that the buckets contained holy water necessary for the performance of various rituals (1992: 66–8; see also Seidl 1985: 45–8).

In a similar way one can interpret the Urartian tree and genie scenes, whose depictions are similar to the Assyrian ones. These depictions are found on helmets, belts, seals, a pyxis lid, and on the above mentioned little bucket. Sacred trees and supernatural beings can be seen on the stone blocks of Kef Kalesi and in the wall paintings at Erebuni and Altıntepe, in typical Urartian style. Hançar connects the Urartian tree to 'a function that encompasses decoration, religious, ritual service and state representation' (1966: 98). Çevik (1997; 1999) discussed the tree in Urartu and proposed that it was a portable ritual object which was used at funeral ceremonies.

## Conclusion

The small seal pictures with two griffins (exceptionally at Ayanis two different beings, one a griffin and the other with a human head) and winged horses, both with human arms, are, according to Seidl (1979: 142, n. 13), probably confined to Urartian art alone. They mirror the particular religious-political ideas and conceptions which the owners of the seal were supposed to realise: to protect the prosperity of the king with the help of the gods by, for instance, expert operation of the sluices. Therefore it is possible that the ritual economic office of $^{LÚ}$A.ZUM-*li* can be 'read' directly from the seal depiction. Here we have a seal that contains the term for the office of 'minister for water' both in the inscription and in the image. This interpretation of $^{LÚ}$A.ZUM-*li* is supported by archaeological findings as well as by the art-historical study of the seal iconography, and by our knowledge of Urartian culture. The $^{LÚ}$A.ZUM-*li* was a person at the royal court of Rusa II, in a priest-like position with administrative responsibilities, who appeared *a-še* A$^{MEŠ}$-*e ši-a-ṣi-ú-l*[*i*] … 'when the waters are enabled to flow (= the sluices are opened)', a ceremony described by Argišti II as well as by Rusa II (*HchI*: 125–6, 156–7).

The $^{LÚ}$A.ZUM-*lis* were probably male members of the royal family, but they offer us no additional information about the order of Urartian kings; it is more likely now that those known were contemporaries of Rusa II (in Bastam, Karmir-Blur, Toprakkale and Ayanis). These observations do not affect the number of rulers of Urartu after Rusa II. The order of the later kings, Sarduri and Rusa son of Erimena, is not certain (Salvini 1995: 116), but, in any case, Rusa II was the only one of these rulers to have exercised any significant power.

**Acknowledgements**

I would like to thank the director of the excavations of Ayanis, Professor Altan Çilingiroğlu, for giving me the opportunity to participate in the Fifth Anatolian Iron Ages Symposium and for his hospitality, both in congress and in an unforgettable visit to Ayanis. I also express my gratitude to Professor Michael Roaf, without whose support the publication of this article would not have been possible.

**Bibliography**

*Abbreviations*

*AHw* = von Soden, W. 1985: *Akkadisches Handwörterbuch* (second edition). Wiesbaden

*HchI* = König, F.W. 1955–1957: *Handbuch der chaldischen Inschriften* (Archiv für Orientforschung Beiheft 8). Graz

*KUKN* = Arutjunjan, N.V. 2001: *Korpus Urartskich Klinoobraznich Nadpisej*. Yerevan

*UKN* = Melikišvili, G.A. 1960: *Urartskie klinoobraznye nadpisi* (second edition). Moscow

*UPD* = Diakonoff, I.M. 1963: *Urartskie pis'ma i dokumenty*. Moscow, Leningrad

Abay, E. 2001: 'Seals and sealings' in A. Çilingiroğlu, M. Salvini (eds), *Ayanis I. Ten years' Excavations at Rusahinili Eiduru-kai 1989–1998*. Rome: 321–53

Arutjunjan, N.V. 1974: 'Problèmes concernant la dernière période de l'histoire d'Urartu' *Acta Antiqua Academiae Scientiarum Hungaricae* 22: 415–28

Bagg, A.M. 2000: *Assyrische Wasserbauten. Landwirtschaftliche Wasserbauten im Kernland Assyriens zwischen der 2. Hälfte des 2. und der 1. Hälfte des 1. Jahrtausends v. Chr.* Mainz

Belli, O. 1997: *Doğu Anadolu'da Urartu Sulama Kanalları — Urartian Irrigation Canals in Eastern Anatolia*. Istanbul

Borger, R. 1986: *Assyrisch-babylonische Zeichenliste*. Neukirchen, Vluyn

Çevik, N. 1997: 'On Urartian priests' *Archäologische Mitteilungen aus Iran* 29: 229–42

—1999: 'Hayat Ağacı'nın Urartu kült törenlerindeki yeri ve kullanım biçimi' *Jahrbuch für Kleinasiatische Forschung* 15: 335–67

Çilingiroğlu, A., Salvini, M. 2001: 'The historical background of Ayanis' in A. Çilingiroğlu, M. Salvini (eds), *Ayanis I. Ten Years' Excavations at Rusahinili Eiduru-kai 1989–1998*. Rome: 15–24

Diakonoff, I.M. 1970: *Hurrisch und Urartäisch*. Munich

Dinçol, A.M. 1976: 'Die neuen urartäischen Inschriften aus Körzut' *Istanbuler Mitteilungen* 26: 19–30

Haas, V. 1984: *Die Serien itkahi und itkalzi des AZU-Priesters, Rituale für Tašmišarri und Tatuhepa sowie weitere Texte mit Bezug auf Tašmišarri*. Rome

Hançar, F. 1966: 'Das urartäische Lebensbaummotiv' *Iraniqua Antiqua* 6: 92–108

Hellwag, U. 2000: '"Sohn der Königin": LÚA.NIN-li oder "Wasserwirtschaftsminister": LÚA.ZUM-li? Überlegungen zu einem "fragwürdigen" Amt am urartäischen Königshof' *Akkadica* 117: 20–43

Hrouda, B. 1964: 'Zur Herkunft des assyrischen Lebensbaumes' *Baghdader Mitteilungen* 3: 41–51

Keel, O., Uehliger, C. 1992: *Göttinnen, Götter und Gottessymbole*. Freiburg, Basel, Wien

Kroll, S. 1984: 'Urartus Untergang in anderer Sicht' *Istanbuler Mitteilungen* 34: 151–70

Lehmann-Haupt, C.F. 1910: *Armenien einst und jetzt* (Band. 1). Berlin

— 1926: *Armenien einst und jetzt* (Band. 2/1). Berlin

Melikišvili, G.A. 1971: *Die urartäische Sprache*. Rome

Merhav, R. 1991: 'Ceremonial buckets' in R. Merhav (ed.), *Urartu. A Metalworking Center in the First Millennium BCE*. Jerusalem: 214–19

Movsisyan, A. 2000: 'An important correction concerning one cuneiform tablet from Karmir blur' *The Countries and Peoples of the Near and Middle East* 19: 133–9

Oppenheimer, A.L. et al. (eds) 1956: *The Assyrian Dictionary of the Oriental Institute of the University of Chicago. Volume VI:H*. Chicago

Piotrovskij, B.B. 1960: 'Urartskie nadpisi iz raskopok Karmir-blura 1939–1958' *Epigraphika Vostoka* 13: 105–9

— 1969: *Urartu/Ourartou*. Geneva

— 1970: *Karmir-blur Katalog*. Leningrad

— 1980: *Urartu*. Munich

Salvini, M. 1978: 'A dedicatory inscription of the Urartian king Išpuini' *Assur* 1: 171–4

— 1979: 'Die urartäischen Tontafeln aus Bastam' in W. Kleiss (ed.), *Bastam I*. Berlin: 115–31

— 1984: 'La bilingue urarteo-assira di Rusa I' in P.E. Pecorella, M. Salvini (eds), *Tra lo Zagros e l'Urmia*. Rome: 79–95

— 1988: 'Die urartäischen Schriftdenkmäler aus Bastam' in W. Kleiss (ed.), *Bastam II*. Berlin: 126–7

— 1995: *Geschichte und Kultur der Urartäer*. Darmstadt

— 2001: 'Inscriptions on clay' in A. Çilingiroğlu, M. Salvini (eds), *Ayanis I. Ten Years' Excavations at Rusahinili Eiduru-kai 1989–1998*. Rome: 279–318

Salvini, M., Wegner, I. 1980: 'Die hethitisch-hurritischen Rituale des LÚAZU-Priesters' *Studi Micenei ed Egeo-Anatolici* 22: 87–95

Seidl, U. 1979: 'Die Siegelbilder' in W. Kleiss (ed.), *Bastam I*. Berlin: 137–49

— 1985: 'Ein assyrisches Eimerchen' *Archäologische Mitteilungen aus Iran* 18: 45–8

— 1988: 'Die Siegelbilder' in W. Kleiss (ed.), *Bastam II*. Berlin: 145–54

— 1998: 'Rezension zu M. Salvini 1995: Geschichte und Kultur der Urartäer' *Klio* 80.2: 509–10

— 2001: 'Siegelabdrücke auf Tonverschlüssen aus Toprakkale' in J-W. Meyer, M. Nowák, A. Pruss (eds), *Beiträge zur Vorderasiatischen Archäologie Winfried Orthmann gewidmet*. Frankfurt: 446–55

Wartke, R-B. 1993: *Urartu — das Reich am Ararat*. Mainz

Wiggermann, F.A.M. 1992: *Mesopotamian Protective Spirits. The Ritual Texts*. Groningen

Wilhelm, G. 1992: 'Hurritische Berufsbezeichnungen auf -li' *Studi Micenei ed Egeo-Anatolici* 29: 239–44

Zimansky, P. 1985: *Ecology and Empire: the Structure of the Urartian State*. Chicago

— 1988: 'MB2/OB5 excavations and the problem of Urartian bone rooms' in W. Kleiss (ed.), *Bastam II*. Berlin: 107–24

— 1995: 'An Urartian Ozymandias' *Biblical Archaeologist* 58.2: 94–100

— 1998: *Ancient Ararat. A Handbook of Urartian Studies*. New York

# The northern border of the Urartian kingdom

## Kemalettin Köroğlu
*Marmara University, Istanbul*

### Abstract

Immediately following its foundation, the kingdom of Urartu expanded in a northerly direction. From the evidence of Urartian royal inscriptions and other remains it appears that Urartian armies reached as far north as the modern southern boundary of Georgia. However, there is a difference both in distribution and in kind between those Urartian remains found in the lake Van basin and those of the upper Kura basin. For example, to the north of the Aras river and to the west of the Arpaçay, in the time of Minua, Argishti I and Sarduri II, only inscriptions have been found. These inscriptions refer only to the name of the king, the areas plundered and the loot taken. Furthermore, in this region there are no known Urartian style rock-cut tombs with several rooms, nor are there square temples or large administrative centres. It seems that the northern boundary for these types of remains runs along or possibly slightly north of the Aras valley. Hence, when drawing the northern boundaries for Urartu we have to choose between an area that includes all inscriptions, even those referring only to looting, and one which takes in only large building works. In this article, the northern boundary and the related issue of the localisation of the land of Qulha are reviewed in the light of known Urartian remains and new evidence from surveys in the Ardahan region.

### Özet

Urartu Krallığı, özellikle yazıtlar ve diğer kalıntılardan anlaşıldığına göre kuruluşunun hemen arkasından ülkenin kuzeyine doğru genişlemeye başlamış ve ordular kuzeyde modern Gürcistan sınırına kadar ulaşmışlardır. Ancak Van bölgesindeki Urartu kalıntıları ile Yukarı Kura havzasındakilerin yapısı ve dağılımı arasında belirgin farklılıklar bulunmaktadır. Örneğin Aras Nehri'nin kuzeyinde, Arpaçay'ın batısında, Minua, I. Argişti ve II. Sarduri donemlerine ait yalnızca yazıtlar bulunmuştur. Bunların hepsi kral adı, yağmalanan yerler ve alınan ganimetlerden söz ederler. Herhangi bir inşaattan veya imar faaliyetinden söz etmezler. Ayrıca bu bölgede Urartu stilinde çok odalı kaya mezarı, kule biçimli kare tapınak veya büyük bir yönetim merkezi bilinmemektedir. Bu türde kalıntıların kuzey sınırı Aras Vadisi veya biraz kuzeyi gibi görünmektedir. Bu nedenlerle Urartu'nun kuzey sınırını çizerken, ordularının ilerleyiş yönünü gösteren yazıtları da kapsayan geniş alan ile büyük yapıların bulunduğu daha dar bölge arasında bir seçim yapmak durumundayız. Bu yazıda, bilinen Urartu kalıntıları ve Ardahan bölgesinden yeni yüzey bulguları ışığında, kuzey sınır problemi ve bununla ilişkili olarak Qulha ülkesinin lokalizasyonu yeniden ele alınacak ve tartışılacaktır.

The land of Urartu consists of a series of mountain plateaux that increase in height as one goes northwards, the exception being the Iğdır, Erivan and Nakhichevan sections of the Aras valley. When one looks at where Urartian remains are located on the map, it is evident that they are not equally distributed between, for example, the Van region and regions in the extreme north such as those around Ardahan and Kars or the area between Iğdır and Horasan.

In this article I will discuss archaeological remains and historical geographical problems of the northern regions of the Urartian kingdom, using evidence obtained from recent surveys conducted in the provinces of Ardahan and Artvin. I will focus especially on the area north of the Aras and west of the Arpaçay, where it seems that the only evidence for an Urartian presence is in the form of inscriptions (fig. 1). I will also consider the equation that has been made between Kolkhis and Qulha.

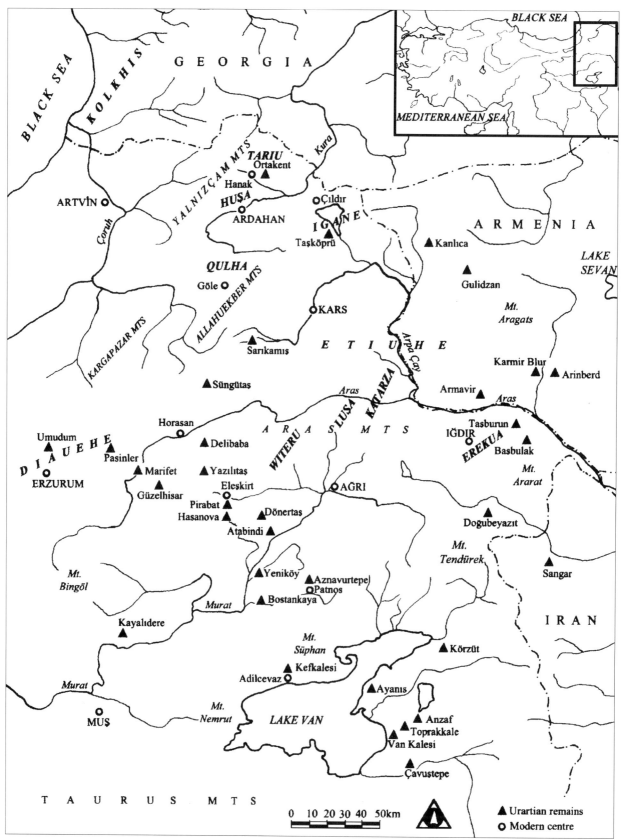

*Fig. 1. Location of remains in the northern area of Urartu*

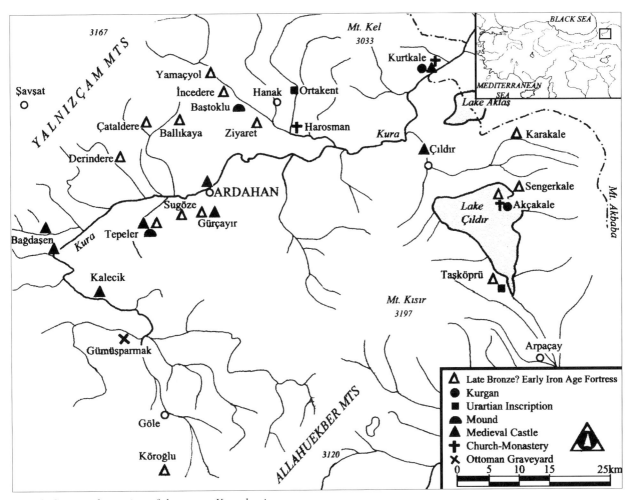

*Fig. 2. Surveyed remains of the upper Kura basin*

First of all it will be useful to look at the campaigns undertaken and the main building activities in this area, in order to clarify the politics of Urartu on its northern boundary.

The first campaigns to the north were made in the founding years of the Urartian kingdom, under Ishpuini (830–810 BC). In this period the first campaigns to distant regions were undertaken, specifically against the tribes of Witeru, Luša and Katarza, and the land of Etiuhe (*UKN*: 20–2) which are placed in or to the north of the Aras mountains (Diakonoff, Kashkai 1981). One of the several inscriptions referring to these campaigns was found near Eleşkirt (*UKN*: 23).

Campaigns in the north against Diauehe and Erekua were conducted under Minua (810–780 BC). It is generally accepted that Diauehe is the region around Erzurum and that Erekua is in the Iğdır region (Diakonoff, Kashkai: 25–6, 31–2). The Yazılıtaş (*UKN*: 36) and Süngütaş (*UKN*: 37: Zivin) inscriptions from east of Erzurum mention these campaigns, whilst the Pasinler (*UKN*: 69), Delibaba (*UKN*: 68) and Pirabat (Dinçol 1989) inscriptions refer to building activities in the same area. It appears from the Yazılıtaş inscription that the land of Diauehe was left under its own ruler but was obliged to pay tribute to Urartu. At the same time, however, Urartian building activities were going on to the east of Diauehe, particularly on the south bank of the Aras. Likewise in the Iğdır region, the Taşburun and Başbulak inscriptions refer to building activities in the area, whose purpose was doubtless to strengthen ties between the region and Tushpa (*UKN*: 30–1, 70).

Under Argishti I (780–756 BC) the Urartian state put emphasis on developing the far northern area and it was in this period that the Urartian armies made their most far reaching advances. The northernmost Urartian inscriptions, found at Ortakent near Hanak (Dinçol, Dinçol 1992), and at Kanlıca (*UKN*: 133) near Leninakan, form the basis for this argument. According to the Horhor inscriptions (*UKN*: 127 I), campaigns to Diauehe and to Luša, Katarza, Witeruhi and Etiuhe again took place as they had under Minua. There were also raiding campaigns to areas such as Tariu, Bia and Huša in the far north. We have some idea about the direction of the campaigns and the lands through which

Fig. 3. Lake Çıldır and Sengerkale

Fig. 5. Ziyaret

Fig. 4. Detail of the walls of Sengerkale

Fig. 6. Detail of the walls of Ziyaret

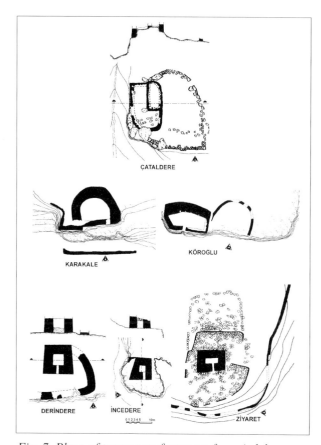

Fig. 7. Plans of tower type fortresses from Ardahan

they passed from the Pirabat (Payne 1996), Sarıkamış (*UKN*: 130) and Hanak inscriptions. Places like Bia, Huša and Tariu, which had previously been located according to the Taşköprü inscription, have now been relocated further north as a result of the discovery of the Hanak-Ortakent inscription (Dinçol, Dinçol 1992). At the same time the cities of Erebuni (Arin-Berd) and Argishtihinili (Armavir-Blur) were built on the fertile land to the north of the Aras river, and the area settled by the Urartians was extended to the left bank of the Aras (*UKN*: 127–8, 137).

The political approach to the northern area did not particularly change under Sarduri II (756–730 BC). According to Sarduri's annals, the Diauehe region required another campaign to bring it back into submission. This would imply that the region had not been brought under direct central government control. Other looting campaigns were made to the north, to places like Iga and Etiune, and also to Qulha (*UKN*: 155–6) which is here mentioned for the first time. The Qulha campaign will be discussed below. Inscriptions of Sarduri II have been found at Güzelhisar (Aydın 1991) and Taşköprü (*UKN*: 159), both of which lie within the region that Argisti I had previously tried to subdue.

Of the later kings, Rusa II carried out major developments in the north, in particular building the new city of Karmir Blur in the lake Sevan basin (fig. 1).

It appears from the northernmost inscriptions that Urartian forces went as far north as the modern border between Turkey and Georgia (Kleiss 1992). However, I would question whether this region ever actually became a part of the Urartian state in the same way as did the south bank of the Aras, or the Erevan plain for example. Before answering this question I will consider the archaeological remains to be found in the Ardahan plain which constitutes the upper Kura basin.

There are three types of fortifications in the Ardahan region. They are to be found in the foothills surrounding the plains of Ardahan, Çıldır, Göle and Hanak (fig. 2).

In the first group can be placed two large walled cities, one being Ziyaret near Hanak, the other being Sengerkale on lake Çıldır. These two centres differ in size and in the type of building found. At both of these sites the outer city wall, which in places reaches a width of 5m, surrounds traces of a civilian settlement. At Sengerkale, which lies on the northeastern shore of lake Çıldır, the citadel is enclosed with a separate wall whilst the lower slopes, running down towards the lake within the city wall, are retained by at least two terrace walls (figs 3, 4). The civilian settlement lies on these terraces. There are entrances to the settlement from at least three directions (north, west and east), and, to the northeast, traces of a man-made ditch can be seen outside the walls. Ziyaret fortress is constructed on the summit of a mountain range which runs in a north–south direction, and it controls the whole area. A tower has been built on the highest point (figs 5–7). Traces of the civilian settlement can be clearly seen on the south, east and northern slopes of the hill. To the west and south, traces of the city wall are still visible (Köroğlu 1998; 1999). The ruins of Ziyaret may help to establish a connection between walled cities and tower type buildings and the dating of these.

The second type of fortress consists of a tower and a small enclosed area adjoining (fig. 7). There are six examples to be found in the Ardahan area. Of these Karakale lies to the northeast of the Çıldır plain, İncedere (fig. 8) stands above the Çotsuyu upstream from Ziyaret, Çataldere and Derindere lie in the eastern foothills of the Yalnızçam mountains to the west of the Ardahan plain, whilst Köroğlu (fig. 9) fortress lies south of Göle in the northern foothills of the Allahuekber mountains.

Ziyaret, Derindere and İncedere fortresses resemble each other in terms of both plan and stone masonry. Köroğlu fortress is architecturally slightly different: in the way the construction conforms to the lie of the land, in its sloping faced east wall and in the four niches to be

*Fig. 8. İncedere*

*Fig. 9. Detail of the walls of Köroğlu*

found in this wall. However the herringbone style of masonry of the east wall is also found at Ziyaret fortress (figs 6, 9). This necessitates viewing them as one group.

The size of the above mentioned towers ranges between 8.30m by 9m for the smallest and 16m by 25m for the largest. In places, the tower walls are still up to 5m high (fig. 7).

Of these six examples Çataldere, and especially Karakale which has a D-shaped plan, are somewhat different to the others in plan. However, all six lie on rocky outcrops and are built from fairly large rough stones without the use of mortar.

In the third group of fortresses the walls follow the contours of the ground and are built from small stones exhibiting little workmanship. The size of these sites ranges from 30m by 40m for the smallest to 70m by 100m for the largest. These fortresses have less in common with each other than did the towers of the previous group. Akçakale and Taşköprü lie in the lake Çıldır region. Gürçayır, Sugöze and Tepeler lie on the south side of the Ardahan plain, and Ballıkaya on its northern side near to Çataldere. Yamaçyol lies northwest of Hanak on the right bank of the Çotsuyu, on a line with the İncedere fortress mentioned above (fig. 2). In two cases, Akçakale and Ballıkaya, rooms lie inside and against the fortification wall (Köroğlu 1997; 1998; 1999; 2001).

When it comes to dating any of these structures we have to rely mainly on the ground-plans and on the type of stonework, since few surface finds have been obtained. At Ziyaret some black burnished ware of Early Bronze Age type, along with some local Early Iron Age scratched ware, was found in an animal den (Köroğlu 1998: fig. 5). From the ground-plans and stonework there is little to indicate that the fortresses are Urartian. The typical Urartian features are missing. The rough stonework and the tendency of the plans to follow the contours of the hillside can be compared with the cyclopean fortresses that became common in Caucasia in the Late Bronze and Early Iron Ages (Mikaelian 1968; Smith 1999; Avetisyan et al. 2000). The standard tower plans found at Ziyaret, Derindere and İncedere have no parallels in Caucasia. To judge from the sherds recovered, Ziyaret seems to be early, but it is still possible that it had more than one period of settlement and that these types of towers are of a later date. Although the evidence is insufficient, we can hypothesise that some of these fortresses could be those referred to in Urartian inscriptions as belonging to local rulers, as for example in the campaign of Argishti I to Tariu or in the Hanak inscription.

To date, excavations such as those at Sos Höyük near Erzurum on the north side of the Aras valley (Sagona et al. 1996; 1997; Parker 1999), at Ani and Dündartepe in the Kars region (Kökten 1944; 1953; Balkan, Sumer 1965) and at Ardahan Höyük (Mellink 1968), together with surveys (Kökten 1943, Güneri 1992), have failed to produce useful evidence for the presence of Urartu in the area. From our own surveys in this region the only examples of Urartian ware recovered are a few pieces of red burnished ware from Tepeler Höyük in the Ardahan plain. Further east, to the east of the Arpaçay, only the excavation at Horom (northwest of mount Aragats) has produced evidence connecting the site to Urartu (Badaljan et al. 1994).

Thus, whilst it seems that Urartian material in small measure reached as far north as the Ardahan region, it can hardly be said that in the source region of the river Kura, where the northernmost inscriptions are to be found, Urartian culture had replaced native elements.

What then can be said about the position of the northern boundary of the Urartian state? And what is the significance of the Urartian inscriptions from the northern area under consideration? To the north of the Aras and to the west of the Arpaçay are to be found inscriptions of Minua, Argishti I and Sarduri II. These all mention the name of the king, the places plundered and the spoil taken. They do not mention building activities, buildings or offerings to the gods of Urartu. Furthermore, in this region there are no known Urartian style rock-cut tombs with several rooms, nor are there square temples or large administrative centres (Zimansky 1985: 62–76). It seems that the northern boundary for these types of remains runs along or possibly slightly north of the Aras valley. It should be noted however that the Kars region has not been well surveyed and new evidence could yet appear.

Thus, when we refer to the northern boundary of Urartu we need to distinguish between that line within which are to be found large building constructions, and the more distant northerly line defining the area used for looting but within which Urartian inscriptions occur. It should be realised that Assyrian kings likewise had a tradition of going abroad and leaving inscriptions behind them. For example, Tiglath-pileser I and also, about 200 years later, Shalmaneser III, left inscriptions at the source of the Tigris high in the Taurus mountains. Tiglath-pileser also left an inscription further north, at Yoncalı on the Muş plain. We also know that Tiglath-pileser III and Sargon II journeyed as far as the central region of Urartu. Such examples indicate that the whereabouts of inscriptions cannot be used to define political boundaries. The corpus of Urartian architectural remains (Kleiss, Hauptmann 1976: map I) indicates that the central government controlled the area up to and possibly slightly beyond the Aras valley, and that the Ardahan region was merely raided when the need arose.

In relation to the northern boundary of Urartu it is also necessary to discuss the whereabouts of the land of Qulha, which was visited in two campaigns of Sarduri II (*UKN*: 155 C, D). Qulha has been equated with ancient Kolkhis, which lay in the Rioni and lower Çoruh valleys (Diakonoff, Kashkai 1981: 68–9), but this equation is based purely on the similarity of the names.

The evidence available does not allow for a geographical location of Qulha beyond northeastern Anatolia. According to the Urartian records, the plunder taken from Qulha was of the same type as that taken from throughout northeastern Anatolia, that is herds of cattle, sheep and horses, and people. The plunder taken in Urartian campaigns must reflect the specific economic and geographic conditions of the area involved (Zimansky 1985: 53–60). Compare, for example, the spoil taken from Mana, to the south of lake Urmia, which included camels (*UKN*: 127–8), the spoil from Qumaha, beyond the Euphrates, which included gold, silver, clothing and copper items (*UKN*: 155 E), and the spoil from the vassal kingdom of Diauehe which likewise included gold, silver and copper (*UKN*: 128). The only point at which the description relating to Qulha deviates from the northeast Anatolian norm is in the second campaign against Qulha where the inscription refers to an iron object, specifically some sort of ring or stamp. But this hardly indicates that Qulha should be considered as the source region for the Urartian iron industry, as has been suggested elsewhere (Salvini 1991: 4–13). Indeed, recent excavations in the Van area demonstrate that there was a developed use of iron from the earliest period of the Urartian kingdom (Sevin, Kavaklı 1996).

In fact it seems there is no evidence that the Urartians ever went north beyond Ardahan. The lower Çoruh valley is steep and narrow and barely suitable for an army containing wheeled vehicles to pass. However, in the campaigning season (i.e. the summer months) there would have been no need to enter such lower valleys to obtain spoil for we can reasonably assume that in Urartian times, as today, the sheep and cattle were summer pastured on the high mountain meadows rather than in the valleys.

According to the Urartian inscriptions, Qulha lay in the neighbourhood of the land of Huša. Since Huša is mentioned on the Hanak inscription, which is the most northerly example known, we should expect that it lay within the area around Hanak, and hence that Qulha too should be nearby. A more suitable region for Qulha would thus be, for example, the modern region of Göle (fig. 1) which is known from medieval Georgian sources as Kola and from medieval Armenian sources as Kol (Edwards 1988; Köroğlu 2001). In this area are to be found the rich pastures necessary to support the flocks and herds mentioned in the Urartian plunder lists. Also in this area are to be found fortresses which could have belonged to local rulers of that period. With this relocation of Qulha, the only reason for connecting the Urartian kingdom with the Black Sea region is removed.

**Acknowledgements**

We thank Adam Smith for sharing his expertise on the Caucasian region with us. I would like to extend my thanks to Margaret R. Pane for her help in writing my paper in English. Finally I would like to express my thanks to Marmara University for giving financial support to our surveys in the Ardahan region.

**Bibliography**

*Abbreviation*

UKN = Melikišvili, G.A. 1960: *Urartskie klinoobraznye nadpisi* (Le iscrizioni cuneiformi urartee) (second edition). Moscow

Avetisyan, P., Badalyan, R., Smith A.T. 2000: 'Preliminary report on the 1998 archaeological investigations of Project Aragats in the Tsakahovit Plain, Armenia' *Studi Micenei ed Egeo-Anatolici* 42/1: 19–59

Aydın, N. 1991: 'Güzelhisar Urartu kitabesi' *Belleten* 213: 323–9

Badaljan, R.S., Kohl, P.L., Stronach, D., Tonikjan, A.V. 1994: 'Preliminary report on the 1993 excavations at Horom, Armenia' *Iran* 32: 1–29

Balkan, K., Sümer, O. 1965: '1965 Yılı Ani kazıları hakkında kısa rapor' *Türk Arkeoloji Dergisi* 14: 103–18

Diakonoff, I.M., Kashkai, S.M. 1981: *Répertoire Géographique des Textes Cunéiformes. 9. Geographical Names According to Urartian Texts.* Wiesbaden

Dinçol, A.M. 1989: 'Yeni Urartu yazıtları ve yazıt parçaları' *Anadolu Araştırmaları* 11: 137–48

Dinçol, A.M., Dinçol, B. 1992: 'Die Urartäische Inschrift aus Hanak (Kars)' in H. Otten et al. (eds), *Sedat Alp'a Armagan Festschrift für Sedat Alp. Hittite and Other Anatolian and Near Eastern Studies in Honour of Sedat Alp.* Ankara: 109–17

Edwards, R.W. 1988 'The vale of Kola: a final preliminary report on the marchlands of northeast Turkey' *Dumbarton Oaks Papers* 42: 119–41

Güneri, S. 1992: 'Doğu Anadolu'da yeni gözlemler' *Türk Arkeoloji Dergisi* 30: 149–95

Kleiss, W. 1992: 'Zur Ausbreitung Urartus nach Norden' *Archäologische Mitteilungen aus Iran* 25: 91–4

Kleiss, W., Hauptmann, H. 1976: *Topographische Karte von Urartu* (Archäologische Mitteilungen aus Iran Ergänzungsband 3). Berlin

Kökten, I.K. 1943: 'Kars'ın tarih öncesi hakkında ilk kısa rapor' *Belleten* 27: 601–13

— 1944: 'Orta, doğu ve kuzey Anadolu'da yapılan tarih öncesi araştırmaları' *Belleten* 32: 659–80

— 1953: '1952 yılında yaptığım tarih öncesi araştırması' *Ankara Üniversitesi Dil Tarih Coğrafya Fakültesi Dergisi* 11: 177–209

Köroğlu, K. 1997: '1995 yılı Artvin-Ardahan illeri yüzey araştırması' *Araştırma Sonuçları Toplantısı* 14.2: 369–95

— 1998: '1996 yılı Artvin-Ardahan illeri yüzey araştırması' *Araştırma Sonuçları Toplantısı* 15.1: 127–56

— 1999: '1997 yılı Artvin-Ardahan illeri yüzey araştırması' *Araştırma Sonuçları Toplantısı* 16.1: 143–60

— 2001: 'Urartu krallığı'nın kuzey yayılımı ve Qulha ülkesinin tarihi coğrafyası' *Belleten* 241: 717–47

Mellink, M. 1968: 'Archaeology in Asia Minor' *American Journal of Archaeology* 72: 134–5

Mikaelian, G.H. 1968: *Cyclopean Fortresses in the Basin of Lake Sevan.* Yerevan

Parker, A. 1999: 'Northeastern Anatolia: on the periphery of empires' in A. Çilingiroğlu, R. Matthews (eds), *Anatolian Iron Ages IV (= Anatolian Studies* 49): 133–41

Payne, M.R. 1996: 'Urartian inscriptions in Erzurum Museum' *Anadolu Araştırmaları* 14: 415–23

Sagona, A., Erkmen, M., Sagona, C., Thomas, I. 1996: 'Excavations at Sos Höyük, 1995: second preliminary report' *Anatolian Studies* 46: 27–52

Sagona, A., Erkmen, M., Sagona, C., Howells, S. 1997: 'Excavations at Sos Höyük, 1996: third preliminary report' *Anatolica* 23: 181–226

Salvini, M. 1991: 'Historical introduction' in R. Merhav (ed.), *Urartu: A Metalworking Center in the First Millennium BCE.* Jerusalem: 4–13

Sevin, V., Kavaklı, E. 1996: *Bir Erken Demir Çağ Nekropolü Van / Karagündüz. An Early Iron Age Cemetery.* Istanbul

Smith, A.T. 1999: 'The making of an Urartian landscape in southern Transcaucasia: a study of political architectonics' *American Journal of Archaeology* 103: 45–71

Zimansky, P.E. 1985: *Ecology and Empire: the Structure of the Urartian State.* Chicago

# Norşun Tepe and Lidar Höyük. Two examples for cultural change during the Early Iron Age

## Uwe Müller

*Eastern Mediterranean University, Gazi Mağusa*

## Abstract

There are only a few sites in the region of the upper and middle Euphrates which can provide an uninterrupted stratigraphy from the end of the Bronze Age through the Iron Age; amongst these are Norşun Tepe and Lidar Höyük. The transition appears to be very different at these two sites. Lidar Höyük reveals an almost unnoticeable development, confirming the political continuity in the region. For Norşun Tepe, on the other hand, previous publications have argued for a radical change caused by the immigration of a new population and marked by a distinct kind of pottery. This paper demonstrates that all the observeable changes can be explained by a restructuring of social, economic and political organisation following the retreat of Hittite government. This view is supported by newly identified links between Bronze Age and Iron Age pottery from Norşun Tepe.

## Özet

Yukarı ve Orta Fırat bölgesinde Bronz Çağı sonlarından başlayıp tüm Demir Çağ boyunca kesintisiz tabakalanması olan ancak birkaç yerleşim vardır. Bunlardan biri Norşun Tepe, biri ise Lidar Höyük'tür. Bu iki yerleşimdeki geçiş dönemleri birbirlerinden çok farklıdır. Lidar Höyük, bölgedeki politik devamlılığı sağlayarak neredeyse hiç hissedilmeyen bir gelişim gerçekleştirmiştir. Diğer taraftan Norşun Tepe ile ilgili yayınlar, Norşun Tepe'de geçiş döneminde radikal değişikliklerin yaşandığını ortaya koyar. Bu değişiklikler bölgeye olan göçler ve özgün bir çanak çömlek türü ile kendini belli eder. Bu çalışma, gözlenebilen tüm değişimlerin Hitit yönetiminin geriye çekilmesinden sonra yeni bir sosyal, ekonomik ve politik yapının oluşturulması çabalarıyla açıklanabileceğini göstermeye çalışacaktır.

The settlement mounds of Lidar Höyük and Norşun Tepe were both excavated as part of the salvage excavation programme conducted during the construction of the Keban and Atatürk dams. The fieldwork at both sites, directed by Harald Hauptmann, took place at Norşun Tepe in the Altınova from 1968 to 1974 (Hauptmann 1969; 1970a; 1970b; 1971; 1972; 1974a; 1974b; 1976a; 1976b; 1979a; 1979b; 1982; 1983; Hauptmann et al. 1976), and at Lidar Höyük in the years 1979 to 1987 (Hauptmann 1987). Both sites were excavated to a considerable depth, and at both sites long stratigraphic sequences were revealed. Together, these two settlement mounds provide the rare opportunity to study and compare uninterrupted sequences from the

Late Bronze Age well into the Late Iron Age. In the district of the large reservoir lakes in eastern Turkey, only Tille Höyük in the Adıyaman region (French 1987; Blaylock, French, Summers 1990; Blaylock 1998; Summers 1991; Summers et al. 1993) has as yet offered a similar opportunity.

Despite these circumstantial similarities however, the Iron Age, and in particular the transition from the Late Bronze Age to the Early Iron Age, has a very different appearance at Lidar Höyük (Müller, forthcoming) compared with Norşun Tepe (Bartl 1988; 1994; 1995; 2001). These differences provide some insight into the diversity and complexity of events following the breakdown of Hittite central power at Hattusha.

## Norşun Tepe

The salvage excavations at Norşun Tepe (fig. 1) were conducted on an extremely large scale.[1] The excavated area extends for more than 300m from north to south and can be roughly divided into three distinct parts: the acropolis, and the northern and southern parts of the terrace. Despite the limited time available for the salvage operations, all the work was extensively documented with drawings, photographs and trench diaries. Practically all of the trenches contained remains of Iron Age structures. More than 10,600 Iron Age pottery sherds have been drawn and described and are going to be analysed and published. This project was supported financially by the German Archaeological Institute (Müller, forthcoming).

Iron Age Norşun Tepe does not exhibit the classic vertical stratigraphic sequence, but a horizontal one. This feature, combined with the fact that previous publications have focused on only a part of the total excavated area, has led to understandable interpretative errors regarding the chronology of the site. Specifically, it has been proposed that a several hundred years' hiatus lay between the Early and Middle Iron Age occupations (Bartl 1988: 122–4; 1994: 480; 1995: 207), whereas, in fact, a study of all Iron Age pottery from all of the trenches clearly demonstrates that this break in occupation never existed. Rather, Norşun Tepe was continously settled throughout the Iron Age and, during this period, it was simply the specific locations of buildings on the site which changed from time to time.

The Late Bronze Age village at Norşun Tepe was situated on the acropolis. There are hints that the terrace was also used at this time: Korbel (1985: 113) mentions Late Bronze Age pottery from an Early Iron Age pit there, and Bartl (2001: 386) interprets the occurrence of a large amount of Late(?) Bronze Age pottery in Early Iron Age levels as evidence for a rather substantial pre-Iron Age occupation. However, no Late Bronze Age architecture has been found on the terrace.

The first Iron Age settlement consisted of a group of widely scattered farmsteads situated in the open, unprotected area of the northern part of the terrace. At a later phase, but still within the Early Iron Age, the acropolis was resettled whilst the dwellings on the terrace were gradually abandoned until, in the Middle Iron Age, the whole terrace reverted to farmland once again. Later on, most probably in connection with the occupation of the Altınova by the Urartian king Menua, a large official building was erected on the southern part of the terrace whilst the village remained on top of the acropolis.

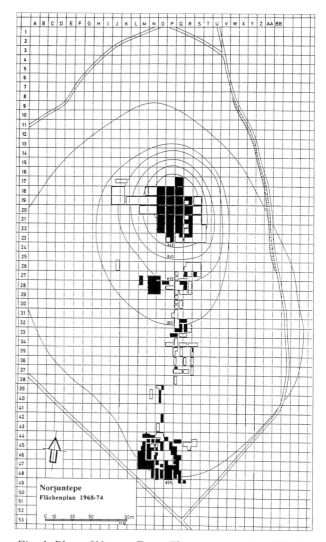

*Fig. 1. Plan of Norşun Tepe. The pottery analysed by the DAI project 'Die Entstehung und Entwicklung der früheisenzeitlichen Keramik in der Osttürkei' comes mainly from the blackened trenches*

The Early Iron Age settlement is very different from its Late Bronze Age predecessor. Not only is there a new building phase, with a new and distinct kind of architecture but the settlement is in a different location and exhibits a different organisational structure. Instead of houses clustered together on the acropolis as in the Late Bronze Age, there are single farmsteads widely separated from each other. It seems that the people built their houses wherever it suited them, which would indicate that the old system of rules and laws which regulated landownership in Hittite times was no longer valid.

The pottery of this village consists of the ribbed/grooved type now known as 'groovy pottery' (compare Roaf, Schachner this volume),[2] which is used

---

[1] Since the work on Norşun Tepe pottery is an ongoing project, the results presented in this paper are preliminary only.

[2] In an email discussion following the Fifth Anatolian Iron Ages Symposium, most colleagues working on such material agreed to use this term, as proposed by Michael Roaf.

by archaeologists as a marker of the Early Iron Age throughout the region. Its appearance indicates much more than simply a change in vessel shapes: it points to a distinct alteration in the whole organisation of ceramic craftsmanship, production techniques and use of the products. In a first phase, handmade ribbed pottery is used side by side with wheel made 'Hittite' vessels, a phenomenon known from other sites in the Keban region (Winn 1980: 155, 162). Later on, all Hittite types disappear to be replaced by a full set of groovy pottery shapes fit for any kind of use.

The new vessel shapes include open bowls or platters of different sizes and forms, used for serving food (fig. 2: 6, 7); and small, deep bowls, most probably drinking cups (fig. 2: 5). There are also pots (fig. 2: 2–4), which often have a typical horizontally grooved handle (fig. 2: 2), and sometimes they bear incised decoration. Some of these pots are recognisable as cooking vessels, from the evidence of secondary firing. A special 'fire-proof' fabric, as found in other regions, is unknown during the Iron Age at Norşun Tepe; rather, all locally made cooking vessels are tempered with the same kind of sand and small stones as the rest of the pottery. There are also high, closed shapes, or bottles, for storing and serving liquids (fig. 2: 1). Some exceptional shapes, for unknown purposes, complete the assemblage.

Besides this change in appearance, the groovy pottery represents a change in the organisation of pottery production. With the groovy pottery there is much less standardisation and a higher variability in shapes and production techniques, distinguishing it from the mass-produced ceramics of Hittite times. However, it would be questionable to interpret this evidence as indicating a change from proto-industrial centralised production to a return to household level production, as is sometimes done.[3] Firstly, only a portion of the groovy pottery assemblage, and that only in the very first phase of the Early Iron Age, is made with the coiling (handmade) technique. Furthermore, these vessels appear together with Hittite type shapes and so we cannot rule out the possibility that the latter were still being produced. Later on, the majority of the groovy pottery is produced on slow rotating turntables, or even on throwing wheels. Even so, it is a common error to consider handmade pottery as being more

primitive than wheel made. Wheel made pottery may be more sophisticated only in the sense that a plastic cup is more developed than a porcelain one: the greater complexity lies only in the technique required to produce it, not in the vessel itself or in the production process. In fact, the production of handmade groovy pottery would have been no less elaborate than Hittite mass production of wheel made vessels, for it takes much longer to produce complex shapes without the aid of a potter's wheel. Furthermore, the burnishing visible on almost every single piece, together with other time consuming surface treatment techniques, demonstrate just how much care and effort the grooved ware potters invested in their work. In addition, there are new techniques visible on the groovy pottery that were unknown or unused by the potters of Hittite times. The frequent use of slips to give the Iron Age pots a particular colour, either whitish yellow or bright red, reveals a highly developed level of craftsmanship and expertise not to be found in the Hittite pottery of the Keban region. In addition to the frequent incised decoration, a fair number of the pots are painted. Again this is a technique unknown to 'Hittite' pottery production, introduced by the potters of supposedly 'primitive' groovy pottery. These painted bowls, pots and bottles certainly deserve to be labelled as the fine ware of the Early Iron Age.

Another significant feature is that the development of these Early Iron Age shapes and wares leads in an unbroken chain to the kind of later Iron Age pottery that used to be called Urartian, Neo-Hittite and Neo-Assyrian; as, for example, at Norşun Tepe from the 12th to the seventh centuries BC, where carinated bowls develop from earlier handmade ribbed types into the later, well known 'Urartian' ones (fig. 3).

One other feature of the groovy pottery has perhaps even more importance. A good many of the cooking pots have narrow spouts which would only have been useful for preparing and pouring thinly constituted hot liquids. Significantly, spouted cooking pots are completely absent from the Hittite repertoire. Thus the groovy pottery cooking vessels demonstrate that in the Early Iron Age there was not only a change in taste for pottery, and in the techniques for producing it, but also that pottery was used for different purposes than before. In the case of the spouted cooking pots this signals a difference in diet. The frequent occurrence of pots of different sizes together with small bowls creates the impression of a regular set of drinking vessels (fig. 4).

In summary, the list of changes occurring at Norşun Tepe with the beginning of the Early Iron Age is quite impressive:

---

[3] In this connection, different ethnographical examples could be cited to support divergent theories. As an illustration of the potential complexities of the situation, consider modern Cambodia, where the author has observed that all traditional pottery is produced in a small group of villages and is distributed countrywide by ox-cart caravans: this centrally produced and far traded pottery is handmade.

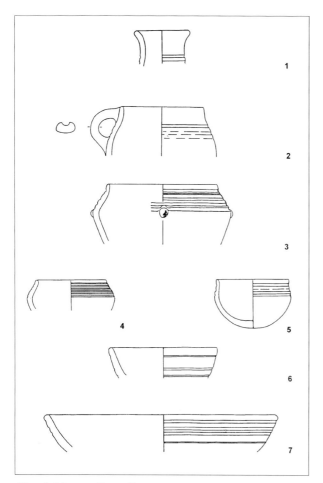

*Fig. 2. Norşun Tepe. Groovy pottery*

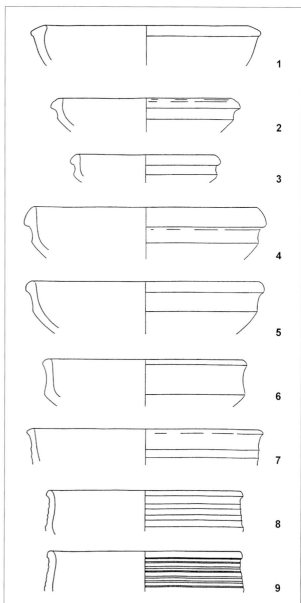

*Fig. 3. Norşun Tepe. Development of Iron Age bowls*

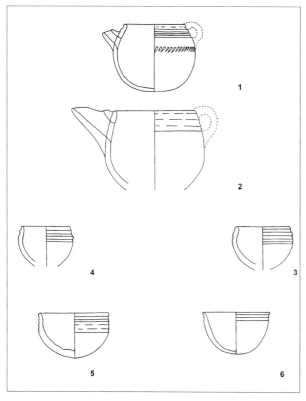

*Fig. 4. Norşun Tepe. Groovy pottery*

1. a new settlement location on the site;

2. the appearance of new architectural forms;

3. the ignoring of old land rights;

4. new shapes and decorations for pottery;

5. different organisation and new techniques of pottery production;

6. a difference in diet.

Consequently, it is understandable that Norşun Tepe was thought to be one of the very few places where a settlement of newcomers, migrating from a foreign country into a region formerly under Hittite control, could be proven. However, there has been no unanimous agreement as to where these newcomers could have come from. Given the relatively close similarities between groovy pottery and ceramics from Late Bronze Age/Early Iron Age Georgia and Armenia, Bartl seems to prefer those regions as the homeland of the groovy pottery producers (Bartl 2001: 397). Other authors connect the appearance of groovy pottery with the movements of Indo-European tribes (Sevin 1991: 97) with a nomadic lifestyle, despite the fact that many regions show an increase in the number of permanent settlements during the Early Iron Age. But another interpretation can be offered in connection with both the groovy pottery known from sites and the material of Transcaucasian type in museums in eastern Turkey. Since this last region was never under Hittite rule, it yields no Hittite type Late Bronze Age ceramics although, as elsewhere, the groovy pottery is thought to signal the Early Iron Age. One should at least consider the possibility that not all the sites with groovy pottery must be dated to the Early Iron Age; rather, this pottery might be in fact nothing other than the typical Late Bronze Age ceramic material of the area. Hence we cannot exclude the possibility that the first Early Iron Age settlers in the Altınova migrated merely from this adjacent neighbourhood, where they had been living in the Late Bronze Age; although only further excavation and the application of scientific dating methods will be able to resolve the problems associated with Transcaucasian chronologies.[4]

But was there a migration at all? Certainly, at first sight, our list of changes in various aspects of life at Early Iron Age Norşun Tepe seems to point towards one. Nevertheless, there is also strong evidence for a continuity of population. Although the majority of the site's Late Bronze Age pottery is similar to material from Hittite assemblages elsewhere,[5] mixed with it in the Late Bronze Age levels

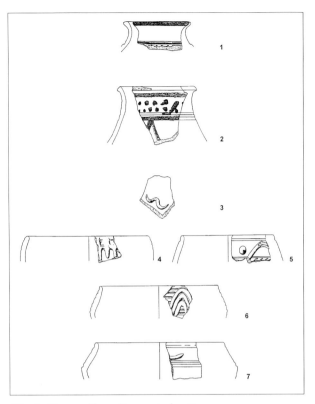

*Fig 5. Norşun Tepe. Decorated pottery*

there is a small but relevant quantity of other, very different ceramics. These include wheel thrown bowls and bottles made from yellow clay. They are red painted and therefore completely un-Hittite in character. Shallow grooves can also be present, mostly arranged horizontally but sometimes forming curving or triangular patterns (fig. 5: 1). Comparison with the painted Early Iron Age bottles from the site (fig. 5: 2) demonstrates that the Late Bronze examples were their direct predecessors: shape, rim form and decorative motifs are virtually identical; even the fabric is similar, except for the fact that the Late Bronze Age bottles were produced on the throwing wheel whilst the later ones are handmade. This painted pottery establishes a clear link between the ceramic assemblage of 'Hittite' times and that of the Early Iron Age.

Furthermore, close examination of some of the Late Bronze Age contexts at Norşun Tepe has revealed examples of groovy pottery from 'Hittite' levels. They are few in number and were previously declared as intrusive material, but since some of them are clearly wheel made there is no reason to doubt their dating to the Late Bronze Age.

Another feature of Early Iron Age pottery leads back to even more remote times. A number of the grooved pots and bowls display applied decoration (fig. 5: 3–7), in a manner strongly reminiscent of the local Middle Bronze Age wares. The large triangular motifs (fig. 5: 5) especially resemble decoration in the Middle Bronze Age Karaz tradition.

---

[4] New investigations will help to clarify these issues (compare the papers by Rubinson, Marcus and by Smith et al., this volume).

[5] This is true for the shapes, but various regional differences occur in the fabrics since potters had to use the locally available raw materials.

Thus, the hypothetical newcomers of the Early Iron Age mentioned above seem to be already present at Norşun Tepe during the Late Bronze Age; or at least, pottery was being produced then according to the same needs and taste but using the Hittite throwing wheel technique. Furthermore, this pottery has strong affinities with the local Middle Bronze Age pottery of northeastern Turkey, which was frequently painted or decorated with applications.[6] The transmission of such decorative motifs and techniques is hardly explicable without a continuity of population. Viewed in this light, it is not the handmade Early Iron Age pottery that appears intrusive and alien to the region but rather the wheel made, mass-produced 'Hittite' wares.

Any historical reconstruction should consider not only the changes but also the strong signs of continuity. A revised reconstruction of events, taking the new evidence into account, might thus look as follows. When Shuppiluliuma I conquered Išuwa to gain access to the metal mines of Ergani, the Hittites imposed their own centrally organised administrative and economic system of control on the region, replacing the local, probably tribally organised, socio-political arrangements. Apart from many other things, this meant that formerly independent potteries were now concentrated in central workshops where wheel made ceramics were mass-produced. In addition to this new production, we have observed above that a small quantity of pottery was made according to the local traditional taste, demonstrating that at least a part of the population was still as it was before the Hittite conquest. Most probably, in fact, only a small number of Hittite administrators moved into the newly conquered region and the mass of the population remained where it was. If then we want to speak about 'migrations', there should be one in the Late Bronze Age when Hittite officials came to the Altınova to reorganise and control the economy and administration of the area. Some time after 1200 BC, when the government at Hattuša collapsed, the Hittites lost control of Išuwa and so the top of the administrative hierarchy there retreated, most probably to places like Melid or Karkamiš where a political continuity is proven. The locals regained control over their land and returned to their traditionally organised economy, apparent both in the founding of small farmsteads in open land and in the return to traditional handmade pottery.

Thus, in this reconstruction, the change in material culture is explained not by an immigration of vast numbers of foreigners, but by the emigration of a small number of administrative officials.

## Lidar Höyük

Only 200km south of Norşun Tepe, at Lidar Höyük, the Late Bronze Age to Early Iron Age transition looks completely different. Short accounts of this are already published (Müller 1999a; 1999b) so here it may suffice to state that the Early Iron Age settlement was located in the same place as its Bronze Age predecessor, with houses clustered together on the acropolis. There is no change in settlement location and structure, and no sign of a change in land rights. Equally, there is not much change in pottery shapes and wares, the vast majority of the Early Iron Age assemblage being more or less identical to the repertoire of Imperial Hittite times (Müller 1999a: Abb. 5; 1999b: Abb. 2–12). Thus there is no indication of a change in economic or social organisation. The archaeological evidence fits perfectly well to the model of political continuity: in this region, the Hittite kings of Karkamiš remained in control after the fall of Hattuša and became Great Kings themselves, founding at least one vice-kingdom, at Melid (Sürenhagen 1986; 1996; Hawkins 1988).

Within this picture of almost complete continuity, only one small group of pottery looks foreign. It is nothing other than our handmade groovy pottery (Müller 1999a: Abb. 6; 1999b: Abb. 5, 8, 11). However, here at Lidar Höyük there is an important difference: instead of the complete repertoire (a full set of different shapes) as found at Norşun Tepe, only cooking pots appear. There is a fair number of them, with narrow spouts and fit for only one special purpose. There are no bowls, mugs, pots or bottles. The grooved Lidar cooking pots are handmade like their northern counterparts but they are manufactured in local cooking pot fabrics, unknown in the north[7] and so, clearly, they were made locally. Unlike the comparanda in the Keban region, they do not belong to the earliest types of groovy pottery but rather to types occurring in the later phases of the Early Iron Age. Archaeologically speaking then, the Iron Age at Lidar Höyük started later than in the north. This fits perfectly well with the chronology based on the seal impressions of Kuzi-Teššub, which were found in the Late Bronze Age levels at the site. Kuzi-Teššub's reign continued well into the period which followed the fall of Hattuša. If the Early Iron Age at Norşun Tepe began with, or shortly after, the destruction of Hattuša around 1180

---

[6] Ongoing work has revealed that there are strong links even in architectural forms between the end of the Early Bronze Age and the Early Iron Age at Norşun Tepe.

[7] Cooking pots at Lidar Höyük are most often tempered with grits of ground minerals with shiny surfaces (without petrographical analysis, it cannot be decided whether these consist of quartz, mica, feldspar or other minerals). This special temper for 'fire-proofing' pots had been common since the Early Bronze Age. By contrast, at Norşun Tepe there is not one single piece of this fabric to be found.

BC, and there is no other reasonable possibility, then the Early Iron Age at Lidar Höyük must have started somewhat later, perhaps two or three generations afterwards. This would bring us to the time of Tiglath-Pileser I of Assyria, whose records include one of the few accounts of events in the general region. The relevant, oft-quoted passage in these records states that the Assyrians had to fight the Mushki,[8] who had conquered the lands of Alzi and Purulumzu 50 years before, and who had subsequently raided in Kutmuhi. Tiglath-Pileser defeated them and settled the survivors in Assyrian controlled territory. The archaeological evidence from Norşun Tepe and Lidar Höyük might reflect this situation quite clearly. In the north, the taking over of control at Išuwa/Alzi by the local population might well have appeared as a conquest to the Assyrians — in any case, the region was no longer Hittite: the return to a traditional local economy shows up as a change in the archaeological record at Norşun Tepe. In the south, at Lidar Höyük, the archaeological evidence remains more or less unchanged, not only because of the political continuity there, but also because a centralised, temple based economic system was already established and had been for many centuries. The groovy pottery of Lidar Höyük is alien in all respects to the vast majority of Neo-Hittite pottery and all its economic and social implications. It could be

one of the rare cases where archaeological evidence can be used to identify one of the many textually attested deportations of prisoners-of-war. This is only possible because the deportees clung to aspects of their own culture, based on different organisation principles than those of their new environment.

Although debate on these topics will undoubtedly continue, the examples of Lidar Höyük and Norşun Tepe demonstrate that there are many more explanations for cultural change than simply invasions. To explain cultural change it is necessary to look closely at the previous history and archaeology of a specific region. Apparently 'new' phenomena may in fact transpire to be old traditions arising again; and single causes such as the breakdown of a central imperial government may produce very different results in different regions of the 'periphery'.

---

[8] The Kizildağ 4 inscription was once thought to contain the first mention of the Mushki (Meriggi 1964) but a recent re-evaluation has shown that this is a misreading of the text (Poetto 1998). Still very often, the Mushki are considered to be identical with the Phrygians (see Summers 1994: 246). The only evidence for this is the equation of Mita of Mushki, mentioned in the Assyrian annals, with Midas of Gordion, but since the name 'Mita' is already attested in Late Bronze Age sources the argument is invalid. Neither does historical geography really support the equation of Mushki with Phrygians: Phrygia proper lies far to the west of the Euphrates and, although the location of its eastern borders are subject to controversy, it is very doubtful (to say the least) that it ever stretched to the east of the central Anatolian plateau. The temple inscription from Ayanis (Salvini 2001: 261) mentions the Mushki as one of the peoples defeated and deported by Rusa II of Urartu, implying that they were located in the immediate neighbourhood of Urartu; thus again, an equation of Mushki and Phrygians seems unlikely. Instead, 'Mushki' might be the name of a local people inhabiting the region subsumed by the Middle Assyrians under the designation 'Nairi Lands'. If the Mushki are not Phrygians then we should take into consideration the fact that groovy pottery appears at the same time as, and in the same region in which, the Mushki are first attested. It is not argued here that groovy pottery is the pottery of the Mushki, but rather that the local inhabitants of the upper Euphrates region, and called Mushki by some of their contemporaries, were amongst those who used this horizontally decorated pottery.

## Bibliography

Bartl, K. 1988: *Norşun-Tepe. Die frühe Eisenzeit.* Unpublished PhD dissertation. Freie Universität Berlin.

— 1994: 'Die frühe Eisenzeit in Ostanatolien und ihre Verbindung zu den benachbarten Regionen' *Baghdader Mitteilungen* 25: 473–518

— 1995: 'Some remarks on the Early Iron Age in eastern Anatolia' *Anatolica* 21: 205–12

— 2001: 'Eastern Anatolia in the Early Iron Age' in R. Eichmann, H. Parzinger (eds), *Migration und Kulturtransfer. Der Wandel vorder- und zentralasiatischer Kulturen im Umbruch vom 2. zum 1. vorchristlichen Jahrtausend.* Berlin: 383–409

Blaylock, S.R. 1998: 'Rescue excavations by the BIAA at Tille Höyük on the Euphrates, 1979–1990' in R.J. Matthews (ed.), *Ancient Anatolia. Fifty Years' Work by the British Institute of Archaeology at Ankara.* London 1998: 111–26

Blaylock, S.R., French, D.H., Summers, G.D. 1990: 'The Adıyaman Survey: an interim report' *Anatolian Studies* 40: 81–135

French, D.H. 1987: 'Tille excavations 1979' in *Lower Euphrates Project 1978–1979* (Middle Eastern Technical University Lower Euphrates Project Publications, Series 1, No. 3). Istanbul: 303–9

Hauptmann, H. 1969: 'Die Grabungen auf dem Norşun-Tepe 1969' *Türk Arkeoloji Dergisi* 18.2: 111–21

— 1970a: 'Die Grabungen auf dem Norşun-Tepe 1968' *Keban Projesi 1968 Yaz Çalışmaları* (Orta Doğu Teknik Üniversitesi Keban Projesi Yayınları, Seri I, No. 1). Ankara: 115–30

— 1970b: 'Norşun-Tepe. Historische Geographie und Ergebnisse der Grabungen 1968/69' *Istanbuler Mitteilungen* 19/20: 21–78

— 1971: 'Die Grabungen auf dem Norşun-Tepe 1969' *Keban Projesi 1969 Yaz Çalışmaları* (Orta Doğu Teknik Üniversitesi Keban Projesi Yayınları, Seri I, No. 2). Ankara: 81–90

— 1972: 'Die Grabungen auf dem Norşun-Tepe 1970' *Keban Projesi 1970 Yaz Çalışmaları* (Orta Doğu Teknik Üniversitesi Keban Projesi Yayınları, Seri I, No. 3). Ankara: 103–17

— 1974a: 'Die Grabungen auf dem Norşun-Tepe 1971' *Keban Projesi 1971 Yaz Çalışmaları* (Orta Doğu Teknik Üniversitesi Keban Projesi Yayınları, Seri I, No. 4). Ankara: 87–99

— 1974b: 'Die Grabungen auf dem Norşun-Tepe 1972. Bericht über die 5. Kampagne' *Türk Arkeoloji Dergisi* 21.1: 59–73

— 1976a: 'Die Grabungen auf dem Norşun-Tepe 1973. Bericht über die 6. Kampagne' *Türk Arkeoloji Dergisi* 23.1: 65–86

— 1976b: 'Die Entwicklung der frühbronzezeitlichen Siedlung auf dem Norşuntepe in Ostanatolien' *Archäologisches Korrespondenzblatt* 6.30: 9–20

— 1979a: 'Die Grabungen auf dem Norşun-Tepe 1973' *Keban Projesi 1973 Yaz Çalışmaları* (Orta Doğu Teknik Üniversitesi Keban Projesi Yayınları, Seri I, No. 6). Ankara: 61–78

— 1979b: 'Kalkolitik Çağdan İlk Tunc Çağının Bitimine Kadar Norşuntepe'de Yerleşmenin Gelişimi' *Türk Tarih Kongresi* 8.1. Ankara: 55–63

— 1982: 'Die Grabungen auf dem Norşun-Tepe 1974' *Keban Projesi 1974–1975 Çalışmaları* (Orta Doğu Teknik Üniversitesi Keban Projesi Yayınları, Seri I, No. 7). Ankara: 41–70

— 1983: 'Neue Funde eurasischer Steppennomaden in Kleinasien' in R.M. Boehmer, H. Hauptmann (eds), *Beiträge zur Altertumskunde Kleinasiens. Festschrift für Kurt Bittel*. Mainz: 251–70

— 1987: 'Lidar Höyük' in D.O. Edzard (ed.), *Reallexikon der Assyriologie und Vorderasiatischen Archäologie* 7.1/2. Berlin: 15–16

Hauptmann, H., Boessneck, J., von den Driesch, A. 1976: 'Die Grabungen auf dem Norşun-Tepe 1972' *Keban Projesi 1972 Çalışmaları* (Orta Doğu Teknik Üniversitesi Keban Projesi Yayınları, Seri I, No. 5). Ankara: 71–100

Hawkins, J.D. 1988: 'Kuzi-Tešub and the "Great Kings" of Kargamiš' *Anatolian Studies* 38: 99–108

Korbel, G. 1985: *Die spätbronzezeitliche Keramik von Norşuntepe* (Institut für Bauen und Planen in Entwicklungsländern. Mitteilungen 4). Hannover

Meriggi, P. 1964: 'Und prima attestazione epicorica dei Moschi in Frigia' *Athenaeum* 42: 52–8

Müller, U. 1999a: 'Die eisenzeitliche Stratigraphie von Lidar Höyük' *Anatolian Studies* 49: 123–31

— 1999b: 'Die eisenzeitliche Keramik des Lidar Höyük' in A. Hausleiter, A. Reiche (eds), *Iron Age Pottery in Northern Mesopotamia, Northern Syria and Southeastern Anatolia*. Münster: 403–34

Poetto, M. 1998: 'Traces of geography in hieroglyphic luwian documents of the late empire and early post-empire period (Boğazköy-Südburg and Kızıldağ IV): The case of Masa' in S. Alp, A. Süel (eds), *Acts of the Third International Congress of Hittitology, Çorum, September 16–22 1996*. Ankara: 469–79

Salvini, M. 2001: 'The Inscriptions of Ayanis' in A. Çilingiroğlu, M. Salvini (eds), *Ayanis I. Ten Years of Excavation at Rusahinili Eiduru-kai 1989–1998*. Rome: 251–319

Sevin, V. 1991: 'The Early Iron Age in the Elazığ region and the problem of the Mushkians' *Anatolian Studies* 41: 87–97

Summers, G.D. 1991: 'Kummuh and Assyria: the evidence from Tille Höyük' *Asia Minor Studien* 3: 1–6

— 1994: 'Grey ware and the eastern limits of Phrygia' in A. Çilingiroğlu, D.H. French (eds), *Anatolian Iron Ages 3* (British Institute of Archaeology at Ankara Monograph 16). Ankara: 241–52

Summers, G.D., Collon, D., Kuniholm, P., Tarter, S., Griggs, C. 1993: *Tille Höyük 4. The Late Bronze Age and the Iron Age Transition* (British Institute of Archaeology at Ankara Monograph 15). Ankara

Sürenhagen, D. 1986: 'Ein Königssiegel aus Kargamiš' *Mitteilungen der Deutschen Orientgesellschaft* 118: 183–90

— 1996: 'Politischer Niedergang und kulturelles Nachleben des hethitischen Großreiches im Lichte neuerer Forschung' in U. Magen, M. Rashad (eds), *Vom Halys zum Euphrat. Festschrift für Thomas Beran*. Münster: 283–93

Winn, M.M. 1980: 'The Early Iron Age pottery' in M.N. van Loon (ed.), *Final Report on the Excavations of the Universities of Chicago, California (LA) and Amsterdam in the Keban Reservoir, Eastern Anatolia 1968–1970*. Amsterdam, New York: 155–75

# The Bronze Age to Iron Age transition in the upper Tigris region: new information from Ziyaret Tepe and Giricano

## Michael Roaf and Andreas Schachner

*Institut für Vorderasiatische Archäologie, University of Munich*

## Abstract

Excavations at Ziyaret Tepe and Giricano (Diyarbakır Province) in 2000 provided new stratigraphic and chronological evidence for the transition from the Bronze Age to the Iron Age in the upper Tigris region. The pottery sequence from these sites matches that of northern Iraq and north Syria in the Late Bronze Age with typical wheel made Mittani and Middle Assyrian pottery, which was replaced in the Early Iron Age by handmade pottery of types widely distributed over east Anatolia. The discovery of 15 cuneiform tablets at Giricano shows that this transition took place after 1069 BC and suggests that the end of Middle Assyrian rule in this region occurred shortly after this date and that the Early Iron Age pottery should be later, but its significance and its precise dating remains disputed.

## Özet

2000 yılında Ziyaret Tepe ve Giricano'da (Diyarbakır İli) yapılan kazılar Yukarı Dicle bölgesi Bronz Çağından Demir Çağa geçiş dönemiyle ilgili yeni stratigrafik ve kronolojik bulgular sağlamıştır. Bu yerleşimlerden ele geçen keramik dizileri Kuzey Irak ve Kuzey Suriye'den bilinen tipik çark yapımı Mittani ve Orta Asur çanak çömlekleri ile özdeşlik göstermektedir. Erken Demir Çağda bu çanak çömlek tipinin yerini el yapımı çanak çömlek tipleri almış ve bunlar tüm Doğu Anadolu'ya yayılmışlardır. Giricano'da bulunan 15 adet çivi yazılı tablet, geçiş döneminin M.Ö. 1069 yılından sonra gerçekleştiğini ve bölgedeki Orta Asur egemenliğinin bu tarihten çok kısa bir süre sonra son bulduğunu düşündürmektedir. Böylece Erken Demir Çağ çanak çömleği aslında daha geç bir döneme ait olmalıdır, ancak önemi ve gerçek tarihi halen tartışılmaktadır.

Assyrian royal inscriptions indicate that, probably in the reign of Shalmaneser I (1273–1244 BC), control of the region along the Tigris downstream from Diyarbakır passed from the control of the kings of Mittani to the Middle Assyrian rulers. Several scholars have recently stressed the importance of this region by suggesting that Ta'idu, the latest capital of the Mittani kingdom, was identical with the Late Assyrian town called Tidu, which lay close to Tušhan (Kessler 1980: 95–105; Karg 1999: 275–6; Radner, Schachner 2001: 756–7).

Archaeological finds from the upper Tigris region — in particular from Ziyaret Tepe and Üçtepe — show a similar development to that observed in sites in northern Iraq and northern Syria (such as Tell Mohammed Arab, Tell al-Rimah, Tell Bderi and Tell Brak), in which levels containing pottery which can be associated with the kingdom of Mittani are followed by levels with pottery typical of the Middle Assyrian period.

In his fundamental work on Mittani and Middle Assyrian pottery, Peter Pfälzner (1995: 228–9, Abb. 135–6) includes two distribution maps showing the extents of the regions in which Mittani and Middle Assyrian pottery were in use. Strangely, in both his maps, these regions are shown stopping at the border between Turkey and Syria. We can now extend the distribution maps to include the upper Tigris region (figs 1, 2; for references see appendices 1, 2), and from the texts found at Giricano we can be sure that this region formed an integral part of the Middle Assyrian Empire, not only ceramically but also administratively and, at least partly, ethnically.

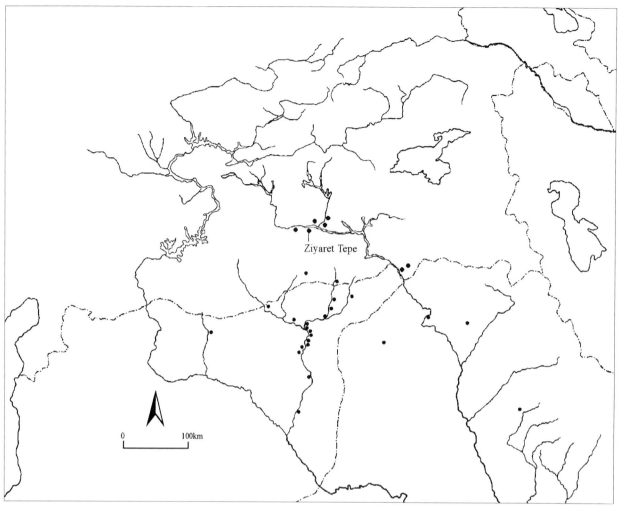

*Fig. 1. Map showing the distribution of sites where Mittani pottery has been found*

**The excavations at Ziyaret Tepe**

The first excavations at Ziyaret Tepe took place in July and August 2000 and were directed by Tim Matney of the University of Akron, Ohio, who had previously carried out extensive surface survey and geomagnetic prospection on the site. Various areas, both on the citadel and in the lower town, were investigated revealing evidence for occupation at various periods including the remains of monumental buildings dating to the Late Assyrian period and in 2002 an archive of Late Assyrian tablets, which may support Karlheinz Kessler's identification (1980: 72–5) of this site with the Late Assyrian provincial capital Tušhan or Tušhu (Matney et al. 2002; 2003).

At the northern end of the east slope of the citadel, a step trench (Operation E) was started in order to investigate the sequence of occupation. Just below the surface were domestic structures of the Middle Assyrian period, with ovens and mud-brick walls. Further down the slope, earlier building levels were exposed dating to the Middle Assyrian period and to the Mittani period. These levels could be dated by the pottery, which is typical of sites of these periods in northeastern Syria and northern Iraq.

Cut into the Middle Assyrian levels was a large pit, about 3m wide and 2m deep with slightly sloping sides, dug from a ground surface which has been eroded away. In this pit was a completely different repertoire of pottery. Whereas the Middle Assyrian pottery was wheel made, with carinated bowls and fine beakers, the pottery from the pit included numerous examples of handmade hemispherical and deep bowls, sometimes with spouts and handles which were decorated with horizontal grooved lines around the rim. This latter type of pottery has been found on numerous sites in eastern Anatolia and has been studied by Veli Sevin (1991; 1999), Uwe Müller (1999; this volume) and Karin Bartl (1994; 2001) who calls it 'grooved-type' pottery (2001: 391) and which we call 'groovy pottery' (a term discussed and agreed to by participants at the Van Congress).

Subsequently, this pit was cut by a rectangular pit lined with mud-brick walls. The latest pottery found within this later feature belonged to the Late Assyrian period. Thus, the groovy pottery pit is securely stratified between the Middle and Late Assyrian periods.

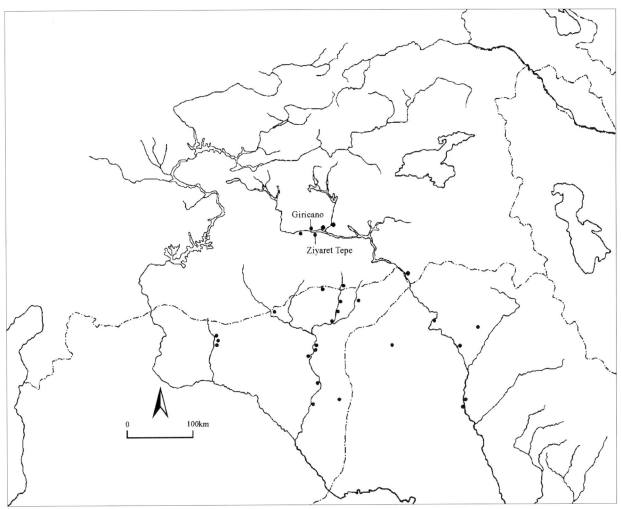

*Fig. 2. Map showing the distribution of sites where Middle Assyrian pottery has been found*

## The excavations at Giricano

The excavations at Giricano are directed by Andreas Schachner. Like the excavations at Ziyaret Tepe, the research at Giricano is carried out under the auspices of the Ilısu Dam Salvage Project in co-operation with the Diyarbakır Museum, and is supported by a grant from the Deutsche Forschungsgemeinschaft for the Northern Frontiers of Mesopotamia Project (Schachner et al. 2002; Schachner 2002). The upper levels of the site are much disturbed by pits, animal holes, roots and weathering, and it was impossible to date with certainty any structures in the top metre or so of the site. There were some later graves and some piles of stones which originally may have belonged to buildings. Amongst the pottery from these surface levels were sherds of groovy pottery (fig. 3). Also in the surface layers were Middle Assyrian sherds, including some complete vessels.

Deeper down where the strata were easier to recognise, various pits were identified, cutting the early second millennium BC monumental buildings; these pits contained typical Middle Assyrian pottery but no examples of groovy pottery.

## The cuneiform tablets from Giricano

Just to the north of the largest of these Middle Assyrian pits, a complete jar was exposed in the surface layers in the edge of the main trench. This jar sat in the section during the visit of the Ministers of Education and Tourism and a few days later it was decided to excavate it. When the bottom of the jar was removed, it proved to contain a group of 15 unbaked clay tablets. In order to preserve these, the jar was removed in a block and then, together with the tablets, it was fired in a local kiln. After cleaning and restoration, the tablets were studied by Karen Radner who identified them as the private archive of Ahuni, son of Kidin-Sin, who is identified as coming both from the settlement Dunnu-ša-Uzibi and from Tušhu (Radner in Schachner et al. 2002; Schachner 2002: 26–7; Radner 2004). The proximity of Giricano (presumably Dunnu-ša-Uzibi) to Ziyaret Tepe supports the identification of Ziyaret Tepe with Tušhan/Tušhu. The tablets record sales of slaves and loans of barley, cattle and silver. Some of the loans were copies but others were still valid and had not been repaid.

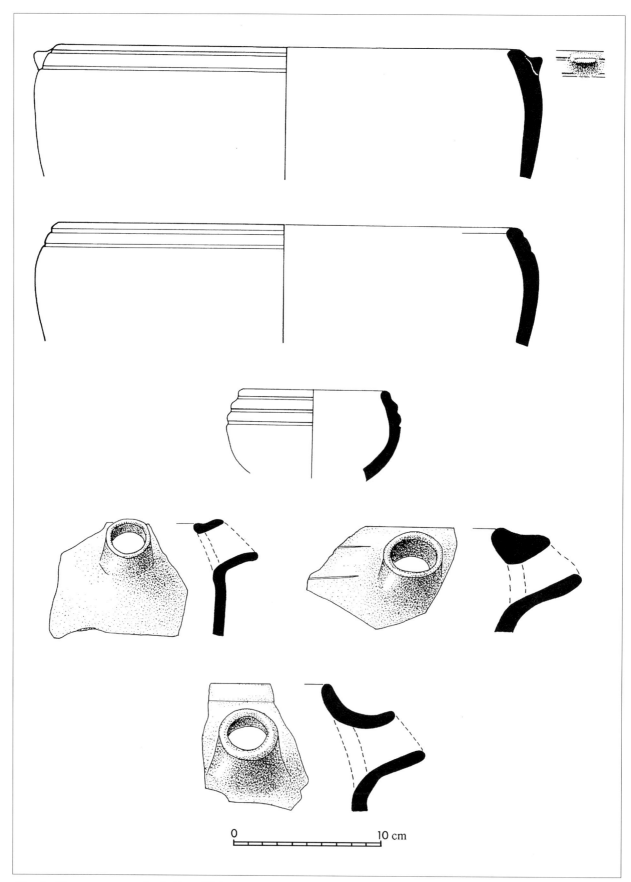

*Fig. 3. Groovy pottery sherds from Giricano*

Perhaps the most interesting feature of these tablets is their date. Eleven of them are dated by the limu-official Ili-iddina, one of the very few Middle Assyrian limu-officials whose date can be fairly closely established because his name is found on the Broken Obelisk of the Assyrian king Ashur-bel-kala (1073–1056 BC). He was probably not one of the first five limu-officials in the reign of Ashur-bel-kala. The Giricano tablets were, therefore, probably written between 1068 and 1056 BC, and until this date Tušhan was under the control of the Assyrians. It is also plausible that the valid documents in Ahuni's archive were left buried in the jar and not recovered because in the following months the Assyrians lost control of the region.

In the year before Ili-iddina was limu (or perhaps in the same year), the Assyrian king relates on the Broken Obelisk that,

> on campaign against the Aramaeans he fought (with them) at the cities . . . which are in the district of the city Šinamu. . . . He conquered the city Hulzu, which is within Mount Kašiari, and the city Erešu, which the people of the land of Habhu held (Grayson 1991: 102 A.0.89.7 iii.13–17).

In the next month he fought against the Aramaeans in Šubru. This is particularly interesting because these places are in or near the upper Tigris region. Šinamu probably lies not far west of Üçtepe, mount Kašiari is the Tur Abdin, Habhu was a neighbouring region and Šubru lay slightly further north.

In the following months the Assyrian king fought against Aramaeans on at least four further occasions (Grayson 1991: 102–3 A.0.89.7 iii.17–32). It is therefore very likely that Aramaeans were responsible for bringing an end to Assyrian rule in the upper Tigris valley. But these Aramaeans, like the 20,000 Mushki defeated by Tiglath-pileser I in the Kashiari mountains some 50 years earlier, were invaders into the region (Grayson 1991: 14, 33, 42, 53).

According to Radner (2004) about two-thirds of the names of the 70 or so people mentioned in the texts have Akkadian etymologies and some are specifically Assyrian. Seven of the names have west Semitic etymologies, but this need not imply that the individuals bearing these names were not Assyrians. Two of the names are Hurrian and 12 cannot be explained. Most of these names were either those of the principals or those of the witnesses, and therefore they belonged to the upper stratum of society and provide no evidence for the majority population living in the region.

## The Kurkh stele and Ashurnasirpal's conquest of the region

When the Assyrians returned to this region in the early ninth century, it was part of the lands of Nairi and was dominated by Aramaeans (Grayson 1991: 261, A.0.101.19 92–6). In 882 Ashurnasirpal II erected a stele in Tušhan and a few years later another stele which was found at Kurkh/Üçtepe. He stated,

> I brought back the enfeebled Assyrians, who because of hunger (and) famine, had gone up to other lands to the land Šubru. I settled them in the city Tuša (Grayson 1991: 202 A.0.101.1 ii 3–9, also 242–3, A.0.101.17 ii 6–28).

The implication of this statement is difficult to determine. Taken at face value there were Assyrians living in Šubru, probably on the north bank of the Tigris. How many years previously they had fled to Šubru, Ashurnasirpal's inscriptions do not reveal.

## Groovy pottery and historical events between 1050 and 900 BC

Between the reigns of Ashur-bel-kala and Ashurnasirpal II, historical sources are silent about what was happening in the upper Tigris region. It appears that the groovy pottery found in the region should be dated to this period.

Bartl (2001: 385, fig. 1) recently published a map showing the distribution of this type of pottery. While the distribution clearly reflects the intensity of archaeological research, it also shows the very extensive region in which this pottery has been found, covering an area some 700km from east to west and 500km from north to south. Recently published reports add more sites where groovy pottery has been identified (see appendix 3), but the overall extent is not much changed (fig. 4).

She also showed that in several regions there was a radical change in the ceramic assemblages between the Late Bronze Age settlements and the Early Iron Age occupations in which groovy pottery occurs. In order to explain this, various scholars have proposed that there was a change in the population and that migrants brought this type of pottery with them; and Bartl, with some hesitation, considers this a plausible theory.

The proposal that the groovy pottery could be identified with the Mushki, against whom Tiglath-pileser I fought in 1115 BC, must be ruled out on historical and geographical grounds (Summers 1994: 245–7). The distribution of groovy pottery corresponds in no way to what is known or surmised about the Mushki.

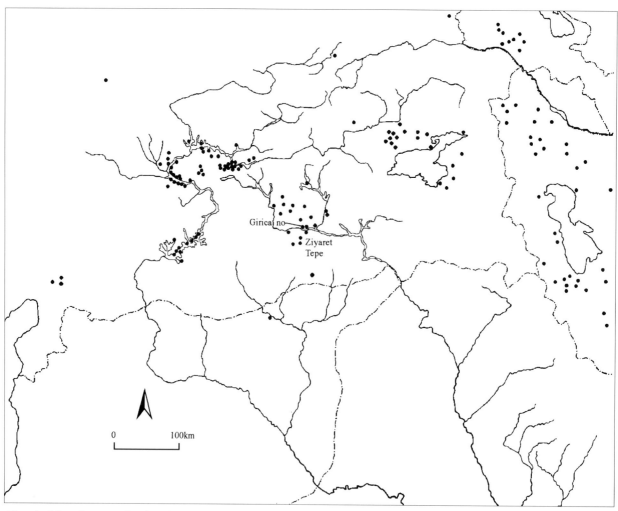

*Fig. 4. Map showing the distribution of sites where groovy pottery has been found*

Even though Middle Assyrian control of the upper Tigris region may have been brought to an end by the Aramaeans there is no reason to associate groovy pottery with Aramaeans, even though in the ninth century the Aramaean kingdom of Bit-Zamani was situated in this region. In fact, of the various peoples and lands mentioned in texts from the 13th to the ninth centuries, only one group corresponds to the known distribution of groovy pottery. These are the Nairi lands. Assyrians and Urartians used this name to describe some very different entities (Salvini 1998), in some cases as equivalent to Urartu or Biainili, in other cases as a land or Assyrian province in the upper Tigris region, but also more generally as a broad, inexact term to describe the mountain lands north of Assyria, covering approximately the area where groovy pottery has been found (see, for example, the map in Salvini 1967: 49). In the inscriptions of Tiglath-pileser I, 23 lands are listed, and in other inscriptions alliances of 30, 40, or 60 kings of the Nairi lands are mentioned (Salvini 1998). It is unlikely, however, that this apparently loose confederation of peoples and lands should be exactly the same as those who used groovy pottery. Moreover, since it is clear that a variety of peoples of various ethnicities used groovy pottery, it should not be associated with only one of them.

**The dating of groovy pottery**

Bartl has discussed also the problems in dating the pottery, and tentatively suggested that it was in use in the Keban dam area between about 1150 and 950 BC (Bartl 2001: 391, 396). In the Karababa dam area, Müller (1999: 404) proposed a date between 1100 and 900 BC for its use at Lidar Höyük, while Blaylock (1999: 267) suggested a rather later date at Tille Höyük ('in the ?10th and ninth centuries, but probably not as late as the eighth century'). There is also evidence to suggest that further east some examples are pre-Urartian (Sevin 1999; Bartl 2001: 396). In the upper Tigris region, however, it seems that the extensive use of groovy pottery must date to after the end of the Middle Assyrian control of the region, i.e. after ca. 1050 BC, but how long after cannot yet be determined.

How late groovy pottery remained in use is still uncertain. It is not the only type of pottery found in the upper Tigris region in the Iron Age, for there are various types of painted and other pottery which have been discussed by Bradley Parker (1997: 240–1; 1998: 436–40 = 2001: 110–11). The dating of these types is still uncertain, but some may be contemporary with the Late Assyrian control of the region. The arrival of the Assyrian army and the re-imposition of Assyrian administration in the upper Tigris region in the early ninth century led to the introduction of new, typically Late Assyrian pottery types, but would not have immediately brought to an end the use of indigenous pottery; but whether the latter was groovy pottery or some other ceramic assemblage is still uncertain.

There are still fundamental questions to be answered about the Early Iron Age in this region. What was the nature of the settlements? If the pit in Ziyaret Tepe is correctly interpreted as a grain storage pit, this would confirm that the region was extensively farmed, as is also indicated in the texts of Ashurnasirpal II. Are there chronological developments in the ceramics within this period? Are there regional differences within the various assemblages currently labelled as groovy? We hope that excavations currently under way in the Ilısu Dam Salvage Project may provide further information on these questions.

## Appendix 1
### Sites in Turkey with Mittani pottery not included in Pfälzner 1995

| | |
|---|---|
| Balpınar: | Algaze 1989: 245 |
| Başorin: | Algaze et al. 1991: 197 |
| Girharrin: | Ay 1995: 16 |
| Girnavaz: | Erkanal, Erkanal 1989: 132 |
| Gre Dimse: | Karg 2001: 686, 669, fig. 8 |
| Gre Hazale (?): | Algaze et al. 1991: fig. 20 C no. 56 |
| Site no. 52: | Algaze 1989: 245 |
| Üçtepe: | Köroğlu 1998: 27, 32, res. 4; Sevin 1989: 106–7, res. 10.6 |
| Ziyaret Tepe: | Matney 1998: 24, fig. 6.12–13 |

## Appendix 2
### Sites in Turkey with Middle Assyrian pottery not included in Pfälzner 1995

| | |
|---|---|
| Başorin : | Algaze et al. 1991: 197 |
| Giricano: | Schachner et al. 2002: 572, fig. 5; Schachner 2002: 32, Abb. 21–6 |
| Girnavaz: | Erkanal 1991: 278; 1989: 279; Erkanal, Erkanal 1989: 132 |
| Gre Dimse: | Karg 2001: 686, 669, fig. 8 |
| Gre Hazale (?): | Algaze et al. 1991: fig. 20 C no. 56 |
| Üçtepe: | Köroğlu 1998: 27–30, 37–49, res. 5–8 |
| Ziyaret Tepe: | Matney 1998: 24, fig. 6.8–9, 25, fig. 9.9 |

Numerous sites with Middle Assyrian pottery in the Batman river valley are mentioned by Algaze (1989: 245), and around Üçtepe by Köroğlu (1998: 74), but the pottery from these sites has not been published.

## Appendix 3
### Sites with groovy pottery not included in Bartl 2001
*Upper Tigris and Batman river region*

| | |
|---|---|
| Aktepe: | Köroğlu 1998: 72–4 |
| Başkale: | Rosenberg, Togul 1991: 245, fig. 10.12 |
| Çubuklu (İshakan): | Köroğlu 1998: 72–4 |
| Eliaçık: | Köroğlu 1998: 72–4 |
| Giricano: | Schachner et al. 2002: 571, fig. 4; Schachner 2002: 25, Abb. 14 |
| Girharrin (?): | Ay 1995: Şekil II.3–13 |
| Gökçetevek: | Köroğlu 1998: 72–4 |
| Gre Dimse: | Karg 2001: 670, fig. 9 |
| Hirbe Tayyar: | Parker 2001: fig. 5.13.H (=1998: fig. 5.11.H) |
| İncirtepe: | Köroğlu 1998: 72–4 |
| Karaçalı: | Köroğlu 1998: 72–4 |
| Kazancı (Kürthacı): | Köroğlu 1998: 72–4 |
| Kenan Tepe: | Parker et al. 2002: 633; 2003: 3 |
| Near Gre Migro no. 4: | Parker 2001: fig. 5.21.F–H (=1998: fig. 5.21.F–H) |
| Pir Hüseyin: | Köroğlu 1998: 72–4 |
| Sivirtepe (Şehaban): | Köroğlu 1998: 72–4 |
| Talavaş Tepe: | Parker et al. 2001: 580, fig. 9.C–E, G |
| Üçtepe: | Köroğlu 1998: 72–4 |
| Yarımca: | Köroğlu 1998: 72–4 |
| Yukarı Bağpınar (Zoğzunç): | Köroğlu 1998: 72–4 |
| Ziyaret Tepe: | Parker 2001: fig. 5.19.G–I (=1998: fig 5.17.G–I); Matney 1998: 24, fig. 7 [already noted in Bartl 2001 with an inaccurate reference] |

*Region between lake Van and the Murat river*

| | |
|---|---|
| Arınçküs: | Özfırat 1999: 3 |
| Çaygeldi: | Özfırat 2000: 197 |
| Elmakaya: | Özfırat 1999: 8 |
| Gümüşpınar: | Özfırat 2000: 197 |
| Haydar Kalesi: | Özfırat 2000: 197 |
| Kırkgöze: | Özfırat 2001: 127 |
| Okçuhan: | Özfırat 2001: 127 |
| Segran Kalesi: | Özfırat 1999: 3 |
| Sütay Yaylası: | Özfırat 1994: çiz. 3 |
| Üçtepe: | Özfırat 2000: 197 |
| Yoncatepe: | Belli, Kavaklı 2001 |

*Sivas region*

| | |
|---|---|
| Kuşaklı: | Müller-Karpe 1996: 79, 81, Abb. 14 |

*Maraş region*

KM 48 Süllümcük:

Swartz Dodd, personal communication

KM 78 Tulhum Çiftlik:

Swartz Dodd, personal communication

KM 104 Beşebli Çiftlik/Karabacakhöyüğü:

Swartz Dodd, personal communication

Lynn Swartz Dodd has re-examined the evidence from the Maraş survey and now considers that groovy pottery is possibly present only at KM 78 and KM 104. For further detail see her contribution to this volume.

## Bibliography

Algaze, G. 1989: 'A new frontier: first results of the Tigris-Euphrates archaeological reconnaissance project, 1988' *Journal of Near Eastern Studies* 48: 241–81

Algaze, G., Breuninger R., Lightfoot, C., Rosenberg, M. 1991: 'The Tigris-Euphrates archaeological reconnaissance project: a preliminary report of the 1989–1990 seasons' *Anatolica* 17: 175–240

Ay, E. 1995: 'Girharrin Höyüğünün arkeolojik değerlendirmesi' in A. Erkanal, H. Erkanal, H. Hüryılmaz, A.T. Ökse, N. Çınardalı, S. Günel, H. Tekin, B. Uysal, D. Yalçıklı (eds), *In memoriam İ. Metin Akyurt ve Bahattin Devam anı kitabı, eski Yakın Doğu kültürleri üzerine incelemeler.* Istanbul: 13–32

Bartl, K. 1994: 'Die frühe Eisenzeit in Ostanatolien und ihre Verbindungen zu den benachbarten Regionen' *Baghdader Mitteilungen* 25: 473–518

— 2001: 'Eastern Anatolia in the Early Iron Age' in R. Eichmann, H. Parzinger (eds), *Migration und Kulturtransfer, Der Wandel vorder- und zentralasiatischer Kulturen im Umbruch vom 2. zum 1. vorchristlichen Jahrtausend.* Bonn: 383–410

Belli, O., Kavaklı, E. 2001: '1999 yılı Van — Yonca Tepe Kalesi ve nekropolü kazısı' *Kazı Sonuçları Toplantısı* 22.1: 369–84

Blaylock, S. 1999: 'Iron Age pottery from Tille Höyük south-eastern Turkey' in A. Hausleiter, A. Reiche (eds), *Iron Age Pottery in Northern Mesopotamia, Northern Syria and South-Eastern Anatolia. Papers Presented at the Meetings of the International Table Ronde at Heidelburg (1995) and Nieborow (1997)* (Altertumskunde des Vorderen Orients. Band 10). Munster: 263–86

Erkanal, H. 1989: '1987 Girnavaz Kazıları' *Kazı Sonuçları Toplantısı* 10.1: 273–86

— 1991: '1989 Girnavaz Kazıları' *Kazı Sonuçları Toplantısı* 12.1: 277–92

Erkanal, A., Erkanal, H. 1989: 'Archäologischer Überblick über die Provinz Mardin' in K. Emre, B. Hrouda, M. Mellink, N. Özgüç (eds), *Anatolia and the Near East, Studies in Honor of Tahsin Özgüç.* Ankara: 129–34

Grayson, A.K. 1991: *Assyrian Rulers of the Early First Millennium BC I (1114–859 BC)* (Royal Inscriptions of Mesopotamia Assyrian Periods 2). Toronto

Karg, N. 1999: 'Gre Dimse 1998: preliminary report' in N. Tuna, J. Öztürk (eds), *Salvage Project of the Archaeological Heritage of the Ilısu and Carchemish Dam Reservoirs Activities in 1998.* Ankara: 272–96

— 2001: 'First soundings at Gre Dimse 1999' in N. Tuna, J. Öztürk, J. Velibeyoğlu (eds), *Salvage Project of the Archaeological Heritage of the Ilısu and Carchemish Dam Reservoirs Activities in 1999.* Ankara: 671–715

Kessler, K. 1980: *Untersuchungen zur historischen Topographie Nordmesopotamiens nach keilschriftlichen Quellen des 1.Jt. v.Chr.* (TAVO B.26). Wiesbaden

Köroğlu, K. 1998: *Üçtepe I, yeni kazı ve yüzey bulguları ışığında Diyarbakır.* Ankara

Matney, T. 1998: 'Preliminary report on the first season of work at Ziyaret Tepe in the Diyarbakır Province' *Anatolica* 24: 7–30

Matney, T., Roaf, M., MacGinnis, J., McDonald, H. 2002: 'Archaeological excavations at Ziyaret Tepe, 2000 and 2001' *Anatolica* 28: 47–89

Matney, T., MacGinnis, J., McDonald, H., Nicoll, K., Rainville, L., Roaf, M., Smith, M., Stein, D. 2003: 'Archaeological investigations at Ziyaret Tepe, 2002' *Anatolica* 29: 175–221

Müller, U. 1999: 'Die eisenzeitliche Keramik des Lidar Höyük' in A. Hausleiter and A. Reiche (eds), *Iron Age Pottery in Northern Mesopotamia, Northern*

*Syria and South-Eastern Anatolia. Papers Presented at the Meetings of the International Table Ronde at Heidelburg (1995) and Nieborow (1997)* (Altertumskunde des Vorderen Orients. Band 10). Munster: 403–34

Müller-Karpe, A. 1996: 'Untersuchungen in Kuşaklı, 1995' *Mitteilungen der Deutschen Orient-Gesellschaft* 128: 69–94

Özfırat, A. 1994: 'M.Ö. II. binyıl Doğu Anadolu boyalı seramik kültürleri üzerine araştırmalar' *Araştırma Sonuçları Toplantısı* 11: 359–77

— 1999: '1997 yılı Bitlis-Muş yüzey araştırması. Tunç ve Demir Çağları' *Araştırma Sonuçları Toplantısı* 16.2: 1–22

— 2000: '1998 yılı Bitlis-Muş illeri yüzey araştırması: Tunç ve Demir Çağları' *Araştırma Sonuçları Toplantısı* 17.2: 193–210

— 2001: '1999 yılı Muş ili yüzey araştırması: Tunç ve Demir Çağları' *Araştırma Sonuçları Toplantısı* 18.2: 123–40

Parker, B. 1997 'The northern frontier of Assyria: an archaeological perspective' in S. Parpola, R.M. Whiting (eds), *Assyria 1995. Proceedings of the Tenth Anniversary Symposium of the Neo-Assyrian Text Corpus Project, Helsinki, September 7-11, 1995.* Helsinki: 217–44

— 1998: The Mechanics of Empire: the Northern Frontier of Assyria as a Case Study of Imperial Dynamics. Unpublished PhD thesis. University of California at Los Angeles

— 2001: *The Mechanics of Empire: the Northern Frontier of Assyria as a Case Study of Imperial Dynamics* (Neo-Assyrian Text Corpus Project). Helsinki

Parker, B., Creekmore, A., Easton, C. 2001: 'The Upper Tigris Archaeological Research Project (UTARP): excavations and survey at Boztepe and intensive survey at Talavaş Tepe, 1999: a preliminary report' in N. Tuna, J. Öztürk, J. Velibeyoğlu (eds), *Salvage Project of the Archaeological Heritage of the Ilısu and Carchemish Dam Reservoirs Activities in 1999.* Ankara: 584–619

Parker, B., Creekmore, A., Easton, C., Moseman, E., Sasaki, R. 2002: 'The Upper Tigris Archaeological Research Project (UTARP): preliminary report for the year 2000' in N. Tuna, J. Öztürk, J. Velibeyoğlu (eds), *Salvage Project of the Archaeological Heritage of the Ilısu and Carchemish Dam Reservoirs Activities in 2000.* Ankara: 631–43

Parker, B., Creekmore, A., Dodd, L. Swartz, Paine, R., Abraham, M. 2003: 'The Upper Tigris Archaeological Research Project (UTARP): an overview of the archaeological research conducted at Kenan Tepe during the 2001 field season' *Kazı Sonuçları Toplantısı* 24.2: 1–20

Pfälzner, P. 1995: *Mitannische und mittelassyrische Keramik, eine chronologische, funktionale und produktionsökonomische Analyse.* Berlin

Radner, K. 2004: *Das mittelassyrische Tontafelarchiv von Giricano/Dunnu-ša-Uzibi* (Ausgrabungen in Giricano I, Subartu). Turnhout

Radner, K., Schachner, A. 2001: 'From Tušhan to Amedi, topographical questions concerning the upper Tigris region in the Assyrian period' in N. Tuna, J. Öztürk, J. Velibeyoğlu (eds), *Salvage Project of the Archaeological Heritage of the Ilısu and Carchemish Dam Reservoirs Activities in 1999.* Ankara: 753–76

Rosenberg, M., Togul, H. 1991: 'The Batman River archaeological site survey, 1990' *Anatolica* 17: 241–54

Salvini, M. 1967: *Nairi e Ur(u)atri: Contributo alla Storia della Formazione del Regno di Urartu.* Rome

— 1998: 'Nairi, Na'iri' *Reallexikon der Assyriologie und Vorderasiatischen Archäologie* 9. Berlin: 87–91

Schachner, A. 2002: 'Ausgrabungen in Giricano (2000–2001), Neue Forschungen an der Nordgrenze des Mesopotamischen Kulturraums' *Istanbuler Mitteilungen* 52: 9–57

Schachner, A., Roaf, M., Radner, K., Pasternak R. 2002: 'Vorläufiger Bericht über die Ausgrabungen in Giricano (Diyarbakır/Türkei) 2000' in N. Tuna, J. Öztürk, J. Velibeyoğlu (eds), *Salvage Project of the Archaeological Heritage of the Ilısu and Carchemish Dam Reservoirs Activities in 2000.* Ankara: 587–611

Sevin, V. 1989: '1988 yılı Diyarbakır/Üçtepe kazısı' *Kazı Sonuçları Toplantısı* 11.1: 103–23

— 1991: 'The Early Iron Age in the Elazığ region and the problem of the Mushkians' *Anatolian Studies* 41: 87–97

— 1999: 'The origin of the Urartians in the light of the Van/Karagündüz excavations' in A. Çilingiroğlu, R.J. Matthews (eds), *Anatolian Iron Ages 4* (*Anatolian Studies* 49): 159–64

Summers, G. 1994: 'Grey Ware and the eastern limits of Phrygia' in A. Çilingiroğlu, D.H. French (eds), *Anatolian Iron Ages 3* (British Institute of Archaeology at Ankara Monograph 16). Ankara: 241–52

# A Phrygian sculptural identity? Evidence from early Phrygian drawings in Iron Age Gordion

## Lynn E. Roller
*University of California, Davis*

### Abstract

This paper discusses a selected number of informal drawings found on the exterior walls of megaron 2, one of the buildings from the late ninth century BC destruction level at Gordion. The drawings were incised in very irregular fashion onto the ashlar blocks of the building, probably before its construction. A variety of subjects can be recognised, including casual marks, signs and symbols, and pictures of animal and human figures and architectural features. Several of the drawings, particularly the animal and human scenes, show a close affinity with the sculptural style and subject matter found in Neo-Hittite sites. Others depict distinctively Phrygian themes, including Phrygian architecture and the predatory bird, a frequent Phrygian religious symbol. Taken together, the drawings provide insight into the artistic subjects and styles, both external and internal, which helped shape the cultural identity of the early Phrygian city.

### Özet

Bu çalışmada, Gordion'da bulunan ve M.Ö. 9. yüzyıl sonlarına tarihlenen yıkım tabakasındaki yapılardan biri olan 2 no.lu megaron yapısının dış duvarları üzerine yapılmış birkaç çizim incelenecektir. Çizimler oldukça kuralsız bir biçimde, olasılıkla yapının inşasından önce, inşaatta kullanılacak olan yontulmuş yapı taşlarının üzerine kazılarak yapılmıştır. Çizimlerde pekçok farklı konu tanımlanabilmektedir. Bunlar gündelik işaretler, damgalar, semboller, insan ve hayvan figürleri ve mimari betimlemelerden oluşmaktadır. Bu çizimlerin, özellikle insan ve hayvan figürleri içerenleri, Neo-Hitit yerleşimlerindeki heykeltraşlık stili ve konu seçimleriyle yakın benzerlikler göstermektedir. Diğerleri çok belirgin bir şekilde Frig temaları ve Frig mimari özellikleri taşımaktadır. Hatta çok yaygın görülen bir Frig dini sembolü olan yırtıcı kuş da bunlar arasında yer alır. Hepsi birarada değerlendirildiğinde, bu çizimler Erken Frig şehirlerinin kültürel kimliğini şekillendirmeye yarayan, hem yerli hem de yabancı sanata ait tema daha yakından anlamamızı sağlayacaktır.

Among the many rich discoveries from Gordion contributing to our understanding of the Anatolian Iron Age is a series of drawings incised onto the exterior surface of megaron 2, the second building recognised in the Phrygian destruction level. The drawings occur on the two side walls and the rear wall of the building. They were positioned on the stone blocks of the walls in fairly random fashion: only rarely is a drawing centred onto a single block, and no drawing extends onto an adjoining block. At the time of its excavation, the southeast corner of megaron 2 was still standing to a height of several courses, and the placement of the drawings here was recorded, but the remaining walls had collapsed in the fire that destroyed the citadel quarter (for excavation of megaron 2, see Young 1957;

1958. For illustration of the back wall of megaron 2 see, Young 1958: pl. 21, fig. 3; 1969: 271, top). Some of the most complex drawings were found on the east side wall, but because the blocks of this wall had tumbled down together into a heap, the relationship of one block to another could not be recovered.

The drawings, first uncovered in 1956 and 1957, were noted in the excavation reports for those years and were the subject of a special study by Rodney Young (Young 1969). Other than that, they have received very little attention. At the time of their discovery, Young formulated an hypothesis to explain them, namely that the drawings were made by a broad cross-section of the population at Gordion who scratched scenes of daily life onto the walls of the building to pass the time while

125

waiting to conduct business in the citadel quarter. His nickname for the incised stones, 'doodlestones', was used in virtually every subsequent mention of them but his explanatory hypothesis was rarely examined. Indeed, Young's casual dismissal of the drawings as 'doodles' tended to imply that the information to be gained from them was limited and it discouraged further attention being given to them (an exception being Mellink 1983).

When I began my study of this material, it quickly became clear that Young's hypothesis was impossible. Even a brief preliminary examination of the material showed that these drawings were not doodles, in the sense of casual scratchings on the wall by idle passers-by. The reconstruction of the back wall of the megaron indicates that many of the drawings were situated either too high or too low on the wall's surface to support the supposition that they were drawn directly onto the standing wall. Several of the drawings were deeply incised, in a few cases almost approaching the technique of relief sculpture (an example is illustrated in Roller 1999a: 144, fig. 2), unfeasible to execute on a standing wall. Moreover, it is highly implausible that private individuals would have had the opportunity to scribble on the walls of an official public building situated in the citadel quarter. This section of the city is surrounded by stone walls and gates designed to limit admission only to those with the right of entry. My own hypothesis to explain the placement of the drawings is that they were incised onto individual blocks before the building was constructed, and that because traffic within this quarter of the city did not normally move around the back of the building, it was not thought necessary to remove the drawings or cover them over (Roller 1999a; a longer work on the incised Gordion drawings will appear in the Gordion publication series).

In this paper I would like to offer a more detailed consideration of the meaning of the drawings and of the information they can give us on the cultural development of Gordion during the Early Iron Age. First, a brief review of the subject matter of the drawings is in order. Some of them can be called 'drawings' only in a very loose sense, for they consist of little more than straight lines and haphazard marks on the stone. The majority, however, consist of complex scenes involving animals, human figures and geometric patterns. Animals are the most frequent subject. The single most common animal is the bird, almost always a bird of prey (published examples include Young 1969: 272, top, 274, top right, 275, top left; Roller 1999a: 147, fig. 5; there are also numerous unpublished examples). Most are drawn in standing profile with curved beaks and talons that emphasise their predatory nature (fig. 1). The lion is the next most frequently represented animal. These too are

*Fig. 1. Four predatory birds, ST 407 and 449 (drawn by L.E. Roller)*

regularly shown in profile. Many are striding forward with open mouth, and prominent curved claws and sharp teeth emphasise the animal's ferocity (fig. 2) (Young 1969: 274, top left [mistakenly identified as a dog]; Roller 1999a: 147, fig. 6, 149, fig. 8). A variety of other animals also appear, including horses, deer, cattle and a goat (Roller 1999a: 147, fig. 6, illustrating a horse and the goat). The animals normally appear as isolated figures, neither interacting with another figure nor forming part of a complex scene.

A smaller number of drawings comprise scenes with human figures. These range in style from almost cartoon-like characters to carefully drawn scenes in which a great deal of detail can be detected (cartoon-like figures include ST 445, unpublished; detailed human figures include Young 1957: pl. 90, figs 11, 13; 1969: 273, middle right; Roller 1999a: 144, figs 1, 2, 146, fig. 4, 147, fig. 5). Often the human figure will be shown in some kind of action, and in a few cases two figures appear who interact with each other. Thus, in contrast to the animal scenes in which the animal figure stands alone and appears to have a simple symbolic value, the scenes with human figures suggest a more complex narrative function.

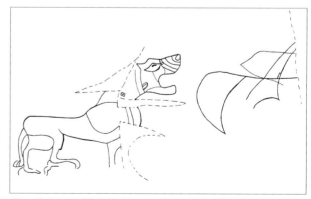

*Fig. 2. Lion, ST 260 (drawn by L.E. Roller)*

Architectural features appear in a small number of drawings. A few blocks depict an end view of a narrow building with a high-pitched roof, pointed gable and curved akroterion, apparently a typical Phrygian megaron such as megaron 2 itself (fig. 3) (ST 263 a, b: Young 1957: pl. 90, fig. 1; again published in Young 1969: 272, top; and in Mellink 1983: 357, fig. 1 — note that this drawing contains several inaccuracies and should be used with caution: a more accurate drawing of ST 263b is given here, fig. 3 — a similar building appears in ST 317, unpublished). This architectural type is not inevitable, however, since at least one different building form is also represented (ST 298, unpublished, depicting a building with a flat roof and central tower).

Another subject that recurs regularly is geometric patterning, ranging from fairly simple motifs, like the five pointed star and X-in-a-square, to complex maze patterns, vertical rows of lozenges and other comparable designs (star: Young 1969: 273, lower right; cross-in-square: Young 1958: pl. 21, fig. 3; maze: ST 283, unpublished; lozenges: ST 297, unpublished).

The variety of subjects, styles, and degrees of artistic sophistication found in the drawings renders their interpretation problematic. One issue is the chronology of the drawings, which are associated with YHSS phase 6 according to the sequence proposed by Voigt and Henrickson (2000: 41): the absolute dates offered for that phase (Voigt, Henrickson 2000: 41) require modification given the recently revised Gordion chronology, derived from radiocarbon samples, which now assigns the Gordion destruction level (YHSS phase 6A) to approximately 830–805 BC, over a hundred years earlier than previously thought (DeVries et al. this volume), clearly forcing a revision of the date of the incised drawings. They cannot be any later than the last quarter of the ninth century BC, the date of the building's destruction, and almost certainly they are earlier. Megaron 2 went through several building phases, indicating that it was in use over a number of years; moreover, it is possible that it was built from blocks reused from an earlier construction level (for a description of the various phases of megaron 2 see Young 1969: 271–2; Roller 1999a: 150–1). These circumstances suggest a tentative date for the drawings in the mid-ninth century BC.

A second issue is the degree of influence from other cultures and other artistic media. Several of the drawings reveal distinct parallels with the artistic style of contemporary Neo-Hittite relief sculpture. One clear example is the hunter who strides forward, sword at his side. In his left hand he holds a captured hare in a bag, while with his right he swings back a mace as if to strike the animal (Roller 1999a: 146, fig. 4.). This hunting scene is a fairly stock element in Neo-Hittite reliefs, and finds a particu-

*Fig. 3. Phrygian megaron with lion, ST 263b (drawn by L.E. Roller)*

*Fig. 4. Human figure striding forward, ST 453 (drawn by L.E. Roller)*

larly close parallel in an Iron Age relief from Kültepe, where the hunted animal is again a hare (Özgüç 1971: 82, fig. 7). Another Gordion drawing, depicting two men squaring off against each other with drawn swords (Young 1957: pl. 90, fig. 11), finds a good parallel in relief sculpture from Tell Halaf (Orthmann 1971: pl. 10c). Some of the Gordion figures are more stately, such as the one in a long gown striding forward (fig. 4) (ST 453), a pose which can be recognised in a relief from Karkamish (Orthmann 1971: pl. 23a). Another depicts a figure in frontal view (Roller 1999a: 144, fig. 1), a pose that finds a close parallel in a Neo-Hittite relief on the base of a large statue from Zincirli (Orthmann 1971: pl. 62e). In each example we sense that the Gordion drawing, while only a basic linear sketch, represents an attempt to capture the same details, such as costume, pointed shoes, and hairstyle, found on the Neo-Hittite models.

In addition to the human figures, the Gordion lions have clear Neo-Hittite prototypes. Like their Neo-Hittite counterparts, they frequently stride forward with open mouth and bared teeth. Specific details, such as the band on the neck, the treatment of shoulder musculature, and prominent curved claws, all of which occur regularly in the Gordion drawings, are standard features of Neo-Hittite lions (compare a Neo-Hittite lion from Malatya, in Orthmann 1971: pl. 29b; with Gordion lions: Roller 1999a: 149, fig. 8; ST 260 [here fig. 3]; S 33, unpublished).

Neo-Hittite influence is also evident in the presence of characters found in hieroglyphic Luwian script. Several of the symbols found in the Gordion drawings, including the row of lozenges and the predatory bird (see above), as well as the tongue (*lingua*) (Young 1969: 273, lower right), occur in Luwian hieroglyphs (for the symbols used in Luwian hieroglyphic script see Hawkins 2000: especially 23–34 and tables 1–4). An intriguing parallel is offered by a series of inscribed lead strips from Kululu (Özgüç 1971: 111–16, pls 50–2). Because the Luwian symbols appear only as random characters in the Gordion drawings, it seems unlikely that they were ever intended to reproduce a specific text. Nevertheless, their presence provides additional evidence for the impact of Neo-Hittite culture on Gordion.

This sampling of parallels strongly suggests that, far from being the random scratchings of an untutored population, at least some of the drawings were the result of attempts to copy Neo-Hittite sculptural style. One may even speculate that they were made under the direct influence of artists brought from the southeastern Anatolian region to Gordion, for the purpose of training local Phrygian artists in Neo-Hittite artistic style. The few sculpted relief panels known from the pre-destruction level of the city (Sams 1989) also show strong influence of Neo-Hittite sculptural style and demonstrate that this was the model that the earliest sculptors of Gordion imitated. Unfinished relief panels from the destruction level (S 79 and S 99, unpublished) further demonstrate that orthostate relief blocks at the site were indeed developed from such two-dimensional drawings as those under consideration here.

At the same time, the subjects represented in the Gordion drawings depart from the Neo-Hittite repertory in a number of significant ways. Furthermore, several themes that were later to play a major role in Phrygian art are already present. The predatory bird, an especially popular subject among the Gordion drawings prefiguring its frequent occurrence in the site's sculpture from later centuries, is substantially more common than the lion, in contrast to the corpus of Neo-Hittite reliefs where lions are the most frequently represented animal. Another distinctively Phrygian theme is the Phrygian megaron. This seems to depict the type of structure actually used in Gordion during the ninth century, one that differs considerably from the typical form found in the Neo-Hittite palaces. Similarly, the interest in complex geometric patterns, found in several of the incised Gordion drawings, prefigures the frequent use of such designs on early Phrygian painted pottery (Sams 1971) and wooden furniture found at Gordion (Young et al. 1981: 62–77, 176–90; Simpson: 1988). Taken together, this suggests that the Phrygian artisans were adapting Neo-Hittite models to create their own distinctive regional style, one that combined themes and forms from southeastern Anatolia with other subjects that could assume a particular meaning within Phrygian culture.

It seems particularly telling that the subjects I have identified in the Gordion drawings as being characteristically Phrygian are themes that were to find prominent expression in Phrygian religious art in later periods. The predatory bird is the regular companion of the Phrygian mother goddess, Matar Kubeliya, and images of birds were frequently used as votive offerings to her (for the cult iconography of the Phrygian mother goddess, see Roller 1999b: 71–105). Similarly, the architectural theme of the Phrygian megaron forms a major subject in Phrygian cult reliefs of later periods; moreover, these cult reliefs are often decorated with elaborate complex patterns, drawn from the Phrygian repertory of geometric art. It seems unlikely that the drawings incised on megaron 2 had a specifically votive intent for they have a very casual, almost humorous character that is readily apparent and would seem to argue against a religious purpose (although Mellink [1983: 356–9] suggested that megaron 2 was a temple, I find this interpretation very doubtful: see Roller 1999a: 151; also Voigt 1997: 428–9). Furthermore, there is no representation of Phrygian Matar, or indeed of any other cult figure, from this level of the city, so we cannot be certain about the nature of Phrygian religious iconography in this period. However, the presence of several themes that were to have a long life in Phrygian art does suggest that the Phrygians who made these drawings were experimenting with the Neo-Hittite style to develop their own visual repertory.

The presence of symbols from Luwian script systems is also intriguing. While no complete word or text can be identified, the regular occurence of random hieroglyphic characters seems too persistent to be accidental. One receives the impression that, as in the case of the complex figured scenes, the Gordion artisans were trying to integrate the Luwian script system into their visual programme. This would imply an interest in creating a writing system that would serve to label the drawings and identify their makers or sponsors, presumably the ruling élite at Gordion, just as the inscriptions on Neo-Hittite reliefs identified the ruling élite responsible for the programmes of relief sculpture.

Thus, rather than a set of cartoonish doodles, we may have here a crude but intriguing reflection of early efforts by the developing Phrygian polity to establish a distinctive visual culture that would advertise the Phrygian state as a major power on the central Anatolian plateau. We need to recall that the Phrygians in the ninth century BC were still relatively recent immigrants into Anatolia, and their presence, language and customs were intrusive into the region (Sams 1995: 1147–8). While we know comparatively little about the Phrygians in their homeland in southeastern Europe it seems highly likely that the earliest Phrygian immigrants had no tradition of monumental art comparable to the contemporary sculptural programmes of the Neo-Hittites and Assyrians, and it is virtually certain that they had no script system with which to write their language. As the Phrygians gained strength and political presence in Anatolia they would surely have wished to cement their impact on their neighbours with a monumental programme of visual arts. Investigations into the stratigraphic sequence of the early Phrygian levels at Gordion reveal that a distinctive monumental stone architecture, indicative of a developing Phrygian state, had appeared within a comparatively short time (Voigt 1994; Voigt, Henrickson 2000: 46–52). I would like to suggest that the leaders of the early Phrygian polity wished to develop a local sculptural programme that was intended to narrate to visitors to the Phrygian capital those topics that were important to the Phrygian state and to Phrygian cultural tradition. Thus certain subjects found in the incised drawings, such as the lion and the armed warrior, would be a natural choice for advertising the growing strength and power of the region. Other themes, including distinctive Phrygian cityscapes and Phrygian cultic symbols, would serve to advertise Phrygian traditions as being separate from those of their Neo-Hittite neighbours. As an early stage in the development of a visual identity, these efforts seem tentative and rudimentary. Yet their survival gives us a small window into the process of creating the visual identity of the Phrygian people in the Iron Age.

**Bibliography**

Hawkins, J.D. 2000: *Corpus of Hieroglyphic Luwian Inscriptions. Volume I: Inscriptions of the Iron Age*. Berlin

Mellink, M.J. 1983: 'Comments on a cult relief of Kybele from Gordion' in R.M. Boehmer, H. Hauptmann (eds), *Beiträge zur Altertumskunde Kleinasiens: Festschrift für Kurt Bittel.* Mainz am Rhein: 349–60

Orthmann, W. 1971: *Untersuchungen zur späthethitischen Kunst* (Saarbrückener Beiträge zur Altertumskunde 8). Bonn

Özgüç, T. 1971: *Kültepe and its Vicinity in the Iron Age* (Turkish Historical Society Publications, fifth series, no. 29). Ankara

Roller, L.E. 1999a: 'Early Phrygian drawings from Gordion and the elements of Phrygian artistic style' *Anatolian Studies* 49: 143–51

— 1999b: *In Search of God the Mother: The Cult of Anatolian Cybele.* Berkeley, Los Angeles

Sams, G.K. 1971: *The Phrygian Painted Pottery of Early Iron Age Gordion and its Anatolian Setting.* Unpublished PhD dissertation. University of Pennsylvania

— 1989: 'Sculpted orthostates at Gordion' in K. Emre, B. Hrouda, M. Mellink, N. Özgüç (eds), *Anatolia and the Ancient Near East. Studies in Honor of Tahsin Özgüç.* Ankara: 447–54

— 1994: 'Aspects of early Phrygian architecture at Gordion' in A. Çilingiroğlu, D.H. French (eds), *Anatolian Iron Ages 3. The Proceedings of the Third Anatolian Iron Ages Colloquium held at Van, 6–12 August 1990* (British Institute of Archaeology at Ankara Monograph 16). Ankara: 211–20

— 1995: 'Midas of Gordion and the Anatolian Kingdom of Phrygia' in J. Sasson (ed.), *Civilizations of the Ancient Near East. Volume II.* New York: 1147–59

Simpson, E. 1988: 'The Phrygian artistic intellect' *Source* 7: 24–42

Voigt, M.M. 1994: 'Excavations at Gordion 1988–89: the Yassıhoyük Stratigraphic Sequence' in A. Çilingiroğlu, D.H. French (eds), *Anatolian Iron Ages 3. The Proceedings of the Third Anatolian Iron Ages Colloquium held at Van, 6–12 August 1990* (British Institute of Archaeology at Ankara Monograph 16). Ankara: 265–82

— 1997: 'Gordion' in E.M. Meyers (ed.), *Oxford Encyclopedia of Archaeology in the Near East Volume 2.* Oxford, New York: 426–31

Voigt, M.M., Henrickson, R.C. 2000: 'Formation of the Phrygian state: the Early Iron Age at Gordion' *Anatolian Studies* 50: 37–54

Young, R.S. 1957: 'Gordion 1956: preliminary report' *American Journal of Archaeology* 61: 322–3

— 1958: 'The Gordion campaign of 1957: preliminary report' *American Journal of Archaeology* 62: 139–54

— 1969: 'Doodling at Gordion' *Archaeology* 22: 270–5

Young, R.S., DeVries, K., Kohler, E.L., McClellan, J.F., Mellink, M.J., Sams, G.K. 1981: *The Gordion Excavations. Final Reports. Volume I: Three Great Early Tumuli* (University Museum Monograph 43). Philadelphia

# Hasanlu IVB and Caucasia: explorations and implications of contexts

## Karen S. Rubinson[1] and Michelle I. Marcus[2]
[1]Barnard College, New York, [2]The Dalton School, New York

## Abstract

This article explores the possibility of learning something about elements of personal identity among some members of the population of Hasanlu IVB in Iran (ca. 1100 to ca. 800 BC) through an examination of select personal ornaments which find parallels at sites in the southern Caucasus. Hasanlu IVB is an ideal place to consider issues of identity because personal ornaments were found both on skeletons in the cemetery and those of individuals left where they had fallen when the settlement was attacked. Many scholars have commented on the use of Assyrian art as a visual model for political status at Hasanlu. Marcus has determined that the mortuary and temple finds have far more in common with local traditions than with Assyria. Here we begin to refine a view of the meaning of 'local' in contrast to 'Assyrian' or 'western' at Hasanlu. The approach we have adopted is to compare two classes of Hasanlu metal bracelets and a pin type with similar objects found in the burials of single individuals primarily from Artik in the modern Republic of Armenia, as a first step towards defining what connections might have existed between Hasanlu and the area of Caucasia. Further classes of ornaments which cluster both at Hasanlu and at excavated sites to the north will need to be systematically accumulated before it will be possible to understand the underlying reasons for these similarities.

## Özet

Bu çalışma, İran'daki (M.Ö. yak. 1100 – M.Ö yak. 800) Hasanlu IVB de yaşayan nüfusun bazı üyelerinin kimlik unsurlarının anlaşılıp anlaşılamıyacağının araştırılması için planlanmıştır. Araştırma, benzerlerine Güney Kafkaslar'daki yerleşimlerde de rastlanan kişisel süs eşyalarından seçilmiş örneklerin incelenmesi ile gerçekleştirile-cektir. Hasanlu IVB bu araştırma için ideal bir yerleşimdir. Çünkü burada kişisel süs eşyalarına hem mezarlıklarda bulunan iskeletler üzerinde, hem de şehir saldırıya uğradığında halkın kaçarken süs eşyalarını geride bırakmış olmaları nedeniyle kolaylıkla ulaşılabilmektedir. Pek çok meslektaşımız Hasanlu'da Asur sanatının politik statünün görsel bir simgesi olarak kullanıldığını düşünmüşlerdir. Marcus, Hasanlu'da mezar ve tapınak buluntularının yerel olarak, Asur geneline kıyasla daha yaygın olarak kullanıldığını ortaya koymuştur. Bu çalışmayla 'yerel' kavramının anlamı 'Asur' veya 'batıya ait' kavramlarıyla karşılaştırılarak açıklanmaya çalışılacaktır. Bu amaçla Hasanlu'da bulunan iki metal bilezik ve bir iğne türü günümüz Ermenistan Cumhuriyeti sınırları içindeki Artik'de kişisel mezarlarda bulunan benzer objelerle karşılaştırılacaktır. Böylece ilk adım olarak Hasanlu ve Kafkasya Bölgesi arasında ne gibi benzerlikler olduğu tanımlanmaya çalışılacaktır. Bundan sonra yapılması gereken şey, hem Hasanlu'da, hem de kuzeye doğru kazısı yapılmış diğer yerleşimlerde sıklıkla görülen süs eşyası türlerinin sistematik bir biçimde toplanması ve bunlar arasındaki benzerliklerin altında yatan nedenlerin anlaşılmaya çalışılmasıdır.

---

Previous scholarship has noted that Hasanlu and nearby Dinkha Tepe in Iranian Azerbaijan, both excavated by the Hasanlu Project directed by Robert H. Dyson Jr., were, in the earlier part of the second millennium BC, part of a culture area tied to greater Mesopotamia, as can been seen through Habur ware ceramics (Hamlin 1974) and certain jewellery types (Rubinson 1991: 384–8). Subsequently, the area was more strongly related to northern Iran, eastern Anatolia and southern Caucasia, as demonstrated by the painted pottery and associated artefacts from Dinkha Tepe (Muscarella 1994: 139; Rubinson 1994).

For the period known as Iron II, or the LWGW (late western grey ware) period, most research has explored the impact of Assyria on the élite arts found at Hasanlu, and at the same time has defined the local art styles at the site: including Muscarella on the ivories (1980), Winter on the unique horse breast-plate (1980) and Marcus on the seals (1996a). Visual relationships to Caucasian material culture have been mentioned, but not explored (for example, Muscarella 1988: 18, 36, 48–50; see also Pogrebova 1977: 43–50, 83, 105–7, 165–7).

Our goal is to pursue these relationships in order to raise larger questions about the personal and/or cultural interrelationships between individuals at Hasanlu and peoples of the Urartian state, which may in fact have their roots in the later second millennium BC. Our approach is embedded in Marcus's published work dealing with the Hasanlu personal ornaments (Marcus 1994; 1996b).[1] Following Mauss (1973) and Bourdieu (1986), we can regard the ways in which we clothe and adorn the body as an active process or technical means for constructing and presenting a bodily self (see also Craik 1994: 1). In this sense, the body is not a given but is actually fashioned through how it is used and projected; it becomes a lived anatomy (Brosz 1990: 43–4). Meskell puts it another way.

> Identity is what is draped over a person by the group of which he or she is a part. Identity is subject to change and is multiple. The person is constituted from a host of identities, all relying on social attitudes to age, sex, class, marital status, ethnicity, nationality, religion, et cetera (Meskell 1999: 32).

In other words, if we assume that personal ornaments are sometimes intimately connected with one's personal or social group identity, being literally attached to the body and hence extensions of the self, then they might be able to tell us more than can other kinds of artefacts about individual identity in archaeology.

A case study we have in mind is Linduff's exami-nation of the burial of Fu Hao, a queen of the late Shang dynasty (about 1200 BC) in China. This woman, a wife of the third Shang king at Anyang, was known from texts to be, amongst other things, a military leader, not a characteristic role for royal wives. Linduff suggested that Fu Hao was a foreigner, from the northern Chinese steppe, where women were sometimes buried with weapons and armour. Although Fu Hao was buried with the typical complement of royal Chinese goods, those

few items closest to her body were knives and mirrors from the steppe, markers, Linduff suggests, of Fu Hao's ethnic identity (Linduff 1996).

The Iron II period at Hasanlu, stratum Hasanlu IVB, about 1100–800 BC (Dyson, Muscarella 1989: 22), is an ideal place to consider issues of adornment and identity because of the unique archaeological contexts of the finds. Personal ornaments were found both *in situ* on 61 skeletons in individual graves in a cemetery, and on another 64 skeletons from burned buildings on the main mound, that is, 'accidental burials' created when the settlement was attacked and destroyed by fire around 800 BC (figs 1–3) ( Muscarella 1989: 32 ).

Having both deliberate and accidental burials provides a rare opportunity to compare the nature of adornment in both living and mortuary contexts, as well as allowing one to link type and style of artefacts with usage. As Hodder has commented, 'As soon as the context of an object is known it is no longer totally mute. Clues as to its meaning are given by its context' (Hodder 1986: 4). At Hasanlu, for instance, it is compelling that ornaments with Assyrian parallels were found primarily in the collapsed debris of what were presumably second floor storage areas in the burned buildings, whereas most of the ornaments found *in situ* on skeletons, both from the cemetery and the burned buildings, were types familiar in western Iran or unique to Hasanlu itself. Thus, Marcus could suggest:

> that for body decoration in mortuary contexts and daily and perhaps temple life, traditional local customs were most appropriate; whereas for promoting the political and administrative power of the ruling elite, Assyrian and other western objects and images were ideologically more useful (Marcus 1995: 2495–7; compare Winter 1977).

For several reasons, in pursuing Caucasian parallels, we have decided for now to consider only those objects with a mortuary context comparable to those from Hasanlu, that is, personal ornaments found in individual burials, not group burials. Although one can successfully explore some cultural relationships across variant burial types — as Sevin has shown by comparing material from Hasanlu and from other sites in Iran with material from the collective burials which he has excavated at Karagündüz (Sevin, Kavaklı 1996: 55, 57) — we have chosen a different approach. We hope that by looking at grave groups from individual burials we might get closer to issues of personal identity.

Furthermore, many classes of Caucasian objects which have been, or which could be, compared to the Hasanlu material are without context altogether. For example, in Kellner's comprehensive study of what he

---

[1] The publication of the full assemblage of personal ornaments from Hasanlu is in preparation for the Hasanlu Special Studies series. The data were collected from the Hasanlu project archives, University of Pennsylvania, Philadelphia, PA.

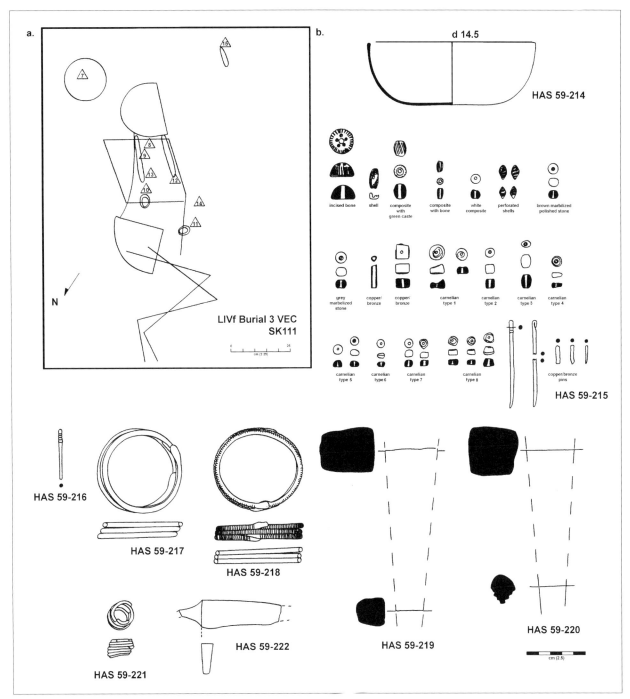

Fig. 1. Skeleton 111 from Hasanlu IVB cemetery.
(a) after the field drawing of SK 111: (7) copper/bronze bowl (HAS 59-214); (8) beads and bronze pins (HAS 59-215);
(9) bronze pin (HAS 59-216); (10) copper/bronze bracelets (HAS 59-217); (11) bronze bracelets (HAS 59-218); (12)
iron near left arm (HAS 59-219); (13) iron near spine (HAS 59-220); (14) copper/bronze rings (HAS 59-221); (15)
iron blade (HAS 59-222). (b) Objects with SK 111

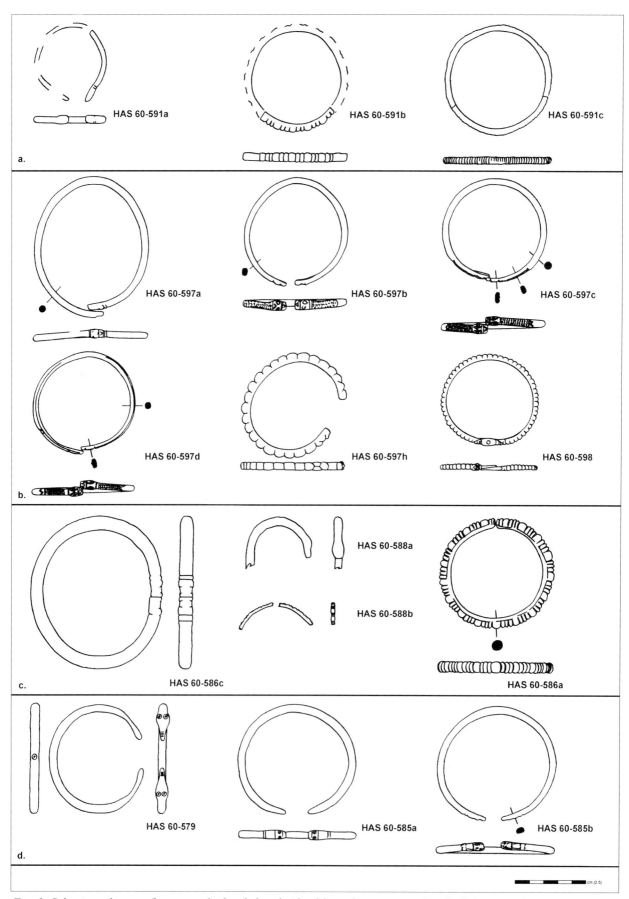

*Fig. 2. Selection of copper/bronze snake headed and ridged bracelets associated with skeletons in burned building II, room 5, Hasanlu IVB: (a) objects with SK 133; (b) objects with SK 135; (c) objects with SK 147; (d) objects with SK 148*

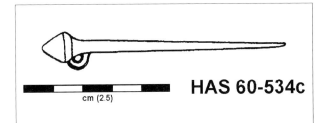

*Fig. 3. Copper/bronze pin associated with SK 136, burned building II, room 5, Hasanlu IVB*

calls Urartian belts, the vast majority are listed as 'findspot unknown' (Kellner 1991: ortsregister). He illustrates 31 belt fragments decorated with rows of repoussé dots, similar to many fragments found at Hasanlu (Kellner 1991: pls 72–9). In his list of 91 belts and belt fragments in the category 'punktbänder', only 12 have known find-spots and two have possible find-spots (Kellner 1991: 70–7). At Hasanlu, several similar belt fragments were found on the floor of burned building II and one was buried with a 25–35 year old male in the cemetery.[2] Perhaps Kellner is correct in calling such belts with rows of repoussé dots Urartian, but there is no evidence that the individuals buried in the Hasanlu IVB cemetery were Urartian (though Medvedskaya [1988: 11–12] does argue for an Urartian presence during Hasanlu IVB). In any event, we believe that comparative objects without context will not serve our particular purposes, nor do justice to the incredible contextual information at Hasanlu.

One site that is especially rich in possibilities for comparative study with Hasanlu is Artik, situated in Armenia near the modern town of Gumri (formerly Lenanikan) (Khachatrian 1979). Of the 600+ individual burials in this cemetery, most can be assigned to the period ca. 1450 to ca. 1150 BC, with some burials forming a later group dated ca. 1150 to 1000 BC (Avetisyan et al. 2000: 25, table 1).

Burial 376 at Artik contained bronze bracelets and rings, as well as a bronze pin, paste and carnelian beads, and two black polished ceramic bowls (fig. 4) (Khachatrian 1979: 72–3, 273).[3] Avetisyan dates this burial to around 1300 BC (personal communication, email dated 26 July 2001). What is particularly interesting from the

viewpoint of Hasanlu IVB is that this burial contains two kinds of personal ornaments which occur also at Hasanlu: a cast bronze pin with bi-conical top and a loop attached to the shaft just below the head; and a bracelet with schematic snake headed terminals. In other words, in a south Caucasian single grave we finally have a combination of artefacts which compares with the Hasanlu material, seemingly much more telling in terms of sound connections than finding individual parallels.

At Hasanlu, a pin with bi-conical top and a loop on the side of the shaft was found on skeleton 136, one of the skeletons found crushed in the building collapse of burned building II (fig. 3). In addition to this pin, the individual was found with two bronze finger rings and two other short pins, as well as 600 small beads of carnelian and shell and 21 bronze beads. Although the skeleton was too crushed to determine its sex on the basis of physical anatomy, such short pins are consistently associated with anthropologically-sexed female skeletons in the cemetery (Marcus 1994:5).[4] The other pins associated with skeleton 136 were typical of Hasanlu and northwest Iran in general in this period, with decorated tops and un-pierced shafts (see, for example, Marcus 1994: fig. 7), in contrast to the toggle pins (pins with pierced shafts) common in the southern Caucasus.

It is the looped bi-conical headed pin which is interesting here. Of the eight pins with bi-conical heads at Hasanlu, this is the only one with a loop attached to the top of the shaft. In fact, it is the only pin found at Hasanlu which has this type of attachment. Although

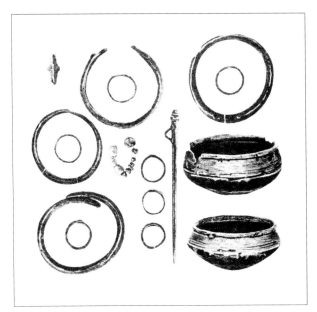

*Fig. 4. Objects from Burial 376 at Artik*

---

[2] The belt from the cemetery is 59-262, found in Op LIE, b 5, skeleton 107. Now MMA 60.20.21a–d (Rogers Fund, 1960) (Muscarella 1988: 47–8, fig. 54a–d) and UPM 60-20-179. The belt was found above the skull together with pottery vessels (HAS 59-255, -258, -259), a copper/bronze spearhead (HAS 59-254) and an iron blade (HAS 59-256). Width 5.8cm.

[3] The text mentions three bracelets and four rings (Khachatrian 1979: 72–3) but the illustration shows seven rings and four bracelets (Khachatrian 1979: 273).

[4] Determinations of sex are based on Rathbun 1972.

the type does not seem to be common in Caucasia, it does occur there. A second, quite similar, pin occurs in burial 118 at Artik, which contained also two black polished pots, a ring and a bracelet (Khachatrian 1979: 37, 160). This grave, according to Avestisyan (personal communication), is to be dated to the same period as grave 376, that is about 1300 BC. Avestisyan (personal communication) has noted three other pins comparable to the Artik examples, one of the same date from tomb 96 at Lori-Berd in Armenia, and two from sites in Georgia: tomb 6 at Pevrebi and tomb 81 at Kviratskhoveli, dated to the 14th to 13th centuries BC. The loop attachment, but with different heads, is also found on other groups of pins from Caucasia, including pins with elongated reeded heads from Artik tombs 2, 6 and 432 (Khachatrian 1979: 19, 20, 79–80, 109, 112, 301), and pins with axe-heads from Artik, Tli and elsewhere (see, for example, Khachatrian 1979: 54, 208; Tekhov 1980: 47, fig. 2, no. 3).

Artik tomb 376 contained not only the pin with loop attachment, but also, as already noted, a bracelet with snake headed terminals. Another bracelet with snake headed ends was found in Artik tomb 541, which is dated to the 14th to 13th centuries BC (Khachatrian 1979: 94, 348–9). Other likely snake headed bracelets at Artik were found in tombs 360, 361, 380, 396 and 446 (Khachatrian 1979: 70, 71, 73, 75, 81, 267, 268, 275, 283, 309).

Of the 268 circlets identified by Marcus, 35 bracelets and three armlets, or 14% of the total, have snake headed terminals. They were mostly associated with nine particular skeletons. One adult female from the cemetery (skeleton 111) had three snake headed bracelets on each wrist (fig. 1a, where the drawing is schematic). In addition, she was buried with two spiral finger rings on her right hand, more than 70 beads at her neck, a needle-headed pin, a dome-headed pin, and some unidentifiable iron fragments at her chest. She was also buried with a bronze bowl and a wooden handled iron knife which might have been used for shearing or fleshing (fig. 1b).

The other skeletons associated with snake headed circlets at Hasanlu were all found in burned building II, which Dyson suggests was a temple on the basis of the architectural plan and nature of the small finds (Dyson 1989: 120). Skeleton 135 was found with a total of 12 bracelets, of which five were snake headed; others were knobbed and ridged (fig. 2b). The individual was apparently also wearing finger rings, two bi-conical pins, three lion pins and beads. Skeleton 148 was wearing 13 bracelets, of which six were snake headed and some others knobbed and ridged (fig. 2d). This body was also associated with two pendants, beads, chain fragments and the fragment of a studded metal plaque.

One particularly well adorned individual (skeleton 147) had more than 35 circlets, of which at least five bracelets and one armlet had snake head terminals; others were knobbed and ridged (fig. 2c). This skeleton was also associated with some gold and bronze buttons, as well as a cylinder seal, a bimetallic pin and a string of beads. The quantity of the metalwork, and the presence of gold and the cylinder seal, all suggest that we have an important individual here.

So far, we have noted many snake headed bracelets on just a few individuals, one from the cemetery and three from burned building II. In addition, another five skeletons from burned building II were each wearing a snake headed bracelet (for example, fig. 2a), and a handful of similar bracelets were in the fill from burned buildings II and IV. At this point, we do not have enough information to link snake headed bracelets with a particular age group or gender; in fact, the available data suggest that there is no such correlation. But their limited distribution on a small percentage of the skeletons found associated with personal ornaments, only nine out of 125 (7%), suggests that they mark some sort of personal or social group identity. Were those nine individuals part of the same family or lineage? Were they all in the service of the same deity? Were the bracelets markers of some connection with southern Caucasia, as Fu Hao's mirrors and knife marked a relationship to the steppe beyond China? Or did the bracelets simply mark a happenstance of trade or some other economic activity? Certainly, based on the evidence we have so far, we are nowhere near presenting an hypothesis. Nevertheless, in light of the inventory at Hasanlu, the combination of the snake headed bracelet with the bi-conical looped pin at Artik is compelling. We believe that the approach we have used will eventually yield enough overlapping patterns of interrelationships to provide concrete proposals for testing.

Above we noted cast ridged bracelets, found four times on skeletons with snake headed bracelets at Hasanlu. Similar ridged bracelets were also found at Artik, for example in graves 246, 284, 300, 301, 310, 318 and 415 (Khachatrian 1979: 55, 60, 62, 63, 64, 65, 77, 212, 230, 239, 240, 244, 245, 248, 291). There, the ridged bracelets are not common although they seem to occur more frequently than snake headed ones.

At Hasanlu, 37 ridged bracelets were found, almost the same number as snake headed ones, although only a small number were associated with skeletons. However, four of the skeletons wearing snake headed bracelets also wore ridged ones: skeleton 147 had five ridged bracelets together with the five snake headed bracelets and a snake headed armlet (fig. 2c); skeleton 135 wore two ridged bracelets with the five snake headed ones (fig. 2b); skeleton 148 wore two ridged bracelets together with six snake headed ones (fig. 2d); skeleton 133 wore two ridged bracelets together with one snake headed one (fig. 2a). Thus, 11 ridged bracelets, about 30% of those recovered and identified, were associated with skeletons which were also wearing circlets with snake headed ends; and that group of skeletons represented about 7% of the total number of skeletons found associated with personal ornaments in Hasanlu IVB. The ridged bracelets do not seem to have parallels elsewhere in Iron Age Iran. Again, and more importantly, they are associated at Hasanlu with skeletons wearing another type of artefact that seems at home in Caucasia.

As we accumulate classes of ornaments that cluster both at Hasanlu and in places like Artik, where there are individual burials in datable contexts, we should be able to talk more convincingly about the nature of the connections and even, perhaps, about elements of identity. Among other categories which seem promising for similar analysis are metal belts, some additional bracelet types, and particular groups of objects which are not personal ornaments and which have been present in the literature for some time (see, for example, Porada 1965: 115, 237, n. 2 of chapter IX). In the light of the evidence we have gathered so far, it might eventually be possible to understand how the people of Hasanlu IVB, evidently destroyed by the military power of Urartu, were related to people from that same region during the fluorescence of Hasanlu IVB's existence.

**Acknolwedgements**

We would like to thank Robert H. Dyson Jr. for permission to work with and publish this material, Maude de Schauensee for invaluable assistance and Denise Hoffman, Ted Hemmaplardh and Christine Chen for preparation of the illustrations.

**Bibliography**

Avetisyan, P., Bedalyan, R., Smith, A.T. 2000: 'Preliminary report on the 1998 archaeological investigations of Project ArAGATS in the Tsakahovit plain, Armenia' *Studi Micenei ed Egeo-Anatolici* 42.1: 19–59

Bourdieu, P. 1986: 'The biographical illusion' *Actes de la Recherche en Sciences Sociales* 62/63: 69–72

Brosz, E. 1990: *Jacques Lacan: A Feminist Introduction.* New York

Craik, J. 1994: *The Face of Fashion: Cultural Studies in Fashion.* New York

Dyson Jr, R.H. 1989: 'The Iron Age architecture at Hasanlu: an essay' *Expedition* 31.2–3: 107–27

Dyson Jr, R.H., Muscarella, O.W. 1989: 'Constructing the chronology and historical implications of Hasanlu IV' *Iran* 27: 1–27

Hamlin, C. Kramer 1974: 'The early second millennium ceramic assemblage at Dinkha Tepe' *Iran* 12: 125–53

Hodder, I. 1986: *Reading the Past.* Cambridge

Kellner, H.-J. 1991: *Gürtelbleche aus Urartu* (Prähistorische Bronzefunde 12.3). Stuttgart

Khachatrian, T.C. 1979: *Artikskii Nekropol: Katalog.* Yerevan

Linduff, K. 1996: 'Art and identity: the Chinese and their "significant others"' in M. Gervers, W. Schlepp (eds), *Culture Contact, History and Ethnicity in Inner Asia* (Toronto Studies in Central and Inner Asia). Toronto: 12–48

Marcus, M. 1994: 'Dressed to kill: women and pins in early Iran' *The Oxford Art Journal* 17.2: 3–15

— 1995: 'Art and ideology in ancient western Asia' in J. Sasson, J. Baines, G. Beckman, K. Rubinson (eds), *Civilizations of the Ancient Near East, Volume 4.* New York: 2487–505

— 1996a: *Emblems of Identity and Prestige: The Seals and Sealings from Hasanlu, Iran. Commentary and Catalog* (Pennsylvania University Museum Monograph 84; Hasanlu Special Studies 3). Philadelphia

— 1996b: 'Sex and the politics of female adornment in Pre-Achaemenid Iran (1000–800 BCE)' in N.B. Kampen (ed.), *Sexuality in Ancient Art.* Cambridge: 41–54

Mauss, M. 1973: 'Techniques of the body' *Economy and Society* 2: 70–87

Medvedskaya, I. 1988: 'Who destroyed Hasanlu IV?' *Iran* 26: 1–15

Meskell, L. 1999: *Archaeologies of Social Life.* Oxford

Muscarella, O.W. 1980 : *The Catalogue of Ivories from Hasanlu, Iran* (Pennsylvania University Museum Monograph 40; Hasanlu Special Studies 2). Philadelphia

— 1988: *Bronze and Iron: Ancient Near Eastern Artifacts in the Metropolitan Museum of Art.* New York

— 1989: 'Warfare at Hasanlu in the later ninth century BC' *Expedition* 31.2–3: 24–36

— 1994: 'North-western Iran: Bronze Age to Iron Age' in A. Çilingiroğlu, D.H. French (eds), *Anatolian Iron Ages 3* (British Institute of Archaeology at Ankara Monograph 16). Ankara: 139–55

Pogrebova, M. 1977: *Iran I Zakavakz'ye v rannem zheleznom veke.* Moscow

Porada, E. 1965: *The Art of Ancient Iran: Pre-Islamic Cultures.* New York

Rathbun, T.A. 1972: *A Study of the Physical Characteristics of the Ancient Inhabitants of Hasanlu, Iran* (Field Research Projects). Miami, Florida

Rubinson, K.S. 1991: 'A mid-second millennium tomb at Dinkha Tepe' *American Journal of Archaeology* 95.3: 373–94

— 1994: 'Eastern Anatolia before the Iron Age: a view from Iran' in A. Çilingiroğlu, D.H. French (eds), *Anatolian Iron Ages 3* (British Institute of Archaeology at Ankara Monograph 16). Ankara: 199–203

Sevin, V., Kavaklı, E. 1996: *Van/Karagündüz: An Early Iron Age Cemetery*. Istanbul

Tekhov, B.V. 1980: *Tliiskii Mogil'nik*. Tbilisi

Winter, I. 1977: 'Perspective on the "local style" of Hasanlu IVB: a study in receptivity' in L.D. Levine, T.C. Young, Jr. (eds), *Mountains and Lowlands: Essays in the Archaeology of Greater Mesopotamia* (Bibliotheca Mesopotamica 7). Malibu: 371–86

— 1980: *A Decorated Breastplate from Hasanlu, Iran* (Pennsylvania University Museum Monograph 39; Hasanlu Special Studies 1). Philadelphia

# The volumes of some Urartian pithoi

## Haluk Sağlamtimur
*Ege University, Bornova-Izmir*

## Abstract

The Urartian kingdom, with its wide extent in eastern Anatolia, western Iran and the Transcaucasian region, possessed a standardised measurement system in order to exercise its central authority. To control the planting and harvesting of crops, and the storage and redistribution of the products from different regions, the central administration needed such an inventory system based on standardised units of measurement. These units of measurement appear in the form of cuneiform inscriptions and/or hieroglyphics on large pithoi found in storerooms at Urartian citadels such as Yukarı Anzaf, Çavuştepe, Karmir Blur, Bastam and Ayanis. However, to what kind of arithmetical calculations this measurement system corresponded is still not fully understood. The aim of this paper is to shed some light upon the issue of volumetric analysis of pithoi, using several of the inscribed examples found at Ayanis since 1989. Filemaker Pro 3.0 database programme was used for our volumetric calculations.

## Özet

Doğu Anadolu, Batı İran ve Kafkasya gibi geniş bir coğrafi alana yayılmış bulunan Urartu Krallığı'nın, merkezi yönetim ve denetim adına kullandığı standart bir ölçüm sistemi olduğu kesindir. Bu nedenle kazısı yapılmış olan Urartu kalelerinde bulunan depo odalarındaki küpler üzerinde çivi yazısı ve/veya hiyeroglif ölçü değerleri görmekteyiz. Küpler üzerinde büyüklük sırasıyla *aqarqi, terusi* ve *liš* temel birimli ölçü sisteminin kullanıldığını gösteren çivi yazıları vardır. Elimizdeki arkeolojik kanıtlar bu ölçü birimlerinin kapların üzerine pişirme işleminden sonra kazınarak yapıldığını göstermektedir. Bu nedenle ölçü birimlerinin, kapların içi doldurulduktan sonra elde edilen farklı hacim değerlerine göre kapların üzerine kazındığını önermekteyiz. Araştırmamızda Ayanis Kalesi depolarında bulduğumuz değişik boyutlardaki küplerin hacimleri bilgisayar yardımıyla hesaplanmıştır. Sonuç olarak küplerin iç kısımlarında yaptığımız matematiksel hesaplamalara dayanarak 1 *aqarqi*'nin 290 litre, 1 *terusi*'nin ise 29 litreye yakın bir değer olduğunu önermekteyiz.

---

As is well known, the state represents the highest level of political organisation. Among the criteria required for such high levels of organisation is a standardised measurement system. It is certain that the Urartian kingdom, with its wide extent in eastern Anatolia, western Iran and the Transcaucasian region, possessed such a system in order to exercise its central authority. Agricultural production would have been difficult in the lands of Urartu, given the high altitudes, the harsh winters, the paucity of good arable land and the insufficient water sources. These difficulties, combined with the labour intensive requirements of agriculture, indicate that the careful management of the agricultural process and its products would have been of crucial

importance to the Urartian central authority. To control the planting and harvesting of crops, and the storage and redistribution of the products from different regions, the central administration needed an inventory system based on standardised units of measurement.

These units of measurement appear in the form of cuneiform inscriptions and/or hieroglyphics on large pithoi found in storerooms at Urartian citadels such as Yukarı Anzaf, Çavuştepe, Karmir Blur, Bastam and Ayanis. However, to what kind of arithmetical calculations this measurement system corresponded is still not fully understood. The aim of this paper is to shed some light upon the issue of volumetric analysis of pithoi, using several of the inscribed pithoi found since 1989 at Ayanis.

139

In the Urartian citadels, storage structures were constructed along with temples and palaces or other types of administrative/religious buildings. Two separate types of storerooms, called *Gie* (*UKN* I: 79) and *(E)ari* (*UKN* II: 419), are mentioned in Urartian inscriptions, but the differences between them are not clearly understood. The storage buildings revealed by archaeological investigations vary in their dimensions and capacities, to some extent due to variations in the topography and overall structural layout at different sites. In some citadels the storage facilities cover areas larger than those of the defensive and administrative installations. At the Ayanis citadel, the belly diameters of some of the storeroom pithoi are greater than the width of the room doorway (Çilingiroğlu 1997: 135). This could indicate either that the vessels were produced elsewhere and then installed in the storerooms before the construction of the store building was completed, or that the vessels were actually made in the storerooms themselves.

The cuneiform inscriptions on the pithoi give the basic units of the measurement system: these are called *aqarqi*, *terusi* and *liš*, graded downwards in that order. Scholarly investigation has focused on calculating the modern equivalent volumes of *aqarqi* and *terusi*. The ratios of these Urartian measurement units to each other, the dependence of these ratios on a decimal scale and the real values of the units are uncertain to us. Hence scholars have proposed differing volumetric values for *aqarqi* and *terusi*. Diakonoff estimated that the maximum unit value of *terusi* was 9. Lehmann-Haupt suggested likewise for the pithoi from Toprakkale; on the other hand, he determined that '9½ *terusi*' was incised on a pithos from Karmir Blur (Klein 1970: 85, n. 20). On the Ayanis storeroom pithoi, '9 *terusi*' is the maximum value we find. These examples are the maximum values known for *terusi* on any Urartian pithos, an incised value larger than 9½ *terusi* is not attested. Given the absence of '10' as a cited value for *terusi*, and the need to complete these *terusi* units to the value of '10', it is possible to assume that 1 *aqarqi* corresponds to 10 *terusi*.

Since the units of *liš* are written after those of *aqarqi* and *terusi*, it is almost certain that *liš* is the smallest and the most insignificant sub-unit of the system and so can be left out of the present discussion. It is also possible to say that the 1:10 ratio of *aqarqi:terusi* does not exist for *terusi:liš*, for on a pithos from the west storage area (Area VII) at Ayanis there is the inscription '2 *aqarqi*, 11 *liš*' (Salvini 2001: 308). Until any evidence appears to the contrary, Salvini's suggestion (Reindell, Salvini 2001: 133; Salvini 2001: 308), which equates 1 *terusi* with 20 *liš*, remains the most acceptable one. The calculations described below are thus made on the assumption that 1 *aqarqi* equals 10 *terusi* and that 1 *terusi* equals 20 *liš*.

Archaeological evidence demonstrates that the Urartian units of measurement were incised on the containers after they were fired. This could indicate that the incising of the measurement values was done after deciding whether to fill the pithoi with dry or with liquid commodities.

Enigmatically, different units of Urartian measurement are inscribed on different pithoi sharing the same volumetric capacity. This raises the question, were units of weight (as opposed to volume) employed in Urartian imperial foodstuff management? It seems impossible to answer this question with any confidence, given the archaeological data available. On the other hand, it should be borne in mind that local villagers in the region today still use volumetric units rather than modern units of weight. According to these rural units of measurement, if one 'tin can' of lentils equals 15–16kg, then one 'çap', a local measurement term approximately corresponding to 80kg of lentils, is equivalent to 5 'tin cans' of lentils. In the same measurement system, 1 'tin can' of barley equals 13–14kg whilst 1 'tin can' of walnuts is about 8–9kg. If some archaeologically unknown units of weight were used in the Urartian measurement system, our problems in understanding the system become more difficult since, to date, scholarly investigation of the system has focused solely on volumetric calculations.

The aim of maximum volume calculations for Urartian pithoi is to discover a standard arithmetical value. However, the Urartian measurement inscriptions used on the pithoi should not be regarded as pure arithmetical operations like multiplication or division. We must take into consideration the type of agricultural product found in the vessel when calculating the constant values for *aqarqi*, *terusi* or *liš*. If the agricultural products filling the pithoi were put into the vessels on the basis of a certain weight, then different types of product would readily change the value of *aqarqi*, *terusi* and *liš*. The modern evidence given above for 1 unit of 'tin can' would explain the existence of different Urartian measurement values found on different jars of nearly the same size.

We must also consider the relationship between the ownership of the various storage structures and the incised measurement system used on the pithoi. Of the marks found on the pithoi from the east storage area (Area VIII), which was interpreted as a 'temple storage area' because of its proximity to the Ayanis temple, none were cuneiform or hieroglyphic inscriptions; *bullae*, which provide evidence for the accounts of incoming and outgoing agricultural products, were not discovered in this area either. It is difficult to accept that the marks on the east storage area pithoi related to the volume or the content of the containers. We can conclude that it was not necessary to use any standard units of measurement on the pithoi owned by the temple itself. Rather, the marks probably specify the kind of storage structure where the commodity was to be kept. The fact that there are many cuneiform and hieroglyphic inscriptions on the pithoi from the west storage area (Area VII) can now be explained. Since Area VII included the formal storage magazines of Ayanis fortress, the vessels there must have been incised in order to form standard measurement values for the central authority for control of both tax collection and the redistribution of resources. Furthermore, the hundreds of *bullae* unearthed in these storerooms give us an idea about the circulation of products (Salvini 2001: 279–319) in the west storage area. The mention of more than one type of storage structure in the Urartian inscriptions becomes understandable.

To date, there is no documentary evidence known that would provide data for indisputably accurate calculations for the volumetric units of *aqarqi* and *terusi*, even though several suggestions have been made. The highest *aqarqi* value yet known from the pithoi inscriptions is 8 *aqarqi*, from the Çavuştepe excavations (Dinçol 1977: 113). In general, the suggested equivalent values for *aqarqi* range from Lehmann-Haupt's calculation of 120–50 litres, based on pithoi from Toprakkale (Lehmann-Haupt 1931: 474), to Piotrovskii's 240–50 litres, based on pithoi from Karmir Blur (Piotrovskii 1952: 74). Other suggestions vary as follows: Klein, 100 litres (Klein 1970: 86); Kroll, 160–80 litres, based on pithoi from Bastam (Kroll 1979: 227); Brasinskij, 208 litres, based on pithoi from Karmir Blur (Brasinskij 1978: 33–49); Salvini, 234 litres, based on pithoi from Ayanis (Reindell, Salvini 2001: 136; Salvini 2001: 294–5).

For our detailed volumetric calculations, the method employed was as follows. The Filemaker Pro 3.0 database programme was used for the calculations. To ensure the complete accuracy of the calculations, a drawing showing the entire cross-section of a complete jar is required. A vertical axis was drawn through the centre of the figure. A series of perpendicular lines was then drawn connecting the vertical axis to the edges of the pithos at regular intervals. The lengths of each of these horizontal lines were calculated, and the sum of all these lengths was then multiplied by two in order to supply the result for the calculation of the total volume of the jar (fig. 1). The programme simply calculates the volumes of a number of imaginary cylinders placed on top of each other inside the jar. The accuracy of the method was tested and proved to be accurate, by means of filling the jar with a known volume of liquid.

The largest value of *aqarqi* found inscribed on a pithos is 8. The dimensions of the pithos found in the Kayalıdere storerooms can be accepted as the greatest known (Burney 1966: 83–4), but the volumetric capacity of this vessel has not been calculated. However a pithos with similarly large dimensions was excavated at Ayanis and for this the volumetric calculations have been made.

Of the 200 jars that we have examined from the Ayanis storerooms, the maximum height of the largest pithoi is 2.15m and the highest *aqarqi* value incised on these is 6. The volume of one of these pithoi, with a diameter of 1.50m and a capacity acceptance up to the lip of the vessel, was calculated at 1,666 litres (fig. 2). Assuming that this maximum size storage jar could contain up to 6 *aqarqi*, 1 *aqarqi* would then equal 260 litres or slightly more. In order to substantiate this assessment, we calculated the volume of a pithos with a height of 1.60m, a diameter of 1.10m and an incised value of '2 *aqarqi*, 1.5 *terusi* and 5 *liš*' (fig. 3). The total volume, leaving about 12cm of the jar empty below the lip, was calculated as being 630 litres. According to this calculation, 1 *aqarqi* equals 290 litres,[1] 1 *terusi* equals 29 litres, and 1 *liš* equals 1.45 litres, the total volume being as follows:

| | | | | |
|---|---|---|---|---|
| 2 *aqarqi* | x | 290 litres | = | 580 litres |
| 1½ *terusi* | x | 29 litres | = | 43 litres |
| 5 *liš* | x | 1.45 litres | = | 7.25 litres |
| ------ | | | | ---------- |
| Total | | | = | 630 litres |

The same calculation method was applied to a large, wide mouthed storage jar which bears hieroglyphs of '7 *terusi*, ½ *terusi* and 5 *liš*' on the inside and outside of the rim (fig. 4) (Çilingiroğlu 1997: 151; Kozbe et al. 2001: 105, pl. xvi, 18; Salvini 2001: 294). Assuming that the inscription on the inside of the rim should have been readable when the container was filled to maximum capacity, a maximum volume of 225 litres was calculated as follows:[2]

| | | | | |
|---|---|---|---|---|
| 7 *terusi* | x | 29 litres | = | 203 litres |
| ½ *terusi* | x | 29 litres | = | 14.5 litres |
| 5 *liš* | x | 1.45 litres | = | 7.25 litres |
| ------ | | | | ---------- |
| Total | | | = | 224.75 litres |

---

[1] Note, however, that for the same pithos Salvini calculated 1 *aqarqi* = 234 litres, which is less than the value I give (Reindell, Salvini: 135).

[2] Note, however, that for the same vessel Salvini calculated a maximum capacity of 183 litres (Salvini 2001: 294).

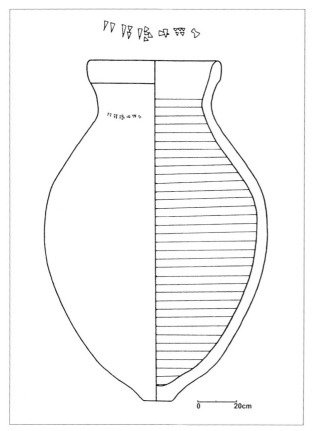

*Fig. 1. Cross-section of a storage jar, showing the method used to calculate volume*

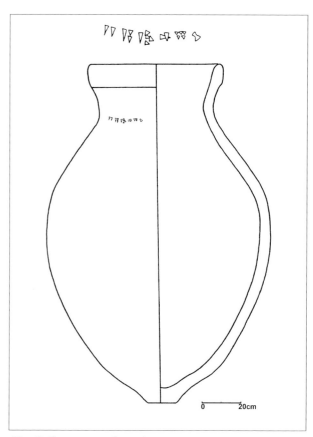

*Fig. 3. Storage jar from Ayanis*

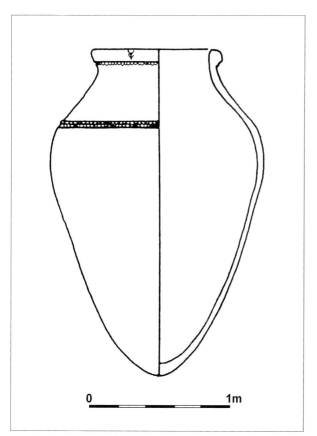

*Fig. 2. Storage jar from Ayanis*

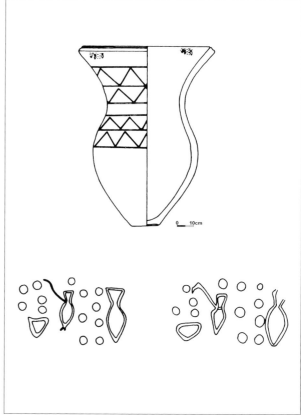

*Fig. 4. Storage jar from Ayanis*

In conclusion, according to our volumetric calculations for pithoi with cuneiform or hieroglyphic inscriptions, from the Ayanis storerooms, we suggest that the value of 1 *aqarqi* is approximately 290 litres.

**Bibliography**

*Abbreviations*

*UKN* I = Melikišvili, G.A. 1960: *Urartskie klinoobraznye nadpisi I (Le iscrizioni cuneiformi urartee)* (second edition). Moscow

*UKN* II = Melikišvili, G.A. 1971: *Urartskie klinoobraznye nadpisi II (Le iscrizioni cuneiformi urartee)* (second edition). Moscow

Brasinskij, J.B. 1978: 'Urartian pithoi: a study in metrology and standardization' *Orientalia Lovaniensia Periodica* 9: 33–49

Burney, C., 1966: 'A first season of excavations at the Urartian citadel of Kayalıdere' *Anatolian Studies* 16: 55–112

Çilingiroğlu, A., 1997: *Urartu Krallığı Tarihi ve Sanatı.* Izmir

Dinçol, M.A. 1977: 'Çavuştepe Kazısında Çıkan Yazıtlı Küçük Buluntular' *Anadolu* 18 (1974): 105–13

Klein, J.J., 1970: 'Urartian hieroglyphic inscriptions from Altıntepe' *Anatolian Studies* 24: 77–94

Kozbe, G., Sağlamtimur, H., Çevik, Ö. 2001: 'Pottery' in A. Çilingiroğlu, M. Salvini (eds), *Ayanis I, Ten Year's Excavations at Rusahinili Eiduru-kai 1989–1998.* Rome: 85–154

Kroll, S. 1979: 'Gefaßmarken in urartäischer Hieroglyphenschrift und Keilschrift aus Bastam' in W. Kleiss (ed.), *Bastam I.* Berlin: 221–8

Lehmann-Haupt, C.F. 1931: *Armenien einst und jetzt. II.2.* Berlin, Leipzig

Piotrovskii, B.B. 1952: *Karmir Blur II.* Erevan

Reindell, I., Salvini, M. 2001: 'Die Urartaischen Hohlmasse für flüssigkeiten' *Studi Micenei ed Egeo-Anatolici* 43.1: 121–41

Salvini, M. 2001: 'The inscriptions of Ayanis. Cuneiform and hieroglyphic' in A. Çilingiroğlu, M. Salvini (eds), *Ayanis I, Ten Year's Excavations at Rusahinili Eiduru-kai 1989–1998.* Rome: 251–320

# Some considerations on Van Kalesi

## Mirjo Salvini

*Istituto di studi sulle civiltà dell'Egeo e del Vicino Oriente (CNR), Rome*

### Abstract

The monumental ruins of Tušpa (modern Van Kalesi), the ancient capital of the Urartian kingdom, are still visible on the Van rock, on the eastern shore of lake Van. The Armenian medieval tradition knows this monumental complex as the 'City of Semiramis'. On the basis of the epigraphic records we can deduce that Van Kalesi was occupied for about 100 years, from Sarduri I (ca. 830 BC) to the end of Sarduri II's reign (ca. 735 BC). During this period, all Urartian kings carried out major works on the site, covering all the surface of the fortress. From Rusa I's reign until the end of the Urartian kingdom (second half of the seventh century BC), Van Kalesi was no more the seat of the Urartian government, but the sacred place for the ideology of Urartian royalty. Especially under Rusa II (ca. 690–660 BC), the Urartian capital was probably itinerant between the new founded cities of Teishebai URU (modern Karmir-blur), Rusai URU.TUR (modern Bastam), Rusahinili Qilbanikai (modern Toprakkale) and Rusahinili Eidurukai (modern Ayanis).

### Özet

Urartu Kralığı'nın antik başkenti Tuşpa'daki (günümüz Van Kalesi) anıtsal kalıntılar Van Gölünün doğu kıyısındaki Van kayalıkları üzerinde halen görülebilektedir. Ermeni Ortaçağ geleneği bu anıtlar topluluğunu 'Semiramis'in Şehri' olarak tanımlar. Epigrafik kaynaklara dayanarak Van Kalesi'nin I. Sarduri (M.Ö. yak. 830) döneminden II. Sarduri (M.Ö. yak 735) dönemi sonuna kadar, yani yaklaşık yüz yıl süreyle iskan edildiğini söyleyebiliriz. Bu süre boyunca tüm Urartu kralları yerleşimde, sur duvarlarının tüm yüzeylerinin kaplanması da dahil olmak üzere, önemli çalışmalar gerçekleştirmislerdir. I. Rusa döneminden Urartu Krallığı'nın sonuna kadar (M.Ö. 7 yüzyılın ikinci yarısı) Van Kalesi Urartu Devletinin yönetim merkezi olmamıştır; ancak Urartu Krallık ideolojisinin kutsal mekanı olmaya devam etmiştir. Özellikle II. Rusa döneminde ( M.Ö. yak. 690 – yak. 660) Urartu başkenti yeni kurulmuş olan Teishebai URU (günümüzde Karmir-blur), Rusai URU.TUR (günümüzde Bastam), Rusahinili Qilbanikai (günümüzde Toprakkale) ve Rusahinili Eidurukai (günümüzde Ayanis) yerleşimleri arasında gidip gelmiştir.

---

Along the coast of lake Van, the ancient 'Upper Sea of Nairi' of the Assyrian records (Salvini 1998), we find — as everyone is aware — the ruins of Tušpa, the ancient capital of the Urartian kingdom (fig. 1) (Salvini 1986; Tarhan 1994). Unlike other Urartian cities such as Ayanis, which has only recently been discovered and excavated (Çilingiroğlu, Salvini 2001), we have always known the site of Van Kalesi with its monumental ruins (the most recent description of the site and of archaeological research there is provided by Tarhan 2001). The memory of its ancient eminence has stayed alive in the minds of those populations which have succeeded each other in this region since the end of the Urartian state,

that is, since the second half of the seventh century BC. The Armenian tradition was established at a very early date by the historian Moses Khorenats'i, who lived during the fifth century AD. He tells of the building of Shamiramakert, the 'City of Semiramis', by the legendary Assyrian queen whom Classical tradition attributes with all kinds of grandiose architectural projects.

It is this tradition which opened the way to the historical research and archaeological discoveries which have continued for almost two centuries now. When, in 1827, the young philosophy professor, F.E. Schulz, arrived in Van to study the ruins of Shamiramakert, he

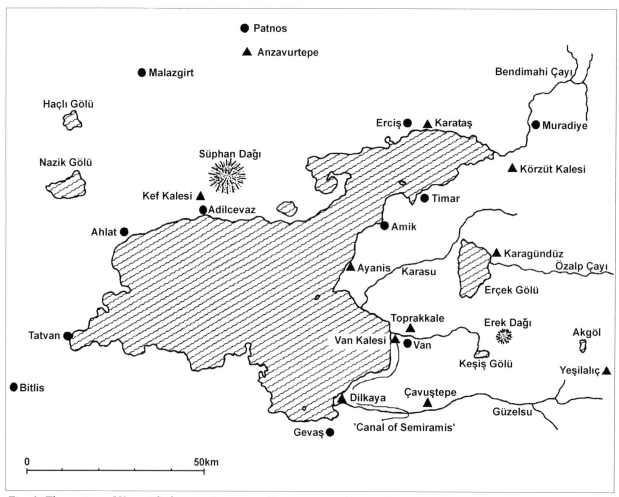

*Fig. 1. The region of Van with the most important Urartian sites (drawn by A. Mancini)*

took with him the history of Armenia by Khorenats'i and the geographical work of Father Indjidjan, which had appeared in Venice in 1809.

What had for some time attracted the attention of scholars, and had led the Iranianist Saint-Martin of the Académie des Inscriptions in Paris to send the young Schulz to explore these sites, was to be found written in chapter 16 of Khorenats'i's work (Saint-Martin 1828; Schulz 1840).

As far as the historical and documentary value of chapter 16 is concerned (not the entire work, but only this chapter, which is the only section concerned with Urartian research), I wish to stress one point. I do not agree with Nina Garsoïan, who interpreted Khorenats'i's description as follows: 'Although clearly fictitious, Movses Xorenac'i's description of the city presumably built at Van by Semiramis . . . is obviously that of a Hellenistic foundation' (Garsoïan 1984-1985: 73). Nor can I agree with Thomson, in his commentary on the *History of the Armenians*, regarding the construction of the 'Canal of Semiramis' (Salvini 1992), where he cites a passage from Diodorus Siculus as a reliable source

(Thomson 1978: 99, n. 6). Mention of Semiramis and the role she plays in the legends of Classical authors must not influence or mislead us in our evaluation of Khorenats'i's Armenian source. Classical mediation, in this case, is limited to the mention of Semiramis' name alone, and her figure corresponds to a legendary literary 'topos'. The concrete description, instead, does not derive from any Classical source, but shows that Khorenats'i or his source had direct knowledge of that real monumental complex.

To see precisely how true this is, I quote some passages from chapter 16, demonstrating through the example of certain figures the precise references found in this text.

…Passing through many places, she arrived from the east at the edge of the salt lake [= lake Van]. On the shore of the lake she saw a long hill [= Van Kalesi] whose length ran toward the setting sun ... To the north it sloped a little [fig. 2], but to the south it looked up sheer to heaven, with a cave in the vertical rock [fig. 3]. ... First she ordered the aqueduct for the

Fig. 2. Van Kalesi, northern slope

Fig. 3. Van Kalesi, southern slope

Fig. 4. Supporting wall of the 'Semiramis canal', built by king Minua around 800 BC

Fig. 5. Van Kalesi, detail of the cuneiform inscription containing Argišti I's annals

river to be built in hard and massive stone [fig. 4] ... on the side of the rock that faces the sun ... she had carved out various temples and chambers and treasure houses and wide caverns [fig. 3] ... and over the entire surface of the rock, smoothing it like wax with a stylus, she inscribed many texts, the mere sight of which makes anyone marvel [fig. 5]. And not only this, but also in many places in the land of Armenia she set up stelae [fig. 6] and ordered memorials to herself to be written with the same script' (chapter 16, 'How after the death of Ara Semiramis built the city and the aqueduct and her own palace'; see Thomson 1978: 98–101).

I think that a comparison between the written description and archaeological reality clearly demonstrates my point: that is to say, such a precise description must be based on reports of ancient travellers or dwellers rather than the works of the Classical authors. So, chapter 16, radically different to the rest of the work, must be seen as a particular mingling in terms both of style and nature, and I believe that this should be borne in mind by Armeniologists commentating on Khorenats'i's work. This, however, is to go beyond my field and is not directly related to the concerns of this discussion.

Fig. 6. Cuneiform stele by Minua (Van Museum)

In this short presentation, I would like to consider the monumental complex of Van Kalesi, and its topographical and archaeological situation from a chronological point of view. I refer to the various chronological phases of the Urartian settlement and, in particular, to the construction of the official buildings. Obviously, I have as my guides only the presence of written documents and their links with certain architectural structures.

## Madir Burçu - Sardursburg (fig. 7)

The oldest building in Van Kalesi which we can date is the so-called 'Sardursburg', defined thus by Lehmann-Haupt who worked there at the end of the 19th century (Lehmann-Haupt 1926: 18ff). This structure forms a right angle, is 12m thick and so solid that, still today, it is in an excellent state of preservation. It is attached to the western slopes of Van rock, not far from the shores of the lake. It consists of huge well squared limestone blocks laid in five regular courses. On both the eastern and western sides of the structure, six cuneiform inscriptions are carved into the blocks, in the Assyrian language and Neo-Assyrian ductus. They are all duplicates of the text of Sarduri I, who must be considered as the founder of the Urartian capital Tušpa (fig. 8).

> Inscription of Sarduri, son of Lutipri, great king, powerful king, king of the universe, king of Nairi, king without equal, great shepherd, who does not fear the fight, king who represses rebels. Sarduri says: I have brought here these foundation stones from the city of Alniunu, I have built this wall (Wilhelm 1986).

With this written document, which was discovered by Schulz, we have the beginning not only of the history of the Urartian kingdom, but also of written documentation for the entire, immense mountainous region stretching across what is now eastern Turkey, Armenia and Iranian Azerbaijan. Sarduri, who was defeated by the Assyrian king Shalmaneser III in the year 832 BC, may be considered as the founder of the Urartian state and its capital Tušpa, even though the name of the city itself does not appear in the document (Salvini 1995: 34–8).

The architecture of Madir Burçu differs from all the other Urartian fortifications known to us. Its position and shape does not even enable us to identify it as a fortress. Nor is Rudolf Naumann's interpretation convincing, namely that this corner platform (12.60m square) formed the foundation of a tower temple (Naumann 1968: 54). I have already put forward the hypothesis — supported moreover by other scholars — that it was, instead, a port structure such as a quay or wharf, assuming that the lake water level at the time of

*Fig. 7. The so-called 'Sardursburg', built by Sarduri I around 840–830 BC at the west end of Van Kalesi*

*Fig. 8. Assyrian inscription of Sarduri I, the first king of the Urartian dynasty*

its construction was a few metres higher than today (fairly rapid increases and decreases in the water level have been noted in various eras). In this period Van Kalesi was perhaps a peninsula.

The presence of a small rock inscription by Minua only a few metres away (Salvini 1973: 279ff) indicates a secondary use of this structure as a grain silo. In fact the text celebrates the foundation of a building called *'ari*, that is to say a silo with a capacity of 23,100 *kapi*, which corresponds to 583m³. This would have been 10m by 10m by 5m in dimension (the calculation is based on the value to be attributed to *kapi*, the Urartian measure used for cereals; see Salvini 1969: 10) and could very well have been constructed on top of the old quay structure now lying above the level of the lake.

However, the 'Sardursburg' also served as a *propylaeum* giving access to the higher levels of the rock, that is to say, the citadel. This may be seen from the rock staircase which still today performs this function.

The square which, according to Naumann, would have formed the base of a tower temple is in fact an isolated architectonic element, an independent structure (fig. 9). Against this, to the south, leans the body of a workroom, constructed with the same large limestone blocks, which links it to the rocky foot of Van rock. The two structural elements are, however, absolutely contemporaneous, given that they bear three duplicates of the same inscription of Sarduri I carved by the same hand (*CICh* 1–3 = *HchI* 1a–c = *UKN* 1–3, and three more duplicates published in Bilgiç 1959: 45ff).

One of the most fascinating and difficult problems that remains to be resolved is that of where these immense blocks came from. About 20 years ago, Oktay Belli published an interesting article in which he announced that he had identified the city of Alniunu, cited in the text by Sarduri I, and the Urartian stone quarry from which the 'Sardursburg' blocks had come (Belli 1982). He located the city of Alniunu and the 'Steinatelier' in the village of Edremit, which lies 17km south of Van Kalesi/Tušpa. The limestone blocks, worked there on the site, would have come from the Harapköy Tepe (1,900m above sea level), 1km southeast of Edremit.

It is likely that the quarry may be, in part, that described and illustrated in Belli's tables VII/2 and VIII, defined as 'Alniunu kenti taş atölyesi', although I have some doubts as to whether the stelae bases shown in tables IX and XIII–XIX, are in fact Urartian. I do not recall having seen anything similar related to Urartian stelae. What is more, Belli makes no mention of the fact that the entire area is occupied mainly by the ruins of the Armenian village of upper Edremit (Artemita on old maps). It is, in effect, covered in broken and half buried stelae from Armenian tombs (*hačkar*), and nearby are the ruins of the small Armenian church transformed into stables. The place is today called Taşkale, or Kıztaşı, whilst Edremit is the modern settlement along the shores of the lake.

Although I have not seen Harapköy Tepe, which is at an altitude of 300m above the level of the lake, I believe I can suggest a far closer source for the limestone blocks used in building the 'Sardursburg'. Roughly 100m from Taşkale there is the bed of a stream, the Kotur Dere, which has cut through the limestone layers, breaking these into flat slabs at numerous points (fig. 10). The more or less constant depth of the layer is approximately 90cm, the height most frequently encountered in the blocks of the 'Sardursburg'. The limestone appears to be the same kind as that of the Van blocks, and the fact that

Fig. 9. The corner section of the 'Sardursburg'

Fig. 10. Broken limestone layers on the bed of the Kotur Dere, by Taşkale (Edremit)

these large stones have a smooth and fairly even surface and almost standard thickness, may have suggested the idea of reducing them still further and transforming them into the huge squared blocks which we find at Van Kalesi. One may imagine that they were made to slip down the stream towards the nearby lakeshore on wooden rollers and then transported by rafts to the coast near Van rock, or even under the rock itself, if it is true that, in Sarduri I's time, the waters of the lake were a few metres higher (see Lehmann-Haupt 1926: 18). For now, however, this is all merely an hypothesis which needs to be checked also from a mineralogical standpoint (Salvini 2001: 302–4).

**The citadel**

The acropolis of the Urartian capital lies on the central section of the rocky crest. It is on the highest point of the rock (approximately 90m high) and must have been built under Sarduri I, although we do not have a foundation inscription to confirm this. The structure does, however, share similar characteristics with the 'Sardursburg'. Its perimeter follows the line of the rock (fig. 11), as may clearly be noted on the south side.

*Fig. 12. Van Kalesi, northern wall of the citadel of Tušpa*

*Fig. 11. Van Kalesi, southern wall of the citadel of Tušpa*

If we ignore the numerous overlying medieval structures, we can still clearly make out the plan of the Urartian fortress. This is in two parts and, at the same time, two phases. The highest and earliest citadel is roughly rectangular, measuring 110m by 45m, with the entrance on the west side (a plan of this inner citadel is published in Tarhan 1994: 32, fig. 8). There is then a second citadel, or a widening towards the west of roughly 350m, the wall of which displays the typical buttresses of Urartian architecture. The Ottoman outer wall, in turn, encloses an area of more than 500m by approximately 80m. The central part of the rock was defended by two cuts or incisions in the rock face which date back to Urartian times and must have defended the city to the east and west. The Ottoman wall then continued eastwards to the end of the rock, thus enclosing the lower city, but this is the section that has suffered the greatest damage.

Returning to the upper citadel, the north wall reveals four different phases (fig. 12). Whilst the upper two are of the Seljuk and Ottoman periods (excluding, of course, modern restorations), the two lower parts date to the Urartian era. The great size and quality of the squared-off stone blocks at the base of the wall show similarities with the 'Sardursburg' and must date back to the time of Sarduri I (ca. 840–830 BC). It is, moreover, unlikely that Sarduri built the quay structure at the base of the rock without fortifying the upper part.

The second phase consists of smaller blocks of friable sandstone, but also dates back to the Urartian period. This is shown by the inscribed stones which are inserted here, even though they are not in their original position (fig. 13). A study of these stones (Salvini 1973: 280–5) has shown that they are fragments of a lengthy inscription by Minua, son of Išpuini, which must have covered the façade of a building which was destroyed and dismantled in medieval times. It is a duplicate of an inscription celebrating Minua's conquests over the lands north of the Araxes. The best preserved example decorated the façade of a tower temple in Körzüt (Dinçol 1976; Salvini 1980).

*Fig. 13. Fragment of an Urartian inscription of Minua, reused in the northern wall of the citadel of Tušpa*

Minua, therefore, is attested on the citadel, but we have no document of his father Išpuini from there, though this does not exclude the fact that Išpuini resided on the citadel, like his father Sarduri and his son Minua. At the eastern edge of Van rock there is the great rock inscription of Tabriz Kapısı (fig. 14) (*CICh* II), by Išpuini, Minua and Inušpua, which must have had a similar function to the rock niches of Meher Kapısı, near Van (Salvini 1993–1997), and Yeşilalıç, 60km east of Van (Sevin, Belli 1976–1977). Like Yeşilalıç, Tabriz Kapısı also makes reference to the construction of a *susi* or 'tower temple' to the god Haldi. As in all the other Urartian cities, and above all in the capital Tušpa, there had to be a 'tower temple' as supreme architectural expression of the state cult. The inscription states that a *susi* temple was built and a 'Gate of Haldi', the latter a definition of the niche itself, 'in front(?) of the City of Tušpa'. This corresponds to the position of the inscription which is outside the citadel perimeter. The question which remains unanswered is the precise location of the temple since no trace of it has yet been found. It may, however, be presumed that it stood in the highest place. The works carried out in 1989–1990 on the perimeter of the upper citadel did not provide any clear results. Tarhan and Sevin, however, believe that they have identified traces of the plan of a temple on the rocky platform (Tarhan, Sevin 1989: 361, figs 8–9; Tarhan 1994: 33).

### The palace of Argišti I

The excavations carried out in 1987–1988 by Tarhan and Sevin brought to light the remains of buildings in the western sector of the rock although these consist of little more than negative imprints on the rock surface (fig. 15) (Tarhan 1988; Tarhan, Sevin 1989). In the entire complex there is not one stone left standing on another, but a stone staircase can be clearly seen, along with the layout of rooms and the thickness of the walls of the so called 'yeni saray' ('new palace'). Although we have no epigraphic documentation, it is almost certain that the work is to be attributed to Argišti I, for topographic reasons. The traces on the rock show that these structures overlooked and dominated the rock chambers of Horhor, the main monument left to us by Argišti I (André-Salvini, Salvini 1992). The long inscription of his annals (see again fig. 5), the most extensive document in Urartian cuneiform epigraphy, is a 'signature', which we can extend to cover the entire western sector of the Van rock. There are no traces of great, external fortifying walls in this lower section of the rock, but this is not surprising. Under the government of Argišti I, the Urartian kingdom attained its greatest extension, and the system of fortresses located throughout the territory,

Fig. 14. Van Kalesi, northeastern corner with the Ottoman structures of Tabriz Kapısı, the rock inscription by Išpuini, Minua and Inušpua

Fig. 15. Van Kalesi, western sector, rock carving for the foundations of Argišti I's palace

together with those controlling access to Van, were far more effective that any simple fortification (Augustan Rome had no need of defensive walls either).

We may therefore deduce that, under Argišti I, the buildings of the capital stretched so far as to cover all of the western surface of the rock which, however, had functioned as the entrance to the upper citadel from the very start.

## The rock terrace of Hazine Kapısı (also known as Analı Kız) (fig. 16)

Returning once more to the eastern sector of Van rock, along the northern slope and only a few metres above the level of the plain, we find a rock terrace about 40m wide and 15m deep. This is known as the 'Gate of the Treasure' due to the two great niches cut in the rock there. That to the east (on the left) is 6.80m high, the one to the west (on the right) 5.70m. Originally they both held inscriptions, but only in the niche to the right are these partially preserved. This is the famous text of the annals of Sarduri II, son of Argišti, which was discovered during the excavations by Marr and Orbeli in 1916 (Marr, Orbeli 1922). The text began on a stele in the left niche, continuing in the right niche on both the rock wall and on a second stele as well as on its basalt base (for the reconstruction of the text of Sarduri II's annals, see Salvini 1995: 63ff; see also the axonometric plan in Tarhan 1994: 29, fig. 6). Today, all of this has been entirely destroyed and the extant fragments are in a pitiable state both *in situ* and in the Van Museum.

*Fig. 16. Van Kalesi, eastern sector, the rock monument of Hazine Kapısı by Sarduri II*

It is still difficult to give an interpretation of the precise function of the terrace, as the cuneiform text provides no information in this regard. The same has to be said for the rock complex of Horhor, in the western sector. The presence of this long rock platform suggests that the terrace marked the point at which important official processions would have arrived in the time of Sarduri. Unlike Horhor, where the rock chambers with the mausoleum of Argišti I were difficult to reach and well guarded since they must have contained precious objects, the complex of Hazine Kapısı lies wide open and is easy to access.

Like the rock inscription of Tabriz Kapısı, Hazine Kapısı also lies outside the perimeter wall of the citadel, indicating that there were no treasures to be safeguarded. The rock terrace of Hazine Kapısı recalls that of Meher Kapısı, built by Išpuini and Minua two generations

earlier on the outskirts of Van, though this clearly served a religious function. On the rock surrounding the entire terrace of Hazine Kapısı there are still clear traces of walls and various structures which it is impossible to reconstruct today. All of this sector of Van rock, however, seems to have been involved in building and construction at the time of Sarduri II.

## Rock tombs

The well known great rock chambers which open mainly onto the southern slope of Van rock have invited various interpretations (see in general Piotrovskij 1966: 299ff). Movses Khorenats'i spoke of 'various temples and chambers and treasure houses and wide caverns'. Today, some of these rock chambers are taken to be tombs, especially the Horhor complex which lies behind the inscribed rock façade containing the annals of Argišti, where the mausoleum of Argišti and his royal family must have been. From the main room, which measures 10.5m by 6m and is 3.5m high, there are entrances into four smaller chambers. All of the walls have niches in the shape of windows, probably to hold ritual offerings (see the photographs published in André-Salvini, Salvini 1992). The same thing may be seen in the princely tombs of Altıntepe (Özgüç 1969) and in the columbarium of Jerevan (Biscione 1994). A rock-cut columbarium also exists in the eastern sector of Van Kalesi and was studied by Sevin in association with the Urartian cremation rite (Sevin 1980). Other small burial chambers are found on various points of the rock, but those which it is most difficult to interpret are the large rooms on the southern slope. The rock chamber of Naft Kuyu — with a 12m high façade (fig. 17) — opens into a series of rooms. The

*Fig. 17. Van Kalesi, southern slope, façade of the rock chamber of Naft Kuyu*

main room measures 9m by 6m and has a barrel vault that is 8m high, with a window above the entrance door. The ceiling of the main chamber in the nearby cave of İçkala is almost 6m high and it too is vaulted. Ingrid Reindell suggests to me that such dimensions and shape may serve to create an acoustic effect which could have been important in certain religious ceremonies. The so-called 'eastern chamber' (fig. 18) is roughly 6m high, but with a flat ceiling.

These measurements do not seem to be compatible with those used in rock tombs. Unfortunately, there are no inscriptions to give us a clue as to their use or to assist in dating them. This is one of the most important unresolved questions regarding Van Kalesi. There is, however, certain evidence that these rock chambers must have had different functions. On the northern slope there is a rectangular rock chamber with the following characteristics and measurements: it is more than 20m long and 9m wide, but only 2.5m high. The entrance is particularly wide, measuring more than 8m. It is self-evident that this could not have been intended for use either as a tomb or as a dwelling. The solution is provided by the inscription at the entrance: 'Minua, son of Išpuini, has made this place a *siršini*'. In the cursing formula there is an explanation of this term and thus of the purpose of this space: 'Minua speaks: he who takes the oxen from here … he who takes the herd from here may the gods destroy them'. Clearly we are dealing with Minua's royal stables, cut into the living rock (Salvini 1986). The Urartian capital must have had other installations of this kind. There is the silo at the westernmost point above the 'Sardursburg', which I mentioned earlier, and I would also add what I call the 'Fountain of Minua', declared to be such by the three epigraphs that mark this site along the north foot of Van rock.

So, we have so far seen how the entire surface and the rock itself of Van Kalesi may be divided into areas linked to the presence and works of the various kings of the dynasty (see table 1). Sarduri I occupied the highest part of the rock and the western extremity between 840 and 830 BC. Išpuini probably built the second citadel west of the first, but his name is attested only in the Tabriz Kapısı inscription. Minua must have resided in the upper citadel, carrying out numerous works on various parts of the rock (the silo, fountain, stables). Argišti I concentrated on the western sector of the rock, building his palace and excavating his own mausoleum. Sarduri II, instead, occupied the sector to the east, celebrating his own achievements as his father had done. It is also likely that he built his own palace there.

These are the works which can be identified and dated. To these we must add the great rock works destined to remain anonymous.

*Fig. 18. Van Kalesi, southern slope, the 'eastern chamber'*

So, we can see that the entire rock was occupied and built on in a century of history which goes from approximately 840/30 to roughly 735 BC, the end of Sarduri II's reign. There are no written documents conserved at Van Kalesi which refer to the later kings. It is clear that, from Rusa I, son of Sarduri, onwards there was no space on the rock for great architectural projects.

One essential problem remains, however: up until what date was Van Kalesi the seat of the Urartian capital Tušpa? Until the end of the kingdom, the kings of Urartu defined themselves as 'Lord of the city of Tušpa', and the Assyrian sources also quote Turušpa on the occasion of the invasion by the Cimmerians and Sargon's eighth campaign in 714 BC.

We must therefore ask ourselves whether Tušpa meant this rock with its ancient constructions or whether, instead, from the end of the eighth century onwards, it indicated a wider concept embracing the entire Van oasis. The sanctuary of Meher Kapısı, dating to the time of Išpuini, also belonged to the capital.

The position of the necropolis (Sevin, Özfırat 2000; 2001), 2km north of Van Kalesi, would seem to fit with the main settlement of the lower city around the rock. In medieval and modern times too, Van did not mean only the ancient city at the foot of the Ghaurab (the fortress), but also the vast garden city, and thus a double city. Toprakkale too, built by Rusa II under the name of Rusahinili, must have been part of the area of the capital Tušpa. It is, however, difficult to explain the gap in the documentation from Sarduri II to Rusa II at Van Kalesi. This, like other open questions, shows how much more there is to study and research at Van Kalesi, a site which has always been known to us, but also always, to some extent, ignored.

| *Assyrian kings* | *Synchronisms* | *Urartian kings* (written records of) |
|---|---|---|
| Shalmaneser III (858–824 BC) | quotes Aramu the Urartian (years 858, 856, 844) | (no written records) |
| Shalmaneser III (year 832) | quotes Seduri, the Urartian (ca. 840–830) | = Sarduri I, son of Lutipri* (* no written records of him) |
| Šamšî-Adad V (823–811) | quotes Ušpina (year 821) | = Išpuini, son of Sarduri (ca. 830–820) |
| | | coregency of Išpuini and Minua (ca. 820–810) |
| | | Minua, son of Išpuini (ca. 810–785/780) |
| Shalmaneser IV (781–772) | quotes Argištu/i | = Argišti I, son of Minua (785/780–756) |
| Aššur-nârârî V (754–745) | is quoted by | Sarduri II, son of Argišti (756–ca. 730) |
| Tiglath-pileser III (744–727) | quotes Sarduri, Sardaurri (years 743, 735?) | = Sarduri II |
| Sargon (721–705) | quotes Ursa, Rusa | = Rusa I, son of Sarduri (ca. 730–714) |
| | quotes Argišta (year 708) | = Argišti II, son of Rusa (713– ?) |
| Sennacherib (704–681) | (no synchronism) | |
| Esarhaddon (681–669) | quotes Ursa (year 673/672) | = Rusa II, son of Argišti (first half of the seventh century) |
| Assurbanipal (669–627) | quotes Rusa (year 652) | = Rusa III, son of Erimena |
| Assurbanipal | quotes Sarduri (year 643) | = Sarduri III, son of Rusa (III) |
| | | Sarduri IV, son of Sarduri (III) |

*Table 1. Urartian chronology*

I would like to conclude by expressing the hope that the authorities will finally decide to bring order to the entire archaeological area and create an open-air museum worthy of its great historical significance. Indeed, Tarhan's old project should be started up again, which had the aim of creating an historical national park at Van Kalesi (see Tarhan 1985).

**Bibliography**

*Abbreviations*

CICh = Lehmann-Haupt, C.F. 1928–1935: *Corpus Inscriptionum Chaldicarum.* 2 Volumes. Berlin, Leipzig

HchI = König, F.W. 1955–1957: *Handbuch der chaldischen Inschriften* (Archiv für Orientforschung, Beiheft 8). Graz

UKN = Melikišvili, G.A. 1960: *Urartskie klinoobraznye nadpisi (Urartian Cuneiform Inscriptions).* Second edition. Moscow

André-Salvini, B., Salvini, M. 1992: 'Gli annali di Argišti I, note e collazioni' *Studi Micenei ed Egeo-Anatolici* 30: 9–23

Belli, O. 1982: 'Alniunu kenti ve taş atölyesinin keşfi / Die Entdeckung der Stadt Alniunu und ihres Steinateliers' *Anadolu Araştırmaları* 8 (1980): 115–30

Bilgiç, E. 1959: 'Birkaç Yeni Urartu Kıral Kitabesi' *Türk Arkeoloji Dergisi* 9: 44–8

Biscione, R. 1994: 'Recent Urartian discoveries in Armenia: the Columbarium of Erevan' *Studi Micenei ed Egeo-Anatolici* 34: 115–35

Çilingiroğlu, A., Salvini, M. 2001: *Ayanis I. Ten Years' Excavations at Rusahinili Eiduru-kai (1989–1998).* Rome

Dinçol, A.M. 1976: 'Die neuen urartäischen Inschriften aus Körzüt' *Istanbuler Mitteilungen* 26: 19–30

Garsoïan, N.G. 1984–1985: 'The early-mediaeval Armenian city: an alien element?' *The Journal of the Ancient Near Eastern Society* 16–17: 67–83

Lehmann-Haupt, C.F. 1926: *Armenien einst und jetzt* Band II/1. Berlin, Leipzig

Marr, N., Orbeli, I. 1922: *Archeologičeskaja ekspedicija 1916 goda v Van. Raskopki dvuch niš na Vanskoj Skale i nadpisi Sardura vtorogo iz raskopok zapadnoj niši'*. St Petersburg

Naumann, R. 1968: 'Bemerkungen zu urartäischen Tempeln' *Istanbuler Mitteilungen* 18: 45–57

Özgüç, T. 1969: *Altıntepe II. Mezarlar, depo binası ve fildişi eserler (Tombs, storehouses and ivories)*. Ankara

Piotrovskij, B.B. 1966: *Il regno di Van (Urartu)*. Rome

Saint-Martin, J. 1828: 'Notice sur le voyage littéraire de M. Schulz en Orient, et sur les découvertes qu'il a faites récemment dans des ruines de la ville de Sémiramis en Arménie' *Journal Asiatique* September 1828: 161–88

Salvini, M. 1969: 'Nuove iscrizioni urartee dagli scavi di Arin-berd, nell'Armenia Sovietica' *Studi Micenei ed Egeo-Anatolici* 9: 7–24

— 1973: 'Urartäisches epigraphisches Material aus Van und Umgebung' *Belleten* 37: 279–87

— 1980: 'Un testo celebrativo di Menua' *Studi Micenei ed Egeo-Anatolici* 22: 137–68

— 1986: 'Tuschpa, die Hauptstadt von Urartu' in V. Haas (ed.), *Das Reich Urartu. Ein altorientalischer Staat im 1. Jahrtausend v. Chr.* (Xenia 17). Konstanz: 31–44

— 1992: 'Il canale di Semiramide' *Geographia Antiqua* 1: 67–80

— 1993–1997: 'Meher Kapısı' *Reallexikon der Assyriologie* Band 8: 21–2

— 1995: *Geschichte und Kultur der Urartäer*. Darmstadt

— 1998: 'Nairi, Na'iri' *Reallexikon der Assyriologie* Band 9, 1/2: 87–91

— 2001: 'Van Kalesi-Sardursburg' *Studi Micenei ed Egeo-Anatolici* 43: 302–4

Schulz, F.E. 1840: 'Mémoire sur le lac de Van et ses environs' *Journal Asiatique*, série III, 9: 257–323

Sevin, V. 1980: 'A rock-cut columbarium from Van Kale and the Urartian cremation rite' *Anadolu Araştırmaları* 8: 151–66

Sevin, V., Belli, O. 1976–1977: 'Yeşilalıç Urartu Kutsal Alanı ve Kalesi' *Anadolu Araştırmaları* 4–5: 367–93

Sevin, V., Özfırat, A. 2000: '1997–1998 Yılı Van/Altıntepe Urartu Nekropolü Kazıları' *Kazı Sonuçları Toplantısı* 21.I: 421–34

— 2001: 'Van-Altıntepe excavations' in O. Belli (ed.), *Istanbul University's Contributions to Archaeology in Turkey (1932–1999)*. Istanbul: 179–83

Tarhan, M.T. 1985: 'Van Kalesi'nin ve Eski Van Şehri'nin Tarihi-Milli Park Projesi üzerinde ön çalışmalar (I): Anıt Yapılar' *Araştırma Sonuçları Toplantısı* 3: 297–355

— 1988: 'Van Kalesi ve Eski Van Şehri Kazıları 1987' *Kazı Sonuçları Toplantısı* 10: 369–91

— 1994: 'Recent research at the Urartian capital Tushpa' *Tel Aviv* 21: 22–57

— 2001: 'Tuşpa-Van Kalesi. Demirçağ'in Gizemli Başkentideki Araştırma ve Kazılar' in O. Belli (ed.), *Istanbul University's Contributions to Archaeology in Turkey (1932–1999)*. Istanbul: 191–200

Tarhan, M.T., Sevin, V. 1989: 'Van Kalesi ve Eski Van Şehri Kazıları, 1988' *Kazı Sonuçları Toplantısı* 11: 355–75

Thomson, R.W. 1978: *Moses Khorenats'i, History of the Armenians. Translation and Commentary on the Literary Sources*. Harvard, London

Wilhelm, G. 1986: 'Urartu als Region der Keilschrift-Kultur' in V. Haas (ed.), *Das Reich Urartu. Ein altorientalischer Staat im 1. Jahrtausend v. Chr.* (Xenia 17). Konstanz: 95–116

# Neo-Assyrian or Neo-Hittite?
# An orthostat in Şanlıurfa Archaeological Museum

## Andreas Schachner[1] and Eyüb Bucak[2]
[1]University of Munich, [2]Şanlıurfa Archaeological Museum

## Abstract

The orthostat published here was found not far to the south of Urfa. Its imagery presents a rare combination: the use of registers, the style and some iconographic details are essentially Assyrian, but the iconology — the general subject of the scenes and, in particular, the representation of the funerary meal — is derived from the indigenous Neo-Hittite tradition. According to this iconological tradition the pictures on the orthostat should be interpreted as being those of a funerary monument. The stylistic and iconographic details of the orthostat favour a rather late dating, most probably in the late seventh century BC.

## Özet

Burada tanıttığımız Urfa Müzesi'nde bulunan ortostat, Asur sanat üslubu ve ikonografisinin Geç Hitit manevi geleneğinde birleştiği nadir örneklerden birini temsil etmektedir. Üslup ve bazı ikonografik detaylar, hemen hemen tamamen Asur sanatına ait olmasına rağmen, sahnelerin genel manası, özellikle ölü yemeği, Geç Hitit sanatının manevi anlayışı çerçevesinde yorumlanabilmektedir. Sadece bu gelenek, sahnelerin gerçek manasını yorumlamaya fırsat vermektedir. Eserimiz Asur üslubunda yapılmış bir kaç stelle beraber M.Ö. 7.yy.'da yoğun bir Arami etkisinin Asur sanatında var olduğunu göstermektedir. Urfa ortostatı sanatsal üslup ve şekliyle daha çok Asur sanatından etkilendiği için büyük bir ihtimalle söz konusu eserler arasında en geç örnek olup, tahminen M.Ö. 7.yy.'ın ikinci yarısına tarihlenmektedir.

Several recent studies have added considerably to our knowledge of the historical developments in northern Mesopotamia, today's borderland between Turkey and Syria, during the first centuries of the first millennium BC. At this time the region was controlled by so-called Neo-Hittite or Aramaean states, and later in the period by the Neo-Assyrian empire.[1]

Some of these recent studies have published new material (Zahlhaas 1995: 76–8, Taf. F; Schachner, Schachner 1996; Kulakoğlu 1999; Balcıoğlu 2000: 111–15; Bonatz 2000: 14–23, A10–A12, B10, C5, C6, C19, C20, C40, C48, C58, C67; Schachner, Schachner,

Karabulut 2002). Others have described the broader historical, political and artistic developments, making use of the known archaeological monuments and the textual evidence (Voos 1985; 1988a; 1988b; Bonatz 2000). The foundations for all such research were laid in the guiding work of Orthmann (Orthmann 1971; note that references to Neo-Hittite monuments given in our paper follow those of Orthmann). Thanks to these efforts, the historical and stylistic developments in the region are comparatively well known.

A major issue is the nature of the relationship between the indigenous Neo-Hittite or Aramaean states, together with their art, and the Neo-Assyrian empire which extended its political and artistic power to the west during the ninth and eighth centuries BC. Whereas the Assyrian side of the coin is well known due to abundant archaeological and textual evidence (Lamprichs 1995; Gerlach 2000), the contributions made by the people of the formerly independent Aramaean states in northern

---

[1] In recent years, a debate has started on the terminology used to describe the ethnic and political situation of the Iron Age city states in north Syria and southeast Anatolia (Voos 1988a: 349; 1988b: 347; Bonatz 2000: 4). We prefer the term Neo-Hittite because it is well established in the literature, even though it does not reflect the ethnic complexity of the region.

Mesopotamia are difficult to determine, mainly due to the lack of adequate archaeological data. Our presentation of a recently found relief may be another piece towards comprehending this complex cultural mosaic (fig. 1).

The relief was acquired by the Urfa Archaeological Museum in 1999. Since the find changed hands several times before reaching the museum, it was impossible to determine the exact find-spot, but it is said to have been found by a farmer ploughing a field between two major sites of the region, Tell Kazane and Harran (the destruction caused by a plough or a pick is still visible on the surface of the orthostat). Before discussing the significance of the relief, it should first be described.

**Description and reconstruction of the scenes**

Height: ca. 54.8cm; width: ca. 54.5cm; thickness: 5.5–6.5cm. Material: very soft white limestone, similar in appearance to that found in the immediate vicinity of Şanlıurfa. Present location: Archaeological Museum, Şanlıurfa.

The orthostat, the original edges of which are partly preserved, is almost square, despite minor variations and breakages at the corners. The regularity of its dimensions indicate that it was carefully made (figs 1, 2). The reverse is roughly smoothed. There are no traces of marks on the reverse or on the sides of the relief to show how it might have been affixed; its shape suggests that it was not freestanding but was incorporated into a wall.

The front side of the orthostat shows several scenes in two registers (figs 1, 2). The upper register measures 40.6–41.2cm by 25.8–26cm, whereas the lower one is only 41.7–42.7cm by 13.5–13.9cm. The ratio of the total surface area of the two registers is almost exactly 2:1 (the total surface area of the relief is about 3,025cm², that of the upper register is about 1,060cm² and that of the lower register about 580cm²). Both are framed by a marginal strip 5.1–6.1cm wide and there is a similar strip between the registers. The reliefs in both registers are of the same fine workmanship. The depth of the carving is only 1–3mm. Since the original surface of the figures is almost nowhere preserved, it is very difficult to recognise details, especially those of the (badly eroded) faces and dress, though some can be reconstructed by comparison with better preserved monuments.

**The upper register** (figs 1–3)

The scene of the upper register is symmetrically framed by two figures facing inwards. On the left, a standing person (no. 1) dressed in a long shirt holds a round object, probably a mirror, in her/his left hand (figs 2, 3). What, if anything, was held in the right hand is not clear. To the right of this figure is the largest individual (no. 2) in the relief.

*Fig. 1. Photograph of the relief (photo: R. Ceccacci)*

*Fig. 2. Drawing of the relief (drawing: C. Wolff)*

*Fig. 3. The upper register (not to scale)*

This main figure (no. 2) of the upper register, and of the whole orthostat, sits on a large, decorated throne which has a tall back and curved arm-rests (whether or not the throne had conical, maybe pine-cone, feet cannot be determined owing to the state of preservation). The throne probably has three horizontal cross-bars below the seat; it may be that these were decorated with ribs or palm capitals where they were fixed to the vertical pieces. The seated person wears a long shirt-like dress without a partition. The feet of the figure rest on a footstool, which has a horizontal cross-bar connecting two vertical legs. Decorative details are not visible. The face and hands of person no. 2 are destroyed but the hairstyle, formed by parallel grooves, is recognisable. The figure holds his/her right arm in front of the body, probably to the height of the chest. The left arm may be slightly visible. Since the general appearance of the figure closely resembles the sitting queen in the famous garden scene of Ashurbanipal, one might assume that the person holds a cup in the right hand and a flower in the left (compare Barnett 1976: pl. lxv).

Although the right side of the table in front of the sitting person is partly destroyed, some details are discernable. The table has a central pole support that is decorated with three large beads arranged vertically on the pole. As with other pieces of furniture in this relief, the upper parts of the table legs are wider than the lower sections. On the right-hand side, the lower part of a tablecloth ends in a two part arrangement. On top of the table lie two clearly visible and separate piles of crescentic objects, though the right pile is partly destroyed. Such objects, and the tablecloth, have close parallels in Neo-Hittite art (compare Maraş B10, B15, B19; Karaburçlu 1; Balcıoğlu 2000: res. 2). The crescents resemble food, probably loaves of bread. In Assyrian art, only a few scenes are known which depict a table prepared for a meal, with different objects such as pots or drinking vessels together with food and other things laid on them; these generally profane scenes indicate that it is exclusively the king who is represented in them. The tablecloth in these Assyrian depictions is very different to those in Neo-Hittite art (Barnett 1961: pl. 98; Barnett, Davies 1970: pl. v, 7; Orthmann 1971: 372 nos 23–27, 388–90).

Between the table and the next figure (no. 3), traces of the legs of a low table or support are visible. Another object might be standing on top of it which, although eroded, can be reconstructed as a jar or a large vessel by comparison with better preserved monuments (Genge 1982: Abb. 1; Bonatz 2000: Taf. xviii, C 48).

To the right again, only the silhouette of the small standing figure (no. 3) is preserved. Its dress is probably the same as that of figures 1 and 2. In its right hand it holds a long object, maybe a fan of the same kind as figure no. 9's in the lower register. No further details are extant.

Another person (no. 4) follows figure 3, holding a flag shaped fan or fly-whisk in its right hand. This individual is larger than figure 3 but smaller than figure 1, and wears the same kind of long dress. Details of the face, the dress and the hairstyle are not visible. In contrast to the flag shaped fan held by figure 11 in the lower register, this example shows no signs of incised lines. The figure stands behind a second table which is plainer than the one in front of figure 2. This overlap-representation incorporates another individual into the rest of the scene, no. 5 on the far right of the register.

In contrast to all other individuals of both registers, this figure no. 5 is bent forward slightly, with both arms stretched out over the table as though working there (unfortunately the surface of the stone immediately above the table here is damaged). The dress of the figure differs from the rest of those in the upper register in that the tunic reaches down to only slightly above the knees. Details of the person's hair, face and hands have not survived.

**The lower register** (figs 2, 4)
On the left side of the lower register an animal, facing right, is flanked by two persons, one of whom (no. 6) is following the animal and is dressed in a short tunic, below which the muscular legs are visible; shoes are not perceptible. The figure has a long beard and therefore is clearly male, with hair reaching down to the shoulders. His left arm is extended over the back of the animal, with the hand open. The right arm is kept in front of the body, holding a stick. Apart from the seated main figure on the right-hand side of the scene, figure 6 is the largest person depicted in the lower register.

The animal (no. 7), in front of figure 6, follows no. 8 who holds it with a rope (or such-like) turned around his right arm. The right-hand part of the animal, including some details of its head, has been partially destroyed by a large gash in the stone, and other surface damage has removed the end of its tail. Nevertheless, some interesting features are visible. The animal's size is proportionately too small in comparison with the human beings on either side of it. The presentation, especially of the head, the pointed ears, the body shape, and the positioning of the legs and hooves, shows that an equid is being depicted; the arrangement of the legs is closely paralleled by scenes of the period of Ashurnasirpal II and Shalmaneser III (Czichon 1992: 31–2, Taf. 2). Only the two humps on its back are unusual. It is impossible to interpret these as representing a carried load, for if this were the case they should be positioned in the middle of

*Fig. 4. The lower register (not to scale)*

the animal's back: a load fixed as shown would be unacceptable to the creature (personal communication with A. von den Driesch). We can also rule out the idea that the relief shows a two humped (Bactrian) camel, because none of the known Bactrian camels in Assyrian art have parallels with the Urfa relief (compare Mitchell 2000). Although the depiction is not clear, two other interpretations are possible. The humps could be explained as a wooden construction for fastening loads to the animal; as Hrouda points out, wooden bars were used to fix loads on mules (Hrouda 1965: 101, Taf. 18.17; compare the Balawat gates of Shalmaneser III: King 1915: pl. xxiii, lower register). However the other and more likely possibility is that a saddle is depicted. As far as we can tell from the Assyrian palace reliefs, this piece of equipment was unknown to Assyrian horsemen. However, saddles comparable to the Urfa relief depiction are attested on monuments dating to the fifth and maybe fourth centuries BC in Anatolia and Iran (see Ghirshman 1973: 94–5, fig. 1, pl. xlviii, 1–2; Nollé 1992: 59, 127, 129, Taf. 8d) and Xenophon mentions a similar saddle which he saw with the Persians (Xenophon, *Kyrupädia* I.IV, 4; *peri hippikes* 12.9).

The animal is led by figure 8, who wears a tunic reaching down to the knees and a belt. It is not clear whether the dress has long or short sleeves. As with 5 and 6, the legs are naked and no shoes are visible. The person has no beard and no traces of the hairstyle are preserved. Since the person is turned to the right, with the right arm holding the animal, the torso is represented frontally.

Figures 6–8 form a group separated from the scene to the right by a space wider than that usually left between two figures. The scene on the right also consists of three persons (nos 9–11).

Figure 9, standing facing right, wears a long dress without a belt. Held in his/her right hand there is a long object, perhaps a fan.

The main person in this part of the relief is a figure (no. 10) sitting on a throne which has a high back and rounded arm-rests. The person is dressed in a long shirt that reaches to the feet. Neither a belt nor any other detail of dress is recognisable. The right arm is clearly visible, holding a now destroyed object in front of the body. The left arm is difficult to discern, again because of the damage to the area in front of the figure. Probably both arms are held in front of the body. The feet rest on a footstool which is only visible as a slightly raised rectangular area; details are lacking which, together with a line between the knees of the figure and the table, may indicate that this part of the relief was not entirely finished. The details of figure 10 have clear parallels with figure 2 in the upper register, such as the hairstyle, the curved profile of the back and the positions of the arms.

In front of the sitting figure 10 stands an elaborate table the details of which are likewise comparable to the one in the upper register associated with figure 2: crescentic objects on top of it, arranged in two piles each of five crescents; bead-on-pole decoration below the table-top; and possibly a tablecloth hanging down on the right-hand side, represented by a line.

Given the marked similarities between figures 2 and 10, and the laid tables associated with them, we suggest that they are depictions of the same person who, for iconographic reasons discussed below, is probably female, as on some Assyrian monuments (for which see Unger 1933; Czichon 1992: 60–5). Nevertheless, it cannot be ruled out that two different persons are being shown, a female (no. 10) and a male (no. 2).

The third person in this scene (no. 11) faces left and is the smallest figure in the lower register. It holds in its right hand a flag shaped fan decorated with parallel horizontal lines. The person wears a long dress. Details of the head are not preserved.

**The iconography and iconology**

The individuals in both registers are depicted in two different ways. Whereas figures 1–4 and 9–11 wear long dresses, figures 5, 6 and 8 are dressed in short tunics which leave the lower leg naked. The dresses of figures 1 and 9 have vertical divisions and figure 8 wears a belt. So far as we can tell, none of the persons wears a head-dress except for figure 10 who has a hair band. Only one (no. 6) has a beard and all the others except for figure 8 seem to have more or less similar hairstyles, which reach down to the shoulder and are sometimes marked by parallel lines.

Given these extant iconographic details, a secure identification of the sex of the persons is difficult to make from the Urfa relief alone. Consideration of the parallels in Neo-Hittite iconography on the one hand, and Assyrian on the other, can lead to variant interpretations in this regard. In Neo-Hittite art, as well as that of the Hittite Imperial period, women usually wear a long, undecorated veil which covers the whole body as well as the head; its antecedents date back to the Old Hittite period (Goetze 1955: 59; Darga 1984: 86–8; compare Orthmann 1971: especially at 276; Schachner, Schachner 1996: 207). In Assyrian iconography on the other hand, though few representations of women exist, they usually wear a long dress (which may be decorated) but no veil: only crowns, bands or diadems around the head are attested (Hrouda 1965: 40–1, 46–7). Hence, if Neo-Hittite artistic conventions were being followed in the Urfa relief, one would assume that all individuals in both registers are male. However, the relief's depictions closely parallel those in Assyrian visual art, indicating that several of the figures could be female.[2]

It is important too to consider the large elaborate thrones upon which the main figures 2 and 10 sit. In Hittite cuneiform texts and Hittite Imperial art, thrones are used exclusively by men or male gods (Symington 1996: 117); women or goddesses sit on stools without arm-rests. However, in Assyrian art, at least in the garden scene of Ashurbanipal, the queen sits on a large and richly decorated throne with rounded arm-rests, closely resem-

*Fig. 5. Schematic line drawing of the relief (drawing: C. Wolff)*

bling the example on the Urfa relief (Barnett 1976: pl. lxv). To conclude then, we identify figures 1–4 and 9–11 as female, given their close relationship to depictions in Assyrian art, and the observation that none of them have beards. However, it cannot be ruled out that figures 2 and/or 10 are male; if they are, then this has consequences for our interpretation of the relief as a whole, as discussed below. Figure 8, although lacking a beard, must be male since the form of his dress is attested for men only, both in the Neo-Hittite and in the Assyrian tradition.

In both registers, the individual figures are grouped according to the position and direction of the standing figures. In the upper register, figures 1, 3 and 4, framing figure 2 and the associated table, form one group to which another table and figure 5 are added by an overlap representation. In the lower register, figures 6 and 8 together with the animal form one group, separated by a small space from the second group which comprises figures 9 and 11 framing the sitting figure 10 and the table. A clear relationship between two sitting and eight standing figures is visible in the relief, since the standing figures all face the sitting persons.[3] Each of the standing figures is characterised by an attribute indicating different functions within the scenes.

---

[2] Note that, at least in the time of Shalmaneser III, the local women of Bit Adini and other parts of Syria are depicted wearing clothes and hairstyles comparable to those in Neo-Hittite art (Wäfler 1975: 139, 202). It cannot be ruled out that after the ninth century BC Assyrian fashion was adopted in the western parts of their empire.

[3] According to the interesting hypothesis of Bonatz, the difference between sitting and standing is more than simply a different way of depicting persons; rather it might be understood as representing the difference between being alive (standing) and dead (sitting) (Bonatz 2000: 108–9).

The sitting individuals are marked out as being the most important in both registers, by their heightened position, by the rich variety of the depicted details and by the large number of servants (figures 1, 3, 4, 9 and 11) accompanying them. Since the tables directly in front of them are also framed by the servants, these too must be associated and interpreted with the sitting persons.

The scene of a sitting figure with a table in front laden with food and/or drink, and flanked by servants with a mirror and/or fans, is well known in Neo-Hittite art. These representations are generally interpreted as showing the funerary meal laid on as part of the activities following the death of an individual, probably of the person depicted. Moreover, these scenes also play an important role in the commemoration of the dead (Orthmann 1971: 366–93; Hawkins 1980: 213–25; Voos 1988a; 1988b: 352–8; Schachner, Schachner 1996: 214–16; Bonatz 2000: 151–8). Hittite and Neo-Hittite texts in particular demonstrate the connection between eating and drinking and the death cult. The table with bread and fruit is to be understood as a symbolic representation of that which was offered to the deities during the ceremonies (Hawkins 1980; for a collection of the most important sources, see Bonatz 2000: 92–5, 66–75). By contrast, in Assyrian art, drinking or eating scenes are only randomly attested, and these involve the king exclusively, and all have a profane meaning. This variation in the interpretation of iconographically similar scenes is due to the different cultural roots of the people of northern Mesopotamia (Orthmann 1971: 388–90; Gerlach 2000).

As pointed out above, the standing figures in the Urfa relief have particular functions characterised by a specific attribute. Figure 1 is associated with a round object with a vertical handle. This, with some certainty, can be identified as a mirror. Mirrors are a frequent attribute represented on Neo-Hittite monuments, and are always associated with women (Bonatz 2000: 82–5, omitting Bossert 1957). In Hittite cuneiform texts the mirror is identified as a symbol of the goddesses of fate (Bossert 1957: 350–2), and the frequent occurrence of mirrors on Neo-Hittite monuments, either alone or held by female figures, shows that this meaning was still understood during the Iron Age.

Figures holding a fan or a fly-whisk are also typical in Neo-Hittite and Neo-Assyrian art. Apart from their functional role, these figures emphasise the importance of the person to whom they are attached, by showing that the individual concerned has the right to a servant with fan (Bonatz 2000: 103–5). On the Urfa relief two different kinds of fly-whisks are represented. The one held by figures 3 and 9 is of the widely known type

operated mainly by an up-and-down movement, typical in Neo-Hittite and Neo-Assyrian art. However the other is the rather rarely attested flag shaped type, which operates by a horizontal movement. Few examples of this last type of fan are known in the art of the Iron Age states of north Syria (they include a stele from Maraş: Schachner, Schachner 1996: 208, 221, fig. 1a; and one from Til Barsip: Thureau-Dangin, Dunand 1936: pl. 14.3). It is not represented in the Neo-Assyrian palace reliefs (for the fly-whisks depicted there, see Hrouda 1965: pl. 32.19–21), but occurs on Neo-Assyrian cylinder seals (Moortgat 1966: nos 660, 662–5, 667, 668; Collon 1987: nos 338, 339), on a fragment of a glazed brick from Niniveh (Campbell et al. 1931: pl. xxxi), and on a helmet of uncertain origin (Born, Seidl 1995: 18, 43, 47, fig. 9, pl. iii). The earlier occurrence of this kind of fan on a Neo-Elamite relief from Susa (Harper et al. 1992: 200, no. 14), on bronze beakers from the western Zagros (Calmeyer 1973: A2–4, 14, 16–18, 22) and on Elamite seals, may indicate an eastern origin.

The scene on the right-hand side of the upper register is unusual for the art of the Neo-Hittite states. Although the surface of the stone is heavily eroded, some details, and in particular the way that person 5 is bending over the table to work, are comparable with representations in Assyrian palace reliefs. Closely similar are scenes showing Assyrian army camps where soldiers are depicted working (Barnett 1961: Taf. 21, period of Ashurnasirpal II). Given these parallels, it is possible that the servant, figure 5, is cutting up a joint of meat; if so, the scene can he interpreted as showing part of the preparation for the funerary meal depicted to the left.

The lower register consists of two different scenes. The group on the right again depicts a funerary meal. The scene on the left, however, is unusual for a grave monument, since equids are only rarely depicted on Neo-Hittite stelae and mainly appear there as symbols of the wealth and status of the person concerned (Bonatz 2000: 100; equids and camels find especial mentioned in the Harran census: Fales 1990: 142). If the two humps are indeed accepted as representing a saddle, the depiction could be viewed as an early representation of the Iranian motif of the horse with empty saddle. Calmeyer interprets the horse or chariot in such motifs as symbolising an invisible yet present god or dead person (Calmeyer 1974: 49, 66–71). The Urfa depiction of one person leading the animal and the other following behind has parallels in Assyrian iconography (compare the Black Obelisk, showing Bactrian camels: Börker-Klähn 1982: Taf. 152, A3, B I).

In both registers of the Urfa relief, the same kind of throne appears with the sitting persons 2 and 10 (our use of the term 'throne' follows Curtis 1996: 168). The decoration of these thrones, and in particular their rounded arm-rests, differentiates them from the chairs and thrones usually depicted on Neo-Hittite monuments, which generally lack arm-rests (compare Kyrieleis 1969: 54–64; Symington 1996: 128–38), with the exception of two relatively late monuments from Zincirli (K2, with edged arm-rests, and Voos 1985: Abb. 14, with rounded arm-rests?). By contrast, arm-rests, and especially rounded ones, are characteristic of the thrones depicted in Neo-Assyrian wall paintings and palace reliefs of the period of Tiglath-pileser III (744–727 BC) or later (Kyrieleis 1969: 9–10; Curtis 1996: 168, fig. 1c, d).

The feet of both the sitting figures rest on footstools. In the upper register, the footstool is represented with fine lines, which probably represent wooden cross-bars, whereas the one in the lower register is only visible as a slight contour.

Unlike the thrones, which are very similar to each other, it is possible to distinguish two different kinds of table. Those in front of the two sitting figures are decorated and have an additional, centrally positioned, vertical support. By contrast, the table at the right-hand side of the upper register is much simpler. Neither type is attested on Neo-Hittite monuments, in which cross legged folding tables are the ones normally depicted and tables with vertical bars are rare (the latter include Karatepe B2, Maraş B10 (?), B17, B20, C4, C5; see also Genge 1982: figs 1, 3; Bonatz 2000: pl. xviii, C48, pl. xxii, C67; Balcıoğlu 2000: res. 2). However, the Urfa orthostat's examples are comparable with tables shown in Neo-Assyrian palace reliefs, where again there is a similar separation between more elaborate examples, associated with representations of the king, and more utilitarian versions (Curtis 1996: 176–8). The decorated tables on the Urfa relief can be compared with the ones used by the Assyrian kings or brought to them as booty; closely similar examples are depicted on a stela from Neirab (Bonatz 2000: 20, Taf. xv, C35), on another in the Aleppo Museum (Bonatz 2000: 23, Taf. xxii, C67) and on one from the vicinity of Mosul (Basmachi 1967: pl. 3).

The iconology of each individual scene in the Urfa relief, and the similarities in their iconographic and stylistic details, show that they each form part of a greater compositional whole, namely a funerary monument as characterised by the main scene located in the upper register. The iconology of this funerary monument clearly lies within the conceptual framework of Neo-Hittite beliefs, although the artistic and stylistic features are closely related to Assyrian art.

## The style and the form

In contrast to Neo-Hittite reliefs, the scenes on the Urfa orthostat are well proportioned. There are no 'squeezed' figures and the individuals are well distributed in the available space. Furthermore, they all stand on the same ground-line. These are stylistic characteristics of Assyrian narrative art (Czichon 1992: 119–20).

Moreover, whereas the depictions on Neo-Hittite monuments have relatively high relief, those on the Urfa orthostat are very shallow in depth, again comparable to the conventions of the Neo-Assyrian palace reliefs and other stone monuments of the same period.

The regularity of the orthostat and of its two registers mark another striking difference to the usually rather irregular shapes of Neo-Hittite grave monuments. Although most of the typical Neo-Hittite funerary stelae were not found in their original contexts, it is highly probable that they were free-standing graveside monuments (Voos 1988a; 1988b: 349, 350–2, fig. 2; Schachner, Schachner 1996: 212–14). By contrast, the square form of the Urfa stone suggests that it was part of a larger structure, perhaps fixed into a wall, which is why it is to be considered an orthostat rather than a stela. Accompanying such a new form of funerary monument there might also have been a change in burial practice and associated structures, and probably a change in the character of the necropolis too.

The meaning of all the individual scenes on the orthostat can be related to the Neo-Hittite funerary meal as indicated above. Furthermore, the organisation and iconography of the main scene have a very close relationship to those on the funerary monuments found mainly in the vicinity of Maraş (Orthmann 1971: 366–95). Despite these general similarities, however, the overall conception of the Urfa orthostat is different from those of the Neo-Hittite reliefs: the funerary meal in the Urfa upper register is incorporated into a larger story, whereas in Neo-Hittite art of the tenth/ninth–eighth centuries BC, generally only rather short scenes are depicted focusing on the funerary meal itself. There are only a few monuments from northern Syria and southeast Anatolia on which the funerary meal is incorporated into such a sequence of scenes, and these are all relatively late in date (Schachner, Schachner 1996: 221, fig. 1). Thus, in comparison to the stelae from Maraş, the Urfa orthostat is a newly identified type, in which the focal main scene is incorporated into a sequence of other scenes containing independently acting persons whose activities are only of secondary importance. It is highly probable that a temporal sequence of events is being depicted, showing the development of the funerary ceremony. In fact, the representation on the orthostat is a combination of two different types of narrative method often used by the

Assyrian artist. One method is the continuous narration of particular events; the other, much more rarely used, shows the same person in different situations within the same event (Czichon 1992: 60–5). In this connection it should be noted that if one interprets the sitting figures 2 and 10 as different persons (rather than as one and the same person as we have proposed above), then the scenes would only make sense if viewed as a variation of the Neo-Hittite type in which a man and a woman are depicted sitting at a table facing each other, as on Karaburçlu 1; Maraş B7; Maraş C2; Zincirli B3; Zahlhaas 1995: 76–8, Taf. F; Balcıoğlu 2000: 111–12, res. 2.

## The dating

The discussion so far has focused on the orthostat itself, its internal features and its meaning, avoiding any statement regarding its date. Although the monument is partly destroyed and many details which might be chronologically significant are unclear, there are some criteria which make it possible to propose a date. The general style of the scenes is closely comparable with the late phase of Assyrian art. The main scene of a woman sitting on an elaborate throne finds its only comparison in the famous garden scene of Ashurbanipal (668–?631 BC), in which the queen is depicted in exactly the same manner as on the Urfa orthostat. The thrones depicted in the Urfa scenes are another indicator, since their comparanda first appear during the reign of Tiglath-pileser III (744–727 BC).

To conclude, the details of the orthostat favour a rather late dating, most probably in the late eighth or seventh century BC; even a date shortly after the collapse of the Assyrian empire in the late seventh or early sixth century BC cannot be completely ruled out.

## Conclusions

The Urfa orthostat is a rare combination: the style and some iconographic details are essentially Assyrian, but the iconology — the general scheme of the scenes, and in particular the representations of the funerary meal — is derived from the Neo-Hittite tradition of the indigenous inhabitants of northern Mesopotamia. Only this Neo-Hittite iconological tradition offers a means of interpreting and understanding the pictures on the orthostat.

The obvious relationship to Neo-Hittite beliefs demonstrate that the orthostat's patron, together with its artist and intended viewers, was well acquainted with this tradition. In this sense, the representations document the development and transformation of Neo-Hittite funerary beliefs in the period dominated by Assyrian culture (Orthmann 1971: 471). Assyrian narrative art was used, as the style in vogue at the time, to convey older beliefs based upon a totally different, indigenous, cultural background. These older beliefs remained strong, despite the heavily Assyrianised environment documented by the textual and archaeological evidence from sites such as Arslantaş, Sultantepe and Harran. The region where the orthostat is said to have been found was densely populated in the Iron Age with a high percentage of indigenous Aramaean or west Semitic people, and it is they who should be seen as the carriers of the pre-Assyrian, Neo-Hittite beliefs and traditions (for the geography of the region, see Lipinski 2000: 165–83; personal names and toponyms mentioned in a village census in the vicinity of Harran, as well as other textual evidence, indicate that the local population was Aramaean in the period following the Assyrian conquest of the region: see Fales, Postgate 1995: xxx–xxxiv; Zadok 1995: 272–3, 275).

The strong iconographic relationship between the Urfa orthostat and the garden scene of Ashurbanipal may indicate that only a high ranking member of a local élite family possessed the right to have such a monument made for her. The fact that mainly women are depicted on the relief, and that the monument was produced for a woman, is striking. In Assyrian art women occur only rarely, in contrast to the tradition of the Neo-Hittite states where women were depicted comparatively often, even as the major element in scenes. Perhaps there was a difference in the status of women in these societies.

The present monument is part of the series of sculptures which covers the entire period extending down from the late Hittite states to the establishment of Assyrian presence in the Urfa region (Kulakoğlu 1999: 174–5; 2000). It also belongs with a small group of other stelae with Neo-Hittite/Aramaean iconology made in an Assyrianised style,[4] though these monuments lie closer to the Neo-Hittite tradition than does the Urfa orthostat; these indicate the strong Aramaean tradition within Assyria. Since not only the artistic style of the Urfa stone but also its form and its iconographical elements show stronger Assyrian influences than the other monuments mentioned, it might be possible that this orthostat is one of the youngest.

## Acknowledgements

We would like to express our gratitude to M. Roaf who read an earlier draft of the article, critically looking over our English and making valuable observations. C. Wolff has drawn the orthostat from sketches (made by A. Schachner) and from the excellent photograph by Roberto Ceccacci. Both deserve our warmest thanks.

---

[4] For which see Basmachi 1967: 144, pls 3, 4 (one bought in Mosul, one from Tall al-Maqir); Orthmann 1971 (Rifa'at 1, Til Barsib B6); Voos 1985: Abb. 14 (Zincirli); Bonatz 2000: Taf. x: C15 (T. Rifa'at ?), xv: C35 (Neirab), xvi: C40 (T. Rifa'at ?), xviii: C48 (T. Rifa'at ?), xxii: C67 (Aleppo Museum, unknown origin).

**Bibliography**

Balcıoğlu, B. 2000: 'Gaziantep Arkeoloji Müzesinde bulunan Geç Hitit Devri Stelleri' *Anadolu Medeniyetleri Müzesi 1999 Yıllığı*. Ankara: 111–15

Barnett, R.D. 1961: *Assyrian Palace Reliefs*. Prague

— 1976: *Sculptures from the North Palace of Ashurbanipal at Niniveh (668–627 BC)*. London

Barnett, R.D., Davies, L.G. 1970: *Ivories from Nimrud (1949–1963). Fascicule II: Ivories in Assyrian Style*. London

Basmachi, F. 1967: 'Miscellanea in the Iraq Museum' *Sumer* 23: 122–4

Bonatz, D. 2000: *Das syro-hethitische Grabdenkmal*. Mainz

Börker-Klähn, J. 1982: *Altvorderasiatische Bildstelen und vergleichbare Felsreliefs*. Mainz

Born, H., Seidl, U. 1995: *Schutzwaffen aus Assyrien and Urartu, Band IV Sammlung Axel Gutmann*. Mainz

Bossert, H.T. 1957: 'Die Schicksalsgöttinnen der Hethiter' *Welt des Orients* 2.4: 349–59

Calmeyer, P. 1973: *Reliefbronzen in babylonischem Stil. Eine westiranische Werkstatt des 10. Jahrhundert v. Chr.* Munich

— 1974: 'Zur Genese altiranische Motive II. Der leere Wagen' *Archäologische Mitteilungen aus Iran* 7: 49–77

Campbell Thompson, R., Hutchinson, R.W. 1931: 'The site of the palace of Ashurnasirpal at Niniveh, excavated in 1929–30 on behalf of the British Museum' *Annals of Archaeology and Anthropology* 18: 79–112

Collon, D. 1987: *First Impressions: Cylinder Seals in the Ancient Near East*. London

Curtis, J. 1996: 'Assyrian furniture: the archaeological evidence' in G. Herrmann (ed.), *The Furniture of Western Asia Ancient and Traditional*. Mainz: 167–80

Czichon, R.M. 1992: *Die Gestaltungsprinzipien der neuassyrischen Flachbildkunst and ihre Entwicklung vom 9. zum 7. Jahrhundert v. Chr.* Munich, Vienna

Darga, M. 1984: *Eski Anadolu'da Kadın*. Istanbul

Fales, F.M. 1990: 'The rural landscape of the Neo-Assyrian empire: a survey' *State Archives of Assyria Bulletin* IV/2: 81–142

Fales, F.M., Postgate. J.N. 1995: *Imperial Administrative Records, Part II. Provincial and Military Administrations* (State Archives of Assyria 11). Helsinki

Genge, H. 1982: 'Die Münchner Borowski-Stele' *Zeitschrift für Assyriologie and Vorderasiatische Archäologie* 81: 274–9

Gerlach, I. 2000: 'Tradition-Adaption-Innovation, zur Reliefkunst Nordsyriens/ Südostanatoliens in neuassyrischer Zeit' in G. Bunnens (ed.), *Essays on Syria in the Iron Age* (Ancient Near Eastern Studies Supplement 7). Louvain, Paris: 235–57

Ghirshman, P. 1973: 'La selle en Iran' *Iranica Antiqua* 10: 94–107

Goetze, A. 1955: 'Hittite Dress' in H. Krahe (ed.), *Corolla Linguistica, Festschrift Ferdinand Sommer*. Wiesbaden: 48–62

Harper, P.O., Aruz, J., Tallon, F. 1992: *The Royal City of Susa*. New York

Hawkins, D. 1980: 'Late Hittite funerary monuments' in B. Alster (ed.), *Death in Mesopotamia* (XXVIe Rencontre assyriologique internationale). Copenhagen: 213–25

Hrouda, B. 1965: *Kulturgeschichte des assyrischen Flachbildes*. Bonn

King, L.W. 1915: *Bronze Reliefs from the Gates of Shalmaneser King of Assyria BC 860–825*. London

Kulakoğlu, F. 1999: 'Late Hittite sculptures from the Şanlıurfa region' in H.I.H. Prince Takahito Mikasa (ed.), *Essays on Ancient Anatolia*. Wiesbaden: 149–66

— 2000: 'Şanlıurfa M. O. I. bin merkezleri yüzey araştırması' *Araştırma Sonuçları Toplantısı* 17.2: 1–11

Kyrieleis, H. 1969: *Throne und Klinen, Studien zur Formengeschichte altorientalischer und griechischer Sitz- und Liegemöbel vorhellenistischer Zeit*. Berlin

Lamprichs, R. 1995: *Die Westexpansion des neuassyrischen Reiches, eine Strukturanalyse* (Alter Orient und Altes Testament 239). Neukirchen, Vluyn

Lipinksi, E. 2000: *The Aramaeans, their Ancient History, Culture, Religion* (Orientalia Louvensia Analecta 100). Leuven, Paris

Mitchell, T.C. 2000: 'Camels in the Assyrian bas-reliefs' *Iraq* 62: 187–94

Moortgat, A. 1966: *Vorderasiatische Rollsiegel* (second edition). Berlin

Nollé, M. 1992: *Denkmäler vom Satrapensitz Daskyleion*. Berlin

Orthmann, W. 1971: *Untersuchungen zur späthethitischen Kunst*. Bonn

Schachner, A., Schachner, S. 1996: 'Eine späthethitische Grabstele aus Maraş im Museum von Antakya' *Anatolica* 22: 203–26

Schachner, A., Schachner, S., Karabulut, H. 2002: 'Vier Sitzbilder aus Bit-Bahiani' *Zeitschrift für Assyriologie and Vorderasiatische Archäologie* 92.1: 2–18

Symington, D. 1996: 'Hittite and Neo-Hittite furniture', in G. Herrmann (ed.), *The Furniture of Western Asia Ancient and Traditional*. Mainz: 111–38

Thureau-Dangin, F., Dunand, M. 1936: *Til Barsip*. Paris

Unger, E. 1933: 'Kinematographische Erzählungsform in der altorientalischen Relief- und Rundplastik' in *Aus fünf Jahrtausenden morgenländischer Kultu, Festschrift Max Freiherr von Oppenheim* (Archiv für Orientforschung Beiheft 1). Berlin: 127–33

Voos, J. 1985: 'Zu einigen spät-hethitischen Reliefs aus den Beständen des Vorderasiatischen Museums Berlin' *Altorientalische Forschungen* 12: 65–85

— 1988a: 'Bemerkungen zum Syrohethitischen Totenkult der Frühen Eisenzeit' in P. Varoušek, V. Soucek (eds), *Šulmu — Papers on the Ancient Near East Presented at the International Conference of Socialist Countries*. Prague: 349–60

— 1988b: 'Studien zur Rolle von Statuen und Reliefs im syro-hethitischen Totenkult während der frühen Eisenzeit (etwa 10.–7. Jh. v.u.Z.)' *Ethnologisch-Archäologische Zeitschrift* 29: 347–62

Wäfler, M. 1975: *Nicht-Assyrer neuassyrischer Darstellungen* (Alter Orient und Altes Testament 26). Neukirchen, Vluyn

Xenophon *Kyrupädia*: R. Nickel (ed.), *Xenophon Kyrupädie, die Erziehung des Kyros*. Darstadt 1992

— *peri hippikes*: K. Widdra (ed.), *Xenophon, Reitkunst*. Berlin 1965

Zadok, R. 1995: 'The ethno linguistic character of the Jezireh and adjacent regions in the 9th–7th centuries' in M. Liverani (ed.), *Assyrian Geography*. Rome: 217–82

Zahlhaas, C. 1995: *Orient and Okzident. Kulturelle Wurzeln Alteuropas 7000 bis 15 v. Chr.* Munich

# The Urartian Ištar-Šawuška

## Ursula Seidl
*Munich*

### Abstract

The main deity on the bronze plaques found near Giyimli, in eastern Turkey, is fashioned after the Neo-Assyrian 'Ištar of Arbela', who represents the Hurrian Ištar/Sa(w)uška. Two minor goddesses, similar to the Hurrian Ninatta and Kulitta, seem to form her entourage. The Urartian name of the goddess is not yet known.

### Özet

Türkiye'nin doğusundaki Giyimli'de bulunmuş olan bronz plakalar üzerindeki asıl tanrı, üslup olarak Hurrilerin Ištar/Sa(w)uška'sını temsil eden Neo-Asur 'Arbela'nın Ištar' ını takip etmektedir. Hurrilerin Ninatta ve Kulitta benzeri, iki daha önemsiz tanrıçası ise onun mahiyetini oluşturmaktadır. Tanrıçanın Urartu dilindeki ismi henüz bilinmemektedir.

Urartian literature, consisting mainly of royal inscriptions and lacking mythological and cultic texts, mentions many deities by name but does not elucidate their characters. The situation is different in visual art, where different deities are characterised by different attributes. Since Urartian style and iconography were modelled on the Assyrian, one can try to define the nature (though not the names) of several Urartian deities with the help of Assyrian prototypes.

My present purpose is to understand the types of divinities represented on the so-called Giyimli votive plaques. These plaques were part of a large bronze hoard found accidentally at Serbar Tepe near Giyimli in 1971 (Erzen 1974). Originally numbering about 2,000 pieces (Taşyürek 1977: 12), the hoard was subsequently dispersed by the art market and the pieces entered museums all over the world.[1] Approximately 1,000 pieces passed through the art market in Munich where H.-J. Kellner, the then director of the Prähistorische (now Archäologische) Staatssammlung, took the opportunity of creating a photographic archive of the bronzes before they were scattered; E. Caner (1998) published about 80% of this corpus. The Giyimli hoard provenance of these bronzes can be deduced with all probability: Kellner (1982; 1983) demonstrated that the Giyimli group can be distinguished from examples from other Urartian sites.

The Giyimli bronzes were produced over a period of at least 200 years (Seidl 2004: 169–98). The oldest known example (Çilingiroğlu 1988: 30) can be dated to the time of Išpuini and Menua, and the most recent ones to after Rusa II's reign, maybe even to after the fall of the Urartian Empire. It is obvious that style and iconography changed during this long period, but the essence remained inherent. The function of the bronzes is not firmly established. The subject of the representations is sacral and the plaques show no signs of depreciation. They were collected in one place, otherwise it would not have been possible to use them again. Thus it seems that the plaques were produced for a single ritual or magical event, and that for every ritual a new plaque was needed, although sometimes an old plaque was taken and reused by providing it with a new chiselled design (Seidl 2004: 178, 187–92, figs 127, 128, 136, 141–4, 147, pls 67, 68). In a broad sense it is not misleading to call them votive plaques.

---

[1] Museums: Ankara (Kulaçoğlu 1990); Adana, Antakya, Gaziantep, Konya, Maraş, Van (Taşyürek 1978a; 1979; 1980); Jerusalem (Muscarella 1981: 175–8); Karlsruhe (Rehm 1997: 169–201, 235–323, figs 417–690); Munich (Caner 1998); Schaffhausen (Ebnöther 1992: 153, nos 9.14, 15); Paris (Amiet 1982: figs 7–10); Venice (Ligabue, Salvatori 1977: 10–14, figs 7–18); in Japan (Tanabe et al. 1982: 71–6, pls 36–64).

The focus of their iconography is an anthropomorphic deity (figs 1–4). This figure is beardless and wears a horned cap, a fringed shawl and a long skirt open at the front to allow freedom of movement. On its back are two crossed quivers with arrows and bows, and sometimes on its left side there are one or two swords. Its right hand is stretched out, whilst the left hand holds a plant, a weapon (bow, arrow, lance or mace) or a string of (?)beads. Very often the deity stands on the back of a lion. On many plaques, a woman faces the divinity. She wears a long dress and a veil covering her hair. Usually she holds a rectangular standard, either with both hands or with her right hand only; in the latter case she holds with her left hand, variously, a string of (?)beads, a bowl, a bucket, a plant (figs 1, 2); sometimes there is an animal (cow or goat) standing by her side (fig. 3); in the rare cases where both her hands are empty, she performs the gesture of prayer (fig. 4). The top rim of the bronze sheets bearing these representations is usually crenellated.

Who is this deity? At a time when the known Urartian iconographical repertoire was still quite meagre, Meyer (1957: 841–4) and Piotrovskii (1959: 223, fig. 68 = 1966: 322ff, fig. 68) decided, on the basis of a belt fragment from Karmir Blur decorated with some divine figures, that the deity on the lion was the god Haldi. Although Riemschneider (1963: 150) had already protested against this identification in 1963, it became the *communis opinio*. Taşyürek (1978b) transmitted the name to the main deity on the Giyimli votive plaques, and in this he was followed by Esayan (1982), who declared that the female figure facing the deity was the goddess Arubani, Haldi's spouse. Kellner (1982: 89ff) refrained from naming the divinity, describing the representations as being of an as yet nameless male god with a female worshipper. Caner (1998: 30, 78) and Rehm (1997: 195–7) followed Kellner in their description of the main deity but they defined his 'worshipper' as the divine spouse.

Let us begin with the last assumption: that the deity on the lion and the facing woman are a divine couple. The divine status of the figure on the lion is clearly expressed by the horned crown and by the other equipment, whereas the veiled woman lacks any divine attribute. It may suffice to look at figs 1 and 4, which show the difference in height and volume of the two figures, expressing a difference in their status. In order to double check, look at figs 6–8 with representations of equally ranked divinities of lower status; or at two plaques showing a meeting of the deity-on-the-lion with a god-on-a-bull (Caner 1998: nos 173, 174). In the last case, not only are height and space equal, but both

*Fig. 1. Votive plaque (Caner 1998: nos 347, 465; drawing: U. Seidl)*

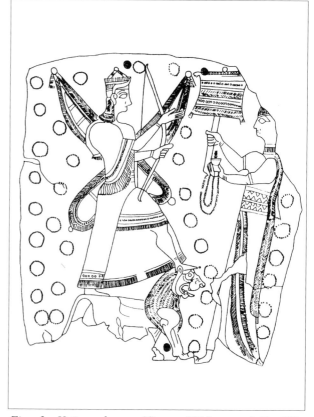

*Fig. 2. Votive plaque (Caner 1998: nos 348, 530; drawing: U. Seidl)*

Fig. 3. Votive plaque (Caner 1998: no. 351; photograph: Archäologische Staatssammlung, Munich)

Fig. 4. Votive plaque in Van (after Taşyürek 1975: pl. 36a)

figures also hold one hand outstretched in the usual gesture of Urartian high ranking deities, as distinct from the prayer gesture seen in fig. 4. These observations show clearly that the female in front of the Giyimli deity is a human being, and thus there is no need to adhere to the idea that the deity is male. In the largest row of Urartian fighting gods on the shield from Anzaf (Belli 1999), the deity with crossed quivers standing on a lion is missing, meaning that it did not play a role in the hierarchy of male gods.

As Urartian visual art is modelled on Assyrian iconography, we may search in the latter place for a model. Nearest comes the image of Ištar, in particular the Ištar of Arbela as represented on a stela found at Til Barsip, dedicated to the 'goddess Ištar who dwells in Arbela' (fig. 5) (Thureau-Dangin 1936: 156ff, pl. xiv). Here the goddess, in an open skirt, stands on a lion; on her back hang two quivers with bows and on her side a sword. She holds her right hand stretched out whilst she grasps a plant and the lion's leash in her left hand. Ištar of Arbela had a similar appearance in the time of Assurbanipal, as seen by a priest (Streck 1916: 116 cylinder B, V 50–5). She is not so much the Babylonian Inanna/Ištar but rather the Hurrian Ištar/Šawuška (Menzel 1981: 6; for the goddess, see Wegner 1981; 1995; and most recently Beckman 1998); and the two servant goddesses Ninatta and Kulitta are associated with her (Frantz-Szabó 1980–1983).

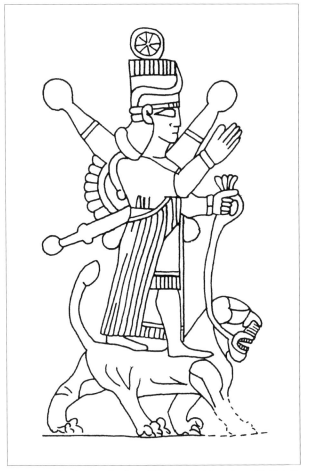

Fig. 5. Relief on stela from Til Barsip (drawing: U. Seidl)

We know of only one representation where the two minor goddesses Ninatta and Kulitta are identified by an inscription: in the Hittite rock sanctuary of Yazılıkaya, where they follow the goddess Ištar/Ša(w)uška (Bittel et al. 1975: 140–2, 173ff, pls 22ff, 57, nos 36–8). They are both dressed in pleated skirts, which are closed as opposed to the open one of Ištar/Šawuška. A similar theme is encountered in a group of the votive plaques from Giyimli (Caner 1998: 5ff, workshops A, B; Seidl 2004: 180–6), executed, of course, in Urartian style. Here, divinities with the same outfit as the great goddess — horned crown, fringed garment and quivers (sometimes in a misunderstood rendering) — occasionally form a pair (figs 6–8): they always carry the rectangular standard; sometimes the two follow each other (fig. 6) (Caner 1998: nos 381–8, 395–401); sometimes they confront each other (fig. 7) (Caner 1998: nos 176–8, 180); and sometimes they visit a seated deity (fig. 8). But most often they are represented alone on single sheets, the outlines of which tend towards the parabolic rather than being rectangular shaped (fig. 9).

*Fig. 8. Votive plaque (Caner 1998: no. 407; photograph: Archäologische Staatssammlung, Munich)*

*Fig. 6. Votive plaque (Caner 1998: nos 145, 393; drawing: U. Seidl)*

*Fig. 7. Votive plaque (Caner 1998: no. 176; drawing: U. Seidl)*

*Fig. 9. Votive plaque, made out of a cheek piece (Caner 1998: nos 87, 429; drawing: U. Seidl)*

These representations of single figures are so much alike that they could have been made in pairs and used as such in rituals or magic, similar to the small Ninatta pictures in Hittite rituals (Wegner 1981: 80). There are further hints that the single representations were made in pairs. In at least one case we can observe that two similar figures were chiseled onto one reused belt sheet (Merhav 1991: 294ff, no. 7), for in separating the two figures a mischance occurred, with parts of the lower figure staying with the upper one. Another hint to their pairing may be that they were sometimes fabricated on reused helmet cheek pieces (fig. 9) (Caner 1998: nos 8, 31, 88, 462, 470, 535). These divine figures are never associated with a lion, never with a worshipper and never with crenellations. Two different anthropomorphic figures are occasionally found in their company: a small swinging acrobat (Caner 1998: no. 178) and a person with pointed headgear (Caner 1998: nos 182, 392, 397, 405). Quite often they are accompanied by a wild goat (*capra aegagrus*) (fig. 9) (which, in contrast to the domestic goat brought by the worshipper, can stand not only at the side of the divine figure but also below it, and with each pair of legs together rather than in the marching pose of the domestic animals) or also by a bird of prey (fig. 9) (compare the falcon in the company of Ištar of Nineveh: Wegner 1981: 11, 57; Haas 1994: 347) or by a cow (fig. 7). The habitation thus indicated is a more unlimited environment, where wild animals are fostered.

In the absence of relevant texts, we do not know the Urartian name of the Ištar-type configuration and her companions. That the Urartians knew such a goddess is confirmed by the writing of the name Sarduri. This name, borne by several Urartian kings, is written in its first part logographically with the name of the goddess Ištar, using the cuneiform signs ${}^d$MÙŠ or ${}^d$XV (Salvini 1998: 95). In some texts of Tiglath-Pileser III, the name is written phonetically as ${}^m$Sa-ar-du-ri (Tadmor 1994: 292) which may provide a link to the Urartian goddess Sardī, mentioned at Meher Kapısı as being the recipient of a cow offering (*HchI*: 10, 22; *UKN*: 27, 22), a practice restricted to female deities (Melikišvili 1965: 442ff). Thus Melikišvili (*UKN*: 440) proposed to connect the Urartian goddess Sardī with the Assyrian Ištar. On the other hand, as the Hurrian name of the goddess 'Šawuška' means 'the Great/Magnificent One' (Wegner 1995), her Urartian name may be a similar appellative in the Urartian language.

Figs 1–4 show the great goddess faced by a standing woman. However, very often on the bronze sheets, one (Caner 1998: nos 184–288) or two (Caner 1998: nos 289–345) women are represented without the goddess being present. The worshippers are always female on the bronze plaques, in contrast to other media where the Ištar figure is equally venerated by a male worshipper, for example on a gold medallion (Kellner 1980). Thus we can conclude that the 'Giyimli votive plaques' belonged to a special cult practised by women. It is difficult to decide whether these women were simple supplicants or priestesses. Some differences in size in the double portraits may point to a difference in status, perhaps within the priesthood (compare the different classes of priestess in the Hurrian cult of Šawuška: Wegner 1981: 151–3) or between a priestess and an outsider. The women carry with their right hand a standard or a twig, and with their left hand a bucket, a string of (?)beads or a domestic animal (goat or calf), in contrast to the wild animals accompanying the minor goddesses. The animal seems to be an offering, and likewise maybe the string of (?)beads and the bucket (or the liquid in it); but the standard is of a different nature.

*Fig. 10. Votive plaque (Caner 1998: no. 655; photograph: Archäologische Staatssammlung, Munich)*

*Fig. 11. Votive plaque: (a) obverse showing worshipper; (b) reverse showing belt decoration, dated approximately to the time of Rusa II (Archäologische Staatssammlung, Munich no. 1971, 1900; photographs: B. Grunewald)*

The shafted square standard regularly held by the minor goddesses and by the women, but only rarely by the great goddess herself, is the essential instrument in this cult and it is never met with outside the Giyimli bronzes. The square is decorated with geometric designs, never with a figural representation; the upper and side borders are concave and tassels are affixed to the four corners. All this shows that a textile is being represented, but it cannot be determined whether it is a simple flag or a double cloth. Whatever the case, we have to envisage a multi-coloured cloth. This brings to mind the importance of red and blue wool, and objects made in wool, in the Hurrian cult of Šawuška (Wegner 1981: 103–5).

Sometime after the reign of Rusa II, the great goddess lost her Assyrian appearance. After some transitional steps, she and her companions came to be represented in frontal view (fig. 10) (Caner 1998: nos 545–814), whilst the human worshipper continued to be depicted in the traditional profile form (fig. 11) (Caner 1998: nos 184–345). By these stylistic means the deities were elevated in a divine sphere without communication with the human, with the human women venerating the remote goddess.

## Acknowledgments

I thank S. Dalley for providing me with the Beckman 1998 reference.

## Bibliography

*Abbreviations*

*Hchl* = König, F.W. 1955: *Handbuch der chaldischen Inschriften* (Archiv für Orientforschung, Beiheft 8). Graz

*UKN* = Melikišvili, G.A. 1960: *Urartskie klinoobraznye nadpisi (Le iscrizioni cuneiformi urartee)* (second edition). Moscow

Amiet, P. 1982: 'Antiquités anatoliennes du Louvre: Les bronzes ourartéens' in Institut français d'études anatoliennes, *Mémorial Atatürk* (Editions Recherche sur les civilisations, synthèse 10). Paris: 13–25

Beckman, G. 1998: 'Ištar of Nineveh reconsidered' *Journal of Cuneiform Studies* 50: 1–10

Belli, O. 1999: *The Anzaf Fortresses and the Gods of Urartu*. Istanbul

Bittel, K., Boessneck, J., Damm, B., Güterbock, H.G., Hauptmann, H., Naumann, R., Schirmer, W. 1975: *Das hethitische Felsheiligtum Yazılıkaya*. Berlin

Caner, E. 1998: *Bronzene Votivbleche aus Giyimli* (Archäologie in Iran und Turan 2). Rahden

Çilingiroğlu, A. 1988: *Die Geschichte des Königreiches Van Urartu*. Izmir

Ebnöther, M. 1992: *Idole Masken Menschen*. Schaffhausen

Erzen, A. 1974: 'Giyimli bronz definesi ve Giyimli kazısı' *Belleten* 150: 191–213

Esayan, S.A. 1982: 'Iskusstvo Portretmogo Izobrajeniya Urartu' *Patma-banasirakan handes* 98.3: 176–190

Frantz-Szabó, G. 1980–1983: 'Kulitta, Ninatta und' *Reallexikon für Assyriologie und Vorderasiatische Archäologie* 6: 303–4

Haas, V. 1994: *Geschichte der hethitischen Religion* (Handbuch der Orientalistik I 15). Leiden

Kellner, H.-J. 1980: 'Ein neues Goldmedallion aus Urartu' *Archäologische Mitteilungen aus Iran* 13: 83–9

— 1982: 'Gedanken zu den bronzenen Blechvotiven in Urartu' *Archäologische Mitteilungen aus Iran* 15: 79–95

— 1983: 'Ergänzungen zu den Blechvotiven in Urartu' *Archäologische Mitteilungen aus Iran* 16: 133–40

Kulaçoğlu, B. 1990: 'Urartu adak levhaları' *Anadolu Medeniyetleri Müzesi Yıllığı* 1989: 176–97

Ligabue, G., Salvatori, S. 1977: 'Oriental bronzes in private collections in Venice' *Rivista di Archeologia* 1: 7–15

Melikišvili, G.A. 1965: 'Die Götterpaartrias an der Spitze des urartäischen Pantheons' *Orientalia* 34: 441–5

Menzel, B. 1981: *Assyrische Tempel* (Studia Pohl SM 10). Rome

Merhav, R. 1991: *Urartu. A Metalworking Center in the First Millennium BCE.* Jerusalem

Meyer, G.R. 1957: 'Die sowjetischen Ausgrabungen in Teschebaini und Ir(e)puni' *Wissenschaftliche Annalen* 6: 834–51

Muscarella, O.W. 1981: *Ladders to Heaven.* Toronto

Piotrovskii, B.B. 1959: *Vanskoe Tsarstvo (Urartu).* Moscow

— 1966: *Il regno di Van, Urartu* (Incunabula Graeca 12). Rome

Rehm, E. 1997: *Kykladen und Alter Orient.* Karlsruhe

Riemschneider, M. 1963: 'Die urartäischen Gottheiten' *Orientalia* 32: 148–69

Salvini, M. 1998: 'Eine urartäische Felsinschrift in der Region Nachicevan' *Zeitschrift für Assyriologie* 88: 94–9

Seidl, U. 2004: *Bronzekunst Urartus.* Mainz

Streck, M. 1916: *Assurbanipal* (Vorderasiatische Bibliothek VII 2). Leipzig

Tadmor, H. 1994: *The Inscriptions of Tiglath-Pileser III King of Assyria.* Jerusalem

Tanabe, K., et al. 1982: 'Studies in the Urartian bronze objects from Japanese collections (1)' *Bulletin of the Ancient Orient Museum* 4. Tokyo

Taşyürek, O.A. 1975: 'Some inscribed Urartian bronze armour' *Iraq* 37: 151–5

— 1977: 'The Urartian bronze hoard from Giyimli' *Expedition* 19.4: 12–20

— 1978a: 'Examples of offering plaques from Giyimli (Hirkanis)' *Belleten* 166: 201–38

— 1978b: 'Die Darstellungen des urartäischen Gottes Haldi' in S. Şahin et al. (eds), *Studien zur Religion und Kultur Kleinasiens (Festschrift F.K. Dörner) Volume II.* Leiden: 940–55

— 1979: 'Eine aus Giyimli stammende Weihplatte' *Zeitschrift für Assyriologie und Vorderasiatische Archäologie* 69: 244–57

— 1980: 'Some Iranian elements on Urartian bronze offering plaques from Giyimli' *Studi Micenei ed Egeo-Anatolici* 22: 201–14

Thureau-Dangin, F. 1936: *Til Barsip* (Bibliothèque Archéologique et Historique 23). Paris

Wegner, I. 1981: *Gestalt und Kult der Ištar-Šauška in Kleinasien* (Alter Orient und Altes Testament 36). Münster

— 1995: 'Der Name der Ša(w)uška' *Studies on the Civilization and Culture of Nuzi and the Hurrians* 7: 117–9

# Southern Caucasia during the Late Bronze Age: An interim report on the regional investigations of Project ArAGATS in western Armenia

## Adam T. Smith[1], Ruben Badalyan[2] and Pavel Avetisyan[2]
*[1]University of Chicago, [2]Institute of Archaeology, Yerevan*

### Abstract

In order to examine the sources of socio-political complexity in the highlands of eastern Anatolia and southern Caucasia prior to the advent of the Urartian kingdom, Project ArAGATS conducted regional investigations in the Tsakahovit plain in western Armenia. This paper discusses the findings of this multi-component field study, including the preliminary results of remote sensing investigations, a systematic intensive survey of the region's elevated flanks and test excavations at several key Late Bronze Age fortress and cemetery sites. Also presented here are the initial results of ongoing XRF analyses of obsidian and INA analysis of regional clays and pre-Urartian ceramics. These investigations have focused on defining the scale and scope of Late Bronze Age polities through analyses of both the shifting landscape associated with the emergence of new political formations and the transformation of patterns of resource exploitation and exchange. The work of Project ArAGATS suggests that we might look to the southern Caucasian polities of the Late Bronze Age for the roots of the political tradition that would later emerge in an amplified form as the Kingdom of Urartu.

### Özet

ArAGATS Projesi Ermenistan'ın batısında bulunan Tsakahovit ovasında bölgesel bir araştırma gerçekleştirmiştir. Amaç, Urartu Krallığının kurulmasından önce Doğu Anadolu'nun dağlık kesimlerinde ve Güney Kafkasya'da gözlenen karmaşık sosyo-politik yapının kaynaklarını araştırmaktır. Bu çalışmada, pek çok değişik uzmanlık alanını içeren arazi çalışmalarının sonuçları tartışılmıştır. Bu değişik alanlar, uzaktan algılama araştırmalarını, ovanın yüksek yan kenarlarında gerçekleştirilmiş yoğun ve sistematik yüzey araştırmalarını ve Geç Bronz Çağa ait bazı kilit sayılabilecek kale ve mezarlık alanlarında yapılan deneme kazılarını kapsamaktadır. Burada, ayrıca halen devam etmekte olan XRF obisidyen analiz ve INA bölgesel kil analiz çalışmalarının ön sonuçları ile, Urartu dönemi öncesi keramiklerinin incelenmesinden elde edilen sonuçlar da açıklanmaktadır. Tüm bu araştırmalar, Geç Bronz Çağı yönetim biçimlerinin boyutlarının ve potansiyellerinin anlaşılması üzerine odaklanmıştır. ArAGATS Projesi Geç Bronz Çağda Güney Kafkasya'da hüküm sürmüş olan yönetim biçimlerine ait politik geleneklerin, daha sonra güçlenerek ortaya çıkan Urartu Krallığına zemin oluşturduğunu düşündürmektedir.

During the summers of 1998 and 2000, the joint Armenian-American Project for the Archaeology and Geography of Ancient Transcaucasian States (Project ArAGATS) conducted regional archaeological investigations in the Tsakahovit plain of western Armenia. The goal of this project was to document the outlines of the Late Bronze Age and Early Iron Age regional landscape, as an initial component of a multi-year examination of southern Caucasia's earliest complex societies (Smith et al. 1999; Avetisyan et al. 2000; Badalyan et al. 2003). We were particularly concerned to develop historically sensitive models of shifting geopolitical practices contributing to the formation of discrete territories of exploitation and control. Such a perspective on the emergence of social and political complexity required a departure from traditional approaches to regional analysis, which have focused rather more upon the locations and sizes of fortified centres to the exclusion of more encompassing accounts of the landscape beyond the fortress walls. We thus performed a systematic, transect based walking survey of the entire highlands surrounding the Tsakahovit plain, complemented by analyses of remote sensing data and by test excavations, at both major and minor fortified settlements and at key cemetery complexes. In this paper we discuss some of the initial findings of our investigations and provide a brief sketch of the models of Late Bronze Age political organisation that are presented in greater detail in a separate publication (Badalyan et al. 2003). These models, amplified by an increasingly refined chronology for the second millennium BC, have refined our understanding of the history and structure of the earliest complex societies of highland Caucasia.

### The Tsakahovit plain

The Tsakahovit plain lies between the northern slope of mount Aragats (4,090m a.s.l.), the southwestern slopes of the Pambak range, and Mets Sharailer mount Kolgat in central western Armenia (fig. 1). At 10–12km across at its maximum extent, the Tsakahovit plain (2,000m a.s.l.) was filled in by Middle Quaternary lava flows and Middle Pleistocene and Holocene riverine and glacial deposits (Zograbyan 1979). The regional landscape is mountain steppe yielding to alpine conditions near the summit of mount Aragats. The plain is used today for irrigation based cultivation, while the surrounding mountain slopes offer pasture for livestock.

Archaeological research in the Tsakahovit plain began with a brief visit to the region by Nikolai Marr in 1893, who recorded several large fortresses on the northern slope of mount Aragats and remarked upon numerous outlying cemetery complexes (Khachatrian 1974). Marr's passage through the region provided a template for non-systematic archaeological and architectural survey that was repeated by Toramanyan (1942), Adzhan et al. (1932) and Kafadarian (1996), all of whom re-recorded several of the major 'cyclopean' fortresses in the region in increasing detail. Only very limited excavations had been conducted in the Tsakahovit plain prior to the commencement of our investigations in 1998. In 1956, Martirosian (1964: 89–93) opened five graves adjacent to the fortress of Gegharot, dating them to the Late Bronze Age. Recent re-analysis of the ceramics pin these materials more precisely to the Late Bronze I and II phases (for which see fig. 2). In 1960, Esaian (unpublished) examined three additional graves from the same complex: the materials uncovered are attributable to two distinct occupation periods, the Late Bronze II phase and one much later grave from the eighth to seventh centuries BC. Both Esaian's and Martirosian's investigations were conducted as salvage operations in advance of major building projects in the village of Gegharot.

### Results of systematic survey

The primary goal of our systematic survey was to define the nature of the Late Bronze Age landscape beyond the restricted confines of the large fortresses. To this end, we walked transects in four zones between fortified centres: the north slope of mount Aragats, the southwest foothills of the Pambak range, mount Kolgat and mount Vardablur (fig. 3). In the course of this survey we discovered several previously unrecorded fortified settlements, including a cluster of small outposts on the Pambak slopes (Tsilkar, Ashot Yerkat and Poloz-Sar) and two fortresses on the Aragats slope (Geghadzor and Sahakaberd). The remains encountered in the hinterland of the fortresses were primarily architectural and included small settlements, extensive irrigation networks, carved stone markers and, above all, cemeteries.

We recorded 193 discrete cemeteries within our two survey zones on the Aragats and Pambak slopes. One hundred and eighty four of these cemeteries were composed of cromlech tombs (stone circles surrounding earthen or stone lined chambers) typical of Late Bronze Age and Early Iron Age mortuary architecture, with a density of 5.3cm per km$^2$. Although a complete census of cemeteries is not feasible due to site formation processes, a conservative estimate of 30 cromlechs per cemetery would yield a total of 4,860 burials within the survey area. Despite the impressive size of the region's Late Bronze Age mortuary population, the most compelling feature of the cromlech cemeteries is their spatial distribution. While the cemeteries are tightly packed within the central 30km$^2$ of the north Aragats slope, extending in an east-west line from 0.5km west of Hnaberd fortress to 3km east of Tsakahovit fortress, they virtually disappear beyond these limits. In order to transform the rather static depiction of settlement provided by our survey into a more nuanced account of Late Bronze Age political and social practices, we have initiated a series of materials analyses, the preliminary results of which enable us to begin the construction of more plausible models of political communities.

### Preliminary results of materials analyses

Discussions of the ties between these local communities and those further afield have traditionally focused on spectacular finds of exotic artefacts in Caucasian contexts, such as the Kassite weight (Khanzadian et al. 1992) or the New Kingdom Egyptian cylinder seal (Khanzadian, Piotrovskii 1992) found in Late Bronze Age levels at Metsamor. While such finds are important reminders of the wider world within which southern Caucasian communities were situated, they tell us very little about what part the region played in this 'global' order, or about the formal and informal ties that bound the players together. To investigate these questions further we must examine the more regularised networks of trade and exchange.

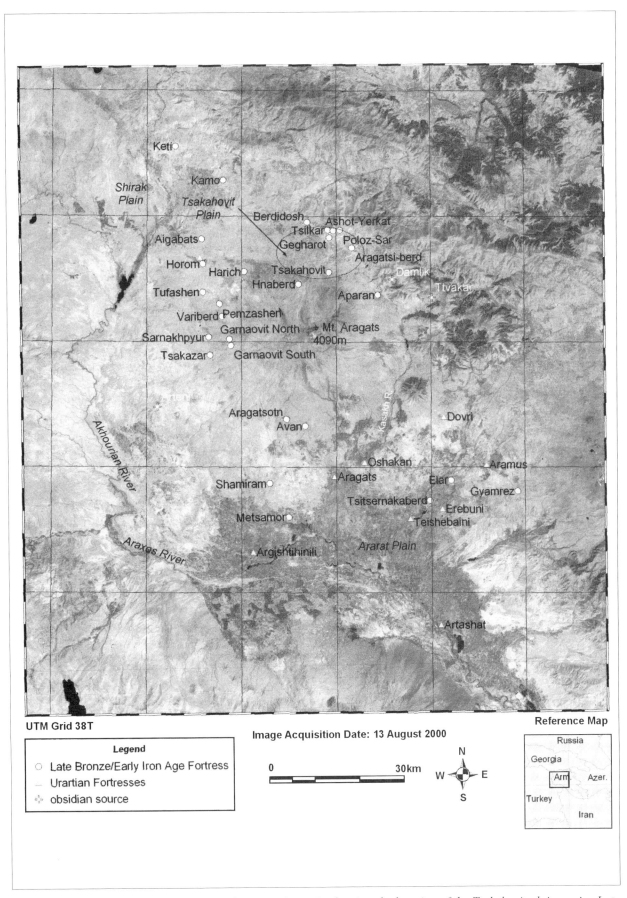

*Fig. 1. Landsat 7 ETM+ satellite image of western Armenia showing the location of the Tsakahovit plain, major Late Bronze Age/Early Iron Age and Urartian fortified sites and obsidian sources mentioned in the text*

| Years B.C. | Periodization | | Horizon Style | | Key Sites | |
|---|---|---|---|---|---|---|
| 200 | Antique Era | ? | Late Yervandid | | Karchaghpyur, Noratus, Astghi Blur, Jujevan Norashen Armavir, Horom, Benjamin Erebuni, Oshakan, Sari-Tepe | |
| 300 | | Yervandid-Orontid (Early Antique) period | | | | |
| 400 | | | Early Yervandid-Achaemenid | | | |
| 500 | | | | | | |
| 600 | Late Iron Age | Late Urartu | "Classic" Urartu | "Local" Urartu | Erebuni, Argishtihinili Karmir-Blur | Metsamor, Horom, Shirakavan, Lori-Berd |
| 700 | Middle Iron Age | Early Urartu | | | | |
| 800 | | | | | | |
| 900 | Early Iron Age | Early Iron II | Lchashen-Metsamor Horizon | | Horom, Elar, Keti, Metsamor Artik (group 3) Dvin (burnt level) | |
| 1000 | | Early Iron I | | | | |
| 1100 | | | | | | |
| 1200 | Late Bronze Age | Late Bronze III | | | Lchashen Artik (groups 1-2) Karashamb, Lori-Berd | |
| 1300 | | Late Bronze II | | | | |
| 1400 | | | | | | |
| 1500 | | Late Bronze I/ Middle Bronze IV | | | Shamiram (burials) Karashamb, Horom, Talin | |
| 1600 | Middle Bronze Age | Middle Bronze III | Sevan, Karmirberd, and Karmirvank Complexes | | Karmirberd, Lchashen, Horom, Uzerlik 2-3 | |
| 1700 | | Middle Bronze II | Trialeti-Vanadzor Culture | | Karashamb (kurgan) Vanadzor (Kirovakan) Trialeti (groups 1-3) Lchashen (120, 123) Lori-Berd, Uzerlik 1 | |
| 1800 | | | | | | |
| 1900 | | | | | | |
| 2000 | | | | | | |
| 2100 | | Middle Bronze I/ Early Bronze IV | "Kurgan" Culture | | Trialeti ("early group") Berkaber (burials 1-3, kurgans 1-2) Stepanakert | |
| 2200 | | | | | | |
| 2300 | Early Bronze Age ? | Early Bronze III | Kura-Araxes Culture ? | | Shengavit (levels 3-4) Garni, Dvin, Karnut, Harich, Elar P3, Kosi Choter, Horom (EBA upper level) | |
| 2400 | | | | | | |
| 2500 | | | | | | |

*Fig. 2. Periodisation and chronology of southern Caucasia from the Early Bronze Age to the Antique Era*

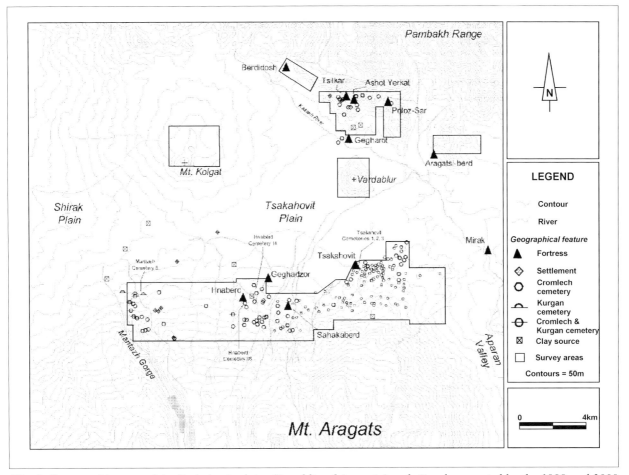

*Fig. 3. Topographic map of the Tsakahovit plain, (Republic of Armenia) and sites documented by the 1998 and 2000 systematic survey of Project ArAGATS*

Field investigations in the Tsakahovit plain have been amplified by a series of ongoing compositional analyses of obsidian and ceramics/clays from Late Bronze Age contexts. These studies are focused upon elucidating the movement of the former into the plain, and of the latter around the plain.

Seven obsidian samples from Tsakahovit fortress and three from Gegharot fortress were analysed using X-ray fluorescence techniques. All of the Gegharot obsidians were surface finds. Four of the Tsakahovit samples were from the surface, while three derived from the Late Bronze Age occupation level excavated on the citadel in 1998. The results of analyses of the Tsakahovit obsidians indicate that four of the seven samples (three surface finds and one from the excavated level) originated in the deposits of the Damlik volcano in the Tsakhunyats range, 15km to the east of Tsakahovit (fig. 1). Two samples (one a surface find, the other from the excavated level) came from the Arteni volcano on the southwest periphery of the Aragats massif. The remaining sample (from the excavated level) was traced to the Ttvakar volcano, again part of the Tsakhunyats range, 20km east of Tsakahovit. All three samples from Gegharot were from the Damlik source.

Although the spatial connections between the Tsakahovit plain and the Tsakhunyats sources are rather immediate, exchange relationships would nevertheless have been required for the movement of the obsidian, either with neighbours to the northeast in the Lori-Pambak region or with polities to the southeast in the Kasakh river valley. Indeed it seems likely that the Tsakahovit plain was a trans-shipment point for the Tsakhunyats obsidian finds known from pre-Urartian contexts in the Shirak plain to the west (for example, at Horom and Harich). The Arteni source is comparatively distant and its obsidian would most likely have been brought to the Tsakahovit plain via the Shirak plain, where Arteni obsidians are well attested at archaeological sites.

These very preliminary results allow us to suggest that the Late Bronze Age polities of the Tsakahovit region served both as mediators within those exchange networks that looked for sources east across the Pambak range, and west beyond the Shirak plain, and as providers of distribution ties west to sites in the Shirak plain which also boast Tsakhunyats obsidians. In addition to obsidian, it is important to note that the Tsakhunyats and Pambak ranges also host considerable copper ore deposits, as well as evidence of mining during the third millennium BC (particularly at Fioletovo). Indeed, a regional geological survey conducted by Arkady Karakhanian in collaboration with our archaeological investigations has indicated the existence of copper sources in the Pambak hills overlooking Gegharot, which may have been utilised during the Bronze Age. Further studies of the region's metal and ore sources might reveal that Late Bronze Age metallurgical and obsidian trade routes were very similar.

To more closely investigate resource movements within the Tsakahovit plain, 270 pottery sherds and samples from seven local clay sources, were submitted to the Phoenix Memorial Laboratory, University of Michigan, for Instrumental Neutron Activation (INA) analysis. Preliminary results (fig. 4a) indicate a primary division of all samples into two main groups, based on the ratio of scandium (Sc) to iron (Fe). Group 1 designates a high scandium to iron cluster. However, all of our clay samples (represented by triangles) appear more closely affiliated with the other, low scandium to iron, group though clay samples from western Aragats sources (Hnaberd East and Mets Mantash) are outliers, falling well outside the confidence interval ellipse for this group. Perhaps more interestingly, there is a weaker separation of the low scandium to iron cluster into two groups, apparent in a bivariate plot of scandium to chromium, based on the amount of chromium (Cr) present (fig. 4b). Group 2 embraces the higher chromium cluster, whilst group 3 includes the low chromium cluster. Clay samples from Norashen and Hnaberd Northwest fall within the confidence interval ellipse for the higher chromium group (group 2). By contrast, all of the Gegharot clay samples are most closely affiliated with the low chromium group (group 3), even though they fall outside (to the left of) the confidence interval ellipse.

These initial results suggest two very preliminary conclusions. Firstly, the analyses indicate three major areas of ceramic production within the late second millennium Tsakahovit plain. Compositional group 2 represents a production source on the southern flank of the plain, probably towards the western end of our study area near Hnaberd. Group 3 can be associated more directly with Gegharot, on the northeastern flank of the plain. The provenance of group 1 remains uncertain at present, but because this source is numerically dominant at Gegharot (representing 37% of the ceramics analysed from that site) it is possible that group 1 represents a clay source near to Gegharot, yet distinct from group 3. Further sampling and analysis of clays from both the eastern and northwestern areas of the plain may help to refine the assignment of group 1.

Secondly, the picture of intra-regional trade that these data present is intriguing. A tabulation of members within these three compositional groups suggests that the high scandium (group 1) and low chromium (group 3) groups consist almost entirely of sherds from Gegharot. By contrast, the high chromium group (group 2) contains sherds from a mix of sites. From the perspective of the sites, Gegharot sherds are well represented in all three compositional groups (fig. 4c), whilst other sites are well represented only in the high chromium group (group 2) (fig. 4d). This suggests that Gegharot drew ceramics and/or clays from sources across the plain whilst neighbouring fortresses, such as Tsakahovit and Hnaberd, drew upon more restricted sources. Thus, the movement of ceramics appears to have been uni-directional, from sites in the southern part of the plain towards Gegharot, a flow more consistent with the movement of goods from satellites to centres rather than between independent political peers.

**Models of Late Bronze Age political organisation**

Together with the results of our survey, these data provide an intriguing perspective on the geography of Late Bronze Age political and social divisions. The crisp boundaries of cromlech cemetery construction revealed by our survey, combined with the evidence for a chronologically compact explosion of occupation in the region during the Late Bronze Age, suggest that the mortuary landscape on the north Aragats slope indexed the spatial extent of sovereignty in the region. That is, the north slope of mount Aragats was part of a single political formation, differentiated from both a southeast Shirak plain formation to the west (comprising sites such as Harich, Artik and Horom) and a Kasakh river valley formation to the southeast (perhaps centred on the fortress at Aparan). While the eastern and western thresholds of this formation emerge from the distribution of cemeteries, the extent to which it extended across the Tsakahovit plain is less clear. However, the unique nature of the Pambak group of fortified outposts, mentioned earlier, suggests two possible models of sovereignty for the plain during the Late Bronze Age.

The first model includes these fortified outposts — Berdidosh, Tsilkar, Ashot-Yerkat and Poloz-Sar — as part of a northeast Tsakahovit polity, centred on Gegharot and autonomous from a southern polity on the slope of mount Aragats (fig. 5a). In support of this reconstruction we can note that the cromlech cemeteries on the Pambak slopes are tightly clustered around Gegharot and do not extend southeast towards Tsakahovit. This interpretation requires that we interpret the fortress at Aragatsi-berd (see fig. 3) as a border post between rival Tsakahovit plain polities (an interpretation supported by a lack of neigh-

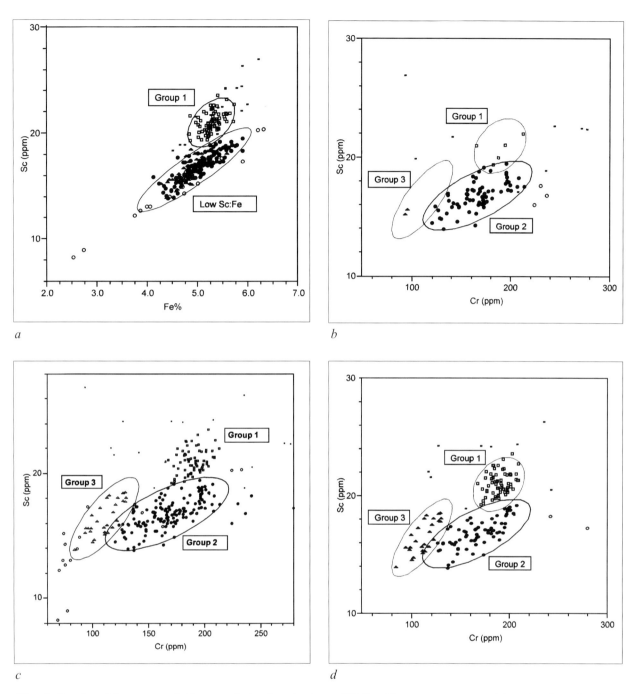

*Fig. 4. Results of Instrumental Neutron Activation Analyses (INA). Clays are represented by triangles, sherds by squares. Sc = scandium; Fe = iron; Cr = chromium. (a) bivariate plot of Sc versus Fe; (b) bivariate plot of Sc versus Cr; (c) bivariate plot of Sc versus Cr, for Late Bronze Age sherds recovered at Gegharot fortress; (d) bivariate plot of Sc versus Cr, for Late Bronze Age sherds from sites on the flank of mount Aragats (Tsakahovit fortress, Hnaberd fortress, Mantash cemetery 8 burial 3)*

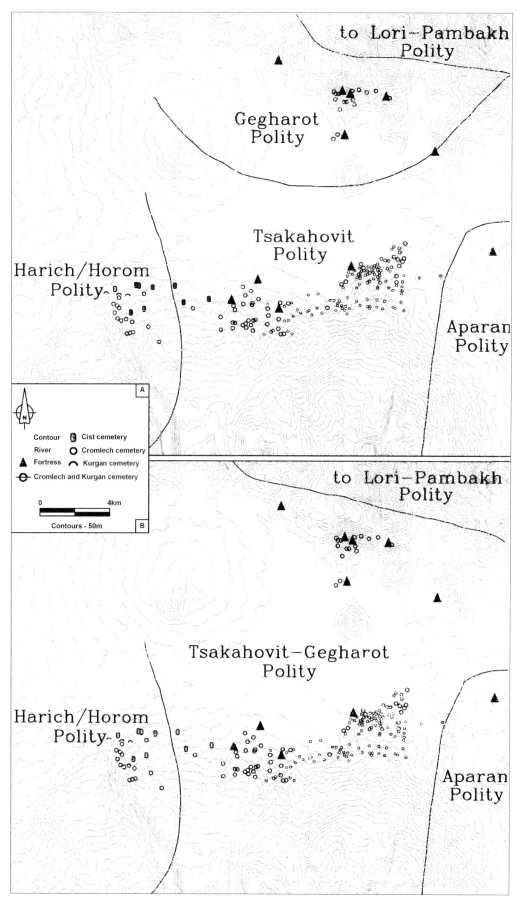

*Fig. 5. Two models of Late Bronze Age political organisation in the Tsakahovit plain: (a) differentiated rival polities; (b) integrated unified polity*

bouring cemeteries that might otherwise have indicated a more enduring commitment to this site). A second model of Late Bronze Age sovereignty takes the entire Tsakahovit plain as a single socio-political community with interlinked centres at Hnaberd, Tsakahovit and Gegharot (fig. 5b). This model can muster support from the preliminary results of our compositional analyses of obsidian and clay/pottery. Gegharot and Tsakahovit appear to have been tied into the same obsidian trade network, drawing upon sources in both the Tsakhunyats range to the east and the Arteni volcano to the southwest. Furthermore, as noted above, the movement pattern of Late Bronze Age ceramics suggests a profound lack of parity, with the fortress of Gegharot drawing materials to it in a uni-directional exchange pattern.

**Results of excavations**

Elaborating upon the results of our regional investigations will depend upon a more refined understanding of the chronology and nature of occupations at the major fortified centres in the region. While extensive excavations will be the focus of the next component of our research, our test soundings have provided us with critical information on the temporal sequence of the major fortresses and of several key cemetery complexes, allowing us to develop a more refined ceramic periodisation tied to an increasing number of absolute radiocarbon dates (fig. 2). To date, we have excavated test trenches at Hnaberd, Tsakahovit and Gegharot, and small soundings at the fortified outposts of Tsilkar and Poloz-Sar above Gegharot in the Pambak range. At Tsakahovit fortress we opened five excavation units: two atop the citadel (C1 and C2) and single units on a western terrace (WT1), in room A of the south settlement (S.A.1), and in room 34 of the southeastern settlement (SE.34.1). Whilst excavations in the settlements demonstrate that these complexes were constructed during the late Urartian or Achaemenid eras, both the citadel and the terrace excavations provided occupation floors sealed by a thick burned layer containing ceramic materials highly diagnostic of the Late Bronze II and III phases.

At Gegharot, we opened three trenches: one against the interior of the eastern wall, one on the north terrace and one east of the fortress. Both the citadel and terrace excavations revealed well preserved Late Bronze Age occupation levels, including terrace architecture preserved to a height of 2.5m.

At Hnaberd, ceramics confirm an original Late Bronze Age construction episode but rebuilding during the first millennium BC has obscured most of the Late Bronze Age level. However, we were able to isolate a Late Bronze Age level in trench F1 on the northwestern interior of the fortification wall.

Ceramics from all three sites indicate close contemporaneity of occupation during the Late Bronze Age II and III phases, highlighted by formal and stylistic parallels with Artik groups 1 and 2, Aparan II, Lchashen, Metsamor and Karashamb. Interestingly, ceramics from the terrace occupation floor at Gegharot amplify Martirosian's findings in the adjacent cemetery, suggesting evidence of a slightly earlier Middle Bronze Age IV/Late Bronze Age I initial occupation, based on key transitional ceramic forms and decorative styles paralleling materials from Nerkin-Getashen, Tsakalandj and Talin, and reminiscent of Karmir-Berd and Sevan-Uzerlik horizon elements (fig. 6).

Calibrated Accelerator Mass Spectrometry dates from all three sites confirm the ceramic sequences, with Late Bronze Age occupations beginning at Gegharot in the early 15th century and ending at Tsakahovit between the late 14th and early 12th centuries. The Late Bronze Age occupations at Tsakahovit were sealed by a thick burned level that appears to mark the destruction of the site and which contributed to the excellent preservation of the occupation floors. On the terrace of the fortress hill we encountered the outlines of burnt beams resting atop two large storage jars (pithoi) and a butter making vessel. In contrast, the citadel trenches uncovered an array of fine wares and bowls, suggesting an emergent segregation of functional areas at the site, perhaps indicative of the initial emergence of those socio-political institutions known from the Urartian era.

Excavations were also undertaken of select burials in order to establish the chronological relationship between fortresses and the mortuary landscape. Excavation of burials in Tsakahovit cemetery 1, Mantash cemetery 8 and Hnaberd cemeteries 14 and 18 revealed ceramics, metals and lapidary remains that reiterated materials recovered from the fortresses, suggesting that the mortuary landscape documented by our survey was formed as part of the same Late Bronze Age socio-political processes that produced the fortresses. What remains to be examined as part of our ongoing research are the social principles governing the clustering of burials into discrete cemeteries, their distribution in the landscape and the significance of these variations for the apparatus of the 'archaic state'. A more extensive report on the regional investigations of Project ArAGATS from 1998–2000 is forthcoming (Smith et al. forthcoming).

**Conclusions**

If Gegharot indeed proves to have emerged as the earliest centre of the fortress based polities on the Tsakahovit plain, this would provide an interesting diachronic framework within which to review the general models of regional political order discussed earlier. We can

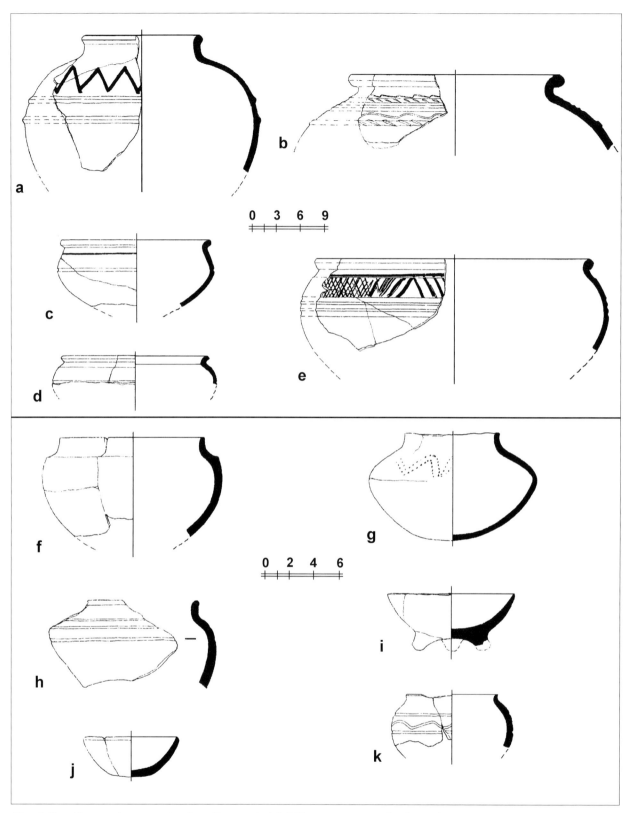

*Fig. 6. Late Bronze Age ceramics from Project ArAGATS excavations at Gegharot fortress in 2000, trench 2, locus 23: (a) black ware closed jar with concentric raised ridges and burnished sawtooth decoration on neck; (b) orange ware closed jar with incised concentric lines and oblique thumbnail decoration; (c) grey ware open jar with concentric pattern burnish; (d) black ware open jar; (e) black ware open jar with irregular hatched/sawtooth pattern burnish; (f) black ware open jar; (g) black ware closed globular jar with wavy punctuate decoration (Late Bronze I phase); (h) black ware open jar with concentric incised lines; (i) orange ware tripod cup; (j) brown ware cup; (k) grey ware cup with concentric incised linear and wavy decoration*

plausibly hypothesise that Gegharot had little competition in its initial period, allowing it a greater geographical expanse within which to exploit local resources. The somewhat later emergence of Tsakahovit and Hnaberd as potential rival seats of authority would have decreased the accessibility of immediately exploitable resources, as emergent regimes sought to limit and control access to those resources within their own territories. Such restrictions on resources could well have been part and parcel of a broader political strategy to force subject populations, generally thought to have been partially nomadic during the Middle Bronze Age, to adopt increasingly sedentary lifestyles. Indeed, the relationship between the, by then, settled regimes situated within the stone walled fortresses, and the subject populations that have left little archaeological traces other than the vast cemeteries, remains the most indelible problem for our understanding of the roots of complex societies in southern Caucasia. Such problems emphasise the need for more systematic surveys in the region to elucidate the broader context within which early fortified political centres emerged. It is hoped that as our investigations in the Tsakahovit plain develop, we will be able to present increasingly refined models of Late Bronze Age social formation and adjudicate the tantalising hypotheses that our initial results currently present.

In conclusion, we have been stimulated by Charles Burney's remarks at this conference (see Burney, this volume) suggesting that we should indeed turn our eyes to southern Caucasia if we hope to understand the milieu from which the Kingdom of Urartu ultimately emerged. This is not to say that the origins of the Urartian state apparatus lay in southern Caucasia, but rather that it is in the Late Bronze Age polities of southern Caucasia that we can see the emergence of a political tradition, a set of institutional forms and strategies for rule, that reverberated into the Iron Age and into Urartian politics (Smith, Thompson forthcoming). The initial emergence of fortress based polities during the mid-second millennium BC in southern Caucasia suggests that complex societies in the highlands may have had a far deeper genealogy and broader geography than has traditionally been suspected.

## Acknowledgements

The material discussed here is based upon work supported by the National Science Foundation under Grant No. 0073519 and by the Wenner-Gren Foundation for Anthropological Research. The authors would like to thank both institutions for their support.

## Bibliography

Adzhan, A.A., Gyuzalian, L.T., Piotrovskii, B.B. 1932: 'Tsiklopichesckii kreposti Zakavkaz'ya' *Soobshchenia Gosudarstvennoi Akademii Istorii Material'noi Kultury* 1/2: 61–4

Avetisyan, P., Badalyan, R., Smith, A.T. 2000: 'Preliminary report on the 1998 archaeological investigations of Project ArAGATS in the Tsakahovit Plain, Armenia' *Studi Micenei ed Egeo-Anatolici* 42(1): 19–59

Badalyan, R.B., Smith, A.T., Avetisyan, P.S. 2003: 'The emergence of socio-political complexity in Southern Caucasia' in A.T. Smith, K. Rubinson (eds), *Archaeology in the Borderlands: Investigations in Caucasia and Beyond.* Los Angeles

Kafadarian, K. 1996: *History of Armenian Architecture* (in Armenian). Yerevan

Khachatrian, T.S. 1974: 'Iz istorii izuchenia drevneyshikh pamyatnikov sklonov Gori Aragats' *Armenovedcheskie Issledovaniya* 1: 109

Khanzadian, E.V., Piotrovskii, B.B. 1992: 'A cylinder seal with ancient Egyptian hieroglyphic inscription from the Metsamor gravesite' *Soviet Anthropology and Archeology* 30(4): 67–74

Khanzadian, E.V., Sarkisian, G.K., Diakonoff, I.M. 1992: 'A Babylonian weight from the 16th century BC with cuneiform inscription from the Metsamor excavations' *Soviet Anthropology and Archeology* 30(4): 74–83

Martirosian, A.A. 1964: *Armenia v Epokhu Bronzi i Rannego Zheleza.* Yerevan

Smith, A.T., Badaljan, R., Avetissian, P. 1999: 'The crucible of complexity' *Discovering Archaeology* 1(2): 48–55

— forthcoming: 'Early complex societies in southern Caucasia: a preliminary report on the 2002 investigations of Project ArAGATS on the Tsakahovit Plain, Armenia' *American Journal of Archaeology*

Smith, A.T., Thompson, T. forthcoming: 'The roots of the Urartian political tradition: institutions and strategies from the Late Bronze Age'

Toramanyan, T. 1942: *Materials for the History of Armenian Architecture* (in Armenian). Yerevan

Zograbyan, L.N. 1979: *Orografia Armyanskogo Nagor'ya.* Yerevan

# The outer town at Ayanis, 1997–2001

## Elizabeth C. Stone
*Stony Brook University*

### Abstract

The Ayanis Outer Town Project was designed to investigate the organisation of an Urartian settlement area. Of especial importance was the determination of the ways in which the residential area was segregated, what role class and wealth played in the articulation of urban life. To this end a number of different and ideally overlapping approaches were taken. Shovel test and magnetic gradiometry surveys were used to select areas for excavation. These sampled both residential areas and a ring of low level public buildings that surrounded the central fortress. Comparison of the architecture, ceramics, faunal remains and objects recovered from these various structures is beginning to build up a picture of this Urartian city.

### Özet

Ayanis Dış Şehir Projesi bir Urartu yerleşim alanının oluşumunu araştırmak üzere planlanmış bir araştırmadır. Bu araştırmanın en önemli amacı, ikamet alanının nasıl bir araya toplanmış olduğunun ve şehir yaşamının oluşumunda sınıfların ve zenginliğin nasıl bir rol oynadığının saptanmasıdır. Bu amaçla birkaç değişik, ancak fikir itibariyle uyuşan yaklaşım kullanılmıştır. Kürek ve magnetik gradiometri ile yapılan ön araştırmalarla kazı yapılacak yerler seçilmiştir. Böylece hem ikametgahların yoğunlukta olduğu alanlar, hem de merkezdeki kaleyi çevreleyen sınıfsal olarak daha düşük seviyeli bir sıra kamu binası incelenebilmiştir. Ortaya çıkan birkaç yapının mimarisinin ve bu yapılarda bulunan keramiklerin, faunal kalıntıların ve objelerin karşılaştırılması ile bir Urartu şehrinin ortaya çıkışının resmi oluşturulmaya başlanmıştır.

Urartian fortresses have been the focus of intense archaeological investigation over the years, but their surrounding urban areas remain much less well understood. Soviet scholars have described Karmir Blur (Oganesjan 1955: 9–17; Piotrovski 1969: 177–8) and Erebuni (Hodjasch 1982) as being accompanied by well planned settlements consisting of both large comfortable dwellings and barrack-like structures, but evaluation of these descriptions is hampered by the lack of plans or photographs. Individual houses were excavated and published from sites like Argištihinilli (Martirosjan 1974: 35–73) and Karmir Blur (Oganesjan 1955: 18–35) but they tend to be isolated buildings making understanding of overall urban planning a little difficult. At Bastam (Kleiss 1988: 11–28) the structures located on the flat land nearest the fortress were investigated, but it is not clear whether this small area represents all that there was to the settlement. Thus, the Ayanis Outer Town Project represents the first attempt to document systematically the organisation of an Urartian city. Our purpose is to determine the character of different parts of the settlement — whether they be administrative or residential — to investigate the nature of social differentiation within the residential area and to understand how these differences may reflect the varying relationships between the residents and the Urartian state establishment. These are obviously ambitious goals and we cannot pretend to have achieved all of them at this time.

How then does one approach issues of large scale urban planning using the rather blunt tools of archaeology? A variety of questions need to be answered. What was the extent of the ancient settlement? How were public buildings and private houses distributed within the city? What was the relationship between the rich and the poor residents of the city, and to what extent were these relationships contingent on differing ties between the various segments of the population and the Urartian state? The work presented here represents the preliminary results of a joint effort by myself and Paul Zimansky, work which would not have been possible without the extraordinary co-operation and generosity that we have received from Altan Çilingiroğlu and his Ege University team.

The first step in such a project is always to conduct a detailed survey, but the juxtaposition of ploughed fields and eroded slopes in the area suggested that quantification of the results of a simple surface pickup might prove misleading. Indeed, comparisons of surface collections and the results of shovel test pits in differing terrains indicate that sherds were much more prominent on the surface of eroded slopes than they were on ploughed fields (Stone, Zimansky 2001: 364). We therefore conducted a shovel test survey over an area that extended 1km east of the citadel and 0.5km in all other directions, with 40 litre excavations placed every 50m (Stone, Zimansky 2001: 366, fig. 3).

If the shovel test survey could tell us the extent of the settlement in the outer town, and provide some spatial information on the distribution of both ceramic densities and wares, it said nothing of the sub-surface architecture. For this we have, like many other archaeologists in Anatolia, turned to magnetic gradiometry. In 1997 Lewis Somers of Geoscan surveyed approximately 5ha, and we were sufficiently impressed with his results that, with the support of the Glen Dash Foundation, we were able to rent a Geometrics gradiometer in 1999 and, in 2001, we borrowed a Geoscan instrument. Altogether some 24ha of the area around the Ayanis citadel have been subjected to magnetic gradiometry, and all decisions on where to place our excavations have been based on the results of this work. In the past two seasons we have excavated single 10m squares in a number of areas exhibiting differing architectural patterns in the magnetic map, in all instances sampling both internal architectural details and external trash deposits. The expansion of selected areas to reveal whole building plans is our goal for future seasons.

Excavation methods must also be adapted to the problem at hand. Ceramic densities are quite low in Urartian sites, the site itself covers an area of up to 80ha, and the buildings consist of a single level of stone architecture. Under these circumstances, we have adopted a programme of rapid excavation and bulk sieving of the excavated soil. Due diligence has enabled us to identify significant stratigraphic changes, especially important in those areas where we encountered post-Urartian occupation. We have also taken a number of micromorphological samples which are being studied by Wendy

Matthews, and from this work we hope to be able to identify better the formation processes that led to our excavated deposits.

Although we like to think that we can tell the difference between those buildings constructed under the guidance of the Urartian state architects and those that were not, on the basis of the regularity of plan and quality of construction, nevertheless it is on the basis of the materials recovered from these structures that we hope to extract information on differential access to wealth, especially as it might relate to ties to the central government.

We have been fortunate in recovering large samples of faunal remains by targeting external trash deposits. Since a key question we are asking here is who got what cuts of meat, we have asked Curtis Marean, a Palaeolithic faunal analyst who specialises in taphonomic approaches, and Melinda Zeder, who has a stronger background in the analysis of faunal assemblages from Near Eastern urban contexts, to develop a programme of faunal analysis designed to answer this question. This entails the expansion and refinement of the analysis through the study of shaft fragments, in addition to the articular fragments that are usually all that are studied at urban sites. Shaft fragments cannot be assigned to a particular species but only to a size category, but since the vast majority of our fauna come from sheep/goat and cattle, which differentiate on the basis of size, this is not a problem. Although this analysis is not yet complete, some significant differences have been noted between samples, and all those so far analysed from the domestic areas seem to lack the best cuts of meat, namely those from the rear upper limb.

But it is the artefacts which are most likely to provide information on whether or not the residents of the outer town had access to the products of state workshops. To answer this question in regard to the ceramics we have initiated a programme of nuclear activation and petrographic analysis on selected sherds. So far these have been completed for red polished diagnostic sherds from the outer town and from Van Kalesi, Altın Tepe, Çavuştepe and Karagündüz. Samples from the Ayanis fortress have yet to be included, and samples from Bastam have only been subjected to preliminary petrographic analysis. The nuclear activation analysis has been conducted by Hector Neff and Michael Glascock at the Missouri reactor, and Melissa Moore has conducted the petrographic analysis. Although our results are still very preliminary, they suggest that the typical Urartian red polished ware pottery was produced locally but in ways that are indistinguishable petrographically throughout the Van basin. This consistency of manufacture suggests to us the employment of highly professional potters and therefore the hand of the

Urartian state. By contrast, the unpolished fine red ware — which shares many of the same forms with the red polished ware — is both petrographically and chemically distinct from the red polished examples and shows more variability. It may therefore represent a less professional copying of the red polished ceramics. At the time of writing, a large selection of coarse ware sherds are in the process of analysis, and we are paying especial attention to buff slipped jars with marks below the rim whose consistency in shape and decoration may also be indications of the products of a state workshop.

Finally, apart from comparing our object inventory with that recovered from the citadel, Christine Bedore is studying the bronzes from both the outer town and the fortress to determine whether they reflect the same traditions of manufacture. Large positive anomalies in our magnetometry data suggest the presence of metallurgical installations, probably smithies, and we plan to test this hypothesis in the forthcoming seasons.

What, then, are the results so far from pursuing these approaches? The 1.5km by 1km area around the citadel chosen for shovel test survey is certainly quite large, but only 524 holes lay both beyond the fortress and away from modern construction. These yielded a total of 550 sherds, all of them seemingly Urartian in date, and a few objects. To the north and east of the survey area we have clearly reached the limit of the settlement but sherds did continue to the south, where we encounter the modern village, and to the west. Nevertheless we estimate the size of the Urartian settlement at between 60ha and 80ha, with some of its area too sloping to have been occupied. In spite of the relatively small number of sherds recovered, there is a clear pattern in their distribution. The major ware types — red polished, medium red-brown, and coarse red-brown wares — show a clear concentration of fine red polished ware in the higher elevations with the coarse wares more common lower down the hill (Stone, Zimansky 2001: 366, fig. 3). Some of the coarse wares from the area below and to the west of the citadel may simply represent wash from the storage areas which are known to have been located in the western part of the fortress (Çilingiroğlu, Salvini 2001: fig. 4).

We used the results of the shovel test survey to choose the areas to be subjected to magnetic gradiometry. Four areas were surveyed: the flattish terrace to the north of the citadel, known as Pınarbaşı, the high slope to the east of the fortress, known as Güney Tepe, the terrace facing the fortress to the south, known as Köy, and the flat area between the fortress and the lake (fig. 1). The magnetic contrast between the limestone walls and the slightly magnetic room fills have highlighted sub-surface architecture in all areas surveyed except the area to the west. On the basis of the magne-

tometry alone, three trends can be identified. One is the presence of often isolated, relatively large, well planned structures located close to the citadel to the north, south and east. Traces of what may be more domestic structures, like those found between similar buildings at Bastam (Kleiss 1988: 20–1), are also seen in those areas. Further up the slope of Güney Tepe is a series of large, roughly square houses, between which are traces of less well organised domestic architecture. Finally, still further up the slope, and stretching towards the south, are more traces of less well planned structures.

We used the results of the magnetometry survey to select areas for excavation. So far we have sampled an area over 1700m$^2$ within ten different structures in the outer town. In nine areas, located close to the north, south and east of the fortress, we identified traces which appear to indicate formal, large scale architecture, five of which have been sampled. Three of these are in the northern area, Pınarbaşı, where a total of 650m$^2$ have been excavated, whereas only single 10m by 10m squares were made in one of the three buildings on the lower slopes of Güney Tepe, the area to the east of the fortress, and in the massive structure located in Köy. Within the area that we interpreted as largely domestic, all of which lies on Güney Tepe, we have cleared 100m$^2$ of one of a series of linear structures located on a low terrace, some 600m$^2$ of two terraces higher up, 125m$^2$ on the highest terrace and a further 100m$^2$ above all modern cultivation. Domestic architecture and associated artefacts were recovered from all but the last sounding, where erosion had removed most architectural traces so that those artefacts recovered lacked a good context.

The more formal structures seen in the magnetometry do indeed seem to represent administrative buildings. All were formally laid out with foundations dug into the ground, buttresses on the exterior wall (except at Köy where our excavation area did not encompass any outside walls), some signs of shaping of the stones used in construction and, in the case of one of the Pınarbaşı buildings, a pair of pillar bases. A paved area in the building on Güney Tepe indicates the presence of a stable. The finds, however, were generally unspectacular. Two seal impressed bullae were recovered from the architecture in Pınarbaşı, and arrowheads (including a bronze trilobate) and a spearpoint from the stable area in Güney Tepe. The original occupation levels of our sounding in Köy comprised a clean floor in a room probably measuring some 20m by 9m, almost devoid of artefacts. Above this were the traces of what we interpret as a squatter occupation dating to a time shortly after the destruction of the fortress. It was marked by scrappy walls sub-dividing the room, a pair of bread ovens and signs of extensive burning which had left one room full of *in situ* pots.

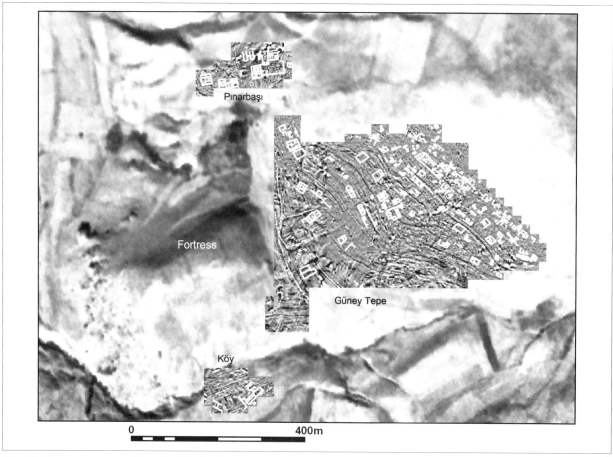

*Fig. 1. The outer town of Ayanis. The background is a Corona image with the magnetometry superimposed. Sketches of architecture visible in the magnetometry are shown in white*

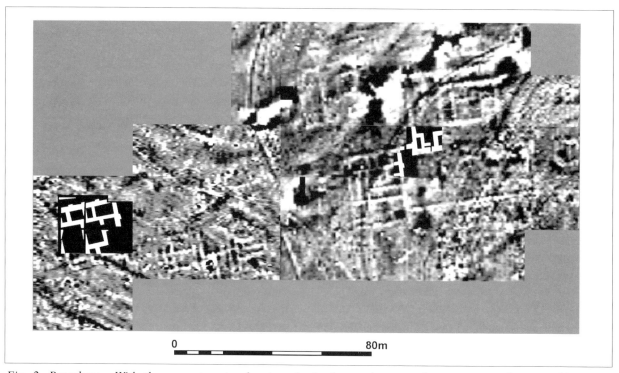

*Fig. 2. Pınarbaşı. With the magnetometry forming the background, excavation areas are shown in black and excavated architecture in white*

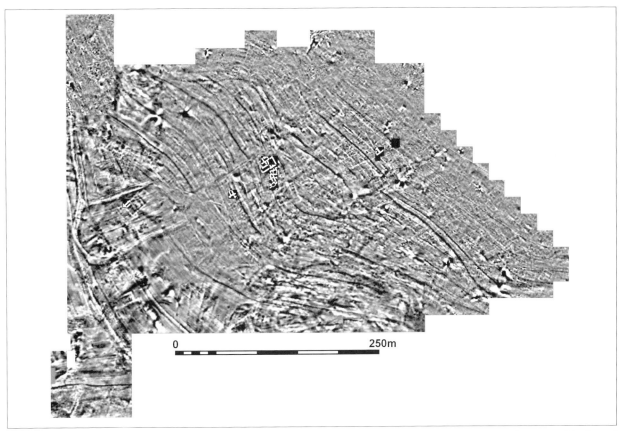

*Fig. 3. Güney Tepe. With the magnetometry forming the background, excavation areas are shown in black and excavated architecture in white*

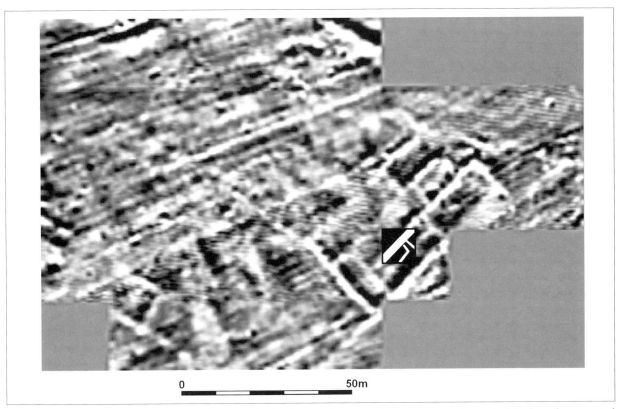

*Fig. 4. Köy. With the magnetometry forming the background, excavation areas are shown in black and excavated architecture in white*

All of these excavations were lacking in precisely those ceramics that are common in the fortress and which we would associate with the hand of the Urartian state — red polished ware and sherds with impressed, stamped or scratched marks (Kozbe, Sağlamtimur, Çevik 2001: 153). Thus, although the architecture and the few objects recovered from these buildings testify to their role in the administrative structure of the fortress, the lack of status goods suggests the presence of low level institutions. The large, well built architectural complex at Pınarbaşı suggests the presence of an institution of some importance to the Urartian state, but the poverty of the associated ceramics and the paucity of objects suggest that it was designed to house individuals of low social status. These data, together with the large number of magnetic anomalies in the area which may indicate the presence of iron working establishments, are not incompatible with the presence of the army. A stronger association with the military can be made for the stable in Güney Tepe on the basis of the weapons found in the trash areas associated with this building. It is tempting to draw parallels between this structure and the Hallenbau excavated at Bastam (Kleiss 1988: 19–28). Both are located close to the gateways of their respective fortresses, and both may have served as the royal chariot house. Too little has been excavated and too little recovered from the original levels of the structure at Köy to say more than that it was a massive building, whose 2m thick walls and very deep foundations more closely resemble the fortress than those of any other building so far excavated in the outer town.

The main residential district covers an area of some 12ha on Güney Tepe, a broad terraced slope that rises opposite the fortress to the east. This can be divided into three zones. Some domestic architectural traces have been found between the areas of more formal architecture close to the fortress, and traces of a series of long, narrow buildings can be seen on the second terrace. A single 10m by 10m square dug into one of the latter revealed a formally built structure which exhibits the same pattern of external buttressing that we have seen with the public buildings discussed above. This structure, however, was heavily modified by its inhabitants, with evidence for the addition of scrappy walls here and there and the blocking of doorways. Higher up the slope, at about the elevation of the top of the fortress, the magnetometry showed clear traces of a number of large buildings, generally about 20m². Less clear traces of architecture were seen between them. Our largest exposure in the outer town encompasses much of one of these buildings and the area between it and the next more substantial structure. Between these two buildings were the remains of a less well planned house, built of smaller

stones, and two trash filled alleyways. Another 125m² excavation area, at an elevation well above the height of the fortress, and in an area characterised in the magnetometry by traces of extensive domestic architecture, none of which is as formal as the large square structures found lower down, also uncovered a large trash filled area, but in this instance part of it had later been encroached upon by architecture.

The finds from these domestic structures differ considerably from those from buildings located closer to the fortress. Typical of all houses were thin, flat iron arrowheads of a form unknown from the fortress. Otherwise, with the exception of the long, narrow house on the lowest terrace, all of the houses yielded pieces of Egyptian blue pigment and small tools and implements in both bronze and iron. Our excavations at the lowest and highest elevations yielded identical items of bronze jewellery — small fibulae and simple hoop earrings. More noteworthy were a piece of decorated bronze — with clear parallels to similar decorative items from the fortress — and an inscribed bulla, both found associated with the large square building excavated halfway up the hill. A bronze bilobate arrowhead, identical with those common at the fortress, was found associated with our highest area of architecture. Unfortunately, it is unwise to read too much into such individual finds, especially since issues of sample size come into play here.

We are in a better position when it comes to an evaluation of the ceramics from the different residential areas. Those from the long, narrow building on the lower terrace are largely similar to those from the public buildings, but the ceramics from the houses at the higher elevations are all characterised by significantly higher percentages of both red polished wares and marked pottery. Associated with the large square building were the highest percentages of red polished ware, but this building had also the lowest percentages of marked sherds. It is possible, however, that the differences in ceramics from the large square structure and from our other excavations on the upper reaches of Güney Tepe might be a product of temporal differences. The stratigraphic information makes it clear that the large square buildings pre-dated the more scrappy architecture that was built between them, and probably also the houses that were built further up the hill.

In conclusion, at this point in the Outer Town Project we see the ancient city as one dominated by the fortress, with subsidiary administrative structures surrounding it on three sides, at least some of which may have been related to the military. The architecture of these buildings testifies to the hand of the Urartian state, but in general the ceramics and objects from them tend to be thoroughly mundane, with the exception of a couple of bullae.

The main residential area was located high on Güney Tepe, mostly at an elevation higher than the top of the citadel as preserved today. Although the excavation of 925m² is certainly not enough to characterise the nature of a 12ha settlement area, our impressions at present are of a residential zone segregated by both elevation and, perhaps, duration of residence. The building with the most clear ties to the Urartian state, in terms of ceramics, access to bronze, Egyptian blue and to writing, was building 1. But though the ceramics from building 3 and from further up the slope have lower percentages of red polished ware they have more marked sherds, and their lack of decorated bronze and writing can be attributed as much to sampling error as to real differences in the assemblages. Most impoverished in terms of both objects and ceramics were the materials recovered from building 6, the linear building at the lowest elevation, but, even there, small bronze items of personal adornment were found. We expect to know a lot more once the analyses of the ceramics, fauna, soils and metals are complete, but these will be no substitute for further excavation — especially the expansion of some of our small soundings and the investigation of areas to the north and south of Güney Tepe.

## Acknowledgements

Our work in the outer town has been supported by generous grants from the National Science Foundation, the National Geographic Society, the Glen Dash Foundation and a generous private donor. I would like to express my gratitude to all the above, as well as to our Turkish colleagues, especially Altan Çilingiroğlu, without whom none of this would have been possible, and to the students — American and Turkish — who helped us with our work. Their tireless effort and good humour have been critical to the success of this project.

## Bibliography

Çilingiroğlu, A., Salvini, M. (eds) 2001: *Ayanis I: Ten Years' Excavations at Rusahinili Eiduru-kai 1989–1998*. Rome

Hodjasch, S.I. 1982: 'Das Leben in der urartäischen Stadt Erebuni' in H. Hirsch, H. Hunger (eds), *Vorträge gehalten auf der 28 Rencontre Assyriologique Internationale in Wien 6–10 Juli 1981* (Archiv für Oreintforschungen, Beiheft 19). Horn: 384–94

Kleiss, W. 1988: *Bastam II: Ausgrabungen in den Urartäischen Anlagen 1977–1978*. Berlin

Kozbe, G., Sağlamtimur, H., Çevik, Ö. 2001: 'Pottery' in A. Çilingiroğlu, M. Salvini (eds), *Ayanis I: Ten Years' Excavations at Rusahinili Eiduru-kai 1989–1998*. Rome: 85–153

Martirosjan, A.A. 1974: *Argištichinili* (Archeologi eskie Pamjatniki Armenii 8). Erevan

Organesjan, K.L. 1955: *Karmir Blur IV: Architektura Tejšebaini* (Archeologi eskie Raskopki ve Armenii No. 6). Erevan

Piotrovskij, B.B. 1969: *The Ancient Civilization of Urartu*. New York

Stone, E.C., Zimansky, P. 2001: 'Survey and soundings in the outer town of Ayanis 1996–1998' in A. Çilingiroğlu, M. Salvini (eds), *Ayanis I: Ten Years' Excavations at Rusahinili Eiduru-kai 1989–1998*. Rome: 355–75

# Aspekte eines neuen Bildes der Entwicklung Anatoliens in der Frühen Eisenzeit (a new understanding of the historical development of Anatolia in the Early Iron Age: the myth of the 'Dark Ages')

**Karl Strobel**
*University of Klagenfurt*

**Abstract**

This paper presents a new understanding of the historical development of Early Iron Age Anatolia, based on a re-evaluation of the archaeological and documentary sources.

**Özet**

Bu çalışma Anadolu Erken Demir Çağının tarihsel gelişiminin anlaşılabilmesi için yazılı ve arkeolojik kaynakları yeniden değerlendirerek yeni bir anlayışın ortaya konmasını amaçlamaktadır.

Das traditionelle Bild vom Ende der Bronzezeit ließ das Hethiterreich im Seevölkersturm zugrunde gehen, der alles, Stadtkulturen, Schriftlichkeit, große und kleine Reiche und entwickelte Wirtschaft wie Verkehrsverbindungen, bis vor die Tore Ägyptens hinweggefegt habe. Das Ergebnis dieses Zusammenbruches waren demnach die 'Dark Ages', die erst wieder im 8. Jahrhundert in Griechenland und in Anatolien überwunden worden seien. Die Ursachen wurden traditionell in Völkerbewegungen des Balkanraumes gesucht (vgl. die Forschungsübersichten bei Bittel 1983; Dobesch 1983; Lehmann 1985; 1996; Ward, Joukowsky 1992; Drews 1993). Die Phryger seien damals wie andere Völkerschaften balkanischen Ursprungs in Anatolien eingewandert und hätten — wenn es schon nicht (mitten im Binnenland) die 'barfüßigen Krieger' der Seevölker selbst waren — Hattuša erstürmt und das Herzland des hethitischen Großreiches überrannt, um sich dann in Phrygien niederzulassen. Graue Keramik, handgemachte Keramik und besonders sogenannte Buckelkeramik wurden als Spuren dieser barbarischen Invasionen balkanischen Ursprungs gesammelt. Daß man dabei allerdings ganz unterschiedliche Phänomene in der lokalen und regionalen Keramik oft sehr unkritisch zu Horizonten vereinigt hat und auch nur oberflächlich ähnliche Erscheinungen mit ganz verschiedenen Wurzeln zusammenfaßte, wurde bereits in den letzten Jahrzehnten durch das Anwachsen des Materials und seine genauere Bearbeitung immer klarer (vgl. besonders Genz 2001). Eigentlich hätten hier vorhandene Probleme schon immer zu denken geben müssen. Doch war das axiomatische Bild zu übermächtigt und führte zu einer Vielzahl von Zirkelschlüssen bei der Interpretation archäologischer Befunde und Materialien, aber auch zu nur scheinbar gesicherten sprachwissenschaftlichen Thesen,[1] die dieses Bild so immer mehr zur Gewißheit zu verfestigen schienen.

Charakteristisch für dieses traditionelle Bild sind die zahlreichen Arbeiten von Fritz Schachermeyr (Schachermeyr 1982; 1986), dessen Rekonstruktionen allerdings bisweilen ins Romanhafte abzugleiten drohen und stets aus eigenen Hypothesen grundsätzlich feststehende Fakten zu machen suchen. Schachermeyr ließ die Seevölker die Wälle von Hattuša erstürmen — ganz unabhängig von der Frage warum sie dann von den Ägyptern als Seevölker charakterisiert worden wären.

---

[1] Dies gilt insbesondere für die Theoriebildung im Bereich der Thrakologie; so sind auch die Bryger-Phryger-Thesen von Petrova 1998 ohne Grundlage und operieren vielfach mit bloßen Namensähnlichkeiten. Ein besonders krasses Beispiel fragwürdiger Schlußfolgerungen bietet Poruciuc 1998.

Oder aber er ließ als Alternative, wie schon angedeutet, die Phryger das hethitische Reich erobern und zerstören. Besonders deutlich werden die traditionellen Züge des Bildes der anatolischen 'Dark Ages', wenn man den Beitrag 'Das dunkle Zeitalter Kleinasiens' betrachtet, den Ekrem Akurgal 1980 Schachermeyr zu dessen 85. Geburtstag gewidmet hat (Akurgal 1983):

> Die Völkerwanderungen, die am Anfang des 12. Jahrhunderts v. Chr. auf dem Balkan und im ägäischen Raum stattfinden, haben der geschichtlichen Entwicklung des anatolischen Landes eine neue Richtung gegeben... Aus den oben dargelegten Tatsachen geht hervor, daß die thrakischen Völker zuerst, um 1200, Troja VIIa, dann um 1180 Hattuša zerstört haben und bei diesen kriegerischen Aktionen um 1170 bis zu der assyrischen Grenze[2] gelangt waren. Bei diesen Wanderzügen haben sich thrakische Stämme in verschiedenen Teilen Anatoliens niedergelassen... Es scheint tatsächlich so, daß Anatolien in der Zeitspanne zwischen 1180 und 750 v. Chr. von nomadischen Völkern besiedelt war, die keine festen Sitzplätze hatten... wir sind genötigt anzunehmen, daß dieses Gebiet [innerhalb des Halysbogens] 400 Jahre lang nur schwach besiedelt war oder überhaupt [als Weideland] nur Besitz der Nomadenstämme wurde.

Die Entstehung des Phrygerreiches setzt Akurgal dabei in traditioneller Weise um 750 v. Chr. an.[3]

Dieses Bild der Akurgal-Schachermeyr-Generation, das auf dem Fehlen entsprechender archäologischer Befunde für diese Zeit (oder auch auf deren Nichterkennen) in der Blütezeit ihrer Forscherzeit aufbaute, hat bis heute eine enorme Wirkung. Es besteht noch immer weithin Konsens, daß um 1200 v. Chr. ein weitgehend einheitlicher Bruch im östlichen Mittelmeerraum eingetreten sei und daß damals eine massive Einwanderung vom Balkan nach Kleinasien erfolgt sei.[4] Die in der antiken Ethnographie und Geographie tradierten Gleichsetzungen von Völkern mit gleichen oder ähnlichen Namen wie Phryges–Bryges, Mysier–Moesier u. a. m. (vgl. dazu etwa Strobel 2001; auch dens. 1998) gelten als die eindeutigen Zeugen für diese Wanderbewegungen nach dem Ende der

Bronzezeit. Mit dem Ende der mykenischen Welt und des Hethiterreiches seien außerdem Stadt- und Schriftkultur aus der Ägäis und dem westlichen wie mittleren Anatolien verschwunden. Die Buchstabenschrift sei durch die Griechen im 8. Jh. oder auch erst um 700 v. Chr. entwickelt worden. Von den Griechen hätte die Schrift dann ihren Weg zu den Völkern Kleinasiens, so zu den Phrygern gefunden, die so das griechische Alphabet übernommen und adaptiert hätten (vgl. etwa Lejeune 1969; Brixhe 1993). Es ist ein grundsätzliches Bestreben der traditionellen Sichtweise, den Griechen die Priorität kultureller Errungenschaften zuzuschreiben (vgl. etwa Muscarella 1989) und insbesondere von einer Erfindung des vokalisierten Alphabets durch die Griechen zu sprechen. (so Wachter 2001).

Auch Gustav Adolf Lehmann führt die von ihm in seiner ungedruckt gebliebenen Studie über die Seevölker vor rund drei Jahrzehnten auf dem damaligen Kenntnisstand entwickelten Vorstellungen nur mit Modifikationen weiter (Lehmann 1970; 1983; 1985; 1996), ohne zu einer grundlegenden Revision aufgrund der neuen archäologischen Befunde bereit zu sein. Dies wurde zuletzt auf dem Kolloquium 'Das Ende der Bronzezeit im östlichen Mittelmeerraum' (Graz, 20. 12. 2001) deutlich. Gleiches gilt im Grunde auch für die Arbeiten von Frau Deger-Jalkotzy (vgl. auch Deger-Jalkotzy 1991). So schreibt Lehmann 1996 in seinem Forschungsbericht erneut, daß die Jahrzehnte um die Wende vom 13. zum 12. Jh. v. Chr. den Höhepunkt des sog. Seevölkersturms markieren würden, daß 'eine erstaunliche Einheitlichkeit der Katastrophenhorizonte um/nach 1200' festzustellen sei, daß durch die Seevölkereinfalle vom Ende des 13. Jh. bis ca. 1180 der gesamte östliche Mittelmeerraum vom griechischen Festland bis zur Levanteküste und bis nach Emar erfaßt worden sei und auf diese tiefe Zäsur in der Geschichte der Kulturreiche in Kleinasien wie in der Ägäis die 'dunklen Jahrhunderte' bis zum 9. Jh. v. Chr. gefolgt seien (Lehmann 1996: bes. S. 1). Dabei kann nach den heutigen Forschungsergebnissen zu Hattuša nicht mehr von dem 'großen Katastrophenhorizont' gesprochen werden, in dem diese Stadt und mit ihr das Hethiterreich untergegangen seien (vgl. Seeher 2001; auch Strobel 2001: 47ff). Ein Zusammenbruch von Staatlichkeit und Urbanität ist im nördlichen hethitischen Kerngebiet und im so benannten Oberen Land innerhalb einer längeren Phase mit offensichtlich unterschiedlichen Ursachen und teils im Kontext innerdynastischer Bürgerkriege erfolgt. Doch kann hier darauf nicht näher eingegangen werden. Nur die Zerstörung von Ugarit ist ein eindeutiger Befund, doch hat sich dessen Kontext und Datierung durch die jüngsten Forschungen ebenfalls deutlich verändert (vgl. auch die Beiträge in Oren 2000). Zerstörungsschichten im Raum Tarsos–Mersin wurden

---

[2] Bezogen auf das Erscheinen der Muški im oberen Tigrisgebiet nach den Annalen Tiglatpilesars I.
[3] So noch bei Högemann (2001: 58) als Wiederbeginn der Geschichtlichkeit Anatoliens angesetzt.
[4] Zu stark geht noch Wittke (1999: 534) in diese Richtung: 'In das luwische Umfeld Westkleinasiens dringen vor oder um 1200 ... namentlich die Phryger ein'.

bisher nach dem Axiom einer als sicher vorauszusetzenden Seevölkerzerstörung entsprechend einheitlich datiert; hier liegt aber, wie auch an zahlreichen anderen Plätzen, ein Zirkelschluß vor, der von der axiomatischen Annahme ausgehend auf immer neue archäologische Befunde ausgeweitet wurde und die relative Chronologie auch des regionalen und überregionalen Fundgutes prägte. Der sogenannte Seevölkersturm, der die Staaten der ausgehenden Bronzezeit hinweggefegt hätte, muß heute als ein überholtes Konstrukt der Forschung gelten (vgl. zum Versuch einer kritischen neuen Zusammenschau Oren 2000; Strobel 2003). Eine Diskussion dieses Problemkreises muß jedoch an anderer Stelle erfolgen.

Besonderes Interesse finden in diesem Zusammenhang die Ausgrabung von Kilise Tepe (vgl. Baker u.a. 1995; Hansen, Postgate 1999)[5] und nun von Kinet Höyük, des antiken Issos (vgl. Gates 1999; 2000; 2001; 2002). In der Phase IV 1 der Spätbronzezeit enden die Perioden 14 und 13 beide in Zerstörungen; ersterer, die eindeutig mit einem kriegerischen Ereignis zu verbinden ist, folgte ein rascher Wiederaufbau. Beide Perioden führen das typische regionale hethitische Fundgut des 13. Jh. v. Chr. bzw. der ausgehenden Großreichszeit. Eine genaue Datierung ergibt sich daraus aber nicht. Die Wiederbesiedlung des Platzes in der Frühen Eisenzeit (Phase III, Periode 12, ?12.–10. Jh.) erfolgte nach einem vollständigen Bruch durch eine neue Bevölkerungsgruppe, deren Ernährungsgrundlage Viehzucht war und die ohne Zweifel aus dem nordsyrischen Binnenland zugezogen ist. Mit einer Einwanderung von mykenischen Griechen oder gar Seevölkern hat dies nichts zu tun. Auch der historische Zusammenhang der Zerstörungen sowie das zeitliche Ende von Phase 13 im 12. Jh. bleiben offen.

In seiner kurzen Darstellung in *Der Neue Pauly* definiert E. Olshausen die Phryger als ein aus Thrakien in Kleinasien eingewandertes Volk, datiert ihre Einwanderung nun aber erst in das 9. Jh. v. Chr. 'als sich um Gordion am Sangarios ein phrygisches Königreich bildete' (Olshausen 2000). Das Phrygische selbst ist, obwohl nur als Trümmersprache überliefert, als ein selbständiger Zweig der indogermanischen Sprachen erkannt (vgl. Neumann 1988; Brixhe 1994; 1999); die Sprache weist nähere Beziehungen zum Griechischen auf, was auf eine frühe Nachbarschaft der beiden Sprachen, genauer zum Attisch–Ionischen und damit zum mykenischen Griechisch, hinweist. Das Thrakische hat dagegen im Phrygischen, was bemerkenswert ist, keine nachweisbaren Spuren hinterlassen; eine linguistische Verwandtschaft ist auszuschließen (vgl. auch Masson 1991; Brixhe 1994). Schon dieser Befund spricht eher für eine frühe Einwanderung der Phryger in Kleinasien und gegen ihre postulierte Anwesenheit bis zum Ende der Bronzezeit auf dem Balkan.

Mit den Muški des 12. Jh. v. Chr. haben die Phryger, wie bereits an anderer Stelle diskutiert, jedoch mit Gewißheit nichts zu tun (vgl. Strobel 2001: ebd., bes. 52ff gegen die Thesen von Börker-Klähn zur 'Europäisierung' Kleinasiens). Eine weitere Klärung des Muški-Problems wird durch den neuen Tatenbericht des urartäischen Königs Rusa II. (ca. 685–645 v. Chr.) im großen Tempel von Ayanis gegeben, in dem die Deportation von Menschen und Rindern (Vieh) aus folgenden Ländern berichtet wird: Assur, Tarquni, Etiuni (Armenien), Tabal, Qainaru, Hate gleich Hatti, Muški und Şiluquni (Şuluqu) (Salvini 2001: 261, Kol. VI 4ff). Unter Hatti ist hier der östliche Teil des ehemaligen hethitischen Kernlandes bzw. das Gebiet um den Oberlauf des Euphrat zu verstehen, nicht jedoch die sonst konkret mit Namen erscheinenden späthethitischen Staaten im Euphrat-Bereich oder Tabal (vgl. auch Karte *Der Neue Pauly* 12/1, 2002: 1027, wo allerdings der Eintrag für *Hate* nicht überzeugt). Diese ethnisch konkret bezeichneten Muški sind sicher nicht mit Phrygern gleichzusetzen,[6] sondern als eine Bevölkerungsgruppe im Murat-und oberen Tigrisbereich zu verstehen. Wichtige Aufschlüsse zu der Entwicklung dieses Raumes in der frühen Eisenzeit geben auch die Untersuchungen von U. Müller (siehe in diesem Band).

Doch wollen wir uns nun die angesprochenen neuen historischen und archäologischen Ergebnisse im Einzelnen ansehen. Heute sind wir in der Lage diese historischen Phänomene im Lichte neuer archäologischer Erkenntnisse schärfer zu umreißen und chronologisch neu zu fassen. Zahlreiche traditionelle Vorstellungen und historisch-archäologische Modelle sind damit überholt oder müssen grundsätzlich neu diskutiert werden. Dabei ist es selbstverständlich an dieser Stelle notwendig, eine Beschränkung der zu betrachtenden Befunde und Phänomene vorzunehmen. Im Mittelpunkt sollen deshalb die neuesten Forschungsergebnisse für Gordion und damit der Problemkreis des Beginns des Phryggerreiches von Gordion stehen. Hier haben die Ausgrabungen der letzten Jahre in Gordion, dem Zentrum des Reiches, und die als zuverlässig zu betrachtenden Ergebnisse naturwissenschaftlicher Untersuchungen, die erst in den letzten Monaten vorgelegt worden sind, zu einer vollständigen Revision des Geschichtsbildes gezwungen (vgl. bereits Strobel 2001; 2002a; 2002b).

---

[5] Die zahlreichen Zerstörungsschichten weisen auf eine Reihe von Auseinandersetzungen, vielleicht bereits beginnend mit dem Bürgerkrieg gegen Tarhuntassa, hin.

[6] Unrichtig noch Çilingiroğlu, Salvini 2001: 19ff.

Bis zu den Ergebnissen der Untersuchungen des Jahres 2001 galt als ein sicherer Fixpunkt für die Chronologie Gordions wie des gesamten anatolischen Raumes — und in der relativen Chronologie weit darüber hinaus! — daß die altphrygische Königszitadelle von Gordion, die Rodney Young ausgegraben hatte, von den Kimmeriern zerstört worden sei, wobei man die Nachricht über den rituellen Selbstmord des Königs Midas mit einer Niederlage gegen die Kimmerier verbunden hatte. Diese angebliche Kimmerierzerstörung, die mit dem 'destruction level' der altphrygischen Königszitadelle von Gordion gleichgesetzt wurde und die man ohne Grundlage auch für das phrygerzeitliche Boğazköy postulierte,[7] hat man traditionell um 700 v. Chr. datiert; einige Ansätze gingen sogar weit in die 1. Hälfte des 7. Jh. hinab (etwa Bossert 1993; 2000: 153ff 158ff, für 674; Parker 1995: für 657 v. Chr. Vgl. hierzu Strobel 2001). Zudem war es für R. Young ein Axiom, das von der älteren amerikanischen Gordion-Schule lange vertreten wurde und in der Forschung noch in den 90er Jahren des 20. Jh. unbesehen übernommen wurde (vgl. DeVries 1990: bes. 391; so noch Drew-Bear 1998), daß auf die Kimm_zerstörung ein längerer Hiat in der Entwicklung der Stadt gefolgt sei und die Neuanlage der Zitadelle wie die ganze mittelphrygische Stadt in Gordion erst in die 1. Hälfte des 6. Jh. zu datieren sei; zuerst hatte R. Young sogar ein Datum erst nach der persischen Eroberung um 540 v. Chr. angenommen. Auf Grund dieses Axioms hat R. Young, wie wir heute sehen werden, bei seinem 'Schliemanngraben' in die altphrygische Königszitadelle hinab die Palastburg des 'Königs Midas', die mittelphrygische Palastzitadelle, zerstört und ihr bei der Ausgrabung und der folgenden Auswertung leider nur ungenügende Aufmerksamkeit geschenkt.

Die Ausgrabungen von Mary M. Voigt seit dem Ende der 80er Jahre haben aber gezeigt, daß ein solcher Hiat nicht vorhanden war, sondern daß die großartige Neuanlage der Königszitadelle unmittelbar auf die Zerstörung des altphrygischen Palastes gefolgt ist (Henrickson 1993; 1994; Voigt 1994; 1997; Voigt u. a. 1994; 1997; Henrickson, Voigt 1998; Voigt, Young 1999; Voigt, Henrickson 2000a; 2000b; auch Gunter 1991). Das Innere der alten Zitadelle wurde meterhoch mit sterilem Lehm aufgeschüttet und der Wall außen mit Geröllmassen angeschüttet, die mit einem mächtigen Stufenglacis verkleidet wurden. Auf der so geschaffenen neuen, über 20m aus der Ebene aufragenden Baufläche wurden Festungswall und Palast neu errichtet. Ebenfalls

wurde die westliche Oberstadt auf einer angeschütteten Lehmterrasse neu errichtet. Auch in der nunmehr von einem mächtigen Wall mit Türmen umzogenen Unterstadt wurden teilweise solche Lehmterrassen zur Errichtung erhöhter Stadtquartiere angelegt. Es handelte sich um eine grandiose Neuanlage, die keinesfalls mit einem im Verfall begriffenen phrygischen Königtum verbunden werden kann.

Auf dieser Grundlage wurde von M.M. Voigt die folgende neue Stratigraphie und Chronologie für Gordion-Yassıhöyük (YHSS) entwickelt (alle Zahlen sind als 'ca.' zu verstehen):

YHSS 10 Middle Bronze Age 2000–1500 v. Chr.
YHSS 9 Late Bronze Age 1500–1400 v. Chr.
YHSS 8 Late Bronze Age/Hittite 1400–1200 v. Chr.
YHSS 7 Early Iron Age 1200–950 v. Chr.
YHSS 6B Early Phrygian B 950–750 v. Chr.
YHSS 6A Early Phrygian A 750–700 v. Chr.
YHSS 5 Middle Phrygian 700–550 v. Chr.
YHSS 4 Late Phrygian/Persian 550–330 v. Chr.

Jedoch wurde bereits seit einiger Zeit bemerkt, daß die Beigaben in der Grabkammer des sogenannten Midas-Tumulus zeitlich offenkundig jünger anzusetzen waren als das im altphrygischen Zerstörungshorizont versiegelte Fundgut. Damit war bereits die bisherige Chronologie in Frage gestellt. Hinzu kamen die dendrochonologischen Daten für das Fälldatum der Hölzer des Grabhaus des Midas-Tumulus und für Balken des altphrygischen Bauhorizontes von YHSS 6A (vgl. Kuniholm 1977; 1993). Das Fälldatum der Hölzer des Midas-Grabes wurde auf ca. 718 v. Chr. bestimmt, das Fälldatum der Hölzer aus dem Terrassengebäude 2A (YHSS 6A) auf 861 v. Chr. Letzteres wurde mit dem Einwand, es seien ältere Balken wiederverwendet worden, wegdiskutiert.

Auf Grund dieser Erkenntnisse wurde dann aber noch im Jahre 2000 eine leicht modifizierte Chronologie vorgeschlagen, die den Übergang von Early zu Middle Phrygian auf 720? ansetzte und auch an eine mögliche assyrische Kriegshandlung dachte (Voigt, Henrickson 2000a).

Die jüngste Adjustierung der dendrochronologischen Daten hat nun ergeben, daß die Datierungen für die Baumringchronologie Anatoliens um 22 Jahre anzuheben sind (Manning u. a. 2001a; 2001b; Reimer 2001). Das Fälldatum der Bäume für das Midas-Grab liegt somit bei 740+4/−7 v. Chr., für die Hölzer von Gebäude Terrace Building 2A bei 883+4/−7 v. Chr. Das Einsetzen einer Anomalie der Ringfolge ist nun auf 1650+4/−7 v. Chr. zu datieren und entspricht jenem jetzt eindeutig mit dem Ausbruch des Thera-Vulkans zu verbindenden Aschenniederschlag im Grönlandeis, der 1645+/−7 v. Chr. datiert. Damit ist für diese ägäische

---

[7] So noch Bossert 2000, wo die neueren Untersuchungen nicht mehr zur Kenntnis genommen sind und insgesamt von völlig falschen chronologischen Annahmen ausgegangen wird.

Katastrophe, deren Spuren nun in einem immer weiteren Umfange festgestellt werden, ein als exakt anzusehendes Datum ermittelt, das zur Anhebung der bisherigen Chronologie im Ägäisraum um mehr als 100 Jahre zwingt und auch die mittlere Chronologie für das altassyrische Reich bestätigt. Doch können diese Konsequenzen hier nicht weiter verfolgt werden (vgl. zu dem Problemkreis Manning 1999; Bietak 2000).

Für den Destruction Level des altphrygischen Gordion ist somit ca. 740 v. Chr. ein *Terminus ante quem*, der bereits jede Verbindung mit dem Erscheinen der Kimmerier in Kleinasien nach 714 v. Chr. ausschließt, gegeben. Die 2001 abgeschlossenen, adjustierten C14-Datierungen für verkohltes Getreide aus dem Zerstörungshorizont haben nun aber ihrerseits geradezu dramatische Daten ergeben, die diese Brandzerstörung in den Zeitraum zwischen 835 und vor 800 v. Chr. setzen. (DeVries u. a. in diesem Band; Bericht K. Sams, Symposium Ankara 2002). Dies bedeutet eine völlige Neubewertung des Befundes von Gordion und eine radikale Änderung der Datierung seiner ältereisenzeitlichen Schichten. Die Konsequenzen erstrecken sich aber auf die gesamte anatolische Chronologie, für die der Befund der Tumuli von Gordion, insbesondere der sogenannte Midas-Tumulus (MM) und der Zerstörungshorizont, bisher den entscheidenden Ansatz der vergleichenden Chronologie um 700 geboten hat (vgl. Muscarella 1967; Sams 1994; Bossert 2000).

Die Neuanlage der Zitadelle, der westlich daran anschließenden Oberstadt und der Unterstadt mit ihren teilweise künstlich aufgeschütteten Terrassen aus sterilem Lehm sowie der Bau der mächtigen, die Unterstadt umziehenden Stadtmauer mit ihren beiden gewaltigen Eckwerken im Süden (Küçük Höyük)[8] und Norden (Kuş Tepe)[9] gehören somit in das 8. Jh. v. Chr. Der Abschluß der großartigen Neuanlage von Stadt und Königszitadelle ist heute, wie auch K. de Vries als ein Vertreter der älteren Gordion-Schule einräumt, vor das letzte Viertel des 8. Jh. v. Chr. zu datieren. Mit der

Neuanlage von Königszitadelle und Stadt wurde in einem ungeheuer aufwendigen, enorme Massen von Arbeitskräften beanspruchenden Bauprogramm bereits kurz vor bzw. um 800 v. Chr. begonnen. Der Zerstörungshorizont der altphrygischen Königsburg, in dem sich keine Hinweise auf ein Kampfgeschehen finden, ist aus heutiger Sicht am ehesten mit einem verheerenden Schadensfeuer in Verbindung zu bringen. Der Wiederaufbau der Palastanlage auf dem künstlich errichteten, monumental befestigten Plateau, das von der westlichen Oberstadt durch einen fast schluchtartigen Straßeneinschnitt abgetrennt war, folgte dabei in charakteristischer Weise dem Plan der zerstörten und nun planmäßig aufgefüllten älteren Anlage.

Diese Neuanlage von Burg und Stadt in Gordion war im 8. Jh. begleitet von der Errichtung des großen mittelphrygischen Zentrums von Hacıtuğrul östlich von Gordion jenseits des Çile Dağı-Gebirges in der fruchtbaren Senke von Polatlı,[10] dessen Ausgrabungen leider bis heute nicht ausreichend publiziert sind. Der gewaltige, vom Verfasser erstmals erkannte, aus Geröll aufgeschüttete Tumulus auf der Paßhöhe der alten Straßenverbindung zwischen Gordion und diesem Zentrum ist vermutlich mit dessen Erbauer in Verbindung zu setzen, der Vorgänger oder Nachfolger des im sogenannten Midas-Tumulus bestatteten Herrschers gewesen sein kann. Die in diesen Tumuli bestatteten Könige von Gordion waren zweifellos Herrscher eines großen, in Blüte stehenden Reiches.

Die neuen Datierungen für den Destruction Level und die Grabkammer des sogenannten Midas-Tumulus (Tumulus MM) haben noch weitere Konsequenzen, die hier kurz angesprochen werden sollen, da sie für die Frage der kulturellen Entwicklung des kleinasiatisch-ägäischen Raumes nach dem Ende der Bronzezeit von großer Bedeutung sind. In beiden Fundkomplexen sind bereits Zeugnisse der voll entwickelten altphrygischen Schrift dokumentiert.[11] Die Übernahme der Alphabetschrift durch die Phryger muß demnach um die Mitte des 9. Jh. v. Chr. schon erfolgt gewesen sein. Die traditionelle Annahme, daß die Phryger die Alphabetschrift

---

[8] Bisher immer als 'lydische (Ziegel-)Bastion' angesprochen und von R. Young seinen Thesen folgend mit dem erneuten Ausbau Gordions unter lydischer Herrschaft in Verbindung gebracht. Die noch heute hoch anstehende Ziegelbastion wurde 546/5 v. Chr. von den Persern mit einem immensen Pfeilhagel überschüttet und in Brand gesteckt. Danach wurde die Bastion mit einem Lehmhügel überschüttet, dessen Deutung als Tumulus für einen toten achaimenidischen Großen nicht überzeugen kann. Vielmehr wurde durch die Zuschüttung der Bastion wie auch des zu Recht im Kuş Höyük zu vermutenden Befestigungswerkes die Verteidigung der Unterstadt von Gordion unmöglich gemacht.

[9] Bisher meist als Tumulus gedeutet; noch keine Untersuchungen; s. o.

---

[10] Die allerdings sehr begrenzten Ausgrabungen im Tell von Polatlı zeigen eine vermutlich große, aber eher dörfliche Besiedlung vom 3. Jt. bis in späte hethitische Zeit (Schichten I-XXXI; die späte hethitische Schicht lag direkt unter der Oberfläche des Tells. Vgl. Seton Lloyd, Gökçe 1951).

[11] Vgl. Brixhe, Lejeune 1984: 73ff, 98ff (erstes Graffito); Roller 1989. Zu den nichtverbalen Zeichen auf Keramikgefäßen in Gordion, die sich unmittelbar von hethitischen Hieroglyphenzeichen ableiten und eine Kontinuität in die Spätbronzezeit anzeigen, vgl. Roller 1987.

von den Griechen übernommen hätten,[12] ist damit völlig in Frage gestellt. Hinzu kommt die Tatsache, daß die Phryger eine Reihe charakteristischer Buchstaben des ionischen Alphabets nicht übernommen haben und daß andererseits aber ein Zeichen im Altphrygischen wie in den frühgriechischen Schriftzeugnissen aus Smyrna gemeinsam vorhanden ist (vgl. Jeffrey 1980: 92), was in eine ganz andere Richtung weist. Zudem sind heute die Unterschiede zwischen der griechischen und der altphrygischen Alphabetentwicklung stärker zu betonen. Dies gilt insbesondere für die angesprochenen, im Griechischen nicht vorhandenen Buchstaben und für Variantenentwicklungen. Es deutet somit alles daraufhin, daß die Übernahme der Alphabetschrift auf dem Landwege in Kleinasien selbst erfolgt ist, und zwar über den mehrsprachigen nordsyrischen und südostanatolischen bzw. kilikischen Raum, wo altaramäische konsonantische Alphabetschrift und ältere Silbenschriften, also mit Vokalschreibungen in Kombination mit Konsonantenzeichen arbeitende Schriften, nebeneinander traten und die Bedürfnisse der indoeuropäischen, vokalbetonten Sprachen empfunden werden mußten. Phönikische und aramäische Inschriften finden wir in den hethitischen Nachfolgestaaten im Süden und Südosten, insbesondere im Pyramos-Gebiet, aber auch in Tuwanuwa (hierogyphenluwische und phönikische Bilingue von İvriz). Die Entwicklung der Vokalzeichen ist heute überzeugend mit der mehrsprachigen, ethnisch gemischten Bevölkerung der Städte Nordsyriens wie Ostkilikiens und mit der Präsenz der Silbenschriften mesopotamischer und hethitischer Tradition zu verbinden; die rein konsonantische phönikische Alphabetschrift muß als Ausgangspunkt für die Entwicklung des vokalischen Alphabets ausgeschieden werden (vgl. Marek 1993: 37f; Naveh 1982). Den Beweis hat die Inschrift auf dem Weihegeschenk des Herrschers von Guzana aus Tell Fekherye am Chabur gebracht (Sader 1987: 23ff), die in die 2. Hälfte des 9. Jh. zu datieren ist und langes I und langes U auch im Wortinneren mit Jod und Waw wiedergibt. Die Weihung einer Pferdestirn aus Bronze mit der aramäischen Inschrift eines Königs von Damaskus vom Ende des 9. Jh. aus dem Heraion von Samos und eine zweite identische Inschrift auf zwei bronzenen Scheuklappen desselben Pferdegeschirrs aus dem Apollonheiligtum von Eretria auf Euboia, wo die

Weihung stratigraphisch noch ins 8. Jh. gehört (Kyrieleis, Röllig 1988: 37ff, 69ff; Marek 1993: 38ff, 42f),[13] zeigen weitreichende internationale Beziehungen an, die von den hethitischen Nachfolgestaaten, die seit 920 v. Chr. schrittweise im syrischen Raum von einer aramäischen Führungsschicht übernommen wurden, ausgingen.

Das griechische Alphabet hat sich, wie heute mit gutem Grund anzunehmen ist, aus dem gleichen Horizont der schriftgeschichtlichen Entwicklung heraus entwickelt (vgl. Marek 1993; auch Lazzarini 1999), wobei die engen Beziehungen Euboias zur Levante, wie sie in Lefkandi deutlich faßbar sind, offenbar von entscheidender Bedeutung waren. In dem Handelsplatz von Al Mina an der Orontesmündung ist die starke Präsenz von Griechen für die Zeit ca. 825-700 v. Chr. gut belegt, wo auch im 8. Jh. frühe griechische Schriftzeugnisse auftreten. Im Raum der Syriens einschließlich der östlichen kilikischen Küste müssen die Griechen aber bereits um 900 präsent gewesen sein, da sie nur so die Bezeichnung der luwischsprachigen Bevölkerung Kappadokiens als 'Weise Syrer' übernommen haben können, die uns Herodot (l, 72) überliefert. Damals müssen sie den Unterschied zwischen den Weißen Syrern, den anatolisch-luwischsprachigen Führungsschichten bzw. Bevölkerungsgruppen und den 'normalen' Syrern kennengelernt und dann auf die luwischsprachige Bevölkerung der im Taurus angrenzenden späthethitischen Staaten und schließlich auf die gesamte luwischsprachige Bevölkerung des kappadokischen Raumes jenseits des Halys ausgedehnt haben. Kurz nach 738 erscheinen Ionier, also Griechen des westkleinasiatisch-ägäischen Raumes, in einem assyrischen Kriegsbericht, da sie vergeblich zu Schiff drei Küstenstädte attackiert hatten (vgl. Braun 1982: 14ff). Ferner ist auf eine bedeutende phönikische Präsenz auf Kreta (Kommos seit spätem 10 Jh. v. Chr.) und auf die Niederlassung von Phönikern auch im griechischen Mutterland und insbesondere auf Euboia hinzuweisen. Euboia erscheint in der griechischen Überlieferung selbst als Ursprung der eigenen Schrift (Herodotus 5, 57f; vgl. Nenci 1998. Vgl. ferner Syll³ 37.38 (Kreta), wo der Schreiber als *Phoinikastas* bezeichnet ist). Die bedeutende Rolle Euboias, dessen Aristokratie internationale Beziehungen unterhielt und zum frühen Zentrum der Kolonisationsbewegung wurde, bei der Verbreitung des Alphabets ist heute klar erkennbar.

Griechische Schriftfunde liegen aus dem 8. Jh. bereits aus dem Westen, aus Italien vor, so daß die Entwicklung des griechischen Alphabets jedenfalls vor der Mitte des

---

[12] So etwa Oettinger 1999 mit der Festellung, daß das phrygische Alphabet unter den kleinasiatischen Alphabetschriften dem frühen griechischen am nächsten stehe. Auch Roller (1989: 57) geht noch davon aus, daß die 17 Buchstaben der ältesten phrygischen Schriftzeugnisse einschließlich des Digamma-Zeichens direkt aus dem Griechischen übernommen seien.

[13] Es ist keineswegs zwingend, daß die Weihenden Griechen waren.

8. Jh. anzusetzen ist.[14] Neben frühen griechischen Schriftzeugnissen tritt in der euboischen Kolonie Pithekussai auch ein aramäischer Graffito auf. In der 2. Hälfte des 8. Jh. können wir mit einer aristokratischen griechischen Oberschicht in der Ägäis und in Mittelgriechenland wie in den Koloniegründungen rechnen, die Litteralität und Epenpräsenz[15] aufweist.

Doch kommen wir nun auf die historischen Konsequenzen aus den Befunden von Gordion zurück. Gordion war nicht das regionale Zentrum dieses Raumes in der Bronzezeit (vgl. Gunter 1991; Voigt 1994). Dieses stellt vielmehr der bisher nur oberflächlich begangene Tell etwas nördlich bei Şabanözü dar. Der gleichnamige Bach strömt vom zentralen Gipfelrücken des Çile Dağ herunter zum Sangarios. Dieser Gipfelrücken ist mit dem antiken Mons Olympus identisch (vgl. Strobel 2002a: 30ff). Der Berg hat somit, wie wir zu Recht annehmen können eine zentrale Bedeutung im regionalen Kult des altanatolischen Berg- und Wettergottes sowie als ein Sitz der Götter gehabt (vgl. auch Haas 1994). In Gordion ist keine Zerstörung am Ende der Spätbronzezeit, die ganz durch die großreichszeitliche hethitische Welt geprägt erscheint, festzustellen. Die Keramik zeigt die charakteristische Serienproduktion; die Größe der hethitischen Siedlung auf dem ursprünglichen leichten Höhenrücken ist nicht zu bestimmen. Die hethitisch geprägte Bevölkerung hat den Ort offensichtlich nach dem Zusammenbruch des hethitischen Machtsystems bald nach 1200 und nach dem entsprechenden Zusammenbruch des bisherigen politischen und wirtschaftlich-sozialen Rahmens aufgegeben.

Es folgte, ohne daß ein längerer Siedlungshiat eingetreten wäre, in YHSS 7B der offenkundige Zuzug eines neuen Bevölkerungselementes, womit ein Wiederaufleben der vorgroßreichszeitlichen, (früh-und) mittelbronzezeitlichen Keramiktraditionen verbunden war, wobei die jüngsten Untersuchungen von H. Genz die direkten Verbindungen dieser Keramik in die östlichen Arzawa-Länder aufgezeigt haben;[16]

Verbindungen in den nördlicher gelegenen Raum sind ebenso möglich, aber mangels dortiger archäologischer Forschungen nicht so klar zu zeigen. Weitere Beziehungen weisen nach Osten bzw. Südosten, auf die mittelbronzezeitliche Keramik Südkappadokiens und Kilikiens bis an den oberen Euphrat. Es ist sehr wohl möglich, daß hier Bevölkerungsgruppen zu fassen sind, die im Zuge der hethitischen Expansionspolitik nach Südosten in diesen westlichen Raum umgesiedelt worden sind. Scheibengedrehte Keramik erscheint erst wieder in YHSS 6B. Die Parallelen zu der Keramik-Entwicklung im Halys-Bogen sind augenfällig.

Der zweite Komplex, der für die Fragen des früheisenzeitlichen Anatolien von ganz entscheidender Bedeutung ist, wird von dem Befund der Büyükkaya-Grabungen in Hattuša gestellt. An dieser Stelle ist es notwendig, den Blick auf die dort erreichten Ergebnisse zu richten. Auf die letzte Phase im Kontext der sich auflösenden Urbanität der Stadt, die mit dem Verschwinden Šuppiluliumas II. ihre Hauptstadtfunktion verloren hatte, folgen 5 Stufen der früheisenzeitlichen Besiedlung des Platzes (vgl. Seeher 1996–2002; Genz 2000; 2001 und in diesem Band). Die naturwissenschaftlichen Daten sichern den Zeitraum 12.–10. Jh. v. Chr. In Stufe I dauert die späthethitische Keramiktradition für kurze Zeit noch an, während zugleich eine neue Bevölkerungsgruppe einsiedelt, für die handgemachte Keramik charakteristisch ist. In Stufe II kommt nur mehr handgemachte Keramik dieser Tradition vor, unter der sich auch sogenannte 'Buckelware' findet. Auch das früheisenzeitliche Alaca Höyük liefert Waren (Noppenverzierung, black burnished), die man nach dem traditionellen Zuordnungsschema als 'balkanisch' einzuordnen hätte. Diese Waren sind auf Keramiktraditionen der Früh- und Mittelbronzezeit im nördlicheren Anatolien zurückzuführen. Stufe III ist die eigentliche Büyükkaya-Stufe, die ins 10. Jh. zu datieren ist. Das neue Keramikinventar der Stufen I–III ist von der Keramik der Früh- und Mittelbronzezeit abzuleiten, ist also eine regionale Entwicklung, die auf die Zuwanderung von Bevölkerungsgruppen offensichtlich aus der nördlich angrenzenden 'Kaskäer'-Zone zurückgeht. Die Keramik des 9. Jh. ist direkt aus dem Inventar der Stufe III abzuleiten und diese ist ihrerseits der direkte Vorgänger der 'klassischen' älterphrygerzeitlichen Keramik im Halys-Bogen, der Büyükkale II bzw. Alişar IVc Ware. Gleichzeitig mit Stufe IV, die ohne Bruch auf Stufe III folgt, ist bereits die Besiedlung von Büyükkale Stufe IIb früh, wohin offensichtlich der größte Teil der Bevölkerung umgezogen ist. Auf dem oberen Plateau von Büyükkaya, wo jetzt die Besiedlung bereits großenteils aufgegeben war, wurde nun eine Abschnittsmauer errichtet, die erste eisen-

---

[14] Übernahme in der 1. Hälfte des 8. Jh. etwa noch bei Marek 1993: 33 angenommen. Vgl. zu dem gesamten Problemkreis Bartonek 1999; Lazzarini 1999.

[15] Sogen. Dipylon-Oinochoe aus dem Kerameikos (Hexameter); Nestorbecher auf Pithekussai (iambischer Trimeter, 2 Hexameter).

[16] Vgl. Genz 2000; ferner in diesem Band. Ich danke Herrn Genz für die ausführlichen Diskussionen. Die tabellarische Aufstellung von typologischen Parallelen in Voigt, Henrickson 2000a: 47 bestätigt einerseits Genz, andererseits sind die angegebenen balkanischen Parallelen (bis nach Makedonien, Serbien und Pylos) bei einer genaueren Überprüfung keineswegs gesichert. Gleiches gilt für die angenommenen 'barbarischen' Troia VIIb2-Parallelen.

zeitliche Befestigung des Ortes, die in Stufe V bereits wieder aufgegeben war. Die Büyükkale IIa-Stufe fand auf Büyükkaya nicht mehr statt. Auf Büyükkale hatte sich eine befestigte Siedlung entwickelt. Der Beginn der jüngerphrygerzeitlichen Büyükkale I-Stufe mit der Glacis-Befestigung ist nach der Korrektur der Datierung des Destruction-Level in Gordion wohl noch in das 8. Jh. zu datieren.

Es zeigt sich heute als ein allgemein verbreitetes Phänomen, daß mit dem Zusammenbruch des hethitischen Großreiches die Einheitlichkeit der Keramikwaren, die auf eine spezialisierte Massenproduktion und ganz bestimmte Wirtschaftsstrukturen zurückzuführen ist, verschwindet und ein Bruch in der Keramiktradition einsetzt. Die spätbronzezeitlichen Traditionen leben mehrfach noch 1–2 Generationen weiter, um dann völlig abzubrechen. Es folgt eine Ausdifferenzierung unterschiedlicher Keramikprovinzen der frühen Eisenzeit (Gordion, Kaman-Kalehöyük, Boğazköy-Tavium, Alişar-Çadır). Die Büyükkaya-Ware ist, wie insbesondere die jüngsten Surveys zeigen, im gesamten Gebiet Amasya-Samsun-Merzifon allgemein verbreitet. Die entsprechenden Entwicklungen sind auch im früheisenzeitlichen Alaca Höyük oder Eskiyapar zu verfolgen.

Die Entwicklung der älterphrygerzeitlichen Keramik im Halysbogen ist also nicht das Ergebnis einer phrygischen Einwanderung, sondern einer regionalen und lokalen Entwicklung. Zudem sind viele Elemente dieser früheisenzeitlichen Keramik aus dem Repertoire der mittelanatolischen Früh- und Mittelbronzezeit abzuleiten. Diese älteren Traditionen wurden zumindest in den städtischen Räumen der hethitisch geprägten Spätbronzezeit unterbrochen, müssen aber außerhalb der hethitischen Macht- oder Wirtschaftsstrukturen, ersteres im nördlicheren Mittelanatolien, letzteres etwa in ländlichen Räumen, fortgelebt haben.

Die früheisenzeitliche Schicht IId in Kaman-Kalehöyük, deren C14-Daten offensichtlich erst relativ spät mit dem 11. und 10. Jh. v. Chr. einsetzen[17] und die 8 Niveaus mit einer Dauer von rund 4 Jahrhunderten umfaßt, weist in den Niveaus 1–4 zuerst eine deutliche Kontinuität zur spätbronzezeitlichen Keramik auf. Typische geometrische Motive und ein Tierstil entwickeln sich als Bemalungsformen. Charakteristisch ist das Auftreten von Grauwaren, die mittelbronzezeitliche Formen vor der Dominanz der standardisierten hethitisch-großreichszeitlichen Keramik wieder aufgreifen. Diese Grauware ist in dem Raum von Kayseri-Kültepe bis in die Ankara-Polatlı-Senke und bis in den Südosten des Großen Salzsees verbreitet. Sie ist eine für die frühe Eisenzeit

charakteristische kulturelle Erscheinung innerhalb und westlich des Halysbogens und keinesfalls mit einer etwaigen phrygischen Einwanderung zu verbinden. Nach einer anfänglichen Kontinuität zur SBZ trat in Kalehöyük in der Frühen Eisenzeit, ohne daß wir Einwanderungsbewegungen fassen können, ein deutlicher Wandel unter Fortführung der scheibengedrehten Keramik ein. Der kulturelle, wieder stärker vereinheitlichende Einfluß der phrygischen Großreichsbildung zeigt sich sehr deutlich in der Präsenz der sogenannten phrygischen Fibeltypen, wobei die gefundenen Gußformen die Herstellung dieser Fibelmode vor Ort dokumentieren. Ebenso erscheint bemalte phrygische Keramik des Destruction-Level, die heute entgegen der bisherigen Datierung, der noch S. Omura folgt, nicht in die 2. Hälfte des 8., sondern in die 2. Hälfte des 9. Jh. zu datieren ist. In den zugehörigen Niveaus findet sich keine handgefertigte Keramik und keine bemalte Keramik in der bisherigen früheisenzeitlichen Tradition mehr. Es entwickelt sich eine neue Grauware mit Glanztonüberzug. Der heute in das 9. Jh. v. Chr. und nicht mehr um 700 zu datierende Anstieg westlicher Einflüsse ist ohne Zweifel auf die machtpolitische Expansion des Reiches von Gordion zurückzuführen, die zur Verbreitung neuer Leitmoden und zur Ausbildung neuer Handelsnetze führte.

Es steht durch diese Untersuchungen fest, daß es entgegen K. Sams und anderen Forschern[18] nicht zum Erscheinen von balkanischen Elementen in Gordion gekommen ist. Balkanische Buckelkeramik als eindeutige Spur einer Zuwanderung ist nur in Troia VIIb zu fassen und für VIIb2 charakteristisch. Selbst im Bereich der Propontis bleibt diese Keramik auf das Gebiet von Troja beschränkt. Bereits in Daskyleion liegt eine eigenständige Entwicklung einer ähnlichen, aber keineswegs zwingend vom Balkan herübergekommenen oder mit einer von dort zugezogenen Bevölkerung zu verbindenden Keramik vor. Das anatolische Plateau hat balkanische Buckelkeramik nicht erreicht.

Was nun die Frage der Chronologie betrifft, so ist YHSS 7B sicher zu Recht in das 12. Jh. zu setzen, endete aber meines Erachtens wahrscheinlich bereits früh im 11. Jh. (s. u.). Die Keramik ist handgemacht. Es handelte sich vermutlich um eine relativ kleine, sich wohl weithin selbst versorgende Gemeinschaft, die jedoch nicht alle gebrauchte Keramik auch lokal hergestellt hat (vgl. besonders Henrickson 1993; 1994; Henrickson, Blackman 1996; Henrickson, Voigt 1998; Voigt, Henrickson 2000a; 2000b).

---

[17] Für weitere Diskussionen danke ich H. Genz.

[18] Vgl. Sams 1994: 19ff; auch Henrickson, Voigt 1998; Voigt, Henrickson 2000a: 46; 2000b räumen sie jedoch ein, keinen wirklichen Beweis für eine Einwanderung der Phryger in YHSS 7B vom Balkan bis nach Gordion erbringen zu können.

In der Schicht YHSS 7A, die von M.M. Voigt 1994, ausgehend von einem Enddatum für YHSS 6A mit 700 v. Chr., auf ca. 1000–950/900? v. Chr. datiert wird[19] und die ohne Hiat oder Bruch auf VIIB folgt, finden wir dann einen charakteristischen Wechsel in der Architektur, in der Technik der Vorratshaltung, im Hausinventar und in einer neuen, in Waren und Technik charakteristischen Keramikproduktion, die sich von nun an kontinuierlich in die altphrygische Zeit entwickelt und die Phase YHSS 6 bestimmt. Allerdings lebte auch die Bevölkerung der Phase 7B mit ihren Traditionen und ihrer Keramik in 7A weiterhin im Ort, bis sie durch Assimilation verschwindet. Offensichtlich ist es in 7A zur Zuwanderung einer Bevölkerungsgruppe gekommen. Die jüngere Gordion-Forschung, welche die Einwanderung der Phryger mit dem Bevölkerungswechsel zu YHSS 7B verbinden möchte, kann für diese Zuwanderung keine wirkliche Deutung geben. Die grauen Waren, welche für YHSS 6-5 charakteristisch werden, sind in 7A nur spärlich vertreten; am Ende der Periode 7A tauchen erst wieder die ersten scheibengedrehten Gefäße auf.

In der folgenden Phase YHSS 6B wurde dann an der Stelle bisheriger Wohnbebauung ein Residenzquartier und die zugehörige erste massive Befestigung der Königsburg, die mehrere Bau- bzw. Umbauphasen aufweist (vgl. DeVries 1990: 373ff), errichtet. In der Architektur zeigt sich deutlich ein Einfluß späthethitischer Vorbilder. Es sind in dem Hofbereich dieses Residenzareals 6 Bau-und Nutzungsphasen dieser Periode festgestellt; in der letzten dieser Phasen wurde eine monumentale Baustruktur errichtet. In 6B entwickelt sich der ältere phrygerzeitliche Keramikkanon. Fragmente von Skulpturen weisen in dieser Phase (Schicht 4) auf engere Beziehungen zur Kultur der hethitischen Nachfolgestaaten hin. In dieser Phase war Gordion ohne Zweifel bereits Sitz eines Königtums von regionaler, eher schon überregionaler Bedeutung. Hier wird somit die Frühphase der Bildung des Reiches von Gordion greifbar. Innerhalb der mächtigen altphrygischen Zitadellenwälle wird dann in YHSS 6A ein großzügig geplantes Palastviertel in einem neuen monumentalen Architekturstil erbaut, das im Destruction Level seinen Untergang fand. Die Errichtung dieses Komplexes muß heute in das beginnende 9. Jh. (Dendrodatum für Terrace Building 2A), sein Ende in die Zeit zwischen 835 und vor 800 datiert werden. In die Phase 6A gehören auch die älteren ausgegrabenen Tumuli der Nekropolen von Gordion. Die ältere Zitadelle der Periode YHSS 6B, die 6 Phasen mit

zahlreichen Bauaktivitäten aufweist und einen längeren Zeitraum umspannt haben muß, ist entsprechend in das 10. Jh. v. Chr. zu datieren und muß eigentlich spätestens ca. 1000 v. Chr. begonnen haben. YHSS 7A ist demnach mit großer Wahrscheinlichkeit dem 11. Jh. v. Chr. zuzuweisen. Damit müssen wir aber auch den Anfang der Reichsbildung von Gordion spätestens in das frühe 10. Jh. v. Chr. setzen und engere Kontakte seiner Führungsschicht zu den zeitgenössischen späthethitischen Staaten und ihrer Kultur voraussetzen.

Zu der Problematik der Phrygerfrage kommt hinzu, daß wir keineswegs von einer einheitlichen Entwicklung eines phrygischen Kulturraums ausgehen können. Vielmehr deutet alles daraufhin, daß wir mit mehreren Gruppen zu rechnen haben, die in der Fremdbenennung von griechischer Seite summarisch als 'Phryges' bezeichnet wurden.[20] Dies ist einmal die Bevölkerungsgruppe Zentralphrygiens, als deren kulturelles Merkmal die phrygischen Felsgräber und Felsfassaden erscheinen, die sich als kulturelles Leitphänomen bis in den Raum von Dorylaion und an den unteren Sangarios und bis nach Pisidien erstrecken.[21] Ihr Verbreitungsgebiet schließt in charakteristischer Weise jenes der phrygischen Tumuli aus, die in Anatolien als eine neue Bestattungssitte erscheinen. Sie sind offenkundig mit der politisch-herrschaftlichen Führungsschicht des Reiches von Gordion zu verbinden. Diese hat im Raum des großen Sangarios-Bogens mit dem Herrschaftszentrum Gordion das Kerngebiet des phrygischen Königtums ausgebildet. Die ältesten bisher erforschten Tumuli gehören nun nach den neuen Daten für Gordion offensichtlich in das 9. Jh. v. Chr. Die monumentale Bestattungssitte der phrygischen Tumulus-Gräber hat sich offensichtlich mit der Machtausbreitung bzw. mit der Ausdehnung der Einflußsphäre dieser Reichsbildung nach Kappadokien (Tabal, Tuwanuwa/Tyana) bis zum Tauros und bis nach Nordlykien (Tumuli von Bayındır) ausgebreitet. Doch auch diese Bestattungssitte der Tumuli ist keineswegs einheitlich. So sind die ca. 20 Tumuli des 9./8.–6. Jh., die dem bedeutenden phrygischen Zentrum Ankyra (Ankara) zugehören (vgl. zu Ankyra jetzt Strobel 2002a: 9, mit Anm. 33), in völligem Gegensatz zu den Bestattungen von Gordion Brandbestattungen; solche Bestattungen erscheinen dort erst in späterer mittelphrygischer Zeit (vgl. Kohler 1980; 1995). Dieser fundamentale Unterschied muß einen für

---

[19] Voigt, Henrickson 2000a: 48: YHSS 6B ca. 900–800; dies erscheint aber bei weitem als zu kurz.

[20] Zur Problematik des Phrygernamens und der modernen wie antiken Bezeichnung phrygisch vgl. Strobel 2001.
[21] Zum nördlichen Pisidien vgl. Fiedler, Taşlıalan 2002. Das Monument am See von Hoyran ist eine Kombination von Kultfassade und Felsgrab des ältesten Typus. Die Datierung in das 8. Jh. ist überzeugend.

uns noch nicht greifbaren religiös-kulturellen, vermutlich auch von verschiedenen Bevölkerungsgruppen getragenen Hintergrund besitzen. Gleiches gilt für die Tatsache, daß Gordion in seiner Glanzzeit in YHSS 6A und 5 keine Parallelen für die ältere und mittlere phygerreichszeitliche Skulptur in Ankyra besitzt, diese sich aber sehr wohl mit jener der hethitischen Nachfolgestaaten in Beziehung setzen läßt. Nur in YHSS 6B haben wir Fragmente vergleichbarer, etwa in das späte 10. Jh. zu datierende Orthostatenbruchstücke wahrscheinlich aus dem jüngeren Torbau der Befestigung (vgl. Sams 1898; Voigt 1994: 271; Voigt, Henrickson 2000a: 50).[22]

Wir haben heute davon auszugehen, daß sich die phrygischen Volksgruppen in Zentralanatolien wie im phrygischen Hochland durch komplexe Prozesse der Ethnogenese und Akkulturation im 11. Jh. v. Chr. gebildet haben.[23] Dabei ist zu beachten, daß die zahlreichen Surveyforschungen im europäischen Teil der Türkei in den letzten Jahren für den Übergang von der Spätbronzezeit zur Eisenzeit gerade keine Phase der Instabilität, der erhöhten Mobilität oder von Abwanderungen aufzeigen.[24] Auch M. Özdoğan verweist darauf, daß die A-Priori-Annahme von Migrationsbewegungen, die sich auf die Aussagen antiker Autoren stützt, keine Bestätigung findet. Ostthrakien und vielleicht ganz Thrakien war im 2. Jt. v. Chr. nur dünn besiedelt; gegenüber der Frühbronzezeit ist ein Rückgang der Siedlungen feststellbar. Während die Frühe Eisenzeit im Nordwesten Anatoliens bisher durch Funde wenig zu fassen ist, trat nun in Ostthrakien ein deutlicher Wandel ein. Es erscheinen zahlreiche Siedlungen, die bezeichnenderweise noch nicht in natürlich geschützten Lagen, wie später üblich, angelegt werden. Ausgenommen von dieser Besiedlung bleiben die Thrakischen Chersones und der nordostägäische Küstensaum, wo die bronzezeitlichen Funde anatolische Prägung aufweisen. Die charakteristische Keramik des thrakischen Raumes (Psenicevo-Gruppe) greift nur in

Troia selbst (VIIb2) aus Kleinasien über. Die Bevölkerungsdichte nimmt in der Frühen Eisenzeit zu, die wirtschaftlichen und sozialen Strukturen erreichen ein neues, höheres Niveau. Zugleich ist auf der asiatischen Seite der Propontis ein Siedlungsrückgang zu bemerken.

Es stellt sich somit die berechtigte Frage, ob die Phryger und die mit ihnen eng verwandten Myser nicht bereits im 2. Jt. v. Chr. die Bevölkerung einer größeren Zone in Nordwestanatolien gestellt haben. So erscheinen sie auch in der Ilias als die Hauptverbündeten Troias und als ein schon lange im Lande ansässiges Volk. Die Phryger verkörpern für Homer auch nicht die Träger der zeitgenössischen Großreichsbildung von Gordion, sondern die Bevölkerung im Bereich der asiatischen Küste der Propontis, wo sie an Ilion angrenzen. Die Phrygisch sprechende Bevölkerung des hellespontischen Phrygien ist heute durch die Zeugnisse aus Daskyleion und anderen Orten gesichert (Bakır, Gusmani 1991; 1993; Bakır 1997; Innocente 1997; Neumann 1997). Das stark befestigte bronzezeitliche Daskyleion kann wohl mit einigem Recht als Zentralort des in den hethitischen Quellen erscheinenden Landes Masa gesehen werden, der auch in der frühen Eisenzeit weiter kontinuierlich besiedelt blieb. Hinzu kommt die Nachricht, daß auch Bithynien ursprünglich phrygisches Siedlungsgebiet gewesen ist. Weder archäologisch noch linguistisch gibt es abgesicherte Beweise für eine phrygische Einwanderung in Kleinasien nach der frühen Bronzezeit.

Nichts spricht also gegen die oben vorgetragene Annahme. Die antike Hypothese einer Einwanderung der Phryger aus Europa, d. h. vom Balkan, ist offenbar auf die Ähnlichkeiten religiöser Rituale und insbesondere auf die in der Antike gebräuchlichen ethymologischen Deutungen bzw. nur onomastisch begründeten Gleichsetzungen zurückzuführen. Ein klassisches Beispiel gibt die bekannte Bryger-Phryger-Gleichsetzung (vgl. dazu auch von Bredow 1997), wobei wir in Wirklichkeit sicher nur von einem gemeinsamen, zugrundeliegenden indoeuropäischen Namensstamm ausgehen dürfen; die zahlreichen daraus gezogenen Argumente der Forschung müssen verworfen werden. Gleiches gilt für die antike Myser-gleich-Moesier-Theorie.[25] Natürlich stellte die Propontis eine Kontaktzone dar.[26] Dies zeigt sich nicht zuletzt im Namensmaterial, wo wir deutlich die Präsenz

---

[22] Sams 1989 hat seine frühere Datierung auf ca. 900 zu ca. 800 korrigiert, dies jedoch mit Rücksicht auf eine Datierung des Endes von YHSS 6A um 700 v. Chr. Die Parallelen legen jedoch eine frühere Datierung nahe.

[23] Vgl. Strobel 1998; 2001; ferner die entsprechende, in der Bibliographie gennante Literatur. Eine Zusammenschau des traditionellen Bildes bieten die Beiträge in Gusmani u. a. 1997; vgl. hierzu auch Strobel 2001.

[24] Vgl. Özdoğan 1993; 1998; Akman 1998; die entsprechenden Berichte in *Araştırma Sonuçları Toplantısı*. Özdoğan weist im übrigen zu Recht darauf hin, daß die frühbronzezeitliche Keramikware sehr leicht mit der früheisenzeitlichen balkanischen verwechselt werden kann. In ersterer ist sehr wahrscheinlich der Ursprung für verschiedene Keramiktraditionen des eisenzeitlichen Nordwestanatolien zu sehen.

[25] Dagegen kennt Herodotus 1, 171 die Myser als Bruderstämme der Lyder und Karer.

[26] Vgl. die differenzierten, gegenüber der 'kanonischen' Sicht eines direkt zusammenhängenden thrakisch-phrygischen Komplexes eher Kritischen Ausführungen: Vassileva 1994; 1998; 2001; zum Kybele-Kult Roller 1999.

thrakischer Bevölkerungselemente in historischer Zeit fassen können, auch wenn bei der Auswertung des Namensmaterials große Vorsicht geboten ist (vgl. Mitchell 1978; French 1994) und bisherige Forschungen oftmals zu stark von der Tendenz, vorgeprägte Annahmen beweisen zu wollen, ausgegangen sind. Erst nach der frühen Eisenzeit scheinen sich die thrakischen Bevölkerungsgruppen mit der Namenswurzel 'Thyn*', die Bithyner, Thyner und Mariandyner, im Norden Kleinasiens ausgebreitet zu haben.[27] In diesem Zusammenhang sind wohl auch die Nachrichten über das Ende der Bebrykes zu sehen, die in der griechischen Mythologie als Volk an der Küste der Propontis noch eine große Rolle spielen und später von den Bithyniern vernichtet wurden (Pliny n. h. 5, 127).

Im 12.–11. Jh. scheinen sich Teile der bronzezeitlichen Bevölkerung Nordwestkleinasiens ins Innere Anatoliens vorgeschoben zu haben, wobei sie offenbar einen Teil ihrer bisherigen Gebiete aufgaben. Nach Gordion sind solche Gruppen offensichtlich als die neue dominierende Schicht mit der Phase YHSS 7A, also wohl relativ früh im 11. Jh. v. Chr., gekommen, haben die vorgefundener Bevölkerung überlagert und überformt und den Impetus zu einer neuen Reichsgründung gegeben, die in vielen Aspekten zum Erbe des hethitischen Großreiches wurde. Für die Ankunft der Gruppen im zentralphrygischen Hochland liegen derzeit keine Datierungshinweise vor. Als Neuerungen brachten sie die religiöse Dominanz der großen, anonymen Muttergottheit, der Matar (Kybeleia), die so im hethitischen Kontext unbekannt gewesen ist und die nun eine wesentliche Rolle in der Königsideologie der Dynastie von Gordion spielte (vgl. etwa Roller 1999).

Abschließend möchte ich noch auf einige weitere, für unsere Frage wichtige Komplexe hinweisen, ohne diese in der Breite ausführen zu können. Dies ist einmal die Tatsache, daß zum Zeitpunkt der beginnenden griechischen Kolonisation an der westanatolischen Küste dort sehr wohl von einem Fortleben der anatolischen Staatlichkeit und Urbanität auszugehen ist. An der Identifizierung von Abasa, der Hauptstadt des Großreiches von Arzawa und nach dessen Ende des Königreiches von Mira,[28] mit Ephesos ist heute nicht mehr zu zweifeln. Die Aufdeckung des bronzezeitlichen Ephesos führt ebenfalls zu einer Revision zahlreicher traditioneller Vorstellungen.

Dieses Alt-Ephesos lag mit seiner befestigten Oberstadt auf dem Ayasoluk-Hügel, an dessen Fuß die entsprechende Unterstadt und der Hafenbereich, verbunden mit der altanatolischen Kultstätte des Artemision, anzunehmen ist (vgl. Büyükkolancı 1997; 2001; 2002; zusammenfassend Höcker, Scherrer 1997). Die Kontinuität der Besiedlung reicht vom 3. Jt. über die protogeometrische und geometrische bis in die archaische Zeit. Die griechische Niederlassung Koressos wurde im späten 11. Jh. in deutlicher Entfernung, und, wie mit gutem Grund anzunehmen ist, mit Duldung durch den Herrscher von Abasa gegründet. Die einheimische Bevölkerung der oberen Stadt wurde schließlich vertrieben (Pausanias 7,2,8; Strabo 14,1,21). Abasa war zu diesem Zeitpunkt bereits als Herrschaftszentrum der Dynastie von Mira, die bereits zu Lebzeiten Suppiluliumas II. die Würde des Großkönigtums erlangt hatte, wohl unter griechischem Druck aufgegeben und das Zentrum nach Sardes verlegt worden. Diese Dynastie können wir sicher zu Recht mit der Herakliden-Dynastie identifizieren, die nach Aussage Herodots bis zu ihrem Sturz durch Gyges ca. 680 v. Chr. 22 Herrschergenerationen oder 505 Jahre geherrscht hatte (Herodotus 1,7,4). Es besteht kein Grund, hier nicht eine in der Herrscherfolge zuverlässige dynastische Überlieferung anzunehmen, die der Halikarnasser Herodot sehr wohl kennen konnte. In Sardes ist die Akropolis im 8. Jh. v. Chr. bereits ausgebaut und das neue Reichszentrum etabliert, wobei sich vermutlich mit Gyges das Ethnikon Lyder durchsetzt.

Doch auch für den zentralanatolischen Kernraum ist nicht von einem völligen Verschwinden politisch-historischer Strukturen zwischen dem Ende des Großkönigtums von Hattuša und der Ausdehnung des Reiches von Gordion östlich des Halys auszugehen. Diese Ausdehnung war, wie die phrygischen Graffiti in Boğazköy und in Pazarlı und nun auch die Steininschrift des 8. Jh. aus Tavium zeigen, mit der Einsiedlung phrygisch sprechender Personengruppen und einer Verbreitung phrygischer Schrift und Sprache verbunden (vgl. Strobel 2002a: 27, 30). Die Forschungen des Verfassers und seiner Mitarbeiter in Tavium, dem altanatolischen Tawinija, und in seinem Territorium, das den gesamten ostgalatischen Raum umfaßte, haben hier in den letzten beiden Jahren zu neuen Ergebnissen geführt. Eine genauere Untersuchung und Aufnahme der Anlage der Çeska Kale etwas nordwestlich von Yozgat, die bisher allgemein als byzantinisch angesehen wurde, haben gezeigt, daß der von einem mächtigen Glacis umzogene Berggipfel und die Felsabarbeitungen des sich über die Glacis-Terrasse erhebenden Felsstocks sowie die in dem Felsen

---

[27] Vgl. Verf., in: *Der Neue Pauly* zu den verschiedenen Lemmata.

[28] Dessen Ausdehnung auch über das Latmos-Gebirge im Südwesten ist durch die hethito-luwische Hieroglypheninschrift am Suratkaya erwiesen; vgl. Peschlow-Bindokat 2002.

getriebenen Gänge und Kammern wesentlich früher zu datieren sind. Die Anlage gehört nach der aufgelesenen und der aus Raublöchern stammenden Keramik eindeutig in das ältere 1. Jt. v. Chr. Einige Funde weisen die Frühgeschichte des Komplexes zumindest bis in das Chalkolithikum zurück. Der stark durch menschliche Eingriffe umgestaltete Felsstock des ehemaligen Vulkangipfels ist von einer Terrasse umzogen, die mit einem durch rechteckige Türme verstärkten Wall befestigt gewesen ist. In das Befestigungssystem einbezogen ist die künstliche Anlage eines großen Zisternenbeckens, das seine direkte Parallele in der Zisterne auf der Kale des Kerkenes Dağ hat. Auch das Glacis entspricht völlig jenem der Kale des Kerkenes, wie ein Vergleich der original erhaltenen Partien zeigt. Gleiches gilt für das Glacis der phrygerzeitlichen Befestigung der Büyükkale. Die gefundene Büyükkale II-Keramik verweist den Ausbau der Çeska Kale in das 9.-8. Jh. v. Chr. Damit ist die von G.D. Summers vertretene Spätdatierung der Kale auf dem Kerkenes nicht mehr haltbar (vgl. Summers 1995; 1997; 2000; 2001). Die Anlage der Kale ist im Gegenteil, wie jetzt mit gutem Grund anzunehmen ist, der Errichtung der gewaltigen Stadtanlage um 600 v. Chr. zeitlich voraus-gegangen. Wir haben in der Anlage dieser Zitadellen mit Glacis-Befestigung offensichtlich eine hier erstmals faßbare politische und historische Entwicklung vor uns, die sich vermutlich von diesem Südrand des nördlichen Kappadokien bis in das Hinterland der pontischen Küste erstreckt hat, wo wir bisher nur den Komplex von Akalan etwas näher kennen (vgl. Strobel 2002a: 29ff). Daß es sich bei dem Land der Kaskäer und der Pläer im Norden des hethitischen Kernlandes nicht um wilde Barbaren gehandelt hat, wie die Topik der hethitischen Quellen zu vermitteln sucht, sondern sich hier in der Spätbronzezeit sehr wohl politische Strukturen und auch befestigte Zentren ausgebildet hatten, das zeigen sehr gut die Survey-Ergebnisse des Paphlagonien-Projektes des BIAA (vgl. Die Web-Datenbank des Paphlagonia-Projektes und die entsprechenden Berichte über die verschiedenen Surveys in *Araştırma Sonuçları Toplantısı*), wobei hier, wie ich meine, keineswegs bei größeren Anlagen eine hethitische Urheberschaft angenommen werden muß. Auch die große Zahl der eisenzeitlichen Tumuli im nördlichen Mittelanatolien werfen die Frage nach der Herkunft dieser Bestat-tungssitte in Tavium, Ankyra und Gordion erneut auf. Diese Fragen können hier nicht weiter diskutiert werden, doch ist mit großem Interesse auf die weiteren Forschungsergebnisse im nördlichen Mittelanatolien zu achten. Die Großreichsbildung von Gordion hat aber wohl auch größere Teile dieses Raumes und der sich in ihm entwickelnden politischen Strukturen erfaßt.

**Bibliographie**

Akman, M. 1998: 'Die Ausgrabung der megalithischen Dolmenanlage in Lalapaşa' in N. Tuna, Z. Aktüre, M. Lynch (eds), *Thracians and Phrygians: Problems of Parallelism*. Ankara: 65–70

Akurgal, E. 1983: 'Das dunkle Zeitalter Kleinasiens' in S. Deger-Jalkotzy (eds), *Griechenland, die Ägäis und die Levante während der 'Dark Ages' vom 12. bis zum 9. Jh. v. Chr.* Wien: 67–78

Baker, H.D. u.a. 1995: 'Kilise Tepe 1994' *Anatolian Studies* 45: 139–91

Bakır, T. 1997: 'Phryger in Daskyleion' in R. Gusmani, M. Salvini, P. Vanicelli (eds), *Frigi e Frigio*. Rom: 229–38

Bakır, T., Gusmani, R. 1991: 'Eine neue phrygische Inschrift aus Daskyleion' *Epigraphica Anatolica* 18: 157–64

— 1993: 'Graffiti aus Daskyleion' *Kadmos* 32: 135–44

Bartonek, A. 1999: 'Das Alphabet der archaischen griechischen Inschriften von Pithekussai' in *XI Congresso Internazionale di Epigraphia Greca e Latina, Atti I*. Rom: 177–81

Bayburtluoğlu, I. 1979: 'Eskiyapar Frig Çağı' in E. Akurgal, B. Alkım, S. Alp, B.S. Baykal, A. Erzi, U. Iğdemir, T. Özgüç, A. Soyalı (eds), *VIII Türk Tarih Kongresi*. Ankara: 293–303

Beck, H., Steuer, H. (eds) 1998: *Germanen, Germania, Germanische Altertumskunde* (Reallexikon der Germanischen Altertumskunde Bd. 11). Berlin, New York

Bietak, M. (ed.) 2000: *The Synchronisation of Civilisations in the Eastern Mediterranean in the Second Millennium BC*. Wien

Bilgi, O. 1999: 'İkiztepe in the Late Iron Age' *Anatolian Studies* 49: 27–54

Bittel, K. 1942: *Kleinasiatische Studien* (Istanbuler Mitteilungen -Beih. 5). Istanbul

— 1983: 'Die archäologische Situation in Kleinasien um 1200 v. Chr. und während der nachfolgenden vier Jahrhunderte' in S. Deger-Jalkotzy (ed.), *Griechenland, die Ägäis und die Levante während der 'Dark Ages' vom 12. bis zum 9. Jh. v. Chr.* Wien: 25–47

Bossert, E.-M. 1993: 'Zum Datum der Zerstörung des phrygischen Gordion' *Istanbuler Mitteilungen* 43: 287–92

— 2000: *Die Keramik phrygischer Zeit von Boğazköy.* Mainz

Braun, T.F.R.G. 1982: 'The Greeks in the Near East' in J. Boardman, N.G.L. Hammond (eds), *The Cambridge Ancient History (2nd edition). Volume III. Part 3 : The Expansion of the Greek World, Eighth to Sixth Centuries BC*. Cambridge: 1–31

Brixhe, C. 1993: 'Du paléo- au néophrygien' *Comptes rendus des séances de l'Académie des Inscriptions et Belles-Lettres* 1993: 323–44

— 1994: 'Le Phrygien' in F. Bader (ed.), *Langues indoeuropéennes*. Paris: 165–78

— 1999: 'Prolegomènes au corpus neo-phrygien' *Bulletin de la Société de linguistique de Paris* 94: 285–315

Brixhe, C., Lejeune, M. 1984: *Corpus des inscriptions paléo-phrygiennes*. Paris

Brunner, K., Merta, B. (eds) 1994: *Ethnogenese und Überlieferung*. Wien, München

Buluç, S. 1979: *Ankara Frig Nekropolünden Üç Tümülüs Buluntuları*. Ankara

— 1992: 'Anadolu'da kremasyon (ölü yakma) geleneği' *Anadolu Medeniyetleri Müzesi 1991 Yıllığı*: 83–101

Büyükkolancı, M. 1997: 'Ayasoluk Tepesi (Eski Efes) 1996 Yılı Kazıları' *Müze çalışmaları ve kurtama kazıları sempozyumu* 8: 69–83

— 2001: 'Selçuk Ayasoluk Tepesi 1999 Yılı Kazıları' *Müze çalışmaları ve kurtama kazıları sempozyumu* 11: 1–4

— 2002: 'St. Jean Anıtı ve Ayasoluk Tepesi 2000 yılı kazı ve onarım çalışmaları' *Müze çalışmaları ve kurtama kazıları sempozyumu* 12: 237–40

Çilingiroğlu, A., Salvini, M. 2001: 'Historical background of Ayanis' in A. Çilingiroğlu, M. Salvini (eds), *Ayanis I*. Rom: 15–24

Cogan, M., Tadmor, H. 1977: 'Gyges and Assurbanipal' *Orientalia* 46: 65–85

Cummer, W.W. 1976: 'Iron Age pottery from Akalan' *Istanbuler Mitteilungen* 26: 31–9

Deger-Jalkotzy, S. (ed.) 1983: *Griechenland, die Ägäis und die Levante während der 'Dark Ages' vom 12. bis zum 9. Jh. v. Chr.* Wien

— (ed.) 1991: *Die Erforschung des Zusammenbruchs der sogenannten mykenischen Kultur und der sogenannten dunklen Jahrhunderte*. Stuttgart

DeVries, K. 1990: 'The Gordion excavation seasons of 1969–1973 and subsequent research' *American Journal of Archaeology* 94: 371–406

Dinçol, A.M. 1998: 'Die Entdeckung des Felsmonuments von Hatip' *TÜBA-AR* 1: 27–35

Dobesch, G. 1983: 'Historische Fragestellungen in der Urgeschichte' in S. Deger-Jalkotzy (ed.), *Griechenland, die Ägäis und die Levante während der 'Dark Ages' vom 12. bis zum 9. Jh. v. Chr.* Wien: 179–230

Dönmez, S. 2001: 'A new look to the pottery of the Late Iron and Hellenistic ages in the Kızılırmak bend region in the view of two painted vessels at the Amasya Museum [türk. mit engl. Zus.]' *TÜBA-AR* 4: 89–99

Drew-Bear, T. 1998: 'Gordion' in H. Cancik, H. Schneider (eds), *Der Neue Pauly: Enzyklopädie der Antike*. Stuttgart, Weimar: 1146

Drews, R. 1993: *The End of the Bronze Age*. Princeton

Fiedler, G., Taşlıalan, M. 2002: 'Un monument rupestre phrygien au bord du lac de Hoyran' *Anatolica Antiqua* 10: 97–112

Fıratlı, N. 1959: 'Ankara Frig nekropolüne ait bir buluntu' *Belleten* 23: 203–11

Francovich, G. De 1990: *Sanctuari e tombe rupestri dell'antica Phrygia*. Rom

French, D.H. 1994: 'Thracians in northwestern Asia Minor' in Fondation Européenne Dragan, Centre Européenne d'Etudes Thraces, Conseil International des Etudes Indo-Européenne et Thraces, *Europa Indo-Europea. Atti del VIo Congresso Internazionale di Tracologia e VIIo Symposio di Studi Traci. Palma da Mallorca 24–28 Marzo 1992*. Rom: 24–8

Frerich, K. 1981: *Begriffsbildung und Begriffsanwendung in der Vor- und Frühgeschichte*. Frankfurt

Gates M.H. 1999: '1997 archaeological excavations at Kinet Höyük (Yeşil-Dörtyol, Hatay)' *Kazı Sonuçları Toplantısı* 20.I: 259–81

— 2000: '1998 excavations at Kinet Höyük (Yeşil-Dörtyol, Hatay)' *Kazı Sonuçları Toplantısı* 21.I: 193–208

— 2001: '1999 excavations at Kinet Höyük (Yeşil-Dörtyol, Hatay)' *Kazı Sonuçları Toplantısı* 22.I: 203–22

— 2002: 'Kinet Höyük 2000 (Yeşil-Dörtyol, Hatay)' *Kazı Sonuçları Toplantısı* 23.II: 55–62

Genz, H. 2000: 'Die Eisenzeit in Zentralanatolien im Lichte der keramischen Funde von Büyükkaya in Boğazköy /Hattuša' *TÜBA-AR* 3: 35–54

— 2001 'Iron Age pottery from Çadır Höyük' *Anatolica* 27: 159–70

Gorny, R.L., McMahon, G., Paley, S., Kealhofer, L. 1995: 'The Alişar Regional Project 1994' *Anatolica* 21: 65–100

Gunter, A.C. 1991: *The Bronze Age* (The Gordion Excavations Final Reports 3). Philadelphia

Gusmani, R., Salvini, M., Vanicelli, P. (eds) 1997: *Frigi e Frigio*. Rom

Haas, V. 1994: *Geschichte der hethitischen Religion*. Leiden u.a.

Hansen, C.K., Postgate, J.N. 1999: 'Bronze to Iron Age transition at Kilise Tepe' *Anatolian Studies* 49: 111–21

Heckmann, F. 1992: *Ethnische Minderheiten, Volk und Nation*. Stuttgart

Henrickson, R.C. 1993: 'Politics, economics, and ceramic continuity at Gordion in the late second and first millennia BC' in W.D. Kingery (ed.), *The Social and Cultural Contexts of New Ceramic Technologies*. Westerville, Ohio: 89–176

— 1994: 'Continuity and discontinuity in the ceramic tradition at Gordion during the Iron Age' in A. Çilingiroğlu, D.H. French (eds), *Anatolian Iron Ages 3* (British Institute of Archaeology at Ankara Monograph 16). Ankara: 95–129

Henrickson, R.C., Blackman, M.J. 1996: 'Large-scale production of pottery at Gordion' *Paléorient* 22: 67–87

Henrickson, R.C., Voigt, M.M. 1998: 'The Early Iron Age at Gordion: the evidence from the Yassıhöyük Stratigraphic Sequence' in N. Tuna, Z. Aktüre, M. Lynch (eds), *Thracians and Phrygians: Problems of Parallelism*. Ankara: 79–106

Höcker, C., Scherrer, P. 1997: 'Ephesos' in H. Cancik, H. Schneider (eds), *Der Neue Pauly: Enzyklopädie der Antike Bd. 3*. Stuttgart, Weimar: 1078–85

Högemann, P. 2001: 'Troias Untergang — was dann?' in *Troia. Traum und Wirklichkeit*. Stuttgart: 58–63

Innocente, L. 1997: 'Questioni di onomastica frigia' in R. Gusmani, M. Salvini, P. Vanicelli (eds), *Frigi e Frigio*. Rom: 33–40

Jefferey, L.H. 1980: 'The graffiti' in M.R. Popham, L.H. Sackett (eds), *Lefkandi I: The Iron Age Settlement, The Cemeteries*. London: 89–93

Kohler, E. 1980: 'Cremations of the middle Phrygian Period at Gordion' in K. DeVries (ed.), *From Athens to Gordion*. Philadelphia: 65–89

— 1995: *The Lesser Phrygian Tumuli I. The Inhumations* (The Gordion Excavations Final Reports 2,1). Philadelphia

Kuniholm, P. 1977: *Dendrochronology at Gordion and on the Anatolian Plateau*. Unpublished PhD thesis. University of Pennsylvania

— 1993: 'A millennium of tree rings from Gordion' *American Journal of Archaeology* 97: 303

Kyrieleis, H., Röllig, W. 1988: 'Ein altorientalischer Pferdeschmuck aus dem Heraion von Samos' *Athener Mitteilungen* 103: 37–42

Lazzarini, M.L. 1999: 'Iscrizioni greche e mondo arcaico. Vecchi e nuovi problemi' *XI Congresso Internazionale di Epigraphia Greca e Latina, Atti I*. Rom: 111–24

Lehmann, G.A. 1970: 'Der Untergang des hethitischen Großreiches und die neuen Texte aus Ugarit' *Ugarit-Forschungen* 2: 39–73

— 1983: 'Zum Auftreten der Seevölker-Gruppen im östlichen Mittelmeerraum — eine Zwischenbilanz' in S. Deger-Jalkotzy (ed.), *Griechenland, die Ägäis und die Levante während der 'Dark Ages' vom 12. bis zum 9. Jh. v. Chr.* Wien: 79–92

— 1985: *Die mykenisch-frühgriechisch Welt und der östliche Mittelmeerraum in der Zeit der 'Seevölker'-Invasionen um 1200 v. Chr.* Opladen

— 1996: 'Umbrüche und Zäsuren im östlichen Mittelmeerraum und Vorderasien zur Zeit der 'Seevölker'-Invasionen um und nach 1200 v. Chr.' *Historische Zeitschrift* 262: 1–38

Lejeune, M. 1969: 'Discussion sur l'alphabet phrygien' *Studi Micenei ed Egeo-Anatolici* 10: 19–47

Lloyd, S., Gökce, N. 1951: 'Excavations at Polatlı' *Anatolian Studies* l: 21–75

Makridi, T. 1926: 'Ankara Hüyüklarindeki hafriyata dair' *Maarif Vekaleti Mecmuası* 6: 38–45

Manning, S.W. 1999: *A Test of Time: The Volcano of Thera and the Chronology and History of the Aegean and East Mediterranean in the Mid Second Millennium BC*. Oxford

Manning, S.W., Kromer, B., Kuniholm, P.I., Newton, M.W. 2001a: 'Anatolian tree rings and a new chronology for east Mediterranean Bronze-Iron Ages' *Science* 294/5551: 2532–5

Manning, S.W., Kromer, B., Kuniholm, P.I., Newton, M.W., Spurk, M., Levin, I. 2001b: 'Regional 14CO$^2$ offsets in the troposphere: magnitudes, mechanisms, and consequences' *Science* 294/5551: 2529–32

Mansel, A.M. 1974: 'Das Kuppelgrab von Kutluca (West-Bithynien)' *Thracia* 3: 207–20

Marek, C. 1993: 'Euboia und die Entstehung der Alphabetschrift bei den Griechen' *Klio* 75: 27–44

Masson, O. 1991: 'Anatolian languages' in J. Boardman, I.E.S. Edwards, N.G.L. Hammond, E. Sollberger (eds), *The Cambridge Ancient History (2nd edition). Volume III. Part 2: The Assyrian and Babylonian Empires and other States of the Near East from the Eighth to the Sixth Centuries BC*. Cambridge: 666–76

Metin, M. 1997: 'Ulus Kazısı 1995' *Müze Kurtuma Kazıları Semineri* 7: 199–220

Metin, M., Akalın, M. 1999: 'Ankara-Ulus Kazısı Frig Seramiği' *Anadolu Medeniyetleri Müzesi 1998 Yıllığı*. Ankara: 141–62

Mitchell, S. 1978: 'Onomastic survey of Mysia and the Asiatic shore of the Propontis' *Pulpudeva* 2: 119–27

Mühlmann, W.E. 1985: 'Ethnologie und Ethnogenese' in *Studien zur Ethnogenese* (Abhandlungen der Rheinisch-Westfälische Akademie der Wissenschaften 72). Opladen: 9–27

Muscarella, O. 1967: *Phrygian Fibulae from Gordion*. London

— 1989: 'King Midas of Phrygia and the Greeks' in K. Emre, B. Hrouda, M. Mellink, N. Özgüç (eds), *Anatolia and the Ancient Near East*. Ankara: 333–42

Naumann, F. 1983: *Die Ikonographie der Kybele in der phrygischen und der griechischen Kunst*. Tübingen

Naveh, J. 1982: *Early History of the Alphabet. An Introduction to West Semitic Epigraphy and Palaeography*. Jerusalem, Leiden

Nenci, G. 1998: 'L'introduction de l'alphabet en Grèce selon Hérodot (V 58)' *Revue des Études Anciennes* 100 : 579–89

Neumann, G. 1988: *Phrygisch und Griechisch*. Wien

— 1997: 'Die zwei Inschriften auf der Stele von Vezirhan' in R. Gusmani, M. Salvini, P. Vanicelli (eds), *Frigi e Frigio*. Rom: 13–31

Niemeier, W.-D. 1998: 'The Myceneans in western Anatolia and the problem of the origins of the Sea Peoples' in S. Gitin, A. Mazar, E. Stern (eds), *Mediterranean Peoples in Transition*. Jerusalem: 17–65

—1999: 'Mycenaeans and Hittites in war in western Asia Minor' *Aegaeum* 19: 141–55

Oettinger, N. 1999: 'Alphabetschriften' in H. Cancik, H. Schneider (eds), *Der Neue Pauly: Enzyklopädie der Antike Bd. 6*. Stuttgart, Weimar: 558–9

Olshausen, E. 2000: 'Phryges, Phrygia' in H. Cancik, H. Schneider (eds), *Der Neue Pauly: Enzyklopädie der Antike Bd. 9*. Stuttgart, Weimar: 965–7

Oren, E.D. (ed.) 2000: *The Sea Peoples and Their World: A Reassessment*. Philadelphia

Özait, M. 2000: '1997 ve 1998 yılı Tokat-Zile ve Çevresi yüzey araştırmaları' *Araştırma Sonuçları Toplantısı* 17: 72–88

Özdoğan, M. 1993: 'The second millennium of the Marmara region' *Istanbuler Mitteilungen* 43: 151–63

— 1998: 'Early Iron Age in eastern Thrace and the megalithic monuments' in N. Tuna, Z. Aktüre, M. Lynch (eds), *Thracians and Phrygians: Problems of Parallelism*. Ankara: 29–40

Özgen, E., Özgen, İ. (eds) 1988: *Antalya Museum Catalogue*. Ankara

Özgüç, T. 1971: *Kültepe and its Vicinity in the Iron Age*. Ankara

Parker, V. 1995: 'Bemerkungen zu den Zügen der Kimmerier und der Skythen durch Vorderasien' *Klio* 77: 7–34

Peschlow-Bindokat, A. 2002, 'Die Hethiter im Latmos' *Antike Welt* 33.2: 211–15

Petrova, E. 1998: 'Bryges and Phrygians: parallelism between the Balkans and Asia Minor through archaeological, linguistic and historical evidence' in N. Tuna, Z. Aktüre, M. Lynch (eds), *Thracians and Phrygians: Problems of Parallelism*. Ankara: 45–54

Poruciuc, A. 1998: 'Phrygian and the southeast European Namebund' in N. Tuna, Z. Aktüre, M. Lynch (eds), *Thracians and Phrygians: Problems of Parallelism*. Ankara: 115–18

Prayon, F. 1987: *Phrygische Plastik*. Tübingen

Reimer, P.J. 2001: 'A new twist in the radiocarbon tale' *Science* 294/5551: 2494–5

Roller, L.E. 1987: *The Non-verbal Graffiti, Dipinti, and Stamps* (Gordion Special Studies 1). Philadelphia

— 1989: 'The art of writing at Gordion' *Expedition* 31: 54–61

— 1991: 'The Great Mother at Gordion: the Hellenization of an Anatolian cult' *Journal of Hellenic Studies* 111: 128–43

— 1999: *In Search of God the Mother. The Cult of Anatolian Cybele*. Berkeley, Los Angeles, London

Romano, I.B. 1995: *The Terracotta Figurines and Related Vessels* (Gordion Special Studies 2). Philadelphia

Rübekeil, L. 1992: *Suebica. Völkernamen und Ethnos*. Innsbruck

Sader, H.S. 1987: *Les états araméns de Syrie depuis leur fondation jusqu'à leur transformation en provinces assyriennes*. Beirut, Wiesbaden

Salvini, M. 2001: 'The inscriptions of Ayanis' in A. Çilingiroğlu, M. Salvini (eds), *Ayanis I*. Rom: 251–319

Sams, G.K. 1989: 'Sculpted orthostates at Gordion' in K. Emre, B. Hrouda, M. Mellink, N. Özgüç (eds), *Anatolia and the Ancient Near East*. Ankara: 447–54

— 1994: *The Early Phrygian Pottery* (The Gordion Excavations Final Reports 4). Philadelphia

Schachermeyr, F. 1982: *Die Levante im Zeitalter der Wanderungen vom 13. bis zum 11. Jahrhundert v. Chr*. Wien

— 1986: *Mykene und das Hethiterreich*. Wien

Seeher, J. 1996: 'Die Ausgrabungen in Boğazköy-Hattuša 1995' *Archäologischer Anzeiger* 1996: 334–62

— 1997: 'Die Ausgrabungen in Boğazköy-Hattuša 1996' *Archäologischer Anzeiger* 1997: 317–41

— 1998: 'Die Ausgrabungen in Boğazköy-Hattuša 1997' *Archäologischer Anzeiger* 1998: 215–41

— 1999: 'Die Ausgrabungen in Boğazköy-Hattuša 1998' *Archäologischer Anzeiger* 1999: 317–44

— 2000: 'Die Ausgrabungen in Boğazköy-Hattuša 1999' *Archäologischer Anzeiger* 2000: 355–76

— 2001 'Die Zerstörung der Stadt Hattusa' in G. Wilhelm (ed.), *Akten des IV Internationalen Kongresses für Hethitologie*. Mainz: 623–34

— 2002: *Hattuša-Führer. Ein Tag in der hethitischen Hauptstadt*. Istanbul

Spalinger, J. 1978: 'The death of Gyges and its historical implications' *Journal of the American Oriental Society* 98: 400–9

Strobel, K. 1994a: 'Galatien und seine Grenzregionen' in E. Schwertheim (ed.), *Forschungen in Galatien* (Asia Minor Studien 12). Bonn: 29–65

— 1994b: 'Keltensieg und Galatersieger' in E. Schwertheim (ed.), *Forschungen in Galatien* (Asia Minor Studien 12). Bonn: 67–96

— 1996: *Die Galater. Geschichte und Eigenart der keltischen Staatenbildung auf dem Boden des hellenistischen Kleinasien I.* Berlin

— 1998: 'Dacii. Despre complexitatea mări milor etnice, politice şi culturale ale istoriei spatiului Dunării de Jos. I' *Studii si cercetări de Istorie Veche şi Archeologie* 49: 61–95

— 2001: 'Phryger - Lyder - Meder: Politische, ethnische und kulturelle Größen Zentralanatoliens bei Errichtung der achaimenidischen Herrschaft' in T. Bakır (ed.), *Achaemenid Anatolia.* Leiden: 43–55

— 2002a: 'State formation by the Galatians of Asia Minor. Politico-historical and cultural processes in Hellenistic central Anatolia' *Anatolica* 28: 1–46

— 2002b: 'Die Staatenbildung bei den kleinasiatischen Galatern' in H. Blum, B. Faist, P. Pfälzner, A.M. Wittke (eds), *Brückenland Anatolien.* Tübingen: 231–93

— 2003 'Das Ende der Bronzezeit und das "Dunkle Zeitalter": Eine Phase der Völkerverschiebungen zwischen Balkan und Zentralanatolien?' in C. Kacso (ed.), *Bronzezeitliche Kulturerscheinungen im Karpatischen Raum, Die Beziehungen zu den benachbarten Gebieten.* Baia Mare: 429–44

Strobel, K., Gerber, C. 2000: 'Tavium (Büyüknefes, Provinz Yozgat) — Ein überregionales Zentrum Anatoliens' *Istanbuler Mitteilungen* 50: 165–215

Summers, G.D. 1995: 'The regional research of Kerkenes Dağ' *Anatolian Studies* 45: 43–68

— 1997: 'The identification of the Iron Age city on the Kerkenes Dağ' *Journal of Near Eastern Studies* 56: 81–94

— 2000: 'The Median Empire reconsidered: a view from Kerkenes Dağ' *Anatolian Studies* 50: 55–73

— 2001: 'Keykavus Kale and associated remains on the Kerkenes Dağ in Cappadocia, central Turkey' *Anatolia Antiqua* 9: 39–60

Temizsoy, İ. Arslan, M., Akalın, M., Metin, M. 1996: 'Ulus Kazısı 1995' *Anadolu Medeniyetleri Müzesi 1995 Yıllığı.* Ankara: 7–36

Temizsoy, İ., Lumsden, S. 1999: 'Gavurkalesi 1998' *Anadolu Medeniyetleri Müzesi 1998 Yıllığı.* Ankara: 53–85

Tezcan, B. 1992: '1969 Göllüdağ Kazısı' *Türk Arkeoloji Dergisi* 30: 1–29

Troia 2001: *Troia — Traum und Wirklichkeit* (Katalog-Handbuch). Stuttgart

Tuna, N., Aktüre, Z., Lynch, M. (eds) 1998: *Thracians and Phrygians: Problems of Parallelism.* Ankara

Vassileva, M. 1994: 'Thrace and Phrygia. Some typological parallels' in Fondation Européenne Dragan, Centre Européenne d'Etudes Thraces, Conseil International des Etudes Indo-Européenne et Thraces, *Europa Indo-Europea. Atti del VIo Congresso Internazionale di Tracologia e VIIo Symposio di Studi Traci. Palma da Mallorca 24–28 Marzo 1992.* Rom: 221–7

— 1998: 'Thracian-Phrygian cultural zone' in N. Tuna, Z. Aktüre, M. Lynch (eds), *Thracians and Phrygians: Problems of Parallelism.* Ankara: 13–17

— 2001: 'Further consideration on the cult of Kybele' *Anatolian Studies* 51: 51–63

Voigt, M.M. 1994: 'Excavations at Gordion 1988–1989: The Yassıhöyük Stratigraphic Sequence' in A. Çilingiroğlu, D.H. French (eds), *Anatolian Iron Ages 3* (British Institute of Archaeology at Ankara Monograph 16). Ankara: 265–93

— 1997: 'Gordion' in E.M. Meyers (ed.), *Oxford Encyclopedia of Near Eastern Archaeology 2.* Oxford: 426–31

Voigt, M.M., Henrickson, R.C. 2000a: 'Formation of the Phrygian state: the Early Iron Age at Gordion' *Anatolian Studies* 50: 37–54

— 2000b: 'The Early Iron Age at Gordion: the evidence from the Yassıhöyük Stratigraphic Sequence' in E.D. Oren (ed.), *The Sea Peoples and Their World: A Reassessment.* Philadelphia: 327–60

Voigt, M.M., Young, T.C. Jr. 1999: 'From Phrygian capital to Achaemenid entrepot: middle and late Phrygian Gordion' *Iranica Antiqua* 34: 192–240

Voigt, M.M., DeVries, K., Henrickson, R.C., Lawall, M., Marsh, B., Gürsan-Salzmann, A., Young, T.C. Jr. 1997: 'Fieldwork at Gordion: 1993–1995' *Anatolica* 23: 1–59

von Bredow, I. 1997: 'Bryges' in H. Cancik, H. Schneider (eds), *Der Neue Pauly: Enzyklopädie der Antike Bd. 2.* Stuttgart, Weimar: 806

Wachter, R. 2001: 'Die Troia-Geschichte wird schriftlich' in *Troia — Traum und Wirklichkeit* (Katalog-Handbuch). Stuttgart: 77–80

Ward, W.A., Joukowsky, M.S. (eds) 1992: *The Crisis Years: the Twelfth Century BC from Beyond the Danube to the Tigris.* Dubuque, Iowa

Wenskus, R. 1961 (ND. 1977): *Stammesbildung und Verfassung. Das Werden der frühmittelalterlichen Gentes.* Köln, Graz

Wittke, A. 1999: 'Frühe Eisenzeit' in H. Cancik, H. Schneider (eds), *Der Neue Pauly: Enzyklopädie der Antike Bd. 6.* Stuttgart, Weimar: 534–5

Zgusta, L. 1964: *Kleinasiatische Personennamen.* Heidelberg

— 1970: *Neue Beiträge zur kleinasiatischen Anthroponymie.* Prag

— 1984: *Kleinasiatische Ortsnamen.* Heidelberg

# Early Iron Age societies of the Black Sea region and Anatolia: some observations

## Gocha R. Tsetskhladze
*University of Melbourne*

### Abstract

The paper gives a general overview of the current state of scholarship concerning the relationship between the Early Iron Age societies of the Black Sea region and Anatolia. Its main aim is to highlight methodological problems and how academics studying each of these regions can enrich the research of those studying the other.

### Özet

Bu çalışma Karadeniz Bölgesi'ndeki Erken Demir Çağı toplulukları ile Anadolu arasındaki ilişkileri inceleyen çalışmaların şu andaki durumlarına genel bir bakıştır. Başlıca amacı metodoloji problemlerini aydınlatmak ve bu bölgelerden herhangi birini inceleyen bir akademisyenin, diğer bölgeyi inceleyen, bir başka akademisyenin çalışmasını nasıl zenginleştirebileceğini ortaya koymaktır.

Interaction of the Early Iron Age societies of the Black Sea region with Anatolia is an academic subject addressed quite frequently. There is not only a large number of articles, papers and notes (see bibliography in Tsetskhladze 1999: 488–96) but also a lengthy book by Jan Bouzek (1997). Despite the popularity of this theme, there are many questions and unsolved problems. The main disadvantage of the existing studies lies largely in the methodological approaches they embody. Specialists in ancient central and eastern Europe look at this problem with respect to their own territories, using material from Anatolia just for simple comparisons to illustrate their own conclusions: they seldom examine the Anatolian material in its own right and its own complexity. Likewise, specialists in Iron Age Anatolia use material from the Black Sea region, especially the Balkans, the Ukrainian steppes and the Caucasus, in a similar fashion. Nevertheless, scholars from each branch of knowledge recognise the importance of the material from the other, and it is obvious that there were very close links between these two regions (Mellaart 1971; Dimitrov 1971; Hoddinott 1986; French 1994; Mihailov 1991; Tuna, Aktüre, Lynch 1998).

From ancient Greek and Roman authors we know that the Black Sea region was populated by Thracians, Getae, Cimmerians, Scythians, Colchians, Mariandyni,

Tibareni, Chalybes, Macrones, etc. Archaeology also demonstrates the very complex ethno-political situation indicated by the written sources (Tsetskhladze 1998: 44–50). Here we face another methodological problem: the information of ancient authors is not contemporary with the Early Iron Age, and it must be used with great care for that period. It is very difficult to establish how far archaeological culture may reflect ethnicity. The problem of ethnicity has been acknowledged by scholars, and more and more work is appearing about it, but the main focus currently is on ancient Greek ethnicity (see, for example, Cohen 2000; Malkin 2001; Morris 2000: 3–36).

To demonstrate how difficult and important it is to establish correlations between written and archaeological evidence, I shall give a few examples. We have written sources, ancient Greek as well as Near Eastern, about the Cimmerians (Ivantchik 1991; 1993; 2001; Sauter 2000: 82–248). According to this evidence, they were a very important and powerful people, playing a prominent role in the history of the kingdoms of the Anatolian Early Iron Age. Archaeologically, we know nothing about the Cimmerians; they are still mysterious for us. Many generations of scholars have tried to identify them, but without much success (Ivantchik 1994; 1995; 1996; Tsetskhladze 1999: 483–5).

Furthermore, in many writings, especially on Anatolian Early Iron Age archaeology, many events are linked to the Cimmerians, despite our archaeological ignorance of them (see, for example, Kuhrt 1995: 499–500, 547–72 with further references). Use is even made of the term 'Cimmerian Destruction Level', but nobody can show that there is anything Cimmerian in these levels (Grantovskii et al. 1997; Kristensen 1988). If something cannot be explained otherwise, it is always ascribed to these mysterious Cimmerians. At the same time, eastern European archaeologists trying to identify the Cimmerians archaeologically have realised that it is an impossible task with our current level of knowledge, and instead use 'pre-Scythian' or 'early Scythian' to describe the cultures of the ninth to eighth centuries BC in a huge territory encompassing the steppes of modern-day eastern Europe (Alekseev et al. 1993; Pogrebova et al. 1998). Another clear example of the difficulties is early Scythian culture. We know much about the Scythians from the Classical period (Ilinskaya, Terenozhkin 1983: 115–200; Alekseev 1992: 113–57; Boardman 1994: 192–217), but the Early Iron Age/Archaic period is full of problems and uncertainties. We do not even know their homeland. Several conflicting theories have been advanced (Chlenova 1997; Murzin 1990; Murzin, Skory 1994; Pogrebova 1993). From written sources we know that they followed the Cimmerians to the Near East, including Anatolia (Pogrebova, Raevsii 1993). Scythian objects, especially those executed in animal style, have very close parallels with the animal style of Anatolia and the whole Near East (see, for example, Blek 1976; Ilinskaya 1976; Ghirshman 1979; Galanina 1991; Kurochkin 1992; Pogrebova, Raevskii 1992; Korenyako 1998). Thus here we face the problem of distinguishing what is purely Scythian when the culture was so heavily influenced by the Near East (Bouzek 2001). At the same time, in the writings of academics studying the Anatolian Early Iron Age, we find many events being linked to the presence and activities of the Scythians there (see Dyakonov 1994; Kurochkin 1994). In reality, we do not know how long the Scythians spent in the Near East, nor what was the extent of their activities. Written sources offer little information, and when they do it is contradictory (Ivantchik 1999). Z. Derin and O. Muscarella (2001: 200–3) recently raised, once more, the important question of the socketed arrowheads recorded at Urartian sites in the seventh century BC and their ethnic attribution. I agree with them in questioning how far modern scholarship can make such an attribution with accuracy when there are so many unresolved difficulties about ethnic identity. Thus, the matter cannot be regarded as solved, and is likely to remain in dispute far into the future. We can record as much new evidence about these arrowheads as possible, but the question is essentially methodological: are they really Scythian or, perhaps, did they belong to other people who borrowed the idea from the Scythians?

With reference to our current theme, what we are finding in the Black Sea region are objects whose origins can be connected mainly with Anatolia. Usually they are of metal, predominantly of bronze: belts, horse ornaments, a few Urartian helmets, objects executed in animal style, etc. (Bouzek 1997; Tsetskhladze 1999). To interpret how these objects got there and what they meant to local societies is a very difficult task. They could have come through trade, as gifts, by chance or reflect the exchange of ideas. Nor can the migration of groups of people or tribes be excluded, bearing in mind that the Black Sea region and Anatolia are adjacent to each other. The Early Iron Age in Anatolia and throughout the Near East was marked by political change and migrations. To establish how these objects arrived, we have to establish many other aspects of culture and everyday life, not just the objects themselves. In the Caucasus, for example, objects of Anatolian origin were found in graves where the funeral rites have Anatolian features — features quite new and alien for local society (Pogrebova 1977; 1984). It is highly likely that this is evidence of migration from Anatolia. Detailed study has indeed demonstrated that metalworking, including goldsmithing, was introduced to Colchis from Anatolia at the end of the seventh or in the sixth century BC (Tsetskhladze 1995: 327).

The question of migration and who went where is very difficult. For example, there has been a long discussion about the origins of the Phrygians. We have ancient written sources — Herodotus (*The History*: 7.73) and Strabo (*The Geography*: 12.3.3, 12.4.4) — but they do not provide a clear picture: the Phrygians may have come from Thrace or somewhere completely different (see Tsetskhladze 1999: 473–5). Resumed excavation at Gordion has unearthed Early Iron Age pit dwellings and a small quantity of handmade pottery (Voigt 1994). The publishers have used them to demonstrate that the Phrygians came from the Balkans (Sams 1994: 18–28, 175–7; Voigt 1994: 285; Henrikson, Voigt 1998: 101–3). However, examination of the bulky eastern European literature and archaeological evidence would have shown that such dwellings so far are unknown in Thrace, where only small-scale surveys and not proper excavations have been conducted: Early Iron Age settlement archaeology is in its infancy in Bulgaria (see, for example, Bouzek 1984; Shalganova, Gotzev 1995; Gotzev 1997) and what we know comes from funeral monuments (see, for example, Delev 1980a; 1980b; Gergova 1989), but is characteristic of a huge area, including the Ukrainian steppes (see Tsetskhladze 2000).

In the literature, the terms 'Thraco-Cimmerian' and 'Caucasian' bronzes are used (Milchev 1955; Bouzek 1983; Chochorowski 1993; Erlikh 1997; Gergova 1980; 1993; Kozenkova 1975). The use of this terminology confuses rather than clarifies the situation. In reality, these bronzes have more in common with Anatolian examples than with their supposed regions of origin. They demonstrate the strong connections of the Balkans, the Caucasus and the Ukrainian steppes with Anatolia, possibly even migration (see Tsetskhladze 1999: 482–6). New excavations and studies bring with them new ideas. Although scholars sometimes recognise stylistic similarities between objects found in the Balkans and those from Anatolia and the Caucasus, they have tended to interpret them as an indication of trade links between the Balkans and the Caucasus (see Stoyanov 2000). Maybe it would be more logical to propose direct links between the Balkans and Anatolia than a relationship conducted via the Caucasus. Geographically it would be much easier for objects to come from Anatolia than from the Caucasus across the widest part of the Black Sea.

Recent years have seen new developments, especially in Anatolian archaeology (see, for example, Pigott 1996; Çilingiroğlu, Matthews 1999; Yalçın 2000; Ramage, Craddock 2000; Bilgi 2001; Yener, Hoffner Jr. 2002; Yakar 2000; Belli 2001). Our knowledge of Phrygians, Lydians, Urartians, etc. is becoming fuller. This was demonstrated very clearly at the Fifth Anatolian Iron Age Symposium. The first volume of the publication of Ayanis gives much material to encourage the rethinking of Urartian archaeology (Çilingiroğlu, Salvini 2001a). The same can be said about other new developments and publications relating to Urartian sites in Turkey and Transcaucasia, demonstrating even stronger Urartian expansion or influence in Transcaucasia than hitherto suspected (Sevin, Kavaklı 1996; Bahsaliyev 1997; Belli 1999; Belli, Sevin 1999; Belli, Konyar 2001; Burney 2002; Potts 2002; Tsetskhladze 2003). Recently, the use of scientific methods to date occupation levels has overturned the entire previously accepted chronology of the Anatolian Early Iron Age, including dating of the so-called 'Cimmerian Destruction Level' at Gordion (for which see DeVries et al. this volume; see contra Muscarella 2003). All of these developments have consequences for the chronology of the Early Iron Age in the Black Sea region too.

Talking about chronology, this is another weak point for the Black Sea region, especially the Balkans and the Caucasus (Tsetskhladze 1995: 309–12; Archibald 1998: 26–48). We still lack a firm chronology for the Early Iron Age of the Black Sea region. What we have is anchored mainly upon local pottery, itself very difficult to date. For example, one Georgian archaeologist has

dated the beginning of iron production in Colchis to the 13th to 12th centuries BC; others have assigned it to the seventh to sixth centuries (see Tsetskhladze 1995: 312). Once again, the problem here is methodological — how to date things when there is no hard evidence (the same can be said, for example, about the first gold objects in Colchis: Tsetskhladze 1995: 323–5; 1999: 479). The only solution is to consider the developments in Anatolian chronology, and see how these might be of use in the Black Sea region, especially since there are considerable quantities of Anatolian or Anatolian type objects from Black Sea sites.

I would like to give some further examples of how developments in Anatolian archaeology can help to solve the problems we are experiencing in the archaeology of the Pontic region in the Early Iron Age. First of all, the long disputed problem of the introduction of iron metallurgy. Some scholars propose a connection between the Hittites and Colchis during the second millennium BC (Pigott 1996: 160–2). However, we lack any hard evidence for dating the introduction of iron objects in Colchis during the second millennium; furthermore, we have no evidence whatsoever for a connection between Colchis (modern western Georgia) and the Hittites. Such evidence as there is indicates links between the Hittites and modern eastern Georgia, the area later known as Iberia (a bronze goblet from Trialeti [Dzaparidze 1981: 11–40; Dschaparidze 2001: 108]; compare a similar goblet from Karashamb, Armenia [Oganesian 1992]). Discussion concentrates on the Chalybes as the people who introduced iron to the entire civilised world (Pigott 1996: 160–2). As far as I am aware, no archaeological exploration has been undertaken in the territory formerly inhabited by the Chalybes (compare Yakar 2000: 283–302). At the same time, Georgian historiography maintains that the Chalybes were one of the Colchian tribes, a view based more on conjecture, speculation and later Graeco-Roman written sources than on firm evidence (see, for example, Mikeladze 1974: 114–49).

Hitherto, we have lacked any archaeological evidence about the Diauehi people, but the joint efforts of an Australian-Turkish team are helping to fill this gap (Sagona 2002). This is very important because Georgian historiography has claimed the Diauehi as one of the Colchian tribes, based mainly on information from Graeco-Roman authors (Mikeladze 1974: 166–72). Detailed publication of the Australian-Turkish investigation (see now Hopkins 2003), and comparison with what we already know of the Colchian culture of western Georgia, will help to clarify matters. Likewise, full and final publication of the unique inscription from the façade of the temple at Ayanis, which (maybe) mentions the Muski, can finally help to locate these people (Salvini

2001: 261; Çilingiroğlu, Salvini 2001b: 20). Yet again, Georgian historiography has considered them as one of the Kartvelian (ancient Georgian) tribes (see, for example, Khazaradze 1984).

The primary aim of this general overview has been to demonstrate that, despite the evidence of connections between Anatolia and the huge Pontic region, our data are so scanty that it is frequently impossible to make a satisfactory interpretation of them. Only a joint effort between specialists studying the Pontic region and Early Iron Age Anatolia will enrich our knowledge of these two regions.

## Bibliography

Alekseev, A.Y. 1992: *Scythian Chronicle (Scythians in the Seventh–Fourth Centuries BC: Historical-Archaeological Essay)*. St. Petersburg (in Russian)

Alekseev, A.Y., Kachalova, N.K., Tokhtasev, S.P. 1993: *Cimmerians: Ethno-Cultural Identity*. St. Petersburg (in Russian)

Archibald, Z.H. 1998: *The Odrysian Kingdom of Thrace*. Oxford

Bahsaliyev, V. 1997: *The Archaeology of Nakhichevan*. Istanbul

Belli, O. 1999: *The Anzaf Fortresses and the Gods of Urartu*. Istanbul

— (ed.) 2001: *Istanbul University's Contributions to Archaeology in Turkey (1932–2000)*. Istanbul

Belli, O., Konyar, E. 2001: 'Excavations at Van-Yoncatepe fortress and necropolis' *Tel Aviv* 28.2: 169–212

Belli, O., Sevin, V. 1999: *Archaeological Survey in Nakhichevan, 1998*. Istanbul

Bilgi, Ö. 2001: *Metallurgists of the Central Black Sea Region. A New Perspective on the Question of the Indo-Europeans' Original Homeland*. Istanbul

Blek, V.B. 1976: 'On the roots of the Scytho-Sarmatian Animal Style' in A.I. Melyukova, M.G. Moshkova (eds), *Scythian-Siberian Animal Style in the Art of the People of Eurasia*. Moscow: 30–9 (in Russian)

Boardman, J. 1994: *The Diffusion of Classical Art in Antiquity*. London

Bouzek, J. 1983: 'Caucasus and Europe and the Cimmerian problem' *Acta Musei Nationalis Pragae, Series A - Historia* 37.4: 177–232

— 1984: 'The archaeological situation in different parts of Thrace during the Early Iron Age' in *Ditter internationaler thrakologischer Kongress II*. Sofia: 73–5

— 1997: *The Aegean, Anatolia and Europe: Cultural Interrelations during the Early Iron Age*. Jonsered

— 2001: 'Cimmerians and early Scythians: the transition from Geometric to Orientalising style in the Pontic

area' in G.R. Tsetskhladze (ed.), *North Pontic Archaeology. Recent Discoveries and Studies*. Leiden, Boston, Cologne: 33–44

Burney, C. 2002: 'Urartu and its forerunners: eastern Anatolia and Trans-Caucasia in the second and early first millennia BC' *Ancient West and East* 1.1: 51–4

Chlenova, N.L. 1997: *Central Asia and Scythians*. Moscow (in Russian)

Chochorowski, J. 1993: *Ekspansja Kimmeryjska na Tereny Europy Srodkowej*. Cracow

Çilingiroğlu, A., Matthews, R. (eds) 1999: *Anatolian Iron Ages 4 = Anatolian Studies* 49. London

Çilingiroğlu, A., Salvini, M. (eds) 2001a: *Ayanis I. Ten Years' Excavations at Rusahinili Eiduru-kai 1989–1998*. Rome

— 2001b: 'The historical background of Ayanis' in A. Çilingiroğlu, M. Salvini (eds), *Ayanis I. Ten Years' Excavations at Rusahinili Eiduru-kai 1989–1998*. Rome: 15–24

Cohen, B. (ed.) 2000: *Not the Classical Ideal. Athens and the Construction of the Other in Greek Art*. Leiden, Boston, Cologne

Delev, P. 1980a: 'Problems of the Thracian Megalithic Culture' *Pulpudeva* 3: 189–92

— 1980b: 'The Megalithic monuments of ancient Thrace' in J.G.P. Best, N.M.W. DeVries (eds), *Interaction and Acculturation in the Mediterranean*. Amsterdam: 197–202

Derin, Z., Muscarella, O.W. 2001: 'Iron and bronze arrows' in A. Çilingiroğlu, M. Salvini (eds), *Ayanis I. Ten Years' Excavations at Rusahinili Eiduru-kai 1989–1998*. Rome: 189–217

Dimitrov, D.P. 1971: 'Troia VII b 2 und die thrakischen und mösischen Stämme auf dem Balkan' *Studia Balcanica* V: 63–78

Dschaparidze, O. 2001: 'Zur frühen Metallurgie Georgiens vom 3. bis zum 1. Jahrtausend v. Chr.' in I. Gambaschidze, A. Hauptmann, R. Slotta, Ü. Yalcin (eds), *Georgien: Schätze aus dem Land des goldenen Vlies. Katalog der Ausstellung*. Bochum: 92–119

Dyakonov, I.M. 1994: 'Cimmerians and Scythians in the Near East' *Rossiiskaya Arkheologiya* 1: 108–16 (in Russian)

Dzaparidze, N. 1981: *Bronze Age Goldsmithing in Georgia (Trialeti Culture)*. Tbilisi (in Georgian)

Erlikh, V.P. 1997: 'Some considerations on the interconnections between Ciscaucasia and middle Europe in the Novocherkassk period' in R.M. Munchaev, V.S. Olkhovskii (eds), *Monuments of Pre-Scythian and Scythian Times in the South of Eastern Europe*. Moscow: 19–34 (in Russian)

French, D.H. 1994: 'Thracians in northwestern Asia Minor' in Fondation Européenne Dragan, Centre Européenne d'Etudes Thraces, Conseil International des Etudes Indo- Européenne et Thraces, *Europa Indo-Europea. Atti del VIo Congresso Internazionale di Tracologia e VIIo Symposio di Studi Traci. Palma da Mallorca 24–28 Marzo 1992.* Rome: 69

Galanina, L.K. 1991: 'Scythian contacts with the Near East (finds from the Kelermes barrows)' *Arkheologicheskii Sbornik Gosudarstvennogo Ermitazha* 3l: 15–29 (in Russian)

Gergova, D. 1980: 'Contributions on the problem of Thraco-Caucasian relations in the Early Iron Age' *Pulpudeva* 3: 296–304

— 1989: 'Thracian burial rites of Late Bronze and Early Iron Age' in J. Best, A. De Vries (eds), *Thracians and Mycenaeans.* Leiden: 231–40

— 1993: 'Some common problems of the interrelations between Thrace and northern Europe' *Pulpudeva* 6: 65–71

Ghirshman, R. 1979: *La tombe princière de Ziwiyé et le début de l'art animalier scythe.* Paris

Gotzev, A. 1997: 'Characteristics of the settlement system during the Early Iron Age in ancient Thrace' *Acta Hyperborea* 7: 407–21

Grantovskii, E.A., Pogrebova, M.N., Raevskii, D.S. 1997: 'Cimmerians in the Near East' *Vestnik Drevnei Istorii* 4: 69–85 (in Russian)

Henrikson, R.H., Voigt, M.M. 1998: 'The Early Iron Age in Gordion: evidence from Yassıhöyük Stratigraphic Sequence' in N. Tuna, Z. Aktüre, M. Lynch (eds), *Thracians and Phrygians: Problems of Parallelism.* Ankara: 79–106

Herodotus, *Histories.* English translation by A.D. Godley (Loeb Classical Library). 4 Volumes. Cambridge Massachusetts, London 1920–1925

Hoddinott, R.F. 1986: 'Thrace, Mycenae and Troy' *Pulpudeva* 5: 125–32

Hopkins, L. 2003: *Archaeology at the North-East Anatolian Frontier, VI. An Ethnoarchaeological Study of Sos Höyük and Yiğıttaşı Village.* Louvain

Ilinskaya, V.A. 1976: 'Current state of the problem Scythian Animal Style' in A.I. Melyukova, M.G. Moshkova (eds), *Scythian-Siberian Animal Style in the Art of the People of Eurasia.* Moscow: 9–29 (in Russian)

Ilinskaya, V.A., Terenozhkin, A.I. 1983: *Scythia in the Seventh-Fourth Centuries BC.* Kiev (in Russian)

Ivantchik, A.I. 1991: 'On the ethnonym "Cimmerians"' *Terra Antiqua Balcanica* 6: 61–73 (in Russian)

— l993: *Les Cimmériens au Proche-Orient.* Freiburg, Göttingen

— 1994: 'On the ethnic identity and archaeological culture of the Cimmerians. I. Cimmerian monuments of the Middle East' *Vestnik Drevnei Istorii* 3: 148–68 (in Russian)

— 1995: 'On the ethnic identity and archaeological culture of the Cimmerians. II. "Early Scythian" finds in Asia Minor' *Vestnik Drevnei Istorii* 1: 3–22 (in Russian)

— 1996: *The Cimmerians. Ancient Near Eastern Civilisations and the Steppe Nomads in the Eighth-Seventh Centuries BC* (enlarged version of Ivantchik 1993). Moscow (in Russian)

— 1999: 'The Scythian "Rule Over Asia": the Classical tradition and the historical reality' in G.R. Tsetskhladze (ed.), *Ancient Greeks West and East.* Leiden, Boston, Cologne: 497–520

— 2001: 'The current state of the Cimmerian question, summary of the discussion' *Ancient Civilizations from Scythia to Siberia* 7.3–4: 307–40

Khazaradze, N. 1984: *Ethnopolitical Problems of the Ancient History of Georgia (Moschi).* Tbilisi (in Georgian)

Korenyako, V.A. 1998: 'On the origin of the Scythian-Siberian Animal Style' *Rossiiskaya Arkheologiya* 4: 64–77 (in Russian)

Kozenkova, V.I. 1975: 'Links of northern Caucasus with the Carpatho-Danubian world (some archaeological parallels)' in A.I. Terenozhkin (ed.), *Scythian World.* Kiev: 52–73 (in Russian)

Kristensen, A.K.G. 1988: *Who Were the Cimmerians and Where Did They Come from? Sargon II, the Cimmerians, and Rusa I.* Copenhagen

Kuhrt, A. 1995: *The Ancient Near East, c. 3000–330 BC. Vol. II.* London, New York

Kurochkin, G.N. 1992: 'Scythian Animal Style and bronze art objects of Luristan' *Rossiiskaya Arkheologiya* 2: 102–22 (in Russian)

— 1994: 'Chronology of the Near Eastern campaign of the Scythians according to literary and archaeological data' *Rossiiskaya Arkheologiya* 1: 117–22 (in Russian)

Malkin, I. (ed.) 2001: *Ancient Perceptions of Greek Ethnicity.* Cambridge Massachusetts, London

Mellaart, J. 1971: 'Prehistory of Anatolia and its relations with the Balkans' *Studia Balcanica* 5: 119–37

Mihailov, G. 1991: 'Thrace before the Persian entry into Europe' in J. Boardman, I.E.S. Edwards, N.G.L. Hammond, E. Sollberger, C.B.F. Walker (eds), *Cambridge Ancient History Vol. III, part 2* (second edition). Cambridge: 591–618

Mikeladze, T. 1974: *Investigation in the History of the Ancient Population of Colchis and the South-western Black Sea Littoral (Second-First Millennia BC).* Tbilisi (in Georgian)

Milchev, A. 1955: 'Thracian-Cimmerian finds in Bulgarian lands' *Izvestiya na Arkheologicheskiya Institut* 19: 359–73 (in Bulgarian)

Morris, I. 2000: *Archaeology as Cultural History. Words and Things in Iron Age Greece.* Oxford

Murzin, V.Y. 1990: *Origin of the Scythians: Main Periods in the Formation of the Scythian Ethnos.* Kiev (in Russian)

Murzin, V.Y., Skory, S.A. 1994: 'An essay of Scythian history' *Il Mar Nero* 1: 55–98

Muscarella, O.W. 2003: 'The date of the destruction of the Early Phrygian period at Gordion' *Ancient West and East* 2.2: 225–52

Oganesian [Hovanesian], V.E. 1992: 'A silver goblet from Karashamb' in P.L. Kohl (ed.), *Recent Discoveries in Transcaucasia* (Soviet Anthropology and Archaeology: Spring: Vol. 30.4). Armonk: 84–102

Pigott, V.C. 1996: 'Near Eastern archaeometallurgy: modern research and future directions' in J.S. Cooper, G.M. Schwartz (eds), *The Study of the Ancient Near East in the 21st Century.* Winona Lake: 139–76

Pogrebova, M.N. 1977: *Iran and Transcaucasia in the Early Iron Age.* Moscow (in Russian)

— 1984: *Transcaucasia and its Links with the Middle East in the Scythian Period.* Moscow (in Russian)

— 1993: 'On the dating of Scythian archaic monuments' *Rossiiskaya Arkheologiya* 2: 84–8 (in Russian)

Pogrebova, M.N., Raevskii, D.S. 1992: *Early Scythians and the Ancient Orient. Towards the History of the Formation of Scythian Culture.* Moscow (in Russian)

— 1993: 'Early Scythians in the light of written tradition and archaeological data' *Vestnik Drevnei Istorii* 4: 110–18 (in Russian)

Pogrebova, M.N., Raevskii, D.S., Yatsenko, I.V. 1998: 'The Cimmerian Problem' *Vestnik Drevnei Istorii* 3: 69–87 (in Russian)

Potts, D.T. 2002: 'Some problems in the historical geography of Nakhchivan' *Ancient West and East* 1.1: 126–42

Ramage, A., Craddock, P. 2000: *King Croesus' Gold. Excavations at Sardis and the History of Gold Refining.* London

Sagona, A. 2002: 'Archaeology at the headwaters of the Aras' *Ancient West and East* 1.1: 46–50

Salvini, M. 2001: 'The inscriptions of Ayanis (Rusahinili Eiduru-kai). Cuneiform and hieroglyphic' in A. Çilingiroğlu, M. Salvini (eds), *Ayanis I. Ten Years' Excavations at Rusahinili Eiduru-kai 1989–1998.* Rome: 251–70

Sams, G.K. 1994: *The Early Phrygian Pottery.* Philadelphia

Sauter, H. 2000: *Studien zum Kimmerierproblem.* Bonn

Sevin, V., Kavaklı, E. 1996: *Van/Karagündüz. An Early Iron Age Cemetery.* Istanbul

Shalganova, T., Gotzev, A. 1995: 'Problems of research of the Early Iron Age' in D.W. Bailey, I. Panayatov (eds), *Prehistoric Bulgaria.* Madison: 327–43

Stoyanov, T. 2000: 'The contacts of northeastern Thrace with Anatolia, the Caucasus and the Near East during the Early Iron Age until the time of Greek colonisation' *Izvestiya na Narodna Muzei Burgas* 3: 50–61 (in Bulgarian)

Strabo, *Geography.* English translation by H.L. Jones (Loeb Classical Library). 8 Volumes. London, New York 1917–1932

Tsetskhladze, G.R. 1995: 'Did the Greeks go to Colchis for metals?' *Oxford Journal of Archaeology* 14: 307–32

— 1998: 'Greek colonisation of the Black Sea area: stages, models, and native population' in G.R. Tsetskhladze (ed.), *The Greek Colonisation of the Black Sea Area. Historical Interpretation of Archaeology.* Stuttgart: 9–68

— 1999: 'Between west and east: Anatolian roots of local cultures of the Pontus' in G.R. Tsetskhladze (ed.), *Ancient Greeks West and East.* Leiden, Boston, Cologne: 469–96

— 2000: 'Note on semi-pithouses and handmade pottery from Gordion' in A. Avram, M. Babes (eds), *Civilisation grecque et cultures antiques périphériques.* Bucharest: 165–71

— 2003: 'The culture of ancient Georgia in the first millennium BC and Greater Anatolia: diffusion or migration?' in A. Smith, K. Rubinson (eds), *Archaeology in the Borderlands: Investigations in Caucasia and Beyond.* Los Angeles: 229–45

Tuna, N., Aktüre, Z., Lynch, M. (eds) 1998: *Thracians and Phrygians: Problems of Parallelism.* Ankara

Voigt, M.M. 1994: 'Excavations in Gordion 1988–1989: the Yassıhöyük Stratigraphic Sequence' in A. Çilingiroğlu, D.H. French (eds), *Anatolian Iron Ages 3* (British Institute of Archaeology at Ankara Monograph 16). Ankara: 265–93

Yakar, J. 2000: *Ethnoarchaeology of Anatolia. Rural Socio Economy in the Bronze and Iron Ages.* Tel Aviv

Yalcın, Ü. (ed.) 2000: *Anatolian Metal 1.* Bochum

Yener, K.A., Hoffner, H.A., Jr. (eds) 2002: *Recent Developments in Hittite Archaeology and History: Papers in Memory of Hans G. Güterbock.* Winona Lake

# Phrygian rock-cut monuments from western Phrygia, with observations on their cult functions

## Taciser Tüfekçi Sivas
*Anadolu University, Eskişehir*

## Abstract

This paper presents some aspects of the religious architecture of Phrygian civilisation, as revealed by our archaeological survey in western Phrygia, conducted from 1992 to 1996 and in 2001. The aim of our fieldwork has been to determine the distribution and character of Phrygian rock-cut monuments within the peripheral zones of the Phrygian highlands. To that end, we have focused our efforts on two regions within Eskişehir and Afyonkarahisar provinces: to the east, Sivrihisar, selected because of its rocky formations and its key position lying between Gordion and Midas City; and İhsaniye in the southern part of the Highlands. As a result, our surveys have not only added a number of Phrygian religious monuments to the known corpus of material, but have also enriched the typological range of this corpus through the discovery and recording of circular rock-cut features and wine presses previously uncharacterised in the region.

## Özet

Bu bildiride 1992–1996 ve 2001 yıllarında Batı Frigya'da gerçekleştirdiğimiz yüzey araştırmaları ışığında Frig dini mimarlığının çeşitli yönleri ele alınmıştır. Arazi çalışmalarına başlarken amacımız Dağlık Frigya Bölgesi'nin yakın çevresinde Frig kaya anıtlarının yayılım alanının ve genel karakterinin saptanmasıydı. Bu doğrultuda çalışmalarımız Eskişehir ve Afyonkarahisar illerinde iki bölgede yoğunlaşmıştır: Doğuda, kayalık yapısı ve Midas şehri ile başkent Gordion arasında geçiş noktası olan Sivrihisar bölgesi; güneyde ise Dağlık bölgenin güney kesiminde yer alan İhsaniye bölgesi. Sonuç olarak araştırmalarımız, sadece bilinen Frig kaya anıtı tiplerinin sayısal olarak artmasını sağlamamış aynı zamanda yuvarlak kaya formları/işaretleri ve üzüm presleri gibi daha önceden tanınmayan anıtlar ile bölgedeki mimari tipolojisini de zenginleştirmiştir.

---

After a scriptless era lasting some 300 or 400 years, Phrygia emerged in the eighth century BC as a powerful Iron Age kingdom in Anatolia. This paper presents some aspects of the religious and ritual architecture of Phrygian civilisation, as revealed by our archaeological survey in western Phrygia, conducted between 1992 and 1996 and in 2001 (fig. 1).

The evidence for Phrygian religious cult indicates that the major divinity was a goddess known to the Phrygians as Matar, the Mother Goddess, mother of the natural world (Roller 1999: 63–115). In western Phrygia, the prominence of Matar is demonstrated by a series of religious rock-cut monuments, of which the monumental rock façades, stepped altars and niches are the most original and impressive types (Haspels 1971: 73–111; Tüfekçi Sivas 1999). The major concentration of these monuments lies in the highlands of Phrygia, the mountainous country near the upper reaches of the Tembris and Sangarios rivers (respectively the modern Porsuk and Sakarya), within a roughly triangular area defined by the modern cities of Eskişehir, Afyonkarahisar and Kütahya (Haspels 1971: 20, fig. 493).

The aim of our fieldwork has been to determine the distribution and character of Phrygian rock-cut monuments within the peripheral zones of the Phrygian highlands. To that end, we have focused our efforts on two regions within Eskişehir and Afyonkarahisar provinces: to the east, Sivrihisar, selected because of its rocky formations and its key position lying between Gordion and Midas City; and İhsaniye in the southern part of the highlands.

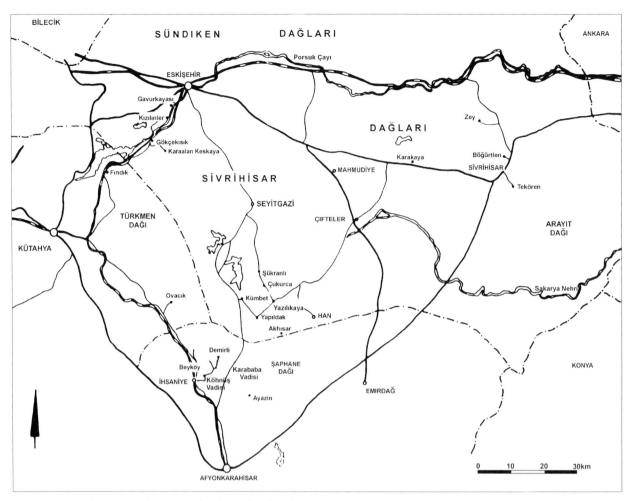

*Fig. 1. Map of western Phrygia (Eskişehir, Afyonkarahisar, Kütahya region)*

## Karakaya

Here, in the Sivrihisar region, in the initial stage of our fieldwork, we had our first encounter with traces of the Phrygians. The small village of Karakaya is situated 20km west of Sivrihisar, with undulating terrain to the north and west of the village, including scattered rock outcrops that belong to the offshoot of a granitic chain which extends northwestwards from the Sivrihisar region to the Eskişehir area, via Kaymaz. Approximately 400m southeast of the village, and just 100m south of the modern cemetery, lies a rock-cut tomb (fig. 2) which, although it had been already plundered, is dateable to the Phrygian Iron Age according to its architectural characteristics.[1] The tomb is situated in an oblong outcrop of

rock, the front (south side) of which has been cut straight and smoothed, and within which is the dromos type entrance, about 1m below present ground level. Within are two chambers, one behind the other, forming a double tomb. Both chambers have pitched ceilings with gables in relief. The floor space of the first chamber is plain; here we found an almost rectangular and carefully worked door stone, the dimensions of which indicate a perfect fit with the entrance to the second (rear) chamber. In the latter, a couch is neatly carved out of the living rock against the back wall, with two lion's-paw-ended legs in relief at the corners; furthermore, not only are the gable and king post carved in relief but also the rafters and beams on the ceiling and the side walls. Closely comparable, in terms of its interior decoration and dromos type entrance below ground level, is a tomb from Midas City (fig. 3).[2]

---

[1] From a close investigation of a large number of rock-cut tombs in the Phrygian highlands, C.H.E. Haspels concluded that the typical Phrygian tomb chamber is a rock-cut imitation of a wooden house, an appropriate dwelling for the dead. The ceiling is usually pitched and is sometimes decorated with carved relief features: rafters, gable, tie beam and king post. The floor space is either plain or has one to three low couches (*klinai*) neatly carved out of the living rock, against the wall/s.

The entrance is a small, almost square opening, tapering upwards slightly, with a door (Haspels 1971: 112–38, figs 530–45).

[2] Excavated by Gürkan Toklu in 1970 on the west side of Midas City; unpublished, see Tüfekçi Sivas 1999: 21.

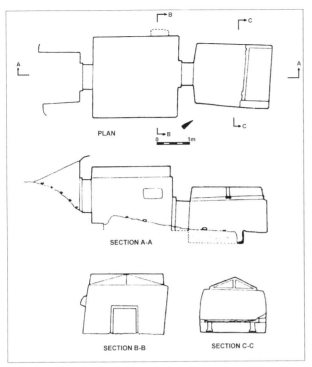

*Fig. 2. Tomb at Karakaya*

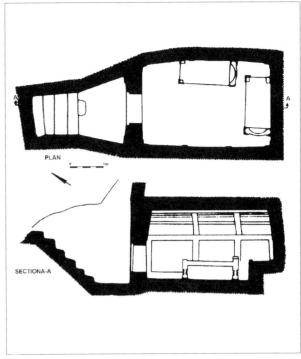

*Fig. 3. Tomb at Midas City*

## Böğürtlen/Balkayası

7km north of Sivrihisar, at the village of Böğürtlen, lies the monument of Balkayası, a small rock façade (2.0m high by 1.5m wide) carved in the vertical face of a steep rocky hill from which it derives its name (fig. 4). It has a low pitched roof and the central area is taken up by the door niche. To date, it is the sole example with evidence of paint, here dark red in colour, used for the geometric decoration on the gable and the side walls. For similar Phrygian small façades, see Haspels (1971: figs 99, 518:1, 246, 526: 2) and Tüfekçi Sivas (1999: pls 84, 85, 88, 89, 102).

## Beypınarı

Almost 1km south of the monument of Balkayası, at Beypınarı, lies another Phrygian tomb. The chamber (fig. 5) is cut low down in the rock, with a small square dromos type entrance about 1m below ground level, as at Karakaya and the Midas City tomb mentioned above. Lying on the ground, at a higher level than the entrance, we found a roughly worked rectangular lid stone (measuring 2m by 1.5m across and 0.2m thick) which would originally have been laid on top of the dromos. The chamber has a pitched ceiling and two couches, one to the left and the other at the rear.

*Fig. 4. Monument of Balkayası*

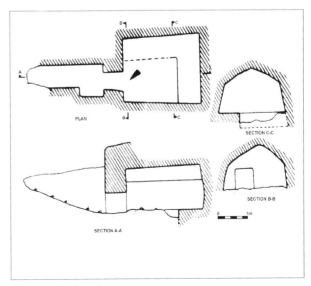

*Fig. 5. Tomb at Beypınarı*

## Zey

Shifting our fieldwork to the north, but in the same region, 1km south of Zey, a small mountain village sited on the northern rocky slopes of the Sivrihisar mountain range and 28km north of Sivrihisar, we found impressive traces of Phrygian Iron Age civilisation: a small necropolis of 12 rock-cut chamber tombs in the east and west sides of a narrow valley; also two stepped altars higher up the cliffs; three circular rock-cut features sited on a smaller rock formation; and settlement remains nearby. Tombs 1 to 7 are cut into the cliffs which border the east side of the valley, and run along more or less in a line.

The first tomb, Zey no. 1, consists of two chambers, one behind the other, forming a double tomb (fig. 6). Both chambers have pitched ceilings with carved gables, beams and rafters. In the first chamber (1.90m by 1.95m across and 1.37m high) there is a low couch against the north wall. The second chamber has a plain interior (2.0m by 1.94m across and 1.42m high), but on the gable the king post is shown in relief (for other examples in the highlands of double chamber tombs with pitched ceilings, see Haspels 1971: 115–16, fig. 532, 116–17, figs 121–3, 533: 2, 3, 5, 126, fig. 576: 2–4).

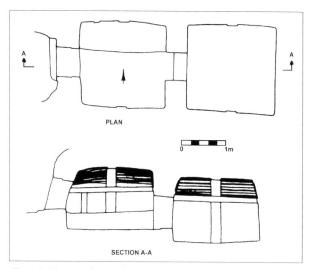

PLAN

0      1m

SECTION A-A

*Fig. 6. Zey tomb no. 1*

Zey tombs nos 2 and 3 are adjacent to each other. Tomb no. 2 is a very simple chamber with plain interior (2.30m by 1.30m across and 1.30m high) and an almost flat ceiling (for other examples of tombs with a plain interior, see Haspels 1971: 118–19, figs 534, 539: 3, 6, 125, figs 540: 5, 7, 541: 4, 5; Sivas 1999: 125–6, figs 1–6). Tomb no. 3 has a spacious chamber (3.60m by 2.40m across and 1.90m high) with pitched ceiling and carved gables, parallel beams and king posts; there is a low couch against the north wall (for other tombs with one couch, see Haspels 1971: 113, fig. 530: 7–9, 122, figs 538: 2, 4, 7–9, 539: 1–2, 7–12).

Zey tombs nos 4 to 7 are grouped together at the end of the valley. Zey no. 4 is a simple tomb with a rectangular chamber (2.20m by 1.70m across and 1.55m high), plain interior and an almost pitched ceiling. Tomb no. 5 has a rectangular chamber (2.20m by 1.70m across and 1.55m high) with pitched ceiling and three low couches against the walls; the empty space between the couches is like a narrow gangway, reached from the doorway by a high step (for examples of tombs with three couches, see Haspels 1971: 114, fig. 530: 3, 6, 120–1, figs 535, 536, 538: 5–6, 125, figs 540: 2, 3, 6, 8–10; Sivas 1999: 126, figs 7–10; 2002: 326–7, figs 1–4).

Zey tombs nos 6 and 7 have regular plans. Zey no. 6 has an almost square chamber (2.60m by 2.26m across and 1.55m high) with an almost pitched ceiling. At the back wall there is a couch with a moulded band along its front. Tomb no. 7 is a simple tomb with a rectangular chamber measuring 1.76m by 1.44m across and 1.22m high. It has a flat ceiling and a low couch on the south wall.

Tombs nos 8 to 12 are grouped high up in the isolated rock on the west side of the valley and are variously arranged side by side and one under the other. Zey no. 8 has a rectangular chamber (2.80m by 2.40m across and 1.78m high) with a roughly executed pitched ceiling and two couches, one at the back wall, the other on the right; probably at a later period, a doorway of normal size was opened in the left wall to provide access into the adjacent tomb, no. 9 (for other examples of tombs with two couches, see Haspels 1971: 121, figs 537, 538: 1, 3, 123, fig. 540: 1, 4).

Zey no. 9 is by far the most spectacular of the chamber tombs (fig. 7). The composition is elaborate and harmonious with careful attention to detail. The chamber is a spacious room (4.10m by 2.10m across and 1.90m high) with pitched ceiling and gables. The well dressed *klinai* against the north and east walls have high, curved head rests, and bull's-hoof-ended legs carved in relief (for similar tombs with spacious chambers containing *klinai* against the walls, see Haspels 1971: 126–34, figs 542–5).

Zey no. 10 comprises a rectangular chamber (2.50m by 2.10m across and 1.42m high) with pitched ceiling and plain interior. Tomb no. 11 has an almost square chamber (2.0m by 2.20m across and 1.52m high) with flattish ceiling. There is a couch on either side of the chamber. Zey no. 12 has a square chamber (2.25m by 2.30m across and 1.35m high) with flat ceiling and it is an exception in having a double couch for two persons, against the back wall.

Since the survey gave no clear evidence regarding the dates of the tombs recorded above, it seems rather hard to offer any absolute chronology. However, the classifi-

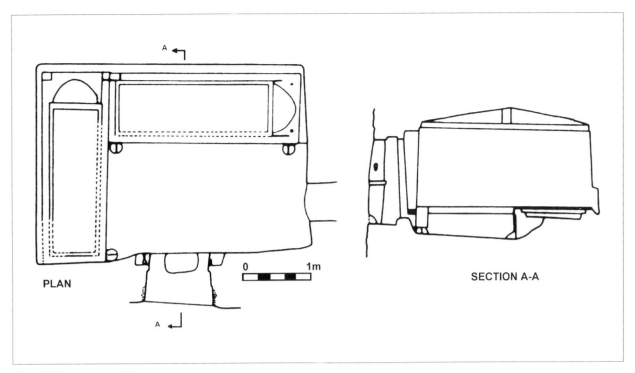

*Fig. 7. Zey tomb no. 9*

cation and dating criteria put forward by Haspels can be taken into consideration to some degree. According to Haspels, Phrygian rock-cut tombs are mainly divided into two groups: group I (Haspels 1971: 112–26, 134–5) comprises simpler forms, of earlier date than the more complex group II examples (for the latter see Haspels 1971: 126–34, 136–8). According to this classification, all the tombs, except for Zey no. 9, belong in group I and could be early in date, from the eighth to the seventh centuries BC. Zey tomb no. 9, with its spacious chamber and neatly carved *klinai*, belongs in group II and can be dated later, to about the sixth century BC.

In the necropolis, on top of the cliffs, positioned directly over Zey tombs nos 6 and 7 and nos 8 and 9, are two Phrygian stepped altars (figs 8, 9) (for a general description of Phrygian altars and further information, see Haspels 1971: 93–6; Naumann 1983: 92–100; Tüfekçi Sivas 1999: 154–73; 2002). A few metres north of Zey tomb no. 1, on a massive isolated rock, there are three circular features cut into the slightly sloping southern face of the rock (fig. 10). They are defined by channels 0.15m wide and 0.15–0.25m deep and have diameters ranging from 0.9m to 1m.

We have recorded a similar circular rock-cut feature from the Midas valley, located just behind the Phrygian chamber tomb of Hamamkaya (Haspels 1971: 113–14, figs 89–90, 531: 1–2), on a flattened rectangular rock platform measuring 5.5m by 3.3m, associated with hollows, cup marks and rectangular basins (fig. 11).

*Fig. 8. Stepped altar at Zey necropolis*

*Fig. 9. Stepped altar at Zey necropolis*

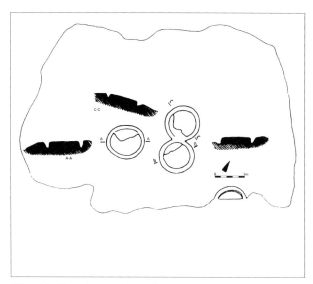

*Fig. 10. Circular rock-cut features at Zey necropolis*

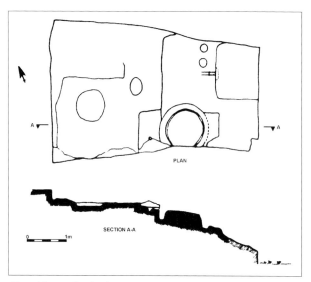

*Fig. 11. Rock platform at Hamamkaya*

These circular features are noteworthy for their monumental quality, and to date these examples seem to be the only ones known in Phrygian rock art. The only analogies are similar rock-cut features found to the east in Urartu, one of the most powerful Iron Age kingdoms of Anatolia, where, on the basis of surveys, it has been determined that a large number occur near to Urartian fortresses, irrigation canals and graves in the Van region; similar rock-cut features have also been found at Horom in Armenia, and at Bastam and Kuh-e Zambil in north-western Iran (see Kleiss 1981; Belli 1989; 2000; 2001; Işık 1995: 43–6). As indicated above, the Phrygian circular rock-cut features are located close to chamber tombs, like a number of the comparanda from Urartu, including some of those at Edremit, Tatvan, Deliçay and all of those at Atabindi, which are located directly above

Urartian rock tombs (Belli 2000: 404; 2001: 366). For the Urartian examples it has been proposed that they are related to a cult of the dead whereby, during the ceremonies conducted at various intervals on behalf of the deceased, some kind of liquid such as water or wine might have been poured over the rock-cut features (Belli 1989: 86; 2000: 405–6; 2001: 368; Işık 1995: 60). Given the special location and curious appearance of the Phrygian examples, these too seem most likely to have had a religious purpose and been part of a cult centre. Although Phrygian funerary practices are hard to distinguish, there is no doubt that both the circular features and the altars at the necropolis at Zey, as well as the rock platform at Hamamkaya by the tomb, were associated with some ritual connected with the cult of the dead. Unfortunately, the nature of this cult remains obscure at present.

In order to determine the location of the settlement associated with the Zey necropolis, a surface survey was conducted in the surrounding region. Approximately 1km south of the necropolis we encountered a rocky site, called by the local villagers Kale (fortress), a landmark in the open, fertile countryside (fig. 12). The summit hardly affords a foothold, the middle section being extremely narrow and the west and east parts crowded with natural round topped rock outcrops. However, on the surrounding slopes, particularly on the south and southeast sides, quantities of Phrygian grey and buff pottery were recovered (see fig. 13). There are also large rectangular hewn blocks lying on the southeast side, which might have been rolled some distance down the slope.

Unlike the well protected Phrygian highlands to the west around Midas City, and the fertile Sangarios valley in the Gordion area, no particular attractions were offered to settlers in the Sivrihisar district. However, our survey indicates that future fieldwork could perhaps determine the precise nature of the Phrygian settlements in this area. Furthermore, such work could shed light on the relationship of the highlands to the important cult centre at Pessinus and the capital city of Gordion.

*Fig. 12. View of Zey Kale*

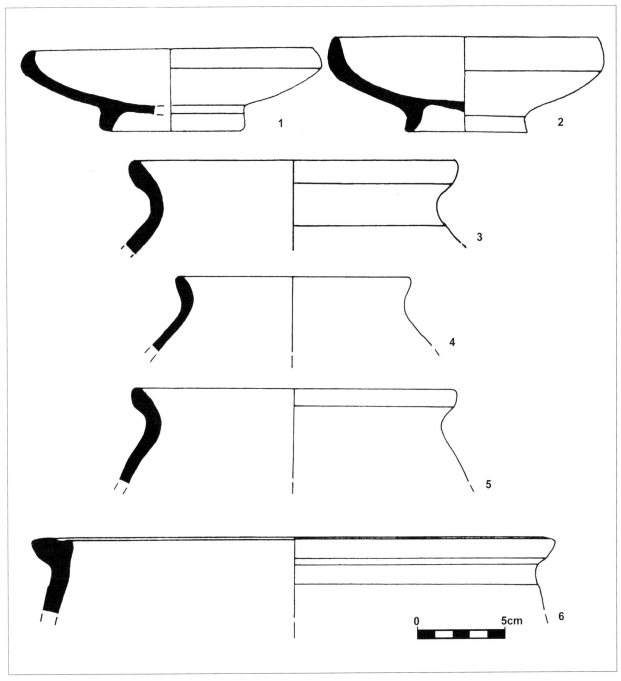

*Fig. 13. Phrygian pottery from Zey Kale*

1. *Plain bowl rim sherd; diameter 15.8cm, thickness 0.5cm; light brown paste; fine sand temper; inner and outer surfaces slipped brownish grey; moderately fired; slightly burnished; wheel made.*

2. *Fragment preserving about half of a plain bowl; diameter 14.8cm, thickness 0.6cm; buff paste; fine sand/mica/grit temper; inner and outer surfaces slipped same colour as the paste; fired variously reddish brown to grey; slightly burnished; wheel made.*

3. *Low necked jar rim sherd; diameter 18cm, thickness 0.8cm; grey paste; medium sand/mica temper; moderately fired; slightly burnished; wheel made.*

4. *Low necked jar rim sherd; diameter 13cm, thickness 0.5cm; grey paste; coarse sand/mica temper; medium fired; wheel made.*

5. *Low necked jar rim sherd; diameter 18cm, thickness 0.6cm; buff paste; medium sand/mica/grit temper; hard fired; slightly burnished; wheel made.*

6. *Ledged rim sherd of a large vessel; diameter 28cm, thickness 1.0cm; grey paste; fine sand/mica temper; slipped surface, polished and fired uniformly very dark grey; wheel made.*

When we moved our survey activities to the Phrygian highlands, the particular focus of the fieldwork was on the southern part of the highlands. In the district of İhsaniye, about 500m southeast of the village of Demirli, grouped in the area of arable land on both sides of the road that leads south to the Köhnüs valley, we discovered some impressive Phrygian religious monuments.

## Menekşekaya

The first group comprises four stepped altars, carved more or less in a row from north to south on the east edge of an isolated, massive, flat topped rock called Menekşekaya. The first altar stands on the northeastern part of the rock where it slopes down towards the road. It faces southeast and consists of three steps leading up to a flat area surmounted by an aniconic idol of Matar the Mother Goddess with a disc shaped head (Tüfekçi Sivas 1999: 171, pl. 152: a, b). Similar schematic images are frequently found elsewhere on the goddess's altars and there is also a series of aniconic idols connected with the goddess's cult (for further information and examples see Naumann 1983: 92–100, pls 9–11; Tüfekçi Sivas 1999: 154–73, pls 115–38). The other three altars lie more towards the south end of the rock, standing next to each other to form a complex (fig. 14). All face east and one of them bears a Paleo-Phrygian rock-cut inscription on the horizontal face of the step (Brixhe, Tüfekçi Sivas 2002: 104–9).

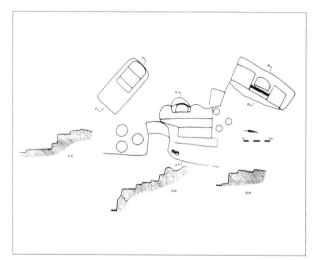

*Fig. 14. Altars at Menekşekaya*

In the light of these newly recorded altars and the inscription we can conclude that Menekşekaya was an extra-urban sanctuary devoted to Matar the Mother Goddess, whose original concern was with the realm of the mountains.

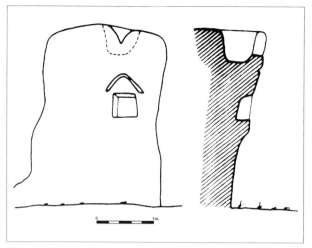

*Fig. 15. Niche at Demirli*

The second group of monuments lies some 300m to the northeast of the Menekşekaya rock, on the opposite side of the road, and includes a small rock-cut façade and a rock-cut niche. The façade is carved out high up on the east side of a pointed rock; it is complete with all the usual elements (Tüfekçi Sivas 1999: 140, pl. 102). Some 100m southeast of the façade, carved in the vertical side of a low, flat topped cliff, lies the niche, rectangular (measuring 0.45m by 0.4m by 0.25m) with an incised gable (fig. 15). The top of the rock forms a kind of rough rectangular rock platform measuring a few metres in width. On this platform, and carved directly above the niche noted earlier, there is a large and deep round depression with an overflow channel (0.4m in diameter and 0.5m deep), very attractive in appearance. Further away from this depression to the west, dispersed on the surface of the platform, there are more rock-cut hollows with overflow channels. These hollows were probably used as containers for libations, their existence indicating the performance of rituals on the rock platform. In religious ceremonies, the overflow channels would have allowed the libation (water or wine) to flow freely over the rock surface, ensuring that a large area of the platform was wetted (for detailed information regarding the cult function and the meaning of hollows and cup marks in Hittite, Neo-Hittite and Urartian civilisation, see Ussishkin 1975; Neve 1977–1978; Işık 1987: 525–6; 1988: 150–1; 1995: 57–8; Gonnet 1993).

## Demirli Kale, Fındık, Akkaya

As well as the newly discovered cult monuments described above, our fieldwork in the İshaniye region has yielded six examples of a type of rock-cut monument previously hardly known in the Phrygian highlands. We have recorded four of these at Demirli Kale, a Phrygian fortress situated nearly 1km north of

Demirli village. The gradually rising open ground around the fortress is full of Phrygian sherds (Haspels 1971: 60–2, figs 171–3, 500: 2) and a short distance to the east of the fortress there lies a fairly low, long rock formation in which are cut four pairs of basins, positioned very close to each other. We found two more such pairs in the northwestern part of the highlands, at the villages of Fındık and Akkaya. Moreover, a similar monument at the village of Tekören has been previously published (Devreker, Vermeulen 1991: 112, 114, figs 11–12), thus giving seven examples in total so far known from the highlands.

Each consists of an upper and a lower basin, connected by a round sectioned conduit through the bottom of the wall that separates them (figs 16, 17). The upper basin, of rectangular plan and 0.4–0.5m higher than the lower basin, is approximately 2.0m by 1.0m across and 0.5–1.0m deep; the floor is inclined down to the lower basin. In five examples, the middle of the upper basin's back wall has a rectangular or square recess cut into it at a point 0.3–0.4m above the floor, measuring 0.25m by 0.3m by 0.3m. The lower basins are almost square or oval in plan at basal level and generally measure 1.0m by 1.5m across and 0.5 to 1.0m deep. Alongside these basins there is also a number of hollows of differing forms hewn out of the rock.

To the south, the surveys conducted by A. Diler in Cilicia and Lycia have yielded a great number of closely comparable rock-cut monuments which were used as wine presses, a type of installation extensively used along the Mediterranean coast of Turkey (Diler 1994: 508–11, figs 15–17; 1995: 83–91, figs 1-5-7, 9-22). A number of similar types of wine press are also known from the Palestinian region, with a long history extending from the Bronze Age down to the Byzantine period (Diler 1995: 90, fig. 24; Ahlström 1978: 20–3, figs 3–8).

Hence we can identify the basins in our survey area as wine presses and it should be no coincidence that the villagers of Tekören still call the double basin there 'Şarapa' (winery). Although it is difficult to offer any absolute date for these installations, their situation in or around Phrygian settlements and monuments indicates that they should date to the Phrygian period and remained in use during later times (for the Hellenistic, Roman and Byzantine periods in the highlands, see Haspels 1971: 147–254). On the other hand, it must remain an open question whether or not the grape harvest was celebrated in the annual festival of in-gathering by the Phrygians. In my opinion, the altar situated just a few metres to the north of the Tekören wine press (Devreker, Vermeulen 1991: 111–12, 114, figs 9–10; Tüfekçi Sivas 1999: 168, pls 139, 140) and

*Fig. 16. Wine press at Demirli Kale*

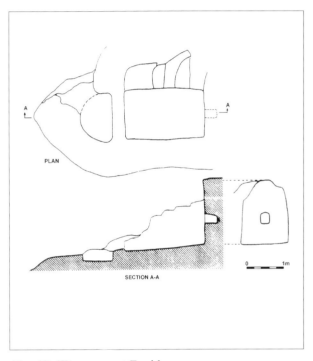

*Fig. 17. Wine press at Fındık*

the steps leading up to a flat platform alongside the Fındık wine press (fig. 17), give some indications regarding these ceremonies. In addition, since the bedrock itself could function as an altar, the hollows around the wine presses may have received the libations of the first-fruit offerings in connection with the grape harvest.

In summary, our surveys have not only added a number of Phrygian religious/ritual monuments to the known corpus of material, but have also enriched the typological range of this corpus through the discovery and recording of rock-cut features previously uncharac-terised in the archaeological literature.

**Bibliography**

Ahlström, G.W. 1978: 'Wine presses and cup marks of the Jenin-Megiddo survey' *Bulletin of the American Schools of Oriental Research* 231: 19–49

Belli, O. 1989: 'Urartu Kalelerindeki Anıtsal Kaya İşaretleri' *Anadolu Araştırmaları* 11: 65–88

— 2000: 'Doğu Anadolu'da Urartu Krallığı'na Ait Anıtsal Kaya İşaretlerinin Araştırılması' in O. Belli (ed.), *Türkiye Arkeolojisi ve İstanbul Üniversitesi.* Ankara: 403–8

— 2001: 'Surveys of monumental Urartian rock signs in east Anatolia' in O. Belli (ed.), *Istanbul University's Contributions to Archaeology in Turkey.* Ankara: 365–9

Brixhe, C., Tüfekçi Sivas, T. 2002: 'Dedicace Paleo-Phrygienne Inedite (Menekşekaya/Demirli)' *Kadmos* 42: 103–16

Devreker, J., Vermeulen, F. 1991: 'Phrygians in the neighbourhood of Pessinus (Turkey)' in *Studia Archaeologica Liber Amicorum J.A.E. Nenquin.* Gent: 109–17

Diler, A. 1994: 'Akdeniz Bölgesi Antik Çağ Zeytinyağı ve Şarap İşlikleri' *Araştırma Sonuçları Toplantısı* 11: 505–11

— 1995: 'The most common wine press type found in the vicinity of Cilicia and Lycia' *Lykia* 2: 83–91

Gonnet, H. 1993: 'Systems de Cupules, de Vasques et de Rigoles Rupestres dans la Region de Beyköy en Phrygie' in M.J. Mellink et al. (eds), *Aspects of Art and Iconography: Anatolia and its Neighbors. Studies in Honor of Nimet Özgüç.* Ankara: 215–24

Haspels, C.H.E. 1971: *The Highlands of Phrygia: Sites and Monuments.* Princeton

Işık, F. 1987: 'Şirinlikale. Eine unbekannte urartäische Burg und Beobachtungen zu den Felsdenkmalern eines Schöpferischen Bergvolks Ostanatoliens' *Belleten* 200: 497–533

— 1988: 'Doğu Anadolu Halk Kültürü'nde İlkçağın Paydaşlığı' *İnönü Üniversitesi II. Battalgazi ve Malatya Çevresi Halk Kültürü Sempozyumu. Tebliğler.* Malatya: 150–6

— 1995: *Die offenen Felsheiligtümer Urartus und ihre Beziehungen zu denen der Hethiter und Phryger.* Rome

Kleiss, W. 1981: 'Felszeichen im Bereich urartäischer Anlagen' *Archäologische Mitteilungen aus Iran* 14: 23–6

Naumann, F. 1983: *Die Ikonographie der Kybele in der Phrygischen und der Griechischen Kunst.* Tübingen

Neve, P. 1977–1978: 'Schalensteine und Schalenfelsen in Boğazköy-Hattuşa' *Istanbuler Mitteilungen* 27/28: 61–72

Roller, L.E. 1999: *In Search of God the Mother. The Cult of Anatolian Cybele.* Berkeley, Los Angeles, London

Sivas, H. 2002: 'Eskişehir-Yenisofça köyünden yeni bir frig kaya mezarı' *Anadolu Üniversitesi Edebiyat Fakültesi Dergisi* 1/3: 323–33

Sivas, T. 1999: 'Eskişehir'den iki Yeni Phryg (Frig) Kaya Mezarı' *Anadolu Üniversitesi Edebiyat Fakültesi Dergisi* 1: 123–33

Tüfekçi Sivas, T. 1999: *Eskişehir-Afyonkarahisar-Kütahya İl Sınırları İçindeki Phryg Kaya Anıtları.* Eskişehir

— 2002: 'Ana Tanrıça /Matar Kubileya Kültü ile Bağlantılı Phryg Kaya Altarları Üzerine Yeni Gözlemler' *Anadolu Üniversitesi Edebiyat Fakültesi Dergisi* 3: 335–53

Ussishkin, D. 1975: 'Hollows, "cup-marks", and Hittite stone monuments' *Anatolian Studies* 25: 85–103

# Phrygia, Troy and Thrace

## Maya Vassileva
*Institute of Thracology, Sofia*

## Abstract

Recent progress in the archaeological studies of both Troy and Gordion offers an opportunity to discuss again the Early Iron Age period and reconsider modern scholarship on Phrygian origins. Gordion Early Iron Age handmade pottery could be considered against the background of the coarse ware problem which is widely discussed for the whole of the Aegean and is still very controversial in terms of historical interpretation and ethnic labels. The parallels between the stamps on the large storage vessels from Gordion and from Thrace, dated to the second phase of the Early Iron Age, are even more compelling. The Early Iron Age ceramic assemblages from Troy, Thrace and Phrygia cannot directly support the literary tradition on Phrygian migration from the Balkans, but they can corroborate a culturally similar environment and can justify the use of the term 'ethno-cultural community'.

## Özet

Hem Troya'da, hem de Gordion'da yakın zamanlarda gerçekleştirilmiş arkeolojik çalışmalar sonucu kaydedilmiş olan ilerlemeler, bizlere hem Erken Demir Çağ dönemini yeniden tartışma fırsatı, hem de günümüz Frigya çalışmalarını yeniden gözden geçirme fırsatı vermiştir. Gordion'daki Erken Demir Çağı el yapımı çanak çömlek, tüm Ege bölgesi için yaygın olarak tartışma konusu olan ve halen tarihsel ve etnik tanımlamalar açısından tartışmalı Kaba Mallar problemi ile bağlantılı olarak ele alınabilir. Gordion ve Trakya'da bulunan ve Erken Demir Çağı ikinci evresine tarihlenen büyük depolama kapları üzerindeki damgalar arasındaki benzerlikler ise daha da zorlayıcıdır. Troya, Trakya ve Frigya Erken Demir Çağ keramik grupları arasındaki benzerlikler Friglerin Balkanlar'dan geldiği yönündeki genel kanıyı doğrudan desteklemese de, kültürel açıdan benzer bir çevre düşüncesini onaylamakta ve "etnik-kültürel topluluk" terimi kullanımını haklı çıkarmaktadır.

Progress made in the archaeological study of Troy during the last decade offers new opportunities for further historical considerations and interpretations in a wider context. Both the Anatolian and the Balkan perspectives now appear better defined. In some respects, however, the new data seem to pose more questions than they resolve. This is especially true for the Late Bronze Age to Early Iron Age transition.

The large number of works on Troy and the Trojan War that have lately accumulated demonstrate just how flexible the chronology of the Hisarlık settlements actually is. The 'lowering' of the second millennium BC Aegean dates influences the Trojan chronology too (see, for example, James 1991: 318). The most recent work to focus on Troy VII gives the following dates: Troy VIIa: 1250–1180; Troy VIIb1: 1180–1120; Troy VIIb2–3: up to 950 BC (Koppenhöfer 1997: 346). Under the consideration of modern scholarship the period of the 'Dark Ages' is getting shorter and shorter. According to Hertel, there is no hiatus between the end of the pre-Greek settlement (around 900 BC) and the beginning of the Aeolian habitation on the Hisarlık, and *The Iliad* echoes precisely this stage of the Aeolian colonisation (Hertel 1992: 177–81).

The attempt at an historical interpretation of the Trojan archaeological data has resulted in the coinage of an important term for Troy VIIb: 'Trojan culture with the imprint of Balkan influences' (Korfmann 1996: 7). It has long been suggested that the inhabitants of the Troy VIIb2 settlement were Mysians and other peoples of

Balkan stock (Dimitrov 1971). Nobody now doubts the importance of the southeastern Balkan lands when considering the pottery from the seventh settlement at Troy, although the coarse ware is simply called 'barbarian'. An important achievement of the last decade of archaeological work at Troy is that the picture of sharp changes leading up to a catastrophe has now been depicted with much milder outlines. The three stages of Troy VIIb flowed smoothly into one another and the different types of pottery were used simultaneously for a certain period (Koppenhöfer 1997: 296, 306–7). The historical interpretation of the archaeological data still tends towards a migration of Balkan tribes, and to an attempt at defining the different migration waves, of which probably two are envisaged (Koppenhöfer 1997: 341). However, it is already clear that an abrupt, destructive invasion did not occur.

The traditional idea of a total catastrophe in the eastern Mediterranean has recently been fundamentally changed as a result of data from newly discovered Hittite texts, as well as by excavations on Cyprus which demonstrate the important role of the island during the 'Dark Ages' (Muhly 1992: 19). There are critical data suggesting that members of the Hittite royal dynasty continued to rule after Supiluliuma II, moving their capital in a southerly direction, to Tarhuntassa (van den Hout 1989: 53–5; Güterbock 1992: 53–5; Hoffner 1992: 46–52). The view that the Phrygian migration put an end to the Hittite Empire can no longer be seriously supported (see Sams 1997: 244).

The results from the study of the early material at Gordion thus assume an important role. Unfortunately the provenance of the Early Iron Age/earliest Phrygian material from the site is known from limited (sondage) excavations and hence it is difficult to work out a precise chronological sequence for the Late Bronze Age to Early Iron Age transition there (Gunter 1991: 1–6, 102–6; Sams 1994: 7), although somewhat better stratified data come from the recent excavations of the Yassıhöyük Stratigraphic Sequence (YHSS) 7B phase, despite the practice of extensive pit digging in the Early Iron Age (Henrickson 1994: 106–7; Voigt 1994: 267–70; Henrickson, Voigt 1998: 85–7, 91–9; Voigt, Henrickson 2000: 42–6). From Gordion at the end of the Bronze Age, there is no destruction layer similar to that known from Hattuşa at about 1200 BC (Gunter 1991: 106), whilst the early handmade pottery is dated +1100 BC, showing definite parallels with Thracian material (Sams 1988: 9–15; 1994: 20–2, 194–6; 1995: 1147).

At Gordion a distinction can be made between coarse handmade pottery and knobbed ware, as proposed also for Troy. However, vessels with well expressed knobs like those from Thrace have not been found at Gordion,

and for the latter it is probably better to speak about 'knobbed-like ware', more detailed comparisons with the Thracian material being prevented.

Closer parallels between Gordion and Thracian ceramics are to be found in the coarse kitchen wares, in use for a long period, though these cannot be very compelling given their common functional characteristics. More telling, perhaps, are the parallels with sherds from much better finished large vessels. At Gordion, horizontal triangular or conical lugs occur, whilst U-shaped lugs are exceptional; in Thrace the latter are more common, usually located on the belly of the vessel (as is probably the case with Gordion pot YH 31721.2). Small rounded or flattened bosses appear occasionally at Gordion (for example, on a bowl sherd and on a utility pot: Sams 1994: 206, 236, nos 64, 413, pls 2, 8). Horizontal fluting can be suggested for two Phrygian bowls, though vertical grooves are not attested; by contrast, an 'horizon of pure fluted pottery' is defined in the Thracian material. Cups and kantharoi type vessels are abundant in the Balkan area, whilst they are almost unattested at Gordion.

The really compelling parallels are in the stamped pottery (Nikov 2002), whose appearance in Thrace is usually assigned to the end of the first and the second stage of the Early Iron Age, the so-called 'Pshenicevo complex' (most recently in Shalganova, Gotzev 1995: 334). Its spread is interpreted as evidence for the 'Hallstattisation' of Thrace and of a possible population movement from the northwest to the southeast. Unfortunately, a precise chronology is difficult to define because the pottery is more often known from pits or burials rather than from well stratified sites.

One of the relatively well stratified contexts of early stamped designs in Thrace suggests a date in the tenth to ninth centuries BC (Stoyanov 1997: 83), whilst more complex patterns appeared later. The earliest examples of stamping at Gordion have previously been assigned to the mid-eighth century BC (Sams 1994: 123–5, 196, tb. 2). However, the carbon 14 dates quite recently obtained for the Gordion 'destruction level' have changed the overall picture, as these are a century earlier than formerly thought, giving a late ninth century BC date for the destruction level, which puts the early stamps at around the mid-ninth century (see DeVries et al. this volume). This revised Gordion chronology still cannot reverse the direction of the assumed inspiration of the pottery decoration. It can, however, contribute to the considerations of a decorative and artistic koine, and hence of a possible cultural community.

Although in Phrygia stamping occurs generally on wheel made pottery, predominantly on big pots and pithoi, the patterns of decoration are sometimes impressively similar to the Thracian designs; this practice is otherwise almost unknown in Early Iron Age Anatolia, an exception being at Midas City (Haspels 1951: 75–7, pl. 33). Another shared feature is the prevailing choice of the upper part of the vessel for the arrangement of the stamped motifs. Circular, square or quadrangular stamps, either in a free form design or arranged in rows, are attested in both areas, though somewhat chaotic stamping is sometimes found at Gordion (for example on vessel P2921). Quadrangular stamps, with semicircles arranged along the long sides to form rhombi in the middle, seem to provide one of the closest parallels in design: compare P3568 from Gordion (fig. 1a), an example from Nebettepe in Plovdiv, southern Bulgaria (fig. 1b) (Detev 1963: fig. 4; Nikov 2002: pl. 8.3) and two more examples from Bulgaria (fig. 2) (Nikov 2002: pls 8.5, 7).

In Thrace, more often than not the stamped design is bordered by incised or pseudo cord impression lines. There are some examples of stamps combined with incised lines at Gordion too (Sams 1994: nos 244, 1022, 'pattern-incised').

There are, however, ceramics from sites in south-eastern Thrace where the typical design of stamped concentric circles connected with incised tangents is absent or scarcely represented, as is the combination of fluting and stamped decoration (Özdoğan 1987: 14; Domaradzki et al. 1991: 130; Stoyanov, Nikov 1997: 197). These thus come closer to the Gordion decorative repertoire.

A number of very similar stamped patterns are found on both Thracian and Phrygian vessels (fig. 3) (examples in Detev 1981: 181, fig. 52.3, 187, fig. 59.5). The most abundant are S-shaped stamped motifs, which seem to be among the earliest to appear both in Thrace and in Phrygia (Sams 1994: 131; Nikov 2002: pls 2, 3.1, 5). These could carry more weight when looking for affinities. Almost all varieties have counterparts in both regions: S-spirals, S-curls, single line S-spirals encased in the outline of the design, etc. Thus, close similarities would appear to be present in both regions whilst still in the early stage of acquiring the stamping practice. A stamp on an amphora from Gordion megaron 4 (Sams 1994: no. 938, pls 134, 170) could be considered a Phrygian development of the S-spiral motif: the tangent, imitating a cord, connects wagon wheels (the design survives on even later examples, including P662).

The stamped image of a goat on a Gordion storage jar (Sams 1994: no. 1000, pls 147, 168) has no parallel in Thrace, although attempts at schematic rendering of animal figures on stamps are attested in the latter region. It seems that birds/water birds were very popular in stylised representations, both in stamped and in cord

*Fig. 1a. Stamp from Gordion: P 3568*

*Fig. 1b. Stamp design from Nebettepe, Plovdiv (photograph after Detev 1963: fig. 4; drawing after Nikov 2002: pl. 8.3)*

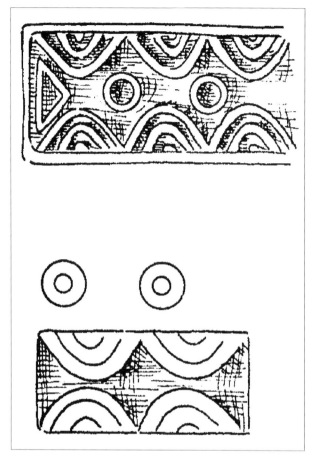

*Fig. 2. Rectangular stamps from Thrace: (a) from Tsepina; (b) from Lenovo (after Nikov 2002: figs 8.5, 7)*

impressed designs (Domaradzki et al. 1991: fig. 17e; Stoyanov, Nikov 1997: figs 30:9, 43:59, 60, 50:5; Nikov 2000: figs 22.1–2; 2002: pl. 5.1–6).

The Thracian repertoire has already been compared to the Protogeometric and Geometric decorative patterns found in the Aegean region (Stoyanov, Nikov 1997: 196, fig. 50; Nikov 2000: 303–8). The geometric patterns and the birds are very similar, although sometimes achieved by a different technique. Regarding simpler geometric motifs, it is hard to claim an origin and direction of spread, although the parallels in the designs are compelling. Probably, a common vocabulary could be suggested for the Aegean and the Balkan areas. Phrygian stamps could well be part of this broader artistic trend, with their own particular contribution to the Greek practice (Sams 1994: 124), while the technique brings them closer to the Thracian examples (on the parallels see Nikov 2002).

Sams' conclusions regarding the 'open lines of communication between Phrygia and Europe' and the existing 'cultural corridor' (Sams 1994: 21; 1995: 1147), and possible cultural exchange with Thrace in later periods, seem to find further confirmation. Future excavations and research could probably define more securely the local variants in Thracian stamping practice. A distinction has already been attempted: it seems that the geographical distribution of stamped circles-with-tangents alternates with that of stamped S-spirals in different areas. According to current knowledge, the border between these two different stamp groups passed somewhere to the north/northeast of the Sakar Mountain in southeastern Thrace (Stoyanov, Nikov 1997: 239, n. 23), with S-spirals to the southeast of this line, though they are absent at Troy and at sites in Turkish Thrace (Özdoğan 1987: 14) (for further distinguishing of the geographical distribution of different stamp motifs in southeastern Thrace, see Nikov 2002). The evidence supports Sams' view that Balkan/Thracian influence on the Phrygian material could have come from different regions and within a certain time span, or implies the existence of tribal peculiarities (Sams 1988: 9, 13; 1994: 21, 176; followed by Bouzek 1994: 220). Whilst knobbed ware and concentric circles-with-tangents seem to have a broader Balkan and Danubian context, the stamps are a peculiar feature that relates the Phrygian and Thracian pottery traditions. To date, one can assume that the most compelling parallels come from southeastern Thrace, in a sense contradicting the ancient written tradition relating the Phrygian emigration as being from Macedonia.

Another key site pertinent to the Thracian, Trojan and Phrygian set of problems is Daskyleion. The site's chronology still requires more precise definition, but grey monochrome pottery together with variants of the knobbed ware have been discovered amongst the second millennium BC material. Turkish scholars interpret these data as evidence for a newly arrived Thracian population after the Trojan War (i.e. after Troy VIIa; Bakır-Akbaşoğlu 1997: 231). Because of the existence of later Phrygian finds there, the earlier material has been assigned to the coming of the Phrygians. Nevertheless, despite common characteristics, this pottery differs from both the Phrygian and the Trojan wares.

Gordion Early Iron Age handmade pottery can be considered against the background of the 'coarse ware problem' which has been widely discussed for the whole of the Aegean region and is still very controversial in terms of historical interpretation and ethnic labelling. Possible explanations vary from northern intruders to socio-economic factors (Rutter 1975 was the first to suggest Thracian origins for this pottery; see also Bankoff, Winter 1984; Small 1990; Bankoff et al. 1996; Genz 1997, arguing against Bankoff et al. 1996, with further references). The recent set of interpretations offered for the Anatolian situation seem to mirror those for mainland Greece and the islands, as similar wares are discovered at more and more Anatolian sites including

*Fig. 3. Stamped pottery from the Razkopanitsa tell (after Detev 1981: figs 52.3, 59.5)*

Kaman-Kalehöyük (Omura 1991), Boğazköy (Genz 2000), Çadır Höyük (Genz 2001) and others (for an emphasis on socio-economic changes, see Henrickson, Voigt 1998: 95; Voigt 1994: 276).

The Anatolian situation is bound up with late second millennium BC developments in the eastern Mediterranean, during the so-called 'crisis years'. The most recent studies of this period show that there was no total catastrophe and that the 'Sea Peoples' could not be responsible for all the changes. The events of the 12th century BC echoed crisis phenomena dating back as early as the mid-13th century (see the articles in Ward, Joukowsky 1992). The range of suggestions on offer demonstrates that it is preferable to think in terms of a whole set of factors, a major one being that the 'palace economies' exhausted their resources (Muhly 1992: 11–12). Both the Mycenaean and the Hittite centres might have lingered for a while, and some of their traditions were certainly adopted by the first millennium BC Mediterranean world. The new iron working technology could have provoked the social changes (Wells 1992).

Reconsideration of the Anatolian, Cypriot and general Near Eastern archaeological material demonstrates how difficult it is to link ethnic names to the changes of the late second millennium BC. The discussions in connection with the so-called 'Sea Peoples' are very instructive in this regard (most recently in Gitin et al. 1998). Could *Masa* and *Moushanach* in the Ramseid inscriptions, relating the events of the battle of Qadesh, be the names of the Mysians and the Mushkians/Phrygians (see Ignatov 1995)? If so, these groups would have been Hittite allies or recruits from western Anatolia. However, the correspondence of ethnonyms and toponyms from the Near Eastern texts to those from the later Greek texts will remain to a great extent hypothetical (for more arguments in favour of this correspondence, see Easton et al. 2002: 94–101).

Turning to western Anatolia, Troy and Beycesultan (Mellaart, Murray 1993: 93–8) are unique sites in many respects: they are Anatolian rather than Hittite or Mycenaean settlements of the second millennium BC. Without overestimating the toponymic parallels, further research into the Hittite texts will probably confirm the place of the Troad within the sphere of Hittite political interest (Easton et al. 2002). A recently discovered bulla with a Luwian inscription from Troy (more probably Troy VIIb2 than VIIb1) has strengthened the view regarding a Luwian speaking Troy (Hawkins, Easton 1996; Korfmann 1996: 3, 27–30; 1998; Easton et al. 2002). Luwian and Thracian elements in the Trojan population have already been suggested (Gindin 1994; 1999 with references). Further research would possibly shed more light on the complex ethnic and cultural situation, and would further confirm multi-cultural interactions in the Troad and in northwestern Anatolia.

The occurrence of Early Iron Age coarse handmade pottery at a number of sites in central Anatolia has generated opposition to the traditionally assumed 'Phrygian' label for this pottery. It has recently been suggested that this handmade repertoire should be related to the Kaška people, the traditional northern enemies of the Hittites (Genz 2000: 40). The idea is predetermined by the nature of the sites, which are mostly Hittite settlements, and is based mainly on negative evidence. The scepticism has affected the interpretation of the later Phrygian pottery from Boğazköy and has prompted the definition 'pottery of the Phrygian period' (Bossert 2000: 174; Genz 2000: 40; though given as 'Phrygian' in Seeher 1998: 73–5). However, the Phrygian epigraphic data, and the evidence provided by the Assyrian cuneiform texts on Phrygian activity in eastern and southeastern Anatolia, should not be completely ignored.

Modern researchers often tend to neglect the Balkan background of Phrygian culture. Some of them consider the Phrygians only as invaders from the east (see for example Drews 1993). Since Blegen, there have been scholars who have looked for Phrygian origins in the Trojan population, but outside the context of the Trojan-Thracian set of problems (Blegen et al. 1958: 37; Mellink 1960; de Graaf 1989). According to others, the Balkan elements are 'distant, but shared traditions' of peripheral importance to the 'distinctive Phrygian culture' (Voigt, Henrickson 2000: 52). Of course one cannot deny the presence of Anatolian features in the Phrygian ceramic assemblage, but the Balkan affinities are not just a minor factor. The amalgam of the 'distinctive Phrygian culture' was certainly more complex than some might think, and the Balkan contribution to this process is worthy of consideration. Those who do not miss the Balkan connection interpret the early handmade pottery at Troy, Daskyleion and Gordion as marking a gradual movement of population, or of different but still related groups of people (Sams 1994: 21, 176). It might be preferable to consider the pottery data as evidence for a cultural exchange taking place at varying intensities in different periods.

The long standing discussion on 'pots and peoples' shows that it is impossible to trace the route of a migration through archaeological material, let alone according to simply ceramics. The attempt to use the matt painted pottery in Macedonia to prove Brygian/Phrygian migration, as related by Herodotus and other ancient authors (Herodotus 7.73; Strabo 7.7.8, 7 fr. 25, fr. 38), failed (the idea had been suggested as early as Hammond in 1976 [152], and was recently revived by Petrova in 1996, followed by Bouzek in 1997 [151–6]; for arguments against such an assumption, see Sams 1994: 134–5 with references). The more compelling comparative archaeological material seems to be concentrated in southeastern Thrace, though further research will probably reveal its distribution in an arc-like area incorporating the northern Aegean, and the Propontic and southwestern Black Sea coasts.

If the parallels between Thracian, Trojan and Phrygian Early Iron Age handmade pottery are kept in mind, parallels that are based on more than just one criterion, then our impressions could change. Probably, the combination of knobbed handmade pottery and coarse kitchen ware would prove to be more diagnostic (in addition to the decorative programmes of the stamped pottery). The knob-like vessels at Gordion could be evidence for a development of the knobbed ware pottery tradition, or of local diversities. A people cannot be named from the ceramics, neither can the whole set of data on the Balkan-Anatolian parallels be simply dismissed. We have a persistent ancient written tradition regarding Thracian tribes living in the northwest of Asia Minor at the end of the second millennium BC and later which cannot be simply ignored as fiction.

In view of the above considerations, it is perhaps preferable to speak of an ethno-cultural community, rather than to specify the ethnonyms or the ethnic features. Displacements and population movements probably occurred at the end of the second and the beginning of the first millennia BC, but they took place within a culturally similar environment. They probably also moved in both directions, west as well as east. 'Thracian-Trojan-Phrygian ethno-cultural community' is possibly a good term to begin with when discussing the Late Bronze Age to Early Iron Age transition in the southeastern Balkans and in northwestern and north-central Anatolia, without attempting to specify the inhabitants, whether Mysians, Phrygians or Bithynians. In terms of cultural interactions, the Early Iron Age handmade pottery can only contribute to the overall picture. Its spread further east should not cause surprise when viewed against the background of the later Phrygian epigraphic and archaeological data relating to that region. In terms of the mid-first millennium BC, and possibly later, we can consider the material discussed above in terms of the 'Thracian-Phrygian cultural zone of interactions' (Vassileva 1998a; 1998b).

## Acknowledgements

I am very grateful to G.K. Sams, Gordion Project Director, who kindly offered me the opportunity to study the Gordion Early Iron Age pottery for three weeks during the 1999 season.

## Bibliography

Bakır-Akbaşoğlu, T. 1997: 'Phryger in Daskyleion' in R. Gusmani, M. Salvini, P. Vannicelli (eds), *Frigi e frigio. Atti del 1o Simposio Internazionale. Roma 16–17 ottobre 1995*. Rome: 229–38

Bankoff, H.A., Meyer, N., Stefanovich, M. 1996: 'Handmade burnished ware and the Late Bronze Age of the Balkans' *Journal of Mediterranean Archaeology* 9.2: 193–209

Bankoff, H.A., Winter, F.A. 1984: 'Northern intruders in LH IIIC Greece: A view from the north' *Journal of Indo-European Studies* 12: 1–30

Blegen, C., Boulter, C., Caskey, J., Rawson, M. 1958: *Troy 4.1.* Princeton

Bossert, E.-M. 2000: *Die Keramik phrygischer Zeit von Boğazköy* (Deutsche Archäologische Institut. Boğazköy-Hattusa Ergebnisse der Ausgrabungen 13). Berlin

Bouzek, J. 1994: 'Late Bronze Age Greece and the Balkans: a review of the present picture' *Annual of the British School at Athens* 89: 219–34

— 1997: *Greece, Anatolia and Europe: Cultural Interrelations during the Early Iron Age* (Studies in Mediterranean Archaeology 122). Jonsered

de Graaf, F. 1989: 'Midas Wanax Lawagetas' in J. Best, N. de Vries (eds), *Thracians and Mycenaeans. Proceedings of the Fourth International Congress of Thracology. Rotterdam, 24–26 September 1984.* Leiden, Sofia: 153–5

Detev, P. 1963: 'Razkopki na Nebettepe v Plovdiv' *Sbornik na Narodnia Arheologicheski Muzei Plovdiv* 5: 27–40

— 1981: 'Le tell Razkopanica' *Bulletin de l'Institut d'archéologie* 36: 141–88

Dimitrov, D.P. 1971: 'Troia VIIb2 und die thrakischen und mösischen Stämme auf dem Balkan' *Studia Balcanica 5. L'ethnogenèse des peuples balkaniques.* Sofia: 63–78

Domaradzki, M., Karaiotov, I., Gotsev, A. 1991: 'L'habitat du premier âge du fer de Malkoto Kale' *Thracia Pontica* 4: 119–32

Drews, R. 1993: 'Myths of Midas and the Phrygian migration from Europe' *Klio* 75: 9–26

Easton, D.F., Hawkins, J.D., Sherratt, A.G., Sherratt, E.S. 2002: 'Troy in recent perspective' *Anatolian Studies* 52: 75–109

Genz, H. 1997: 'Northern slaves and the origin of Handmade Burnished Ware: a commentary on Bankoff et al. (*JMA* 9 [1996]: 193–209)' *Journal of Mediterranean Archaeology* 10.1: 109–11

— 2000: 'Die Eisenzeit in Zentralanatolien im Lichte der keramischen Funde vom Büyükkaya in Boğazköy/Hattuşa' *Türkiye Bilimler Akademisi Arkeoloji Dergisi* 3: 35–54

— 2001: 'Iron Age pottery from Çadır-höyük' *Anatolica* 27: 159–70

Gindin, L.A. 1994: 'Thrace et Troie: La population da la Troie Homerique' in Fondation Européenne Dragan, Centre Européenne d'Etudes Thraces, Conseil International des Etudes Indo- Européenne et Thraces, *Europa Indo-Europea. Atti del VIo Congresso Internazionale di Tracologia e VIIo*

*Symposio di Studi Traci. Palma da Mallorca 24–28 Marzo 1992.* Roma: 63–8

— 1999: *Troja, Thrakien und die Völker Altkleinasiens. Versuch einer historisch-philologischen Untersuchung.* Innsbruck

Gitin, S., Mazar, A., Stein, E. (eds) 1998: *Mediterranean Peoples in Transition. Thirteenth to Early Tenth Centuries BCE. In Honor of Professor Trude Dothan.* Jerusalem

Gunter, A.C. 1991: *The Bronze Age* (Gordion Excavations Final Reports 3). Philadelphia

Güterbock, H.G. 1992: 'Survival of the Hittite dynasty' in W.A. Ward, M.S. Joukowsky (eds), *The Crisis Years: The 12th Century BC. From Beyond the Danube to the Tigris.* Dubuque: 53–5

Hammond, N.G.L. 1976: *Migrations and Invasions in Greece and Adjacent Areas.* New Jersey

Haspels, C.H.A. 1951: *Phrygie 3. La Cité de Midas. Céramique et trouvailles diverses.* Paris

Hawkins, J.D., Easton, D.F.A. 1996: 'Hieroglyphic seal from Troia' *Studia Troica* 6: 111–18

Henrickson, R.C. 1994: 'Continuity and discontinuity in the ceramic tradition of Gordion during the Iron Age' in A. Çilingiroğlu, D.H. French (eds), *Anatolian Iron Ages 3* (British Institute of Archaeology at Ankara Monograph 16). Ankara: 95–129

Henrickson, R.C., Voigt, M.M. 1998: 'The Early Iron Age at Gordion: The evidence from the Yassıhöyük Stratigraphic Sequence' in N. Tuna, Z. Akture, M. Lynch (eds), *Thracians and Phrygians: Problems of Parallelism. Proceedings of an International Symposium on the Archaeology, History and Ancient Languages of Thrace and Phrygia. Ankara: 3–4 June, 1995.* Ankara: 79–106

Hertel, D. 1992: 'Fundstätten und Funde griechischer Vorzeit. Zum Problem der Historizität der Sage vom Trojanischen Krieg: Kämpfe in der Frühphase der Äolischen Kolonisation Nordwestkleinasiens als historisches Substrat der Tradition' in J. Herrmann (ed.), *Heinrich Schliemann. Grundlagen und Ergebnisse moderner Archäologie 100 Jahre nach Schliemanns Tod.* Tübingen: 177–81

Hoffner, H.A. 1992: 'The last days of Khattusha' in W.A. Ward, M.S. Joukowsky (eds), *The Crisis Years: The 12th Century BC. From Beyond the Danube to the Tigris.* Dubuque: 46–52

Ignatov, S. 1995: 'Dardanians, Moesians and Phrygians in the Qadesh Inscriptions of Ramses II' *Thracia 11. Studia in Honorem Alexandri Fol.* Serdicae: 108–12

James, P. 1991: *Century of Darkness.* London

Koppenhöfer, D. 1997: 'Troia VII – Versuch einer Zusammenschau einschliesslich der Ergebnisse des Jahres 1995' *Studia Troica* 7: 295–353

Korfmann, M. 1996: 'Troia – Ausgrabungen 1995' *Studia Troica* 6: 1–63

— 1998: 'Stelen vor den Toren Trias. Apaliunas – Apollon in Truisa/Wilusa?' in G. Arsebuk, M.J. Mellink, W. Schirmer (eds), *Light on Top of the Black Hill. Studies Presented to Halet Çambel.* Istanbul: 471–88

Mellaart, J., Murray, A. 1993: *Beycesultan 2.2* (British Institute of Archaeology at Ankara Occasional Publications 12). London

Mellink, M.J. 1960: 'Review of Troy IV by C. Blegen et al.' *Bibliotheca Orientalis* 17: 249–53

Muhly, J.D. 1992: 'The crisis years in the Mediterranean world: transition or cultural disintegration' in W.A. Ward, M.S. Joukowsky (eds), *The Crisis Years: The 12th Century BC. From Beyond the Danube to the Tigris.* Dubuque: 10–26

Nikov, K. 2000: 'Bird-images on Early Iron Age pottery from southeastern Thrace' in L. Nikolova (ed.) *Technology, Style and Society. Contributions to the Innovations between the Alps and the Black Sea in Prehistory* (BAR International Series 854). Oxford: 303–8

— 2002: 'Stamped decoration pithoi in southern Thrace from the Early Iron Age' *Archaeologia Bulgarica* VI.1: 19–44

Omura, S. 1991: '1990 yılı Kaman-Kalehöyük kazıları' *Kazı Sonuçları Toplantısı* 13: 319–36

Özdoğan, M. 1987: 'Taşlıcabayır. A Late Bronze Age burial in eastern Thrace' *Anatolica* 14: 5–30

Petrova, E. 1996: *The Briges in the Central Balkans: 2nd–1st Millennium BC.* Skopje

Rutter, J. 1975: 'Ceramic evidence for northern intruders in southern Greece at the beginning of the Late Helladic IIIC period' *American Journal of Archaeology* 79: 30–1

Sams, G.K. 1988: 'The Early Phrygian period at Gordion: toward a cultural identity' *Source* 7. 3/4: 9–15

— 1994: *The Early Phrygian Pottery. The Gordion Excavations, 1950–1973* (Gordion Final Reports 4). Philadelphia

— 1995: 'Midas of Gordion and the Anatolian kingdom of Phrygia' in J.M. Sasson (ed.), *Civilizations of the Ancient Near East. II.* New York: 1147–59

— 1997: 'Gordion and the kingdom of Phrygia' in R. Gusmani, M. Salvini, P. Vannicelli (eds), *Frigi e frigio. Atti del 1o Simposio Internazionale. Roma, 16–17 ottobre 1995.* Rome: 239–48

Seeher, J. 1998: 'The Early Iron Age settlement on Büyükkaya, Boğazköy: first impressions' in N. Tuna, Z. Akture, M. Lynch (eds), *Thracians and*

*Phrygians: Problems of Parallelism. Proceedings of an International Symposium on the Archaeology, History and Ancient Languages of Thrace and Phrygia. Ankara 3–4 June, 1995.* Ankara: 71–8

Shalganova, T., Gotzev, A. 1995: 'Problems of research on the Early Iron Age' in D.W. Bailey, I. Panayotov (eds), *Prehistoric Bulgaria* (Monographs in World Archaeology 22). Madison, Wisconsin: 327–43

Small, D.B. 1990: 'Handmade Burnished Ware and prehistoric Aegean economics: an argument for indigenous appearance' *Journal of Mediterranean Archaeology* 3.1: 3–25

Stoyanov, T. 1997: '*Sboryanovo'. Early Iron Age Tumular Necropolis.* Sofia

Stoyanov, T., Nikov, K. 1997: 'Rescue trench excavations of the Early Iron Age settlement and sanctuary near the village of Rogozinovo, Harmanli district (preliminary report)' in K. Leshtakov (ed.), *Maritsa Project 1.* Sofia: 171–240

van den Hout, Th. P.J. 1989: 'A chronology of the Tarhuntassa-treaties' *Journal of Cuneiform Studies* 41: 100–14

Vassileva, M. 1998a: 'Thracian-Phrygian cultural zone' in N. Tuna, Z. Akture, M. Lynch (eds), *Thracians and Phrygians: Problems of Parallelism. Proceedings of an International Symposium on the Archaeology, History and Ancient Languages of Thrace and Phrygia. Ankara 3–4 June, 1995.* Ankara: 13–17

— 1998b: 'Interactions in the Thracian-Phrygian cultural zone' in P. Roman (ed.), *The Thracian World at the Crossroads of Civilizations 2. Proceedings of the Seventh International Congress of Thracology in Constanta-Mangalia-Tulcea, 20–26 May 1996.* Bucharest: 300–5

Voigt, M.M. 1994 'Excavations at Gordion 1988–89: the Yassıhöyük Stratigraphic Sequence' in A. Çilingiroğlu, D.H. French (eds), *Anatolian Iron Ages 3* (British Institute of Archaeology at Ankara Monograph 16). Ankara: 265–86

Voigt, M.M., Henrickson, R.C. 2000: 'Formation of the Phrygian state: the Early Iron Age at Gordion' *Anatolian Studies* 50: 37–54

Ward, W.A., Joukowsky, M.S. (eds) 1992: *The Crisis Years: The 12th Century BC. From Beyond the Danube to the Tigris.* Dubuque

Wells, P.S. 1992: 'Crisis years? The 12th century BC in central and southeastern Europe' in W.A. Ward, M.S. Joukowsky (eds), *The Crisis Years: The 12th Century BC. From Beyond the Danube to the Tigris.* Dubuque: 31–9

# The cities of Rusa II and the end of Urartu

**Paul Zimansky**
*Boston University*

## Abstract

In the second quarter of the seventh century BC, Rusa II launched a building programme of unprecedented scale, constructing the largest royal centres in Urartu. Most of these were associated with large settlements populated in part by foreigners, and their creation appears to have been part of a restructuring of the kingdom. Possible motives for this transformation are considered. As Rusa II was the last Urartian king to have undertaken significant building projects and the violent destruction of his citadels contrasts with the orderly abandonment of the settlements, could the demise of the kingdom have been a reaction to his policies?

## Özet

M.Ö. 7 yüzyılın ikinci çeyreğinde, II. Rusa Urartu sınırları içerisindeki en büyük krallık yerleşimlerinin inşası için, görülmemiş ölçekte bir inşaat programı başlatmıştır. Öncelikle önemli sayıda yabancının yaşadığı yerleşimler bu programa dahil edilerek, krallığın yeniden yapılandırılması yolunda önemli adımlar atılması planlanmıştır. Bu çalışma ile bu değişim gereksinimini tetiklemiş olası nedenler değerlendirilmiştir. II. Rusa'nın kayda değer inşaat projeleri başlatmış son Urartu kralı olması ve diğer taraftan onun zamanında kalelerin şiddetli saldırılarla yıkılması ile yerleşimlerin belli bir düzen dahilinde boşaltılması arasındaki tezat, akıllara krallığın son bulmasına acaba II. Rusa'nın politikalarına gösterilen tepkiler mi neden olmuştur sorusunu getirmektedir.

There is something quite extraordinary about the sheer mass of material that survives from the reign of Rusa II in the first half of the seventh century BC. Even allowing for the point that evidence is generally more abundant for the ends of empires than for earlier phases of their history, one cannot deny a conspicuous and growing lopsidedness in the archaeological record: more artefacts are datable to Rusa's reign than to the reigns of all the other Urartian kings combined. This imbalance cannot be dismissed as an anomaly in a statistically inadequate corpus of materials — the Urartians were lavish in their expenditures on bronze and in their creation of military and ceremonial architecture throughout their history, and their works are sufficiently distinctive to have been identified in quantity in excavation and survey. The conclusion that one particular king, in the first half of the seventh century BC, marshalled the resources of Urartu's highly integrated imperium at significantly higher intensity than any of the previous rulers in his line is inescapable.

In this contribution I will focus on one particular aspect of Rusa's efforts — the construction of large royal centres with attached settlements. To judge by the extant inscriptions, all of his predecessors from the time of Sarduri I (ca. 830 BC) onwards established new fortified sites, and to a certain extent one can plot the progress of the state's expansion by these foundations. But when it came to creating major centres, these kings seem to have focused their efforts on one or two places that were conspicuous as citadels rather than cities. These they generally named after themselves — for example, there is only one Minuahinili,[1] Sardurihinili

---

[1] The newly discovered Ayanis temple inscription also mentions a Minuai-URU.TUR ('Minua's small city'), and the parallel with Rusai-URU.TUR, i.e. Bastam, demonstrates that such a site need not, in fact, have been small. However, the site itself has not been identified.

and Argištihinili.[2] In contrast, Rusa erected at least five great sites — Toprakkale (Rusahinili Qilbanikai), Karmir Blur (URU Teišebai), Kef Kalesi near Adilcevaz, Bastam (Rusai-URU.TUR) and Ayanis (Rusahinili Eidurukai). These centres, which include the largest and richest of the known sites in Urartu, are for the most part associated with extensive extra-mural settlements. In creating them, it would appear that Rusa was effecting a transformation of the structure of the kingdom he inherited. Moreover, there is a conspicuous absence of new foundations after his reign, and Rusa's efforts may well have represented a kind of climactic over-extension that contributed to Urartu's demise. While there is much that is tentative in this argument, particularly given the current uncertainties about the chronology and agency of Urartu's final destruction,[3] it is worth presenting if only to stimulate discussion of the historical implications of Rusa's actions, which have so far received minimal scholarly consideration.

It must be stressed that archaeological evidence is largely responsible for this newly won understanding of the significance of Rusa II. Until the Second World War, Urartian history was reconstructed almost wholly through texts, and relatively few royal display inscriptions of the seventh century BC were known. Before archaeologists began working systematically in Urartu, Sargon's eighth campaign (714 BC) and the nearly simultaneous incursion of the Cimmerians were thought to have been catastrophic for the Urartians, destroying a large part of their kingdom. Since Assyrian references to Urartu are infrequent after the reign of Sargon and Urartian display inscriptions nearly disappear for a generation, the conclusion that the kingdom had suffered a major setback was not unreasonable. Perhaps in residual deference to this now discredited view, some have chosen to characterise Rusa II's reign as a 'restoration' or 'reconstruction' (e.g. Smith 1999: 49–50). However, there are grounds for viewing Rusa's creation of multiple centres with large settlement areas as a departure from earlier traditions.

## The settlements at Rusa's centres

The five great sites mentioned above probably represent only a part of Rusa's building activity. For example, there is a lengthy list of projects in the inscription on the façade of the Ayanis temple. Curiously, this does not include any reference to the other centres we know archaeologically. If the thesis that Ayanis was the last of the known citadels to be built is correct,[4] one would have to explain this omission by assuming the list had a purely local focus, and that there might indeed have been comparable activities in other areas. In any case, the quality and character of the evidence for settlements in association with Rusa's primary foundations are uneven. In three instances — Karmir Blur, Bastam and Ayanis — we can be certain that there were substantial urban populations. The possibility of their existence at the other two sites remains open.

At Karmir Blur the settlement on the lower elevations beside the fortress is well defined, and covers an area of approximately 40ha. Piotrovsky suggests that it was laid out according to a pre-existing plan, with regular blocks of standardised housing (Piotrovsky 1969: 177–8). He identifies a wall that went partially around the settlement, and suggests that it was never completed. He notes discrepancies between larger houses and smaller ones, attributing these to class distinctions. In the one area of housing for which there is a full publication (Martirosjan 1961), some of the walls do not meet at right angles, for which construction by prisoners of war (POWs) has been offered as an explanation. Smallfinds were relatively sparse, no doubt because, unlike the citadel, the settlement appears to have been abandoned rather than destroyed[5] — a characteristic of all of Rusa's settlements.

Bastam is certainly one of the most ambitious and impressive of Rusa's projects. The citadel is probably the largest ever created in Urartu by a single ruler (for site size comparisons, see Kleiss 1983). The main area

---

[2] There are actually two different sites named Argištihinili, but each appears to be associated with a different Argišti. The most famous and best attested was founded by Argišti I at Armavir in the early eighth century. The other appears to be on the northern shore of lake Van and is mentioned only in passing in a single inscription by Argišti II around the beginning of the seventh century (see Diakonoff, Kashkai 1981: 9–10). The longevid Argišti I did create at least two major centres however, since in addition to the Argištihinili near Armavir he also founded Erebuni.

[3] There have been two significant developments in this regard since this paper was prepared for presentation at the Symposium. The first was the publication of the first volume of the Ayanis site reports (Çilingiroğlu, Salvini 2001) which contains an extended discussion of the sequence in which Rusa constructed his centres. The second was the proposed revision of the dendrochronological sequence to put the construction of Ayanis in the 670s — 22 years earlier than previously thought — and thus increasing the interval between the date it was finished and the demise of the kingdom.

[4] The order of construction has been considered in detail by Çilingiroğlu and Salvini (2001: 15–24) who conclude, with the caveat that no datum is entirely secure, that the most probable sequence is: (1) Karmir Blur; (2) Bastam; (3) Kef Kalesi (?); (4) Toprakkale; and (5) Ayanis.

[5] Piotrovsky believed that the settlement was evacuated when its inhabitants withdrew to the citadel in the face of enemies who had come to besiege it (1969: 179).

of settlement lies below and to the north of the citadel rock, and its size, although difficult to estimate because it includes many non-residential structures, appears to be roughly the same as Karmir Blur. The excavation team devoted most of its effort to uncovering public buildings around the perimeter of this area: the Nord-Gebäude, the Hangbebauung and the Hallenbau.[6] The houses in the centre of the settlement (Kleiss 1988: 19–23) look much more like the chaotic agglutinative structures of the eastern area at Karmir Blur than the regularly laid out row houses Piotrovsky reported in his western exposures. Smallfinds were comparatively few, except in a rubbish dump that was actually outside any roofed living area (Kleiss 1988: 90).

Although Rusa's fortress at Ayanis is on the same scale as Karmir Blur, the extra-mural structures are spread out over a larger area than at any other site that has yet come to light, covering approximately 80 hectares (Çilingiroğlu, Salvini 2001: 355–75). Excavations at various locations in the outer town have established that it was constructed by placing formal houses at intervals along the slope and these were modified as time went by. The spaces between buildings were later filled in with less formally planned and executed structures. The houses themselves contained little material of archaeological interest, but in the streets beside them there were massive deposits of occupation debris including many sherds and animal bones, similar to the rubbish deposits of the Bastam settlement. In some areas beside the citadel there are buildings that one would characterise as public, whereas private housing appears on the slopes of Güney Tepe to the east. To judge by the animal bones there were different patterns of consumption in different areas but, in all parts of the outer town, people were using pottery and other artefacts that we would call Urartian. Despite a passage in the temple inscription indicating, if correctly construed, that large numbers of foreign peoples were brought here (Çilingiroğlu, Salvini 2001: 261), we have yet to discover traces of their ethnicity in the archaeological record.

The two instances in which the existence of a substantial area of housing is less clear are Kef Kalesi and Toprakkale. The archaeology of the latter is vexed by the fact that the site was more plundered than excavated in the 19th century. It is only 4km from the citadel rock at Van, and it would not be unreasonable to assume that the original capital of ancient Tušpa itself was the city with which it was associated. This is neither confirmed nor denied by the testimony of the Keşiş Göl inscription which, in recording the construction of hydraulic works to serve the area, makes a distinction between the place name of Rusahinili and the people of Tušpa. There is one text that has sometimes been taken to suggest that a substantial population resided in its vicinity — the personnel list excavated by Lehmann-Haupt on Toprakkale, which enumerates various categories of people totalling 5,507 individuals (Diakonoff 1963: no. 12). Although this is dated to the year in which the god Haldi established Rusa as king in Rusahinili Qilbanikai (for a recent translation of the year name, see Çilingiroğlu, Salvini 2001: 17) and there is no doubt that the latter is the ancient name for Toprakkale, it does not explicitly associate the enumerated people with the site. If one does assume a linkage, the modest dimensions of the citadel rock itself could hardly have accommodated a group this large.

Kef Kalesi, above Adilcevaz, is the most enigmatic foundation of Rusa II. Results of the excavations there in the 1960s are incompletely published. In terms of the standard inventory of a Rusa II site — bronzes, bullae, etc — Kef Kalesi was a disappointment. Although traces of burning on the citadel are everywhere, Baki Öğün, the excavator, reports that there was little in the way of smallfinds to recover because the site was thoroughly looted before it was set ablaze (Öğün 1982: 219). An inscription partially duplicating the temple inscriptions of Karmir Blur and Ayanis was found re-used in a medieval building in Adilcevaz and may have come from the site, although the possibility of another settlement in Adilcevaz itself remains open (Salvini 2001: 301–2). The text mentions the place of dedication as the 'city of Haldi in the land of Ziuquni' (Salvini 2001: 301) and has a list of captive peoples similar to the one in the Ayanis inscription. At Kef Kalesi itself, Charles Burney identified a 'town area' in his initial description of the site (Burney 1957: 50–1). It is no larger than about 10ha and its position within the fortifications is not typical of the other settlements of Rusa. Outworks to the north of the citadel indicate that not everyone lived within the walls, however (Burney, Lawson 1960: 188–9). In any case, no excavation of houses has been undertaken here, and the area within the walls offered little promise should anyone attempt to do so in the future (Öğün 1967: 484).

Thus at three of these sites founded by Rusa — Karmir Blur, Bastam and Ayanis — there have been archaeological investigations of settlements constructed in immediate proximity to the fortresses. It has been suggested that a settlement also existed at or near Kef

---

[6] A case can be made that the latter, which was as close to the entrance of the citadel as one could take a wheeled vehicle, was where the royal chariot was housed. It contained a large stable — a room with a very wide door — next to which was a much smaller stable area in close proximity to a fodder storeroom in which there were pithoi scratched with an abbreviated version of the name of the city.

Kalesi and the case for Toprakkale remains open. All of these sites were new foundations and the settlements appear to have come into existence at the same time as the fortresses. The settlements also appear to have been abandoned shortly after the fortresses were destroyed.[7] Although some other Urartian sites, like Erebuni (Oganesjan 1973: chapter 5), Altıntepe (Summers 1993), Horom (Kohl, Kroll 1999) and Van itself, saw new occupation and construction after the kingdom's collapse, Rusa's centres were deserted by all but a few squatters and totally forgotten.

## Urartian settlements prior to Rusa II

In order to evaluate Rusa's innovations, we must consider what is known of Urartian settlement prior to his reign. The best evidence is textual, provided by the Assyrians in the penultimate decade of the eighth century. Sargon's letter to the god Assur, outlining the itinerary of his celebrated campaign of 714 BC (for a summary of literature on the eighth campaign, see Chamaza 1994; 1995–1996), describes a countryside broken up into discrete provinces in each of which settlements are clustered. Scores of habitation sites or *alani* surrounded each fortified site, and there was at least one, and usually more fortified sites per province (Zimansky 1985: 40–6). These outlying hamlets, encampments, farmsteads, or whatever they were, have not been identified archaeologically and had they been at all substantial it is hard to see how they would have escaped notice in modern surveys. They may indeed have been quite small and perhaps impermanent. Espionage reports of the Assyrians dating to the same time show that these provinces were ruled by provincial governors who enjoyed a measure of autonomous power that one would never expect if one had only Urartian royal inscriptions to judge by. They commanded troops of their own and sometimes acted in concert with each other, independently of the Urartian king (Zimansky 1985: 89–94). One assumes that this arrangement reflects a survival of power configurations predating the creation of the Urartian state. Empires, particularly those that come into existence as rapidly as Urartu, generally make use of existing governmental mechanisms and only get around to creating uniformity in their administration after some time has passed.

[7] Post-Urartian remains are not altogether absent in the Ayanis and Bastam settlements. Kroll reports a modest amount of 'Median' pottery from floors in the Hallenbau that cover the remains of the pithoi in one of the storerooms (Kroll 1979). In the Pınarbaşı area of Ayanis there was some re-use of building stones and a scattering of post-Urartian pottery. In neither case, however, does the evidence make a case for anything more than a modest squatter occupation.

It would be enlightening to have a substantial body of comparative archaeological evidence for Urartian settlements dating to the eighth century, but it does not really exist. There are indeed settlement areas at sites that we know were founded by the predecessors of Rusa II, such as Anzaf, Argištihinili and Erebuni (Martirosjan 1974; Hodjash 1999), but in most cases we cannot be certain that what survives to be excavated does indeed date to the earlier phase of Urartu's history. If we could confidently locate a single site that Sargon or the Cimmerians destroyed it would give us a baseline for the late eighth century, but clear evidence of discontinuity of settlement within the Urartian period is hard to find. In any case, there is no question of any of the known settlements at earlier sites approaching the size of the ones at Karmir Blur, Bastam and Ayanis, and many prominent eighth century citadels, such as Çavuştepe, appear to have no associated settlements at all. Thus extra-mural residential areas beside citadels were probably not a new concept with Rusa II, but no one else in Urartu's history was so concerned with creating them. Had they been a priority of earlier kings, surely there would be more evidence for them and the contrast between Rusa's efforts and those of all of his predecessors would not be so great.

## Innovation and integration in Rusa's cities

What motives lay behind this massive construction effort? It is customary to discuss earlier fortress building in Urartu in terms of colonisation and defence. Places like Argištihinili and Erebuni are thought to have been created to establish an Urartian presence in a new area, to exploit local resources and to defend territory. These explanations simply will not serve for the building programme of Rusa II. He was not moving into new territory at all, and his most ambitious creations were within sight of existing Urartian centres. The proximity of Toprakkale to Van is obvious, and it has been suggested that it was set up on more defensible ground than the Van citadel as a second capital of the kingdom (Burney 1957: 40). But the other sites share the same proximity to existing establishments. From the heights of the Ayanis settlement on Güney Tepe, one can easily see both the Van citadel and Toprakkale. One can also see the Adilcevaz plain from Ayanis and Van, and presumably spot a fire signal should anyone choose to send one. Karmir Blur was constructed on the opposite side of modern Erevan from Erebuni, in territory that had been firmly in Urartian hands for a century. Only in the case of Bastam might the argument for exploitation of a new area be made, but given that such nearby sites as Kale Oğlu date to a very early period in Urartian history, it seems more likely that the Qara zia-eddin plain was controlled by Van long before Rusa created his 'little city' there.

Another point is that some of these new centres were situated beside rather small pockets of alluvium, at least in comparison to the pattern of fortress building in earlier eras. The irrigable areas around Ayanis and Adilcevaz are tiny and cannot have sustained the population of the new sites. The plain over which Bastam looks out is a little larger, but not nearly so large as those others the Urartians controlled in what is now northwest Iran — Maku, Khoy, Shahpur, Ushnu/Solduz and Urmia. Bullae found at Ayanis confirm that foodstuffs were being brought in from elsewhere. It is possible that the reason bullae are so common for the latest period in Urartian history, and virtually unknown otherwise, is that new forms of administration had been created to sustain these centres.

This raises the issue of human resources. Eastern Anatolia has never supported a particularly dense population, and one must ask where the people who created and maintained these new centres came from. The annals that we have from the eighth century show an overwhelming concern for securing POWs, who presumably were put to work building the fortresses and irrigation systems that provided defence and enhanced the agricultural capacities of the kingdom. A few inscriptions, such as those concerned with the founding of Erebuni, are explicit about the settling of captive populations in newly created cities. While Rusa II has provided us with no annals, the new Ayanis inscription does give a list of lands from which he claims to have taken captives: Assur, Targu, Etiuni, Tabal, Qainaru, Hatti, Muški and Siluquni. A building and settlement programme as profound as the one Rusa undertook thus involved moving a great many foreigners into the kingdom. More fortresses, particularly large and lavishly appointed ones like Ayanis, Bastam and Karmir Blur, meant there had to be more soldiers to garrison them and more supplies to feed them.

In introducing concentrations of population not seen in earlier periods of Urartian history, in close proximity to new royal foundations which were themselves of considerable size, Rusa II appears to have been bent upon changing the cultural geography of his own heartland. These foundations integrated the settlement and defensive networks of the state and promoted more direct and visible connections between the population and royal authority than would have prevailed in the more dispersed eighth century settlement pattern described by Assyrian inscriptions. They may perhaps be seen as an attempt to make the empire more territorially unified, eliminating vestiges of provincial independence and integrating disparate populations under firm state control. On the other hand, their creation undoubtedly taxed the resources of the kingdom and may have engendered vulnerabilities that eventually led to Urartu's destruction.

## Rusa's programme and the end of Urartu

In any event, all the evidence makes it clear that in the long run Rusa's programme did not work. He is the last of the kings of Biainili to have done any significant building. Not just the kingdom but the very culture of Urartu vanished shortly after he died, and neither Rusa nor his works were long remembered. Greek historians were unaware that a great empire had existed in eastern Anatolia less than two centuries before Herodotus, and nothing transmitted by local tradition found its way into the work of Moses Khorenats'i.

In retrospect it is not difficult to identify factors that might have created a dangerous tension in what had previously been a rather resilient empire: importation of large groups of foreigners who had no particular loyalty to the state; the almost military imposition of a state assemblage; resources stretched to the limits to build sites that existed primarily for display and which had to be supported by long distance transportation of basic foodstuffs; and a burgeoning bureaucracy. It would not take much of a spark to bring the whole edifice down.

Perhaps it is not surprising that the violence so evident in the archaeological record of Urartu's demise is strikingly and specifically directed at the citadels created by Rusa II. Those were the ones that were put to the torch and not re-occupied. Their subsequent neglect did not come about because the inhabitants were all slaughtered. Rusa's sites are not like Hasanlu or Nineveh — there are few traces of victims in the ruins. The towns beside the citadels were not burned, but apparently peacefully abandoned. Could it be that the destruction of Urartu was something personal, directed at Rusa's creations if not at Rusa himself? There is, of course, too little solid evidence to make this anything more than a suggestion. Much work remains to be done on the question of settlement in Urartu, but it is increasingly evident that the ruins of extra-mural houses present a perspective on the kingdom's demise quite different from what is seen in the ashes of the citadels themselves.

## Bibliography

Burney, C.A. 1957: 'Urartian fortresses and towns in the Van region' *Anatolian Studies* 7: 37–53

Burney, C.A., Lawson, G.R.J. 1960: 'Measured plans of Urartian fortresses' *Anatolian Studies* 10: 177–96

Chamaza, G.W.V. 1994: 'Der VIII. Feldzug Sargons II. Eine Untersuchung zu Politik und historischer Geographie des späten 8. Jhs. v. Chr. (Teil I)' *Archäologische Mitteilungen aus Iran* 27: 91–118

— 1995–1996: 'Der VIII. Feldzug Sargons II. Eine Untersuchung zu Politik und historischer Geographie des späten 8. Jhs. v. Chr. (Teil II)' *Archäologische Mitteilungen aus Iran* 28: 235–67

Çilingiroğlu, A., Salvini, M. (eds) 2001: *Ayanis I: Ten Years' Excavations at Rusahinili Eiduru-kai, 1989–1998*. Rome

Diakonoff, I.M. 1963: *Urartskij pis'ma i dokumenty*. Moscow, Leningrad

Diakonoff, I.M., Kashkai, S.M. 1981: *Geographical Names According to Urartian Texts* (Beiheft zum Tübinger Atlas des Vorderen Orients, Reihe B [Geisteswissenschaften] Nr. 7/9. Répertoire Géographique des Textes Cunéiformes. Band 9). Wiesbaden

Hodjash, S. 1999: 'Urartäische Siedlungen: Erebuni, Argistihili, Tesabaini' in Eskicağ Bilimleri Enstitüsü, *Çağlar boyunca Anadolu'da yerleşim ve konut uluslararası sempozyumu (International Symposium on Settlement and Housing in Anatolia through the Ages)*. Istanbul: 255–8

Kleiss, W. 1983: 'Grössenvergleiche urartäischer Bergen und Siedlungen' in R.M. Boehmer, H. Hauptmann (eds), *Beiträge zur Altertumskunde Kleinasiens: Festschrift für Kurt Bittel*. Mainz: 1: 283–90

— 1988: *Bastam II: Ausgrabungen in den urartäischen Anlangen 1997–1978* (Teheraner Forschungen, Band 5). Berlin

Kohl, P., Kroll, S. 1999: 'Notes on the fall of Horom' *Iranica Antiqua* 34: 234–59

Kroll, S. 1979: 'Meder in Bastam' in W. Kleiss (ed.), *Bastam I: Ausgrabungen in den urartäischen Anlagen, 1972–1975* (Teheraner Forschungen, Band 4). Berlin: 229–34

Martirosjan, A.A. 1961: *Gorod Tejšebaini*. Erevan

— 1974: *Argištichinili* (Archeologiceskie Pamjatniki Armenii 8). Erevan

Oganesjan, K.L. 1973: *Erebooni*. Erevan

Öğün, B. 1967: 'Die Ausgrabungen von Kef Kalesi bei Adilcevaz und einige Bemerkungen über die urartäische Kunst' *Archäologische Anzeiger* 1967: 481–503

— 1982: 'Die urartäischen Paläste und die Besattungsbräuche der Urartäer' in D.H. Papenfuss, V.M. Strocka (eds), *Palast und Hütte*. Mainz am Rhein: 217–36

Piotrovsky, B.B. 1969: *The Ancient Civilization of Urartu*. Geneva

Salvini, M. 2001: 'Progetto Urartu' *Studi Micenei ed Egeo-Anatolici* 43/2: 275–306

Smith, A.T. 1999: 'The making of an Urartian landscape in southern Transcaucasia: a study of political architectonics' *American Journal of Archaeology* 103: 45–71

Summers, G.D. 1993: 'Archaeological evidence for the Achaemenid period in eastern Turkey' *Anatolian Studies* 43: 85–108

Zimansky, P. 1985: *Ecology and Empire: The Structure of the Urartian State* (O.I.C. Studies in Ancient Oriental Civilization 41). Chicago